Case, argument structure, and word order

Routledge Leading Linguists

Edited by Carlos P. Otero, ***University of California, Los Angeles, USA***

1. **Partitions and Atoms of Clause Structure**
   Subjects, Agreement, Case and Clitics
   Dominique Sportiche

2. **The Syntax of Specifiers and Heads**
   Collected Essays of Hilda J. Koopman
   Hilda J. Koopman

3. **Configurations of Sentential Complementation**
   Perspectives from Romance Languages
   Johan Rooryck

4. **Essays in Syntactic Theory**
   Samuel David Epstein

5. **Comparative Syntax and Language Acquisition**
   Luigi Rizzi

6. **Minimalist Investigations in Linguistic Theory**
   Howard Lasnik

7. **Derivations**
   Exploring the Dynamics of Syntax
   Juan Uriagereka

8. **Towards an Elegant Syntax**
   Michael Brody

9. **Generative Grammar**
   Theory and its History
   Robert Freidin

10. **Theoretical Comparative Syntax**
    Studies in Macroparameters
    Naoki Fukui

11. **A Unification of Morphology and Syntax**
    Investigations into Romance and Albanian Dialects
    M. Rita Manzini and Leonardo M. Savoia

12. **Aspects of the Syntax of Agreement**
    Cedric Boeckx

13. **Structures and Strategies**
    Adriana Belletti

14. **Between Syntax and Semantics**
    C.-T. James Huang

15. **Regimes of Derivation in Syntax and Morphology**
    Edwin Williams

16. **Typological Studies**
    Word Order and Relative Clauses
    Guglielmo Cinque

17. **Case, argument structure, and word order**
    Shigeru Miyagawa

Case, argument structure, and word order

Shigeru Miyagawa

Routledge
Taylor & Francis Group
NEW YORK LONDON

First published 2012
by Routledge
711 Third Avenue, New York, NY 10017

Simultaneously published in the UK
by Routledge
2 Park Square, Milton Park, Abingdon, Oxon OX14 4RN

Routledge is an imprint of the Taylor & Francis Group, an informa business

Library of Congress Cataloging-in-Publication Data

Case, argument structure, and word order / Shigeru Miyagawa.
p. cm. — (Routledge leading linguists; 17)
Includes bibliographical references and index.
1. Grammar, Comparative and general—Case. 2. Grammar, Comparative and general—Syntax. 3. Grammar, Comparative and general—Word order. I. Title.
P240.6.M59 2011
415—dc23
2011035160

ISBN13: 978-0-415-87859-3 (hbk)
ISBN13: 978-0-203-12684-4 (ebk)

Typeset in Sabon by IBT Global.

Printed and bound in the United States of America on acid-free paper by IBT Global.

To my parents

Contents

	Introduction	1
1	**Numeral quantifiers and thematic relations**	17
2	**Telicity, stranded numeral quantifiers, and quantifier scope**	44
3	**Argument structure and ditransitive verbs in Japanese** WITH TAKAE TSUJIOKA	64
4	**Nominalization and argument structure: Evidence for the dual-base analysis of ditransitive constructions in Japanese**	92
	Appendix to Chapter 4: Challenges to the dual-base analysis of ditransitives	112
5	**Genitive subjects in Altaic and specification of phases**	122
6	**The genitive of dependent tense in Japanese and its correlation with the genitive of negation in Slavic**	146
7	**Blocking and Japanese causatives**	169
8	**Blocking and causatives revisited: Unexpected competition across derivations**	195
9	**Historical development of the accusative case marker**	217
10	**The Old Japanese accusative revisited: Realizing all the universal options**	259
	Notes	275
	References	301
	Index	319

Introduction

According to a UNESCO report (Bjeljac-Babic 2000), there are some 6,000 spoken languages in the world. Anyone who has worked in the field in Africa, Italy, South Asia, or many other parts of the world may rightly feel that this is an underestimation. Whatever the actual number, the variations we can witness are enormous, and this diversity is something to celebrate.[1] A part of our work as linguists is to delve deeply into the workings of a particular language in order to try to come to an understanding of its internal logic. At the same time, as linguists working in the generative tradition, we want to know what these languages have in common, for the basic tenet that guides our work is that each language exemplifies a general structure employed by all human languages (Chomsky 1975, 77). The combination of looking deeply into a particular language and at the same time keeping the universality of human language in mind naturally leads to a way to do our work that is both interesting and illuminating. When studying a language, we tend to focus on some element that is unusual about that language, and we take it up as a challenge to try to figure out how the chosen element works. We see this pattern repeated over and over in linguistics research, with studies of such phenomena as the unusual transitive expletive construction in Icelandic, the mysterious auxiliary selection in Romance, and the extraordinary agreement system in Bantu. It is quite a feat simply to elucidate how, for example, the Bantu agreement system works, and one can devote a lifetime to such a task without coming even close to a full understanding of the system at work. These unusual features of a particular language are inherently interesting because they represent the diversity of human language, how languages can vary, and vary greatly. At the same time, as we learn the inner workings of these unusual facets of a particular language, we begin to explore how they tap the resource of the general linguistic structure, thereby illuminating what the underlying universal system holds. In this way, the unique properties of a particular language do not comprise what are essential only to that language, which would isolate the language from the rest, but rather, they demonstrate the possibilities of the general system at work, thereby uniting the language under study with the untold others that are spoken around the world.

In this book, I have assembled five topics that I have worked on over the past thirty years, topics that center primarily on Japanese but with reference also to a variety of other languages. Each topic comprises something unusual that is found in Japanese, although by no mean limited to Japanese, and the topics all relate in varying degrees to issues of case, argument structure, and word order. Each topic is presented as a pairing of an "earlier" published work and a new work that extends the earlier work, including responses to other linguists' criticisms of the original analysis. I have "earlier" in quotations because, while some of the previously published chapters date back to the 1980s, others are quite new, as in the case of Chapter 5 on nominative–genitive conversion, which is in fact a 2011 article (but is based on work done much earlier). In writing the new chapters, I made it a point to summarize parts of the original work sufficiently, sometimes quite substantially, in order for the analysis in the new work to make sense.

STRANDING OF NUMERAL QUANTIFIERS AS EVIDENCE FOR A-MOVEMENT, WITH SPECIAL REFERENCE TO THE PREDICATE-INTERNAL SUBJECT POSITION

Chapters 1 and 2 take up the topic of numeral quantifiers. A numeral quantifier (NQ) is composed of a numeral and a classifier that agrees with the type of entity being counted. NQs are found in many languages in Asia and, although there is variation in when they must appear, in Japanese, they are inevitably required when counting people, animals, or objects. While a NQ typically occurs adjacent to its associate noun phrase, as in (1), a striking property of NQs is that they can also occur away from their NP, as in (2).

(1) Kodomo-ga futa-ri hasitta.
child-NOM two-$\text{CL}_{\text{PERSON}}$ ran
'Two children ran.'

(2) Hon-o kodomo-ga ni-satu yonda.
book-ACC child-NOM two-$\text{CL}_{\text{BOUND VOLUME}}$ read
'The child read two books.' (Lit. 'Books, the child read two.')

It is not the case that the NQ can occur anywhere relative to its associate NP. While the object-oriented NQ *ni-satu* in (2) above can occur away from the object NP, being separated from it by the subject, a subject-oriented NQ usually cannot be separated from the subject by the object (Haig 1980; Kuroda 1980).

(3) *Gakusei-ga sake-o san-nin nonda.
student-NOM sake-ACC three-$\text{CL}_{\text{PERSON}}$ drank
'Three students drank sake.'

In Chapter 1, which is an abridged version of the second chapter of my 1989 book, *Structure and case marking in Japanese*, I present my original work on this topic, where I proposed that the NQ and its associate NP must observe strict locality. Where a NQ stands alone, as in (2) above, there is an unpronounced copy of the moved associated NP next to it that fulfills the requirement of strict locality. I further showed that based on this approach to NQs, we can find evidence for A-movement, in that NQs can be stranded precisely where we expect to find a copy of A-movement in passive and unaccusative constructions.

Chapter 2, which is new work, takes up a number of counterexamples that have appeared in the literature as challenges to the strict-locality proposal. Virtually all of these counterexamples take the form of a subject-oriented NQ separated from the subject NP with unexpected grammaticality. What I demonstrate, extending the work in Miyagawa and Arikawa 2007, is that these counterexamples are actually predictable under an important development that occurred in linguistic theory, namely, the hypothesis of the predicate-internal subject position. This is another A-position that hosts a copy of A-movement. The puzzle then becomes, why is (3) above still judged ungrammatical? Kuroda gave this example in an era when we did not have the predicate-internal subject position in the theory, so its ungrammaticality was expected. But given the modern theory, we expect the NQ in (3) to meet the strict-locality requirement with the copy of the subject in the predicate-internal subject position. What I argue in Chapter 2 is that the copy of the subject in the predicate-internal subject position in Japanese is only visible under a particular aspectual interpretation, specifically, telic aspect. While (3) above is interpreted as atelic, so that the copy in the predicate-internal subject position is not visible and the example is ungrammatical, the following, which differs minimally from (3) by the addition of 'already', naturally invites a telic interpretation, and the sentence becomes perfectly acceptable.

(4) Gakusei-ga sake-o **sudeni** san-nin nonda.
student-NOM sake-ACC already three-CL drank
'Three students already drank sake.'

In this example, the copy of the subject is visible next to the NQ, thereby fulfilling the locality requirement; the object has scrambled to a position above this predicate-internal subject position. Although evidence for the predicate-internal subject position has been given using quantifier float in English and French (Sportiche 1988), that analysis has been challenged (see, for example, Bošković 2004). The analysis of NQ stranding I present in Chapter 2 provides evidence for what has come to be one of the centerpiece notions in recent linguistic theory.

DITRANSITIVE CONSTRUCTIONS AND ARGUMENT STRUCTURES

Chapters 3 and 4 take up the topic of argument structure and ditransitive verbs. Scrambling, which is a defining property of Japanese, has played a key role in the literature on this topic. The two internal arguments of a ditransitive verb may occur in either order, and the pioneering work on this issue by Hoji (1985) gave compelling arguments that one order is basic, and the other derived by scrambling (I have glossed the particle *-ni* as simply NI and will explain this below).

(5) a. Taroo-ga tomodati-ni tegami-o okutta.
Taro-NOM friend-NI letter-ACC sent
'Taro sent a friend a letter.'

b. Taroo-ga tegami-o$_i$ tomodati-ni ___$_i$ okutta.
Taro-NOM letter-ACC friend-NI sent

According to Hoji, the *-ni -o* order in (5a) is basic, and the *-o -ni* order in (5b) is derived by scrambling. In Chapter 3, which is a *Journal of East Asian Linguistics* article (2004) coauthored with Takae Tsujioka, we note that, on the simplest interpretation of this "standard" approach, the ditransitive verb in Japanese is associated with just one argument structure with the word order *-ni -o*, and the other order is simply a surface-word-order transform of this singular argument structure. Given the pervasiveness of scrambling in Japanese, this single-base view appears not only plausible, but intuitively right, and it is why this approach has been enormously influential. But if this is correct, we should not find any evidence that there is more than one argument structure associated with ditransitive verbs. Such a distinction is found in the literature on English ditransitive constructions: there is a restriction on the goal phrase in the double-object construction that does not show up in the dative construction (see, e.g., Bresnan 1978, 1982b; Harley 1995b; Mazurkewich and White 1984; Pinker 1989). The following is taken from Bresnan 1978.

(6) a. I sent the boarder/*the border a package.
b. I sent a package to the boarder/the border.

In the double-object construction in (6a), the goal must be animate, but no such restriction is observed with the *to* goal phrase in the dative construction in (6b). In one body of literature, this distinction is correlated with a *dual-base analysis*, according to which in the double-object construction, the goal is interpreted as the possessor of the theme (*package*), while the *to* goal in the dative is associated with the meaning of a simple goal. As a possessor, the goal in the double-object construction should most naturally be a sentient entity, hence the animate *boarder* is fine but the inanimate *border* is not. In the argument structure representing the dative construction, the *to* phrase is simply a goal, and no animacy restriction is placed on the kind of phrase that occurs in this position. The two goals not only differ in their meaning, but they also differ in lexical category: the possessor goal in the double-object construction is an NP (or DP) while the goal in the dative construction is a PP. As it turns out, the same NP–PP difference shows up in Japanese, and we can detect it with NQ float.

It has been noted that a NQ occurs with an NP that is case-marked, but not with an NP accompanied by a postposition, because this is a violation of locality (see Chapter 1 and references therein).

(7) *Hito-ga tiisai mura-kara futa-tu kita.
people-NOM small village-from two-CL came
'People came from two small villages.'

In Chapter 3, Takae Tsujioka and I note the following distinction.

(8) a. Taroo-ga **tomodati-ni futa-ri** nimotu-o okutta.
Taro-NOM friends-DAT two-CL package-ACC sent
'Taro sent two friends a package.'

b. *Daitooryoo-ga **kokkyoo-ni futa-tu** heitai-o okutta.
President-NOM borders-to two-CL soldiers-ACC sent
'*The President sent two borders soldiers.'

In (8a), the NQ is able to be construed with the animate goal 'friends', but this is not the case in (8b) with the inanimate goal 'borders', despite the fact that both goal phrases have the particle *-ni*. Following Sadakane and Koizumi (1995), we postulate two kinds of *-ni*, one a dative case marker, which is what we find in (8a), and the other a postposition, which we see in (8b). As a case-marked phrase, the goal in (8a) is an NP, while the goal with the postposition in (8b) is a PP. This is precisely the distinction we find in English between the two types of argument structures associated with the double-object and dative constructions. Although there is no overt distinction among ditransitive constructions in Japanese, the evidence for a difference in category between two types of goal phrase indicates that a dual-base analysis of "the ditransitive construction" in Japanese holds promise.[2] What is particularly interesting about (8) is that, once we remove the NQ that forces the goal phrase to be an NP and creates a grammaticality problem in (8b), the word order is the same in both: *-ni -o*. We argue that the possessive goal phrase only occurs in this *-ni -o* order but the simple goal phrase is compatible with either order, *-ni -o* or *-o -ni*.

In Chapter 4, I explore further the consequences of adopting the dual-base analysis for the ditransitive construction in Japanese. Kayne (1984) pointed out that only the dative construction can undergo nominalization.

(9) a. present the ball to John ⇒
b. the presentation of the ball to John
c. the ball's presentation to John

(10) a. present John the ball ⇒
b. *the presentation of John of the ball
c. *John's presentation of the ball

We can observe the same difference in Japanese in the so-called *-kata* 'way' nominalization.

(11) a. Itiroo-no Hanako-e-no nimotu-no okuri-kata
Ichiro-GEN Hanako-to-GEN package-GEN send-way
'Ichiro's way of sending a package to Hanako'

b. *Itiroo-no Hanako-no nimotu-no okuri-kata
Ichiro-GEN Hanako-GEN package-GEN send-way

In (11a), the goal phrase is accompanied by the postposition *-e* 'to', and the nominalization is fine, but in (11b), the fact that the genitive *-no* occurs directly on the goal *Hanako* indicates that this goal is an NP, thus a possessor, and the nominalization is impossible, showing that the dual-base analysis again makes the correct prediction, this time with nominalization.[3] I pursue the analysis of nominalization based on Pesetsky's zero-syntax work (1995), showing that not only does it make the correct prediction with regard to nominalization in English and Japanese for ditransitive verbs, it also correctly predicts a difference that occurs between the two languages with another construction involving the causative verb.

NOMINATIVE–GENITIVE ALTERNATION AND PHASE DOMAINS

In Chapters 5 and 6, I take up so-called nominative–genitive (*ga–no*) conversion, a phenomenon first noted by Harada (1971). Certain environments allow the subject, which is typically accompanied by the nominative *-ga*, to be marked instead by the genitive case marker *-no*.

(12) [$_{RC}$ Hanako-**ga/-no** katta] kuruma
Hanako-NOM/-GEN bought car
'the car that Hanako bought'

As shown, the genitive subject may occur in a relative clause, and this is the most typical environment for it. While T is the licensor of nominative case marking, it is not immediately clear what licenses the genitive option. This alternation between nominative and genitive on the subject is also found in other Altaic languages such as Dagur (Hale 2002), Sakha (Kornfilt 2008), and Uighur (Asarina and Hartman 2011; Kornfilt 2008), but it is in the literature on Japanese that a debate has arisen over how to license the genitive subject, and this debate has had an impact on the analysis of the same phenomenon in other languages. On the surface, the structure in which these two case markers occur appears to be the same, and the debate in its essence boils down to whether that is true or not. In Chapter 5—an article of mine (Miyagawa 2011a) that appeared in *Lingua* in 2011, which was a work based on Miyagawa 2008, which in turn was an extension of Miyagawa 1993—I address this controversy. On the surface, the nominative and the genitive appear to occur in exactly the same structure, with the alternation being entirely optional. The so-called *C-licensing approach* (Watanabe 1996; Hiraiwa 2001, 2005) essentially assumes that the two case markers are licensed in the same structure. Even the licensing head is the same: a special kind of C found within the relative clause and other constructions where the alternation occurs licenses both possibilities. So, in the C-licensing approach, the two options are essentially two sides of the same coin.[4] However, in Chapter 5, using Hale's (2002) analysis of Dagur as a starting point, I provide arguments for the D-licensing analysis of the genitive subject, showing that the structures that license these case markings are fundamentally different. In its essence, the approach I present is about domains that are opaque for the purpose of licensing elements in them from outside—in this case, the genitive case—versus domains that are transparent for this purpose. The structures for the two case markers, nominative and genitive, are given below (I leave out irrelevant portions, including the head of the relative clause).

(13) Nominative

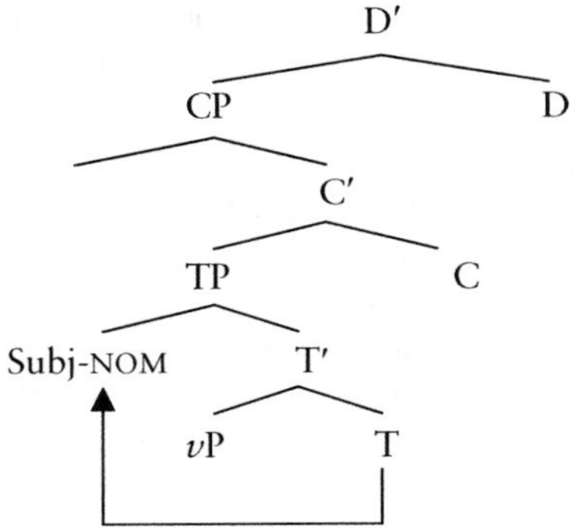

(14) Genitive

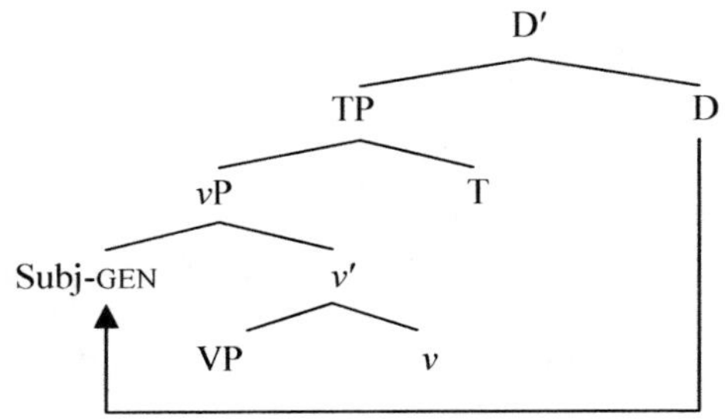

The nominative case marker occurs within a full CP; the CP, being a *phase*, is opaque from the outside, and the D that selects it cannot reach into this domain. This excludes the subject from being marked by the genitive, which must be licensed by the D head. In this structure the nominative is licensed by the T selected by C. The bare TP in (14), which is the structure for the genitive, is transparent from the outside by virtue of not being a phase. This makes it parallel to the ECM construction in English (e.g., *Mary wanted* [$_{TP}$ *him to come*]). In both constructions, the case on the subordinate subject inside a TP is licensed from outside by an external head. In the Japanese case it is D, which licenses genitive, and in the English case it is *v*, which licenses accusative. There are other similarities between these two constructions that I note in Chapter 5.

In Hale's (2002) analysis of the genitive in Dagur, we can see the connection between D and the genitive subject clearly because the D head agrees with the subject.

(15) [**mini** au-sen] mer^y-min^y sain.
 1SG.GEN buy-PERF horse-1SG.GEN good
 'The horse I bought is good.' (Hale 2002, 109)

The head noun *mer*^{y} 'horse' is accompanied by the agreement morpheme *-min*^{y} (1SG.GEN), which agrees with the genitive subject. Hale also points out that the phrase in Dagur in which the genitive subject occurs is an Aspect Phrase (AspP), as indicated by the fact that the verb can only inflect for aspect, not tense. The reduced nature of this relative clause allows the D head to "reach in" and license the genitive case marking. In the Japanese case, I assume that the reduced structure is TP, and the T is defective in not being able to assign the nominative because the T is not selected by C. We will see that, like in Dagur, this defective nature of T extends to its interpretation, being limited to a type of stative meaning.

In Chapter 6, which is the new work on nominative–genitive conversion accompanying Chapter 5, I propose that there is an entirely different genitive in Japanese that is not licensed by D. Watanabe (1996) and Hiraiwa (2001, 2005) give some intriguing counterexamples to the D-licensing approach that provide the impetus for this new proposal. The following is taken from Hiraiwa 2001.

(16) John-wa [ame-**ga/-no** yamu made] office-ni i-ta.
 John-TOP rain-NOM/-GEN stop-PRES-ADN until office-at be-PAST
 'John was at his office until the rain stopped.'

The subject in the embedded temporal clause may alternate between the nominative and the genitive, and as Hiraiwa correctly points out, there is no nominal head on the temporal clause, so that the genitive case, which is an option here, cannot be viewed as being licensed by D. However, while this example is fine, Takahashi (2010) points out that the following, which is similar to Hiraiwa's example, is ungrammatical with the genitive marking (I changed Takahashi's example slightly).

(17) John-wa [Mary-ga/?*-no wara-u made] odotteita.
John-TOP Mary-NOM/-GEN laugh-PRES until was dancing
'John was dancing until Mary laughed.'

What is the difference between these two examples? Drawing on observations by Fujita (1988) and Miyagawa (1989), Takahashi points out that while the verb in Hiraiwa's example is unaccusative ('fall'), the example in (17) contains an unergative verb ('laugh'). She further notes that many, though not all, of the counterexamples to D-licensing are of the same specific kind as Hiraiwa's, with a verb that is unaccusative. In Chapter 6, I extend Takahashi's insight by showing that the distribution of this non-D-licensed genitive in Japanese virtually matches the distribution of the so-called genitive of negation in Slavic. In both constructions, the genitive occurs on internal arguments—unaccusative subjects, passive subjects, and objects, although in Japanese, the occurrence of this genitive on objects is limited to transitive stative constructions. The generalization about this type of genitive both in Japanese and Slavic is that it occurs with two things in combination: a type of "weak" *v* (which I define as a *v* that does not assign accusative case) and . . . something else. In Slavic, this something else is negation. In Japanese, what combines with the weak *v* is instead *dependent tense*, which is a form of tense whose reference is dependent on the tense of the matrix clause.

This difference between Japanese and Slavic in the combination that licenses the genitive accounts for one distributional difference: while the Slavic genitive of negation may occur in the matrix clause, the corresponding genitive in Japanese can only occur in subordinate clauses.

(18) *Ame-no futta.
rain-GEN fell
(Intended: 'It rained.')

This is, very simply, because negation occurs in both matrix and subordinate clauses but dependent tense only occurs in subordinate clauses.

CAUSATIVE VERBS AND THE ARCHITECTURE OF GRAMMAR

In Chapters 7 and 8, I take up the topic of causative verbs. Japanese is an agglutinative language, and verbs host any number of suffixes. A typical suffix that occurs is the causative suffix, which often takes the form of *-sase* or *-sas* on the verb stem; the initial *s* is deleted when one of these forms attaches to a consonant-ending stem, and epenthetic *i* is inserted after *-sas* in certain environments.

(19) a. Hanako-ga kodomo-o/-ni kaer-**ase/asi**-ta.
Hanako-NOM child-ACC/-DAT go home-CAUS-PAST
'Hanako made/let her child go home.'

b. Taroo-ga gakusei-ni ronbun-o yom-**ase/asi**-ta.
Taro-NOM student-DAT paper-ACC read-CAUS-PAST
'Taro made/let the student read a paper.'

When the causative morpheme attaches to an intransitive verb, as in (19a), the case marking on the causee (here *kodomo* 'child') may often alternate between the accusative *-o* and the dative *-ni*, and this alternation leads to a difference in meaning: the example with *-o* has the meaning of 'make' and the *-ni* example has the meaning of 'let'. If the verb stem is transitive, as in (19b), the causee may only be marked with the dative *-ni*, and the sentence is ambiguous between 'make' and 'let'. Starting with the pioneering work of Kuroda (1965), which became the basis for important work by Kuno (1973) and Shibatani (1973), the causative construction became one of the best-studied constructions in Japanese. The particular observation about causative verbs that I focus on is due to Shibatani (1973): some causative verbs enter into competition with other causative verbs. The following example is taken from that work (346–347).

(20) a. Taroo-ga isu-o ugok-**asi**-ta.
Taro-NOM chair-ACC move-CAUS-PAST
'Taro moved the chair.'

b. *Taroo-ga isu-o ugok-**ase**-ta.
Taro-NOM chair-ACC move-CAUS-PAST

The causative verb in (20a) has the *-sas* causative morpheme, and it takes as its object the inanimate 'chair'; in the virtually identical (20b), the causative verb is formed from the other causative morpheme, *-sase*, and the example is ungrammatical. Shibatani observes that this difference is a difference between lexical causative and analytical causative: in the latter, the causation is indirect, and the causee must be "animate and self-propelled," that is, it must have its own will to carry out the activity named by the verb. This requirement is incompatible with *isu* 'chair'. If (20b) is changed to have a human causee, the sentence is perfectly acceptable because the *-sase* causative verb is able to function as an analytical causative.

(21) Taroo-ga kodomo-o ugok-**ase**-ta.
Taro-NOM child-ACC move-CAUS-PAST
'Taro made the child move.'

Shibatani points out that the unaccusative verb in these examples, *ugok* 'move', does not have a monomorphemic lexical-causative counterpart, and suggests that the *-sas* causative verb moves into this lexical-causative space. The *-sase* causative cannot function as a lexical causative even in the absence of a monomorphemic lexical causative. It remains an analytical causative because it is attached to the verb stem in syntax and we would not expect it take on a lexical-causative meaning. Lexical causatives belong to the lexicon.

In Chapter 7, which is a 1984 *Lingua* article based on my doctoral dissertation, I extend Shibatani's insight and show that even causative verbs formed from *-sase* enter into competition with corresponding monomorphemic lexical-causative verbs. For example, in idioms that contain causative verbs, there is a competition between the *-sase* causative, which is supposed to be an analytical causative formed in syntax, and the corresponding monomorphemic lexical causative if one exists. The following are taken from Zenno 1983.

(22) ago-o das-u/*de-sase-ru
chin-ACC push out-PRES/come out-CAUS-PRES
'to give up'

(23) hana-o sak-ase-ru
flower-ACC bloom-CAUS-PRES
'to succeed'

The idiom in (22), 'to give up', is formed from the monomorphemic lexical causative *das* 'push out' that takes the object 'chin'. As shown, the *-sase* causative formed from the unaccusative counterpart of *das*, *de* 'come out' (*de-sase-ru*) is ungrammatical. In (23), on the other hand, the idiom 'to succeed' is successfully formed from *-sase* attaching to the unaccusative verb 'bloom' and the resulting *-sase* causative verb *sak-ase-ru* takes 'flower' as its object. The difference between *de-sase-ru* in (22) and *sak-ase-ru* in (23) is that while the former has a corresponding lexical causative *das* 'push out', the latter lacks such a correspondent. On the assumption that an idiom must be formed from lexical items registered in the lexicon, this observation leads to the view that a causative verb created from *-sase* may occur in the lexicon if it does not compete with a corresponding lexical causative. Adopting a term from Aronoff 1976, I describe this phenomenon of competition as *blocking*.

This leads to a paradox. On the one hand it has always been assumed that the *-sase* causative verb is formed in syntax, and, indeed, it has a number of syntactic properties; yet it also has the property of being in competition with monomorphemic lexical causatives in the lexicon, which shows that it may exist in the lexicon. I concluded that the *-sase* causative verb is formed in the lexicon, contrary to the standard view that this causative verb is formed in syntax.

In response to my observations about blocking of *-sase* causative verbs, which I first presented in my 1980 dissertation, Kuroda (1981) suggested that the *-sase* causative verb is formed in syntax, as proposed in the standard approach, but in certain instances, the syntactically formed *-sase* verb is allowed to loop back and be registered in the lexicon. Broadly speaking, Kuroda was arguing for a less sharp line of demarcation between the lexicon and syntax. In Chapter 8, I pursue Kuroda's original insight by adopting ideas from Distributed Morphology (Halle and Marantz 1993), which is a framework in which word formation takes place in syntax, effectively breaking down the boundary between "lexical" and "syntactic" processes, as Kuroda originally suggested. In this new work, which is based in part on Miyagawa 1994, 1998 as well as Harley 1995a, 1995b, 2008, I argue that not only the causative verbs formed from *-sase/-sas* but also monomorphemic lexical causatives such as *das* 'push out' are formed in syntax. If all forms of the causative reside in one component—syntax—it is not surprising to find that one form enters into competition with another that corresponds to it in meaning and function. I pursue consequences of this new analysis for the acquisition of causatives in Japanese and also for the analysis of causative verbs in English.

CASE MARKING, UNIVERSAL GRAMMAR, AND LANGUAGE CHANGE

In the last two chapters of this book, Chapters 9 and 10, I take up the issue of language change. Like many languages of the world, Japanese has case markers that are morphologically separate from the noun phrase that they attach to. With few exceptions, a noun phrase occurs in a sentence with a case marker or some other particle such as the topic marker *-wa*.

(24) Taroo-**ga** Hanako-**ni** tegami-**o** okutta.
Taro-NOM Hanako-DAT letter-ACC sent
'Taro sent Hanako a letter.'

These case markers have been a major topic of study from the earliest work on Japanese within generative grammar (Kuroda 1965). Although the invariable appearance of the case marker is a fact in modern Japanese, it was not always so. As has been widely observed in the traditional study of the language, in the Japanese of the eighth to twelfth centuries (Old Japanese–Early Middle Japanese), noun phrases often appeared without any such marking. The following are examples from the *Man'yōshū*, a collection of poems compiled in the eighth century A.D. (in Old Japanese the accusative marking was pronounced as *-wo* instead of the modern *-o*).

(25) Ware-ha imo ___ omohu.
I-TOP wife think
'I think of my wife.'

(26) [sima-**wo** miru] toki
island-ACC look when
'when I look upon the island'

In (25), the object *imo* 'wife' occurs bare without any marking, while in (26), *sima* 'island', which is the object of *miru* 'look', occurs with the accusative *-wo*. In the *Man'yōshū*, both the bare form of the object and the form with *-wo* are common, which has led one traditional grammarian to suggest that the case marking *-wo* was unstable at the time (Kobayashi 1970, 226) or that it was simply optional (Wrona and Frellesvig 2009).

In Chapter 9, which was the sixth chapter of my 1989 book, I show, based in part on the work of Matsunaga (1983), that the distribution of *-wo* in Old Japanese is predictable from the type of inflection on the verb. Old Japanese (and Early Middle Japanese) employed two cross-linguistically common ways to mark the object: abstract case, which results in a bare object without any case marking, as exemplified in (25) above, and morphological case, which in this type of language results in objects marked with *-wo*, like in (26). Through language change that is well documented, this dual case-marking system in earlier forms of Japanese was reduced to a single possibility of morphological case marking, which is what we find in modern Japanese. The distribution of abstract case and morphological case in Old Japanese and Early Middle Japanese is the following (Chapter 9, Section 3.3).

(27) Distribution of abstract and morphological case
The *conclusive* form assigns abstract case while the case-assigning feature of the *attributive* form must be manifested overtly as *-wo*.

The conclusive form of the verb is typically found in the main clause, though not always. This is what we see in (25), thus the object has abstract case, while the attributive form is found typically, though not always, in the subordinate clause, as we see in (26). The conclusive form is a true verb form that possesses the ability to assign abstract case, while the attributive form is nominal in nature, which makes it incapable of assigning abstract case, necessitating the insertion of *-wo* on the object.

This analysis based on verbal inflections in older Japanese was able to account for much of the data in the eighth-century *Man'yōshū*. The analysis also provided a straightforward explanation of the change that occurred that resulted in modern Japanese, which marks virtually all its objects with *-wo* (or some other particle). Through language change that occurred over several hundred years starting with the Early Middle Japanese of the tenth century, the conclusive form, which assigned abstract case, was lost, having been supplanted by the attributive form. The attributive form required the morphological *-wo*, and this explains the spread of *-wo* throughout the language, transforming Japanese from an abstract- and morphological-case-marking language to the strictly morphological-case-marking language that we find today.

In Chapter 10, which is my new work on the topic, I respond to Kinsui's (1993) criticism of the original work. Kinsui points out that in the

Man'yōshū, there are objects of the conclusive verb that occur with *-wo* instead of abstract case, and there are objects of the attributive verb that occur "bare" without *-wo*. Both are contrary to the prediction made in (27). Regarding conclusive objects with *-wo*, it is well known that abstract case is assigned under adjacency with the verb (Stowell 1981). The conclusive counterexamples noted by Kinsui virtually all involve objects that for one reason or another occur away from the verb, necessitating the insertion of *-wo*. The following is one such example.

(28) sore-**wo** ware masarite iha-mu to
it-ACC I more than speak-intend COMP
'that I speak about it more than (others do)'

The verb *iha-mu* 'intend to speak' is in the conclusive form and its object *sore* 'it' is accompanied by *-wo*. In this example, the object is focused, and it has undergone focus movement to the head of the sentence away from the verb. In this instance the verb cannot license abstract case on the object and *-wo* is inserted on the object.

For objects of the attributive verb that occur "bare" as if assigned abstract case, contrary to (27), some of the explanations given in Chapter 10 are reproduced from Miyagawa and Ekida 2003. However, the most interesting cases are those that Yanagida (2007) points out (see also Yanagida and Whitman 2009). Yanagida observes that most of the counterexamples to the idea that the attributive form of the verb cannot assign abstract case, necessitating the insertion of *-wo*, involve objects that are single words. The following quoted in Yanagida and Whitman 2009 shows this (I use their romanization).

(29) Saywopimye-no kwo-ga pire puri-si yama.
Sayohime-GEN child-NOM scarf wave hill
'the hill where Sayohime waved her scarf'

The object of the attributive verb 'wave' is 'scarf', and this object, which lacks *-wo*, is a single word as opposed to a multiword phrase. What Yanagida argues is that this indicates yet a third way to license case on the object along with abstract and morphological case. As noted by Baker (1988), some languages license case on the object by incorporating the object into the verb. This is a form of morphological word formation in syntax, and it is typically limited to a single word, or a "head." In Chapter 10, I replicate Yanagida's discovery, which she made based on the eighth-century *Man'yōshū*, by using data from Miyagawa and Ekida 2003, which presents an analysis of case marking on the object in the works of prose of tenth-century Early Middle Japanese (the *Murasaki Shikibu diary* and *Izumi Shikibu diary*). With few exceptions, Yanagida's hypothesis accounts for the "bare" occurrence of objects with the attributive form—these objects are single words.

What we can see from all of this is that the older Japanese employed all three possibilities available in universal grammar for case on the object: abstract case, morphological case, and incorporation. Through language change, only the morphological-case option survived, leading to the morphological-case-marking language we find today.

ACKNOWLEDGMENTS

A large number of people pitched in to help with various parts of the new chapters. I regret that I can only acknowledge some because of limited space. The new analysis of numeral-quantifier stranding in **Chapter 2** owes thanks to Bronwyn Bjorkman, Yusuke Imai, Toshiaki Inada, Beth Levin, Masako Maeda, Hiroki Maezawa, Nobuaki Nishioka, DaeYoung Sohn, Hiroaki Tada, and Yukiko Ueda. A group of graduate students at Kyushu University went through the key examples in an earlier version this work, and their careful judgments identified numerous empirical issues attendant to the examples. This paper was presented at MIT, Kyushu University, and Nagoya University in May–June 2011, and I received a number of helpful comments that helped to shape the final version of this chapter. For the analysis of nominalization of ditransitive constructions in **Chapter 4**, I am grateful to Yoko Sugioka for extensive discussions, as well as to Hideki Kishimoto and Yoko Yumoto. The analysis of the genitive of dependent tense in **Chapter 6** benefited from comments by Alya Asarina, Masha Babyonyshev, and Hisako Takahashi. I presented an earlier version at Nagoya University in June 2011, and received a number of helpful comments from the audience. For the analysis of causatives and blocking in **Chapter 8**, I am grateful to Adam Albright, Heidi Harley, Beth Levin, Alec Marantz, Keiko Murasugi, the audiences at the Georgetown Linguistics Society Conference, FAJL 5, held at UC Santa Cruz, and the Morphology in Linguistic Theory conference at the University of Arizona. For the analysis of historical change in accusative case marking, I am grateful to David Lightfoot and John Whitman for helpful comments on an earlier version of **Chapter 10**.

Finally, I am grateful to David Hill for extensively copyediting the final manuscript and making numerous suggestions that have greatly improved the work.

Chapter 1 is a condensed version of Miyagawa 1989, chap. 2. **Chapter 9** is also taken from the same 1989 book (chap. 6). I am grateful to Elsevier LTD for giving me permission to use these chapters. **Chapter 3** was cowritten with Takae Tsujioka, and was published in 2004 in the *Journal of East Asian Linguistics* (vol. 13: 1–38). I am grateful to Springer for permission to use it in this book. **Chapter 4** is a longer version of Miyagawa 2009, which appeared in Japanese. I thank Kuroshio for permission to include it. **Chapter 5** was first published in *Lingua* in 2011 (vol. 121: 1265–1282), as a substantially revised version of Miyagawa 2008. I thank Elsevier LTD for permission to use this article in this book. A shorter version of **Chapter 6** will appear as "Genitive of dependent tense in Japanese and genitive of negation in Slavic" in a volume in honor of Toshiaki Inada. I thank Kaitakusha for giving me permission to include the longer version in this book. **Chapter 7** was originally published in 1984 in *Lingua* (vol. 64: 177–207). I thank Elsevier LTD for permission to use this article in this book.

GRAMMATICAL GLOSSES

ABS	absolutive
ACC	accusative
ADN	adnominal
ATTRIB	attributive
CAUS	causative
CL	classifier
COMP	complementizer
CONCL	conclusive
CONJ	conjunctive
COP	copula
DAT	dative
DITR	ditransitive
EMPH	emphatic
EXCL	exclamation
FEM	feminine
FUT	future
GEN	genitive
INTR	intransitive
LOC	locative
MASC	masculine
NEG	negation
NEUT	neuter
NL	nominalizer
NL_{FACT}	factive nominalizer
NOM	nominative
PASS	passive
PAST	past
PERF	perfect
PL	plural
PRES	present
REQ	request
SG	singular
TOP	topic
TR	transitive
TRAV	traversal
UNACC	unaccusative
1SG (etc.)	first person singular (etc.)

1 Numeral quantifiers and thematic relations[1]

1 INTRODUCTION

In Japanese, the act of counting people, animals, or things invariably invokes the use of a numeral quantifier (NQ). A NQ consists of a numeral and a classifier that agrees with the type of entity being counted. For example, to count people, one would use the classifier *-nin,* as shown in (1). To count bound volumes such as books and magazines, the classifier *-satu* is used, as shown in (2).[2]

(1) Sensei-ga **san-nin** kita.
teacher-NOM three-CL came
'Three teachers came.'

(2) Hanako-ga hon-o **ni-satu** katta.
Hanako-NOM book-ACC two-CL bought
'Hanako bought two books.'

The number of these classifiers is quite large. In fact, there are over 150 classifiers attested, though the inventory of those most commonly used is considerably smaller, possibly less than 30 (Downing 1984, 12–15). When fifteen informants were asked by Downing to choose the classifiers that they use from a list of 154, all chose the 27 listed in (3). They were also asked to list the entities that the classifier can count. Understandably, not all speakers agreed on exactly what entities can be counted with these classifiers. Those entities listed in parentheses are entities that not everyone listed. (Some explanatory notes have also been added in square brackets.)

(3) 1. dai furniture, machines, land and air vehicles
2. hiki animals [excluding birds, for some speakers]
3. hon long, slender objects, such as pencils, trees, threads, roads, and lines; (items that follow a trajectory, such as TV programs, letters, telephone calls, and baseball hits)

4.	kabu	rooted plants, roots and bulbs, shares of stock
5.	ken	buildings or parts of buildings that act in some functional capacity, such as a home or shop
6.	ken	incidents, occurrences, such as robberies, fires, and accidents
7.	ki	airplanes, (other air vehicles, such as helicopters and rockets)
8.	ko	small objects of roughly equivalent extension in all three dimensions, such as fruits, candies, and stones; also coins [general inanimate classifier, for some speakers]
9.	ku	haiku [seventeen-syllable poems], (other short poems)
10.	kyoku	pieces of music
11.	mai	flat, thin objects such as sheets of paper, pieces of cloth, dishes, items of clothing, phonograph records, leaves, rugs, and coins
12.	mei	human beings [honorific]
13.	mon	questions, problems
14.	mune	buildings
15.	nin	human beings
16.	satu	books, magazines, notebooks, books of tickets, pads of paper
17.	seki	large boats
18.	soku	pairs of footwear
19.	soo	small boats
20.	syoku	meals
21.	teki	drops of liquid
22.	ten	points in a score, items in an inventory, works of art
23.	too	large animals
24.	toori	methods, opinions
25.	tu	inanimates, concrete or abstract [general classifier]
26.	tubu	small, grainlike objects such as grains of rice, grapes, gems, pills, and drops of liquid
27.	tuu	letters and postcards, documents, (telephone calls)

The fact that NQs occur in Japanese is consistent with what has been observed cross-linguistically. A number of linguists have noted that a NQ system and obligatory plural marking are in complementary distribution: a language can have one of them, but rarely both (Greenberg 1972; Sanches and Slobin 1973; T'sou 1976). Although Japanese has plural markers (*-tati*, *-ra*), they are certainly not obligatory because a noun without such marking can typically denote a singular entity or a collection of entities. The word *gakusei,* for example, can mean 'student' or 'students'. For this reason, the plural markers rarely surface, except when a specific reference to a plurality of entities is required and contextual information alone does not suffice.

For a NQ to function properly, it must of course be construed with the appropriate noun phrase whose referent is being counted. In most cases this is not a problem because the classifier identifies the type of entity being counted. In (4), the NQ *yon-satu* 'four$_{\text{BOUND VOLUMES}}$' can only be construed with the object NP *hon* 'books' because the classifier *-satu* is used exclusively to count bound volumes.

(4) Gakusei-ga hon-o **yon-satu** katta.
student-NOM book-ACC four-CL bought
'The students bought four books.'

One would not attempt to relate this NQ to the subject, *gakusei* 'students', because 'student' is incompatible with the classifier *-satu*. But if one wishes to count 'students' here, it is not enough to simply change the classifier.

(5) ?*Gakusei-ga hon-o **yo-nin** katta.
student-NOM book-ACC four-CL bought

The classifier *-nin* is used to count people, hence it should be appropriate with 'students'. But as shown, this construal is impossible. To make it possible, the NQ must be positioned next to the subject.

(6) Gakusei-ga **yo-nin** hon-o katta.
student-NOM four-CL book-ACC bought
'Four students bought books.'

The grammatical examples up to now, (4) and (6), happen to have the NQ adjacent to its NP. Is it the case that adjacency is the condition required? If so, not much more needs to be said. As shown in the following examples, however, successful NP–NQ construals need not always involve adjacency (see Haig 1980 and Kuroda 1980 on examples such as (8)).

(7) Gakusei-ga kyoo **san-nin** kita.
student-NOM today three-CL came
'Three students came today.'

(8) Hon-o Taroo-ga **ni-satu** katta.
book-ACC Taro-NOM two-CL bought
Lit. 'Books, Taro bought two.'

In (7), the time adverb *kyoo* 'today' intervenes between the subject NP and its NQ. In (8), the object NP has been scrambled to the head of the sentence, resulting in the subject NP intervening between it and its NQ. Examples such as (7) and (8) demonstrate that the NP and its NQ are syntactically independent phrases. Otherwise, an adverb, as in (7), or a subject NP, as in (8), could not possibly intervene.[3]

In all of the examples that we have seen thus far, the NP and the NQ are separate phrases. There is an alternative construction in which the two occur in the same phrase. As shown in (9a), in this construction the

NQ is in the modifier position of the NP headed by the "counted" noun. The construction with the NQ occurring separately is given in (9b) for comparison.

(9) a. [$_{NP}$ **San-nin**-no gakusei]-ga kita.
three-CL-GEN students-NOM came
'Three students came.'

b. Gakusei-ga **san-nin** kita.
students-NOM three-CL came
'Three students came.'

The existence of these two constructions has led many linguists to claim that the construction in (9b) is transformationally derived from (9a) by the rule of quantifier float (see, e.g., Okutsu 1974; Shibatani 1977, 1978). I briefly review this literature in the next section.

In this chapter, I look at the syntactic and semantic factors that govern the construal of the syntactically separate NQ with its NP. In other words, my primary concern is the construction exemplified in (9b), in which the NQ is clearly syntactically separate from its NP. I propose that the NQ in examples such as (9b) can be related to the appropriate NP by the theory of predication (Williams 1980; Rothstein 1983; Culicover and Wilkins 1984).

The theory of predication provides the conditions necessary for the construal of "small clauses" in English, such as *raw* in the following example:

(10) John ate the meat **raw.**

In the theory of predication, *raw* is considered a predicate that modifies (is predicated of) the object NP *meat*. A small clause can also modify the subject.

(11) John ate the meat **nude.**

While a NQ may not transparently qualify as a predicate, we can nevertheless note similarities between the small clause and the NQ. First, the small clause and the NQ are syntactically separate from the NP that they modify. We saw this for the NQ in (7) and (8), where an independent phrase intervenes between the NP and the NQ. Second, neither the small clause nor the NQ is an argument of the verb because the verb does not assign a thematic role to it.[4] Finally, both most commonly modify subjects and direct objects. My contention is that this parallelism between NQs and small clauses is not coincidental, but rather it is because both are governed by the theory of predication.[5]

In looking at the NQ, one goal is, of course, to formulate a viable analysis of the NQ. It is not enough, however, to just propose such an analysis. For the research to have a true impact on the study of Japanese in particular and universal grammar in general, it is necessary to look at the consequences of the proposed analysis for the entire Japanese language. In turn, we must reflect on yet other consequences, this time for the theory of universal grammar. The particular perspective on the NQ proposed in this chapter has a number of significant consequences both for the analysis of the Japanese language and for universal grammar, some of them quite unexpected. Among others, the analysis of the NQ provides evidence that the regular passive in Japanese involves movement, and that the so-called unaccusative[6] verbs (Burzio 1981, 1986; Perlmutter 1978) also involve movement, even in Japanese. As I demonstrate, this evidence for movement in the passive and unaccusative constructions constitutes one of the strongest pieces of empirical evidence found for an important theoretical object, the NP trace (see, e.g., Chomsky 1977, 1981).

The analysis of the NQ based on the theory of predication assumes that the NQ has not been moved by quantifier float. Instead, the syntactically separate NQ is seen as base-generated in its position to begin with. In this chapter, I provide support for this analysis and look at its consequences for a number of constructions including the passive and the topic constructions.

The next sections are organized as follows. Section 2 gives an overview of past studies of the NQ. In Section 3, I present an analysis of the NQ that is based on the theory of predication. Based on this analysis, I argue in Section 4 that both the direct-passive and unaccusative constructions in Japanese involve the movement of the underlying object to the subject position, leaving behind a trace in the original object position.[7]

2 PAST STUDIES OF THE NUMERAL QUANTIFIER

Virtually all of the past literature on the NQ centers on the relationship between the two constructions exemplified in the following pair of examples. The assumption is that the rule of quantifier float derives a construction such as (13) from (12).

(12) San-nin-no kodomo-ga kita.
three-CL-GEN children-NOM came
'Three children came.'

(13) Kodomo-ga san-nin kita.
children-NOM three-CL came
'Three children came.'

There are three hypotheses proposed in the literature for the relationship between (12) and (13). For present purposes, I call them the *grammatical-relations hypothesis*, the *surface-case hypothesis*, and the *extended grammatical-relations hypothesis.* The grammatical-relations hypothesis is found in works such as Okutsu 1969, 1974; Harada 1976c; and Kuno 1978. Shibatani (1977, 1978) proposes the surface-case hypothesis. And finally, Inoue (1978a) proposes the extended grammatical-relations hypothesis.

For each hypothesis, it is possible to abstract away from its assumptions about the issue of quantifier float and look at the condition it imposes on "derived structures" such as (13). I prefer this approach because the analysis of the NQ presented later in this chapter does not assume the rule of quantifier float. The proposed analysis focuses on the structural and semantic constraints imposed on constructions such as (13). For ease of exposition, I henceforth refer to the NP modified by the NQ as the *antecedent* of the NQ, following the terminology of Culicover and Wilkins 1984, 1986.

2.1 The grammatical-relations hypothesis

The grammatical-relations hypothesis (Okutsu 1969, 1974; Harada 1976c; Kuno 1978) states that the antecedent of a NQ must be either a subject or an object. Thus, while (14) and (15) are well formed, (16), in which the antecedent is the indirect object, is ill formed.

(14) Gakusei-ga **san-nin** hon-o katta.
students-NOM three-CL book-ACC bought
'Three students bought a book. '

(15) Gakusei-ga hon-o **san-satu** katta.
student-NOM book-ACC three-CL bought
'A student bought three books.'

(16) (?)Hanako-ga kodomo-ni **futa-ri** okasi-o ageta.[8]
Hanako-NOM children-to two-CL candy-ACC gave
'Hanako gave candies to two children.'

Further support for the grammatical-relations hypothesis is the following contrast between two "verbs of receiving" constructions (Harada 1976c):

(17) Taroo-wa sensei-ni **futa-ri** suisenzyoo-o
Taro-TOP teachers-DAT two-CL recommendation letters-ACC
kaite moratta.
write had
'Taro had two teachers write (him) recommendation letters.'

(18) *Taroo-wa sensei-ni **futa-ri** hon-o moratta.
Taro-TOP teachers-from two-CL book-ACC got
(Intended: 'Taro got books from two teachers.')

In (17), the antecedent of the NQ *futa-ri* can be analyzed as the subject of the embedded verb *kaite* 'write', thus the sentence is well formed. On the other hand, in (18), the same antecedent cannot function as the subject because the sentence is uniclausal, thus the NQ cannot take *sensei(-ni)* '(from) teachers' as its antecedent.[9]

The same phenomenon is observed in the indirect and direct passives (Harada 1976c). In the indirect passive, the NP marked by the dative *-ni* can be viewed as the subject of the embedded verb, while in the direct passive it cannot (Kuno 1973). Therefore, the *-ni*-marked NP can be the antecedent of a NQ in the indirect passive but not in the direct passive.

(19) Boku-wa kodomo-ni **futa-ri** sin-are-ta. Indirect passive
me-TOP children-DAT two-CL die-PASS-PAST
'I had two children die on me.'

(20) *Taroo-wa sensei-ni **futa-ri** sikar-are-ta. Direct passive
Taro-TOP teachers-by two-CL scold-PASS-PAST
(Intended: 'Taro was scolded by two teachers.')

2.2 The surface-case hypothesis

Shibatani (1977, 1978) rejects the grammatical-relations hypothesis, and argues that what is crucial is the surface case marking of the antecedent. In particular, only the nominative (*-ga*) and the accusative (*-o*) NPs can function as the antecedent of a NQ. His argument rests crucially on two tests for subjecthood, reflexivization and subject honorification. The latter inserts the discontinuous morpheme *o- . . . -ni-nar* on the verb (cf. Harada 1976b). Shibatani's point is that these two tests identify certain dative-marked NPs as subjects, yet the same NPs cannot function as antecedent of a NQ.[10] The NP can function as such if marked by the nominative *-ga*. The following are examples taken from Shibatani 1977:

(21) Reflexivization
Sensei-ni(-wa) **zibun**-ga wakar-ana-i.
teacher-DAT(-TOP) self-NOM understand-not-PRES
'The teacher does not understand himself.'

(22) Subject honorification
Sensei-ni(-wa) eigo-ga o-wakari-**ni-nar**-u.
teacher-DAT(-TOP) English-NOM $\text{understand}_{\text{HONORIFIC}}$
'The teacher understands English.'

As Shibatani notes, despite the fact that the dative NP in (21) and (22) is identified as the subject, the same NP cannot function as the antecedent of a NQ.

(23) *Korerano kodomatati-ni **san-nin** eigo-ga wakaru.
these children-DAT three-CL English-NOM understand
(Intended: 'These three children understand English.')

These examples indicate a discrepancy between grammatical relations and what can function as the antecedent of a NQ. Shibatani views this discrepancy as a demonstration of the invalidity of the grammatical-relations hypothesis and uses it to support his surface-case hypothesis. In particular, he notes that the possible antecedent can only have the nominative *-ga* or the accusative *-o*. Hence, unlike (23), example (24) with the nominative case on the subject is acceptable.

(24) Korerano kodomotati-ga **san-nin** eigo-ga wakaru.
these children-NOM three-CL English-NOM understand
'These three children understand English.'

Example (24) is identical to (23), except that in (24) the subject is marked with the nominative *-ga* instead of the dative *-ni*.[11]

2.3 The extended grammatical-relations hypothesis

Inoue (1978a, 172–174) proposes what I term an *extended* grammatical-relations hypothesis that incorporates what she calls *quasi-objects* as possible antecedents of the NQ along with the subject and the object. The following examples are from her work. (I provide the word-for-word gloss and the English translation.)

(25) Watakusi-wa dantaikyaku-o tomeru **yadoya-ni ni-san-gen**
me-TOP group of guests-ACC let stay inns-DAT two-three-CL
atatte mita.
inquired
'I inquired at two or three inns that let groups of guests stay.'

(26) Watakusi-wa hasi-o **futa-tu-ka mit-tu** watatta-to
me-TOP bridges-TRAV two-CL-or three-CL crossed-COMP
kiokusite iru.
remember
'I remember that I crossed two or three bridges.'

Inoue notes that both the dative NP of *ataru* 'inquire' in (25) and the traversal NP, marked with *-o*, of the verb *wataru* 'cross' in (26) are subcategorized

NPs. This, she contends, is the reason why they can function as the antecedent of a NQ. These NPs are labeled quasi-objects to distinguish them from regular direct objects and also indirect objects. Indirect objects in her analysis cannot function as the antecedent; the following example is from her work (1978a, 29; I have provided the English gloss and translation).

(27) *Watakusi-wa kono zisyo-o **syoonentati-ni** **suu-nin**
me-TOP this dictionary-ACC boys-to few-CL
presento-sita.
presented
(Intended: 'I presented this dictionary to a few boys.')

The indirect object here is not subcategorized by the verb (it is not a necessary phrase), hence it is incapable of being the antecedent. Based on this distinction between indirect objects and quasi-objects, Inoue extends the list of possible antecedents of NQs to include quasi-objects along with subjects and direct objects.

An important insight of Inoue's study is the distinction between subcategorized and nonsubcategorized NPs; she argues that only the subcategorized ones can function as the antecedent. In more recent terminology, this is the distinction between *arguments* and *adjuncts* (see, e.g., Chomsky 1981; Huang 1982). I shall focus on this distinction and show that the crucial factor is not grammatical relations or surface case but instead whether an NP receives a thematic role from an external source such as the verb. This analysis follows automatically from the theory of predication and is therefore most compatible with Inoue's extended grammatical-relations approach. Also, among the studies reviewed in this section, Inoue's is the only one that explicitly rejects the rule of quantifier float, instead viewing the NQ as being base-generated in its position. This, too, is a view that I share.

3 MUTUAL-C-COMMAND REQUIREMENT ON PREDICATION

In order for a predicate such as the NQ to successfully modify an NP, a particular structural relationship must hold between the predicate and the NP. The following exemplify cases where a NQ successfully modifies an NP:

(28) **Gakusei-ga** **san-nin** hon-o katta.
students-NOM three-CL book-ACC bought
'Three students bought the book.'

(29) Hanako-ga **pen-o** **san-bon** katta.
Hanako-NOM pen-ACC three-CL bought
'Hanako bought three pens.'

In (28) the NQ *san-nin* modifies the subject NP *gakusei* 'students', and in (29) the NQ *san-bon* modifies the object NP *pen* 'pen'. If we simply consider the linear order of words, we see that in both examples the NQ is adjacent to the NP that it modifies. It is well known, however, that adjacency is not always required. For example, an adverbial phrase can intervene between the NP and the NQ.

(30) **Gakusei-ga** kyoo **san-nin** hon-o katta.
students-NOM today three-CL book-ACC bought
'Three students bought the book today.'

(31) Hanako-ga **pen-o** kyoo **san-bon** katta.
Hanako-NOM pen-ACC today three-CL bought
'Hanako bought three pens today.'

The fact that the NQ in these two examples successfully modifies an NP despite the intervening adverb suggests that the relevant condition cannot be formulated on the basis of surface word order. Instead, it points to a condition that relies on abstract sentential structures.

3.1 Mutual-c-command condition

Although a time adverbial such as *kyoo* 'today' can intervene between the NP and the NQ, as we saw in (30) and (31), other types of phrases obstruct predication if placed between the NP and the NQ. Observe the contrast between the following examples (cf. Kamio 1977).

(32) **Tomodati-ga futa-ri** Sinzyuku-de Tanaka-sensei-ni atta.
friend-NOM two-CL Shinjuku-in Professor Tanaka-DAT met
'Two friends met Professor Tanaka in Shinjuku.'

(33) ****Tomodati-ga** Sinzyuku-de Tanaka-sensei-ni **futa-ri** atta.
friend-NOM Shinjuku-in Professor Tanaka-DAT two-CL met
(Intended: 'Two friends met Professor Tanaka in Shinjuku.')

The NQ *futa-ri* is intended to modify the subject NP *tomodati* 'friends' in both examples, but the predication is accomplished only in (32). To see why the NQ in (33) cannot modify the subject NP, let us compare the structure of these two sentences. (I exclude the postpositional phrase *Sinzyuku-de* 'in Shinjuku' since it has no bearing on the argument.)

(34) = (32)

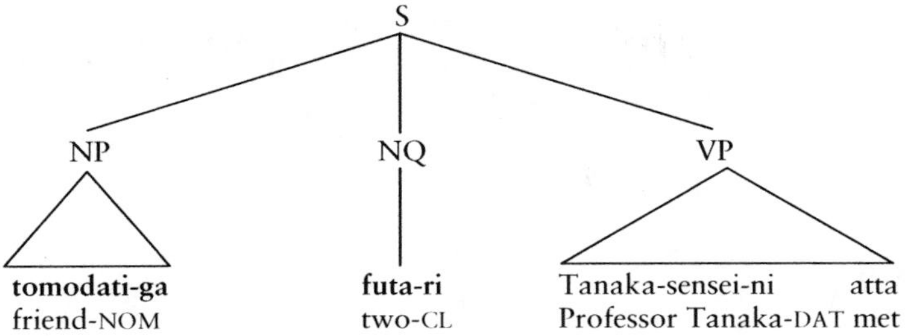

(35) = (33)

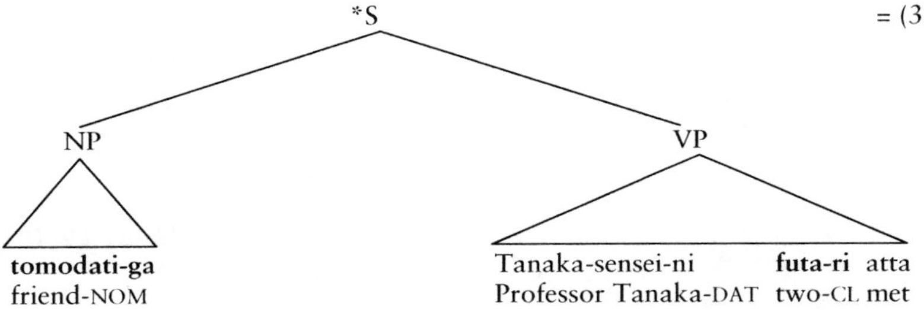

The crucial difference between these two structures is that, in the grammatical example in (34), the NQ occurs outside the VP, but in the ungrammatical example in (35), the same NQ occurs inside the VP. To be more precise, in the ungrammatical structure in (35), the NQ does not c-command the NP that it modifies. The following is the definition of c-command (Reinhart 1979).

(36) *A* c-commands *B* if neither of *A*, *B* dominates the other and the first branching node dominating *A* also dominates *B*.

In (35) the NQ *futa-ri* cannot c-command the subject NP because the first branching node, VP, that dominates it fails to dominate the subject NP. On the other hand, in the grammatical structure in (34) the NQ does c-command the subject NP because the first branching node that dominates the NQ, namely S, also dominates the subject NP.

It is evident then that the NQ must c-command the NP for predication to take place. This is the reason why (32) is fine but (33) is ungrammatical. The question now is whether this is a sufficient condition to cover all cases of possible and impossible predication structures. The following example demonstrates that another condition must also be included.

(37) *[$_{NP}$ **Tomodati-no** kuruma]-ga **san-nin** kosyoosita.
friend-GEN car-NOM three-CL broke down
(Intended: 'Three friends' cars broke down.')

The NQ *san-nin* is intended to modify the NP *tomodati* 'friends', but this predication is somehow blocked. Note that while the NQ c-commands the NP, the NP does not in turn c-command the NQ.

(38)

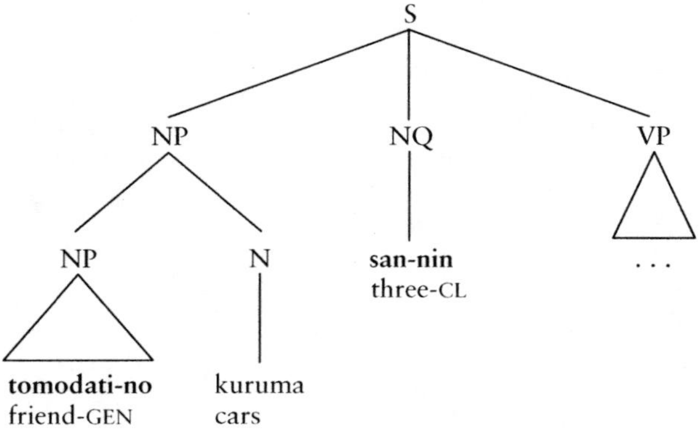

Based on this, I propose the following condition (cf. Williams 1980).

(39) Mutual-c-command requirement

For a predicate to predicate of an NP, the NP or its trace and the predicate or its trace must c-command each other.

The mutual-c-command requirement accounts for all of the grammatical and ungrammatical sentences that we have seen, including the examples in (30) and (31) in which a time adverb occurs between the NP and the NQ.[12] Again consider example (30), repeated here as (40).

(40) **Gakusei-ga** kyoo **san-nin** hon-o katta.
students-NOM today three-CL book-ACC bought
'Three students bought the book today.'

The time adverb *kyoo* 'today' occurs between the subject NP and the NQ. A time adverbial can occur virtually anywhere in the sentence. It need not have a special node to which it attaches, any available node being sufficient. By this assumption, the relevant structure of (40) is (41).

(41)

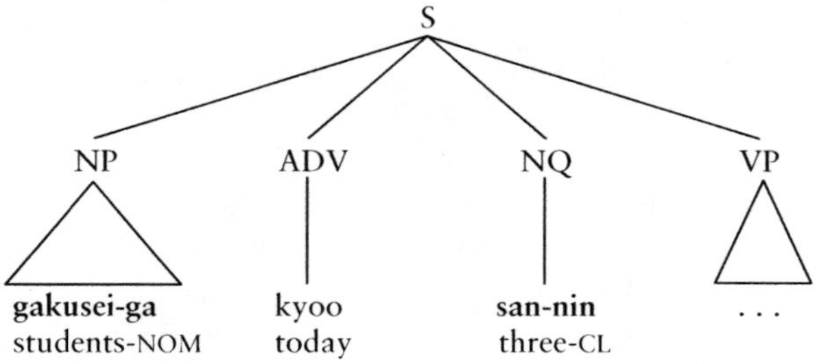

In (41) the NP *gakusei* 'students' and the NQ *san-nin* c-command each other because neither dominates the other, and the first branching node, S, that dominates one also dominates the other.

The mutual-c-command requirement also accounts for the following grammatical example:

(42) **san-mai,** kodomo-ga **sara-o** watta (koto)
three-CL child-NOM plates-ACC broke fact
'(the fact that) the child broke three plates'

Here, the NQ *san-mai* is allowed to modify the VP-internal NP *sara* 'plates' despite the fact that the NQ is clearly outside the VP. Example (42) meets the mutual-c-command requirement if we assume the following structure:

(43) $[_S$ san-mai$_i$ . . . $[_{VP}$ sara-o t_i . . .]]
three-CL plates-ACC

The structure in (43) readily fulfills the mutual-c-command requirement if we allow the trace to participate in the c-command relationship with the NP. Likewise, the following example, in which the object NP has moved from its original position in the VP, can be accounted for if we allow its trace to participate in the c-command relationship with the NQ.[13]

(44) **Hon-o**$_i$, Taroo-ga $[_{VP}$ t_i **ni-satu** katta].
book-ACC Taro-NOM two-CL bought
'Taro bought two books.'

3.2 The mutual-c-command requirement and the postpositional phrase

One clear agreement among the past treatments of the NQ is that a NQ cannot take as its antecedent an NP that is within a postpositional phrase (PP).

(45) a. *Hito-ga **tiisai mura**-kara **futa-tu** kita.
people-NOM small villages-from two-CL came

b. Hito-ga futa-tu-no tiisai mura-kara kita.
people-NOM two-CL-GEN small villages-from came
'People came from two small villages.'

(46) a. *Gakuseitati-wa **kuruma**-de **ni-dai** kita.
students-TOP cars-in two-CL came

b. Gakuseitati-wa ni-dai-no kuruma-de kita.
students-TOP two-CL-GEN cars-in came
'Students came in two cars.'

(47) a. *Hanako-wa **kooen**-e **futa-tu** itta.
Hanako-TOP parks-to two-CL went

b. Hanako-wa futa-tu-no kooen-e itta.
Hanako-TOP two-CL-GEN parks-to went
'Hanako went to two parks.'

The grammatical-relations hypothesis correctly excludes the intended predication because the antecedent is neither the subject nor the direct object (nor the quasi-object). The surface-case hypothesis excludes it because the intended antecedent is not marked with the nominative *-ga* or the accusative *-o*.

In the theory of predication, the ungrammaticality of (45a), (46a), and (47a) automatically follows from the syntactic structure without any reference to grammatical relations or case marking. The mutual-c-command condition on predication excludes any structure in which the antecedent is embedded within a PP, since such an NP cannot c-command the NQ external to the PP, as shown in (48).

(48)

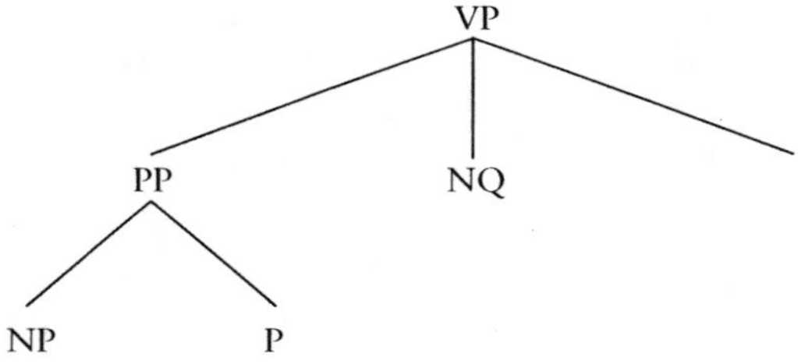

3.2.1 Case marking and postpositions

This analysis of the NQ based on mutual c-command has an immediate consequence for the structural analysis of the Japanese NP + particle sequence. In Japanese, every NP in a sentence is accompanied by a particle, either a case marker such as the nominative *-ga* and accusative *-o* or a postposition such as *-kara* 'from' and *-de* 'in, at; with, by'. The mutual-c-command analysis makes a clear distinction between these two types of particles based on whether they project a maximal node under which the potential antecedent NP occurs: a postposition does project such a node (PP) whereas case markers such as the nominative *-ga* and the accusative *-o* do not.

As demonstrated in the prior section, an NP with a postposition is incapable of functioning as the antecedent of a NQ because of the PP node that is projected from the postposition. This PP node prohibits the NP from c-commanding the NQ. In contrast, if an NP can function as the antecedent of a NQ, the accompanying particle has no projection but rather is cliticized onto the NP. These two structures are shown in (49) and (50) for phrases both internal and external to the VP.

(49) PP structure

a.

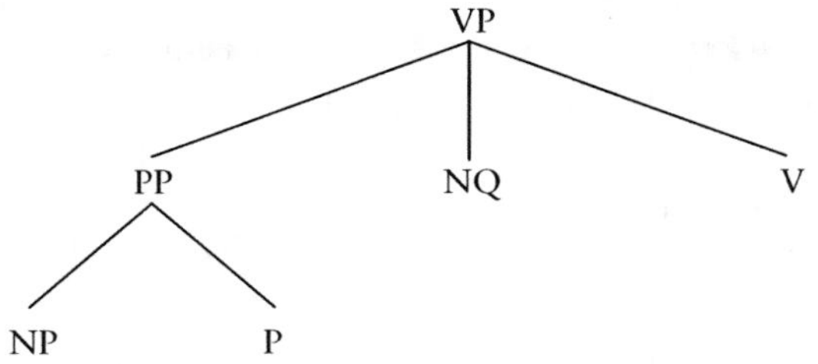

b.

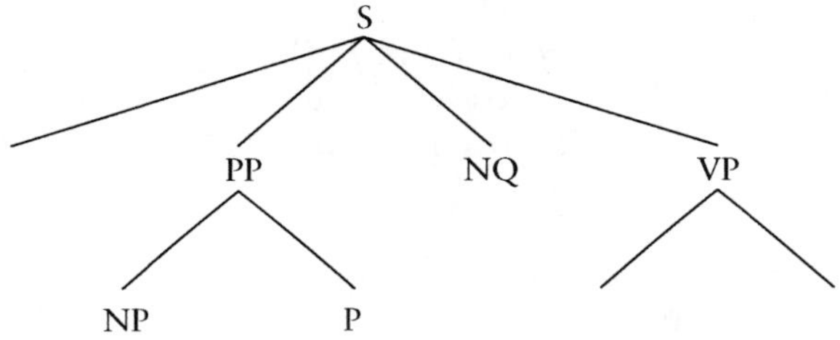

(50) Cliticized structure

a.

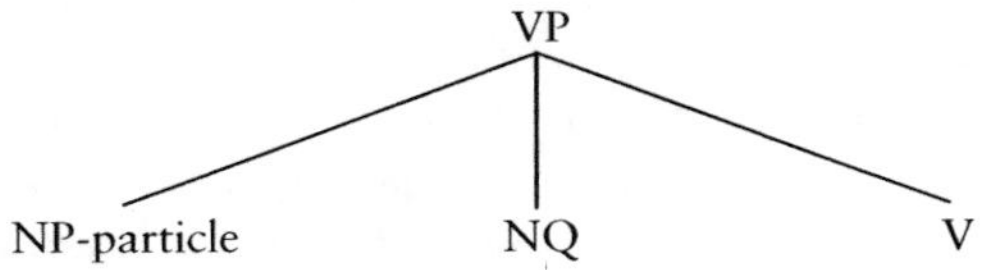

b.

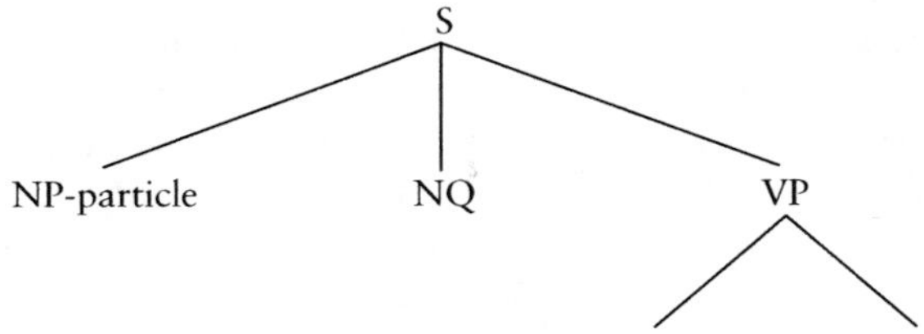

I have already discussed why the NP under the PP in (49) cannot be the antecedent to the NQ. In (50), the particle has no projection, instead cliticizing onto the NP. Because of this, the NP is capable of c-commanding the NQ in both (50a) and (50b). If the particle in (50) were to have a projection, it would be impossible to construe the NQ as intended.

What are the particles that cliticize directly onto an NP as in (50)? The two that immediately come to mind are the nominative *-ga* and the accusative *-o*. These two particles, unlike postpositions such as *-kara* 'from', share one crucial property. The NP to which *-ga* or *-o* attaches receives its thematic role not from the particle but from an external source: if the NP occurs in the subject position (marked by *-ga*), the thematic role is assigned by the VP (cf. Chomsky 1981; Marantz 1984); if it occurs within the VP, the thematic role is assigned directly by the V (the NP here has *-o*).

(51) [Taroo-ga [$_{VP}$hon-o katta]].
Taro-NOM book-ACC bought
'Taro bought a book.'

In (51), the phrase *Taroo-ga* receives the agent thematic role from the VP node (the agent of 'bought a book'). The phrase *hon-o* receives its thematic role directly from the verb (the theme of 'bought').

In contrast, the object of a postposition such as *-kara* receives its thematic role, namely ablative, directly from the postposition itself. We therefore have the following generalization:

(52) If a particle assigns a thematic role to the NP, the particle has a projection (postposition); if the NP receives its thematic role from an external source, the particle has no projection but instead cliticizes onto the NP (case marking).

The distinction in (52) is, at its core, the common distinction between arguments and adjuncts. In brief, an argument is a phrase that bears some grammatical relation, most commonly subject or object, whereas an adjunct phrase does not. In this sense, the grammatical-relations approach to the NQ captures the correct generalization. Our approach differs from the grammatical-relations approach in that I do not draw a *direct* correlation between grammatical relations and the antecedent of a NQ but focus instead on the syntactic structure as defined by mutual c-command. A subject, for example, can function as the antecedent not because it has the grammatical relation of subject but because, being a subject, it has the cliticized NP-particle structure that is amenable to predication according to the mutual-c-command condition. In other words, a NQ seeks out a subject NP (for example) as its antecedent not by grammatical relation but simply by structural affinity, due to the nonprojecting status of the particle.

3.2.2 *Case theory and the two particle structures*

The distinction drawn between the PP structure and the case-cliticization structure is a natural one when we consider the function of the various particles. Take, for example, the postposition *-kara* 'from'. This postposition has semantic content that is fully realized in combination with its object NP, for example, *uti-kara* 'from the house'; the postposition takes the NP as its argument and assigns the thematic role of ablative. For this to happen, the NP must occur in the object position of the postposition, as in (53).

(53)

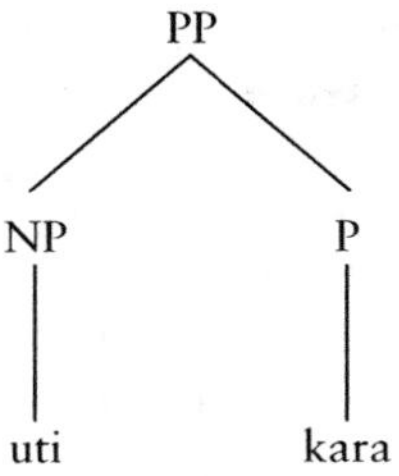

This structure, in particular the PP projection, is necessitated by the function of the postposition that requires it to have an NP object, to which the ablative thematic role is assigned.

In contrast, the nominative *-ga* and the accusative *-o* do not have semantic content, so the thematic role that the NP with these particles has is provided by a source external to the case-cliticization structure. As pointed out for (51), the subject NP with *-ga* receives its thematic role from the VP whereas the direct-object NP with *-o* receives its thematic role directly from the verb. If *-ga* and *-o* do not provide a thematic role to their NP, why do these particles need to occur at all? In order to answer this question, it is necessary to turn to a universal linguistic principle.

The appearance of these case markings can be accounted for if we view them as having just one function: to provide case to the NP. The subtheory of universal grammar pertinent to case marking is case theory (Chomsky 1981; Stowell 1981), which requires that every overt NP have case. This is formalized into what is called the case filter, one version of which is given below.

(54) Case filter (Chomsky 1981)
*NP if NP has phonetic content and has no case.

This principle marks as ungrammatical any sentence containing a caseless NP. Nominative *-ga* and the accusative *-o* occur to fulfill the requirement that the overt NPs be case-marked. Because these case particles do not themselves require an NP argument in the way that we saw for postpositions, we would not expect them to project a phrasal node of their own. Instead, they simply cliticize onto the NP in order to fulfill their sole function as the provider of case. I will henceforth refer to particles such as *-ga* and *-o* as case markers and those such as *-kara* 'from' as postpositions.[14]

3.2.3 Arguments and adjuncts

Returning to the NQ, the case cliticization of *-ga* and *-o* accounts for the observation made by the grammatical-relations hypothesis that the subject and direct-object NPs can function as the antecedent of the NQ. The cliticized case-marking structure makes the subject and object NPs amenable to the mutual-c-command requirement. Because the present analysis does not depend on grammatical relations but only on structure, I predict that any NP, including the subject and the direct object, whose thematic role is provided by an external source rather than the particle can function as the antecedent of the NQ. This makes it possible to also incorporate the observation made by Inoue (1978a)—what I term the "extended grammatical-relations" hypothesis—that certain nonsubject, non-direct-object NPs can function as the antecedent. Two such NPs are the traversal object and certain dative NPs.

(55) Taroo-wa **hasi-o** **futa-tu** watatta.
Taro-TOP bridges-TRAV two-CL crossed
'Taro crossed two bridges.'

(56) Boku-wa **yuumei na gakusya-ni** **san-nin** atta.
me-TOP famous scholars-DAT three-CL met
'I met three famous scholars.'

Inoue observes that these antecedent NPs (termed quasi-objects) are required by the verb. From our perspective, these are arguments of the verb and thus receive a thematic role directly from the verb instead of from the particle. The function of the particle is therefore simply to provide case to the NP, so that the particle is a case marker that cliticizes onto the NP as we saw for the subject and direct-object NPs.

Our analysis predicts, then, that any NP internal to the VP that can function as the antecedent is an argument of the verb. For example, while we have seen that the NP marked with *-ni* is an argument for verbs *au* 'meet' and *ataru* 'inquire' (examples (25) and (32) as well as (56)), the following examples show that the goal NP, marked with *-ni* for the verbs *iku* 'go' and *kuru* 'come', is not an argument of these verbs; hence it is an adjunct.

(57) a. *Kodomotati-wa **kooen-ni** **futa-tu** itta.
children-TOP parks-to two-CL went

b. Kodomotati-wa **futa-tu-no** **kooen-ni** itta.
children-TOP two-CL-GEN parks-to went
'The children went to two parks.'

(58) a. *Kyonen, Hanako-wa **paatii-ni** **mit-tu** kita.
last year Hanako-TOP parties-to three-CL came

b. Kyonen, Hanako-wa **mit-tu-no** **paatii-ni** kita.
last year Hanako-TOP three-CL-GEN parties-to came
'Last year, Hanako came to three parties.'

These show that the particle *-ni* 'to' with *iku* 'go' and *kuru* 'come' is a postposition that projects the PP node, thereby making it impossible to obtain the mutual-c-command relationship between the NP and the NQ.[15]

It is also worth noting that the same verb can select a *-ni*-marked phrase either as an argument or as an adjunct. As pointed out by Nobuko Hasegawa (personal communication), the verb *katu* 'win' can take a *-ni* phrase that either denotes the person/team that the subject won against (beat) or the type of game that the subject won. Only the latter, however, can be the argument of the verb.

(59) *Taroo-ga Amerikazin-ni **san-nin** katta.
Taro-NOM Americans-*NI* three-CL won
(Intended: 'Taro beat three Americans (in a game of some sort).')

(60) Taroo-ga geemu-ni **futa-tu** katta.
Taro-NOM game-*NI* two-CL won
'Taro won two games.'

As also noted by Hasegawa, although Japanese allows both of these phrases to occur with the same particle, English allows only the counterpart of (60): *John won the game/*Henry.*

3.2.4 *Mutual c-command and the surface-case hypothesis*

Recall from Section 2.2 that Shibatani (1977) gives examples of what he calls "dative subject" to support the idea that the antecedent of a NQ is not decided by grammatical relations. In particular, he notes that NPs that qualify as a subject by the reflexivization and subject-honorification tests can function as the antecedent if marked by the nominative *-ga* but not the dative *-ni.*

(61) Korerano kodomotati-**ga/*-ni san-nin** eigo-ga hanaseru.
these children-NOM/-DAT three-CL English-NOM can speak
'These three children can speak English.'

Our analysis predicts that the NP *korerano kodomotati* 'these children' is the subject NP only if marked by *-ga*. If the dative *-ni* appears instead, the particle projects the PP node that blocks mutual c-command. Being a PP, the dative phrase is not the subject. Saito (1982) in fact argues independently that the dative subject is a PP.

3.3 Passive formation

I now apply the mutual-c-command analysis to the passive formation. In Japanese, there are two types of passives, commonly called *direct* and *indirect* (or *pure* and *adversative*, cf. Kuno 1973). Both types of passives are formed by attaching the bound passive morpheme *-(r)are* to a verb. The direct passive is similar to the English passive in that the passive morpheme attaches to a transitive verb and the subject is the original object NP of the transitive verb. The agentive phrase is marked by *-ni* 'by'.

(62) Kodomo-ga oya-ni sikar-are-ta.
child-NOM parents-by scold-PASS-PAST
'The child was scolded by his parents.'

The indirect passive differs from the direct passive in that the attachment of the passive morpheme *-(r)are* results in the addition of an experiencer NP. In the indirect passive, the passive morpheme can attach to intransitive and transitive verbs.

(63) Taroo-ga ame-ni fur-are-ta.
Taro-NOM rain-DAT fall-PASS-PAST
'Taro was rained on.'

(64) Hanako-ga sensei-ni kodomo-o sikar-are-ta.
Hanako-NOM teacher-DAT child-ACC scold-PASS-PAST
'Hanako had her child scolded by the teacher.'

The referent of the added experiencer phrase (*Taroo* in (63), *Hanako* in (64)) is understood to be somehow affected by the action, usually in an adverse fashion (cf. Kuno 1973).

3.3.1 Direct passive

There are two analyses proposed in the literature for the direct passive that presuppose a simplex structure throughout the derivation. The first is a movement analysis (Kuno 1973), which regards the subject of the passive as having moved to that position from the object position, very much like the analysis proposed for the English passive (Chomsky 1981). Under this analysis, the passive sentence in (62) above has the structure in (65).

(65)

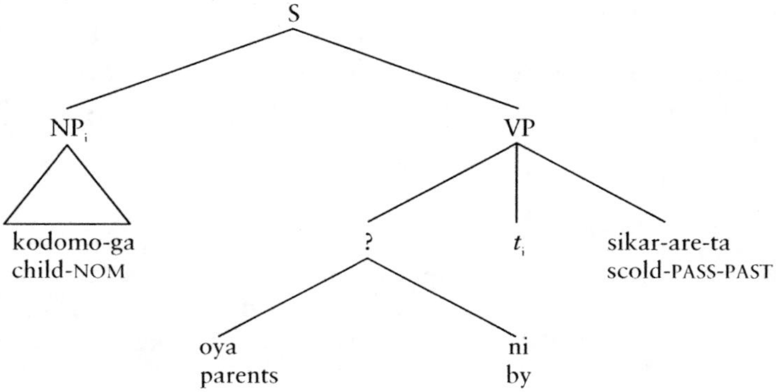

The other approach is a strictly lexical one (e.g., Miyagawa 1980). In this analysis, it is assumed that no movement has occurred; the passive verb simply takes as its subject what corresponds to the object of the transitive verb. An analysis of this sort has been proposed for English as well (e.g., Williams 1981a).

The mutual-c-command requirement on NQ predication helps us to choose between these two possible accounts. As we shall see, the movement account is more promising than the lexical account.

The crucial example is the following:

(66) Yuube, **kuruma-ga** doroboo-ni **ni-dai** nusum-are-ta.
last night cars-NOM thief-by two-CL steal-PASS-PAST
'Last night, two cars were stolen by a thief.'

The important point to note is that the NQ *ni-dai* occurs in the VP, *and* it successfully modifies the subject NP *kuruma* 'car' (see also Ueda 1986). Example (66) sharply contrasts with a nonpassive example such as (67).

(67) ***Tomodati-ga** Sinzyuku-de Tanaka-sensei-ni **futa-ri** atta.
friend-NOM Shinjuku-in Professor Tanaka-DAT two-CL met
(Intended: 'Two friends met Professor Tanaka in Shinjuku.')

Just as in (66), there is a NQ, *futa-ri,* in the VP that is intended to modify the subject NP. Unlike (66), (67) is ungrammatical because the NQ fails to c-command the subject NP.

There can only be one reason why (66) is grammatical. The NQ somehow manages to c-command the subject NP. The NQ obviously cannot directly c-command the NP in the subject position because of the intervening maximal projection VP. The only choice open to us is that the subject NP starts out in the object position and is moved to the subject position, leaving behind a trace. The relevant portion of the structure for (66) is thus the following:

(68)

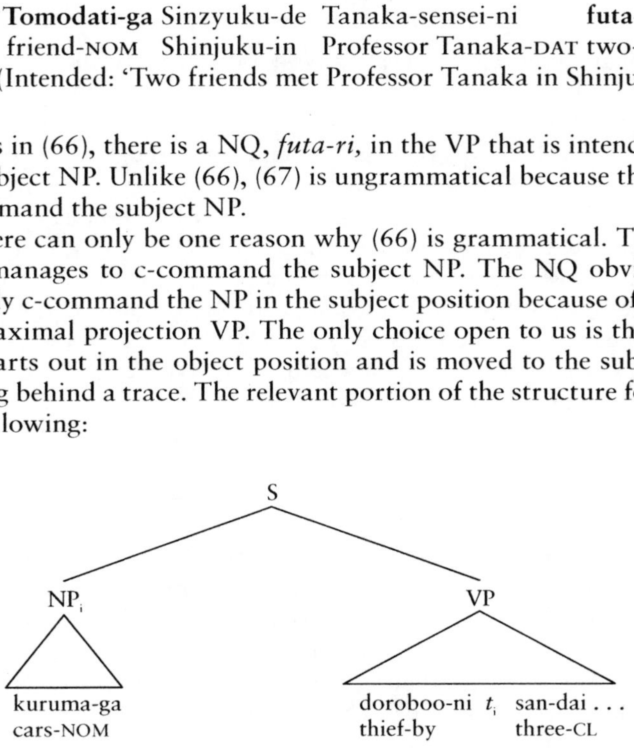

Before the movement, the NP and the NQ mutually c-command each other directly because both occur in the VP. After the movement, the mutual-c-command relation is maintained by the trace left by the NP. The following are other passive examples similar to (66):

(69) Kinoo, **gakusei-ga** ano otoko-ni **futa-ri** koros-are-ta.
yesterday students-NOM that man-by two-CL kill-PASS-PAST
'Yesterday, two students were killed by that man.'

(70) Gakkoo-no mae-de, **kodomo-ga** kuruma-ni **futa-ri**
school-GEN front-in children-NOM car-by two-CL
run over-PASS-PAST
hik-are-ta.
'Two children were run over by a car in front of school.'

(71) Ano mise-de-wa, **takai** **konpyuutaa-ga** okyakusan-ni **ni-dai**
that store-at-TOP expensive computer-NOM customer-by two-CL
kowas-are-ta.
break-PASS-PAST
'At that store, two expensive computers were broken by a customer.'

The movement analysis of the direct passive assumes that the bound passive morpheme lexically attaches to a transitive verb. According to the movement analysis of the passive in English (Chomsky 1981), the addition of the passive morphology does two things: it "suppresses" the original agentive role of the transitive verb; and it "absorbs" the case-assigning ability of the transitive verb. The latter causes the object NP to be without case, thus forcing it to move to the subject position in order to receive case from INFL (inflection). Suppression of the external thematic role allows the object NP to move to the subject position because the subject position is not associated with a thematic role. Otherwise, the NP would have two thematic roles, the thematic role originally assigned to it as an object NP (theme) and the agent role assigned by the transitive verb to its subject position. I provisionally assume this analysis for the Japanese direct passive. The important point, of course, is that the analysis predicts movement of the object NP to the subject position, leaving a trace, which allows the mutual c-command to be maintained.

It is important to note that the argument given above for the movement analysis of the direct passive hinges on the assumption that the agentive phrase (marked by the particle *-ni* 'by') is in the VP. Otherwise, there is no guarantee that the NQ that follows the agentive phrase is itself in the VP, hence making it questionable that its ability to take the subject NP as its antecedent is due to the existence of the trace within the VP.

The assumed VP-internal status of the passive agentive phrase is upheld if we follow Jaeggli's (1986) analysis of the passive. In particular, he proposes that the passive morpheme subcategorizes for the 'by' NP in that the passive morpheme, which absorbs the external θ-role of the verb, in turn discharges this θ-role onto the PP via the preposition 'by' (see his work for details). This accounts for the fact that the agentive NP of the passive is not always "agentive." It is whatever corresponds to the external θ-role of the verb. For example, in *the package was received by John, John* can be interpreted not as the agent but as the goal, which is an option open for the external role in the nonpassivized form of the verb. This assignment of the absorbed external thematic role by the passive morpheme presumably occurs under government, hence the 'by' phrase must be in the VP, since Jaeggli argues that the passive morpheme subcategorizes the PP headed by 'by'.

We see a similar phenomenon in Japanese. In the following example, the NP marked with *-ni* is the experiencer, which is the original external role of the verb *sinpaisuru* 'worry'.

(72) Sono koto-ga **minna-ni** sinpais-are-ta.
that matter-NOM everyone-by worry-PASS-PAST
Lit. 'That matter was worried by everyone.'

The *-ni* phrase here can only have this experiencer role if the phrase occurs in the VP, and it receives this thematic role from the passive morphology, as argued by Jaeggli (1986).

3.3.2 *Indirect passive*

Unlike the direct passive, the indirect passive does not switch the order of the arguments. Instead, it adds an experiencer NP, which then becomes the subject of the passive verb. What is involved here is not movement but simply the addition of an extra argument (the experiencer argument). Certainly, we cannot conceive of an NP movement from within the VP to the subject position as we did for the direct passive. This predicts that a NQ within the VP cannot modify the subject NP of the passive because there is no trace coindexed with the subject NP. This is borne out in the following:

(73) ***Kodomo-ga** ame-ni **futa-ri** fur-are-ta.
children-NOM rain-DAT two-CL fall-PASS-PAST
(Intended: 'Two children were rained on.')

(74) *[$_S$ **kodomo-ga** [$_{VP}$ ame-ni **futa-ri** fur-are-ta]] = (73)
children-NOM rain-DAT two-CL fall-PASS-PAST

The NQ *futa-ri* occurs in the VP without the benefit of a VP-internal trace coindexed with the subject NP *kodomo* 'children'. The NQ therefore fails to c-command the subject NP that it is intended to modify in violation of the mutual-c-command requirement.

The behavior of the NQ coupled with the mutual-c-command requirement shows that the direct passive is best accounted for by movement. The indirect passive involves no such movement and is characterized simply by the addition of the experiencer NP (cf. Miyagawa 1980).

4 UNACCUSATIVE[16] VERBS

Note that the following example appears to be a blatant violation of the mutual-c-command requirement on predication:

(75) Kinoo, **tekihei-ga** ano hasi-o **ni-san-nin**
yesterday enemy soldiers-NOM that bridge-TRAV two-three-CL
watatta (no-o mita).
crossed NO-ACC saw
'(I saw that) yesterday, two to three enemy soldiers came across that bridge.'

The problem posed by this example is that the NQ *ni-san-nin* occurs in the VP, yet it is able to be construed with the subject NP. We have already seen that similar examples are ungrammatical.

(76) ?***Tomodati-ga** ie-o **san-nin** katta.
friend-NOM house-ACC three-CL bought
(Intended: 'Three friends bought houses.')

Note that there is a difference in the thematic role of the subject NP in these two examples. In (76) the subject is an agent, but in the acceptable (75) the subject is a theme, which is a thematic role most commonly associated with the object NP. In fact, if we can show that a "theme subject" such as in (75) originates in the object position and is moved to the subject position, leaving behind a trace in the VP, (75) need not be considered a counterexample to the mutual-c-command requirement. I intend to demonstrate this here.

Linguists have argued that the subject NP of certain intransitive verbs in Italian originates in the VP (Belletti and Rizzi 1981; Burzio 1981; Perlmutter 1978). These verbs are called *unaccusative* (Perlmutter 1978) or *ergative* (Burzio 1981, 1986). As one piece of evidence, Burzio notes that the partitive clitic *ne* can only go with the object of transitive verbs and the subject of unaccusatives.

(77) Gianni **ne** ha insultati due.
Gianni of them has insulted two
'Gianni has insulted two of them.'

(78) ***Ne** telefonano molti.
of them telephone many
(Intended: 'Many of them telephoned.')

(79) **Ne** arrivano molti.
of them arrive many
'Many of them arrive.'

In (77), *ne* goes with the object of a transitive verb. In (78), the clitic is intended to go with the subject of the unaccusative verb *telefonano*, but, as shown, the sentence is ungrammatical. In contrast to this, (79), which is also an intransitive construction, allows the clitic to be construed with the subject NP. Following Perlmutter, Burzio suggests that the subject of *arrivano* is in fact the object of the verb at D-structure, thereby making it possible to have the generalization that *ne* can only go with (deep) objects. He shows that this is true for other unaccusative verbs.

Let us then suppose that the subject of the verb *watatta* 'crossed' in (75) originates in the object position and is moved to the subject position by Move α at S-structure. Presumably, what motivates this movement is the lack of case that the verb can assign to the object. Akin to the direct passive, the object must move to the subject position where the nominative *-ga* is assigned. The resulting structure is given in (80).

(80)

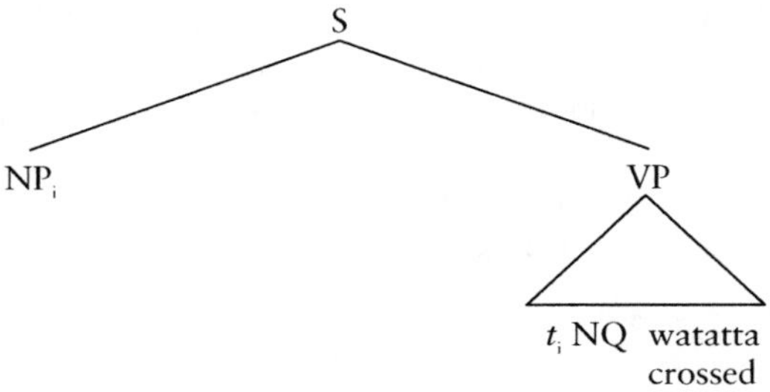

The trace left by the NP allows this structure to fulfill the mutual-c-command requirement, just as we saw for the direct passive. The following are other examples of unaccusative verbs together with a NQ in the VP. I assume the same subject-trace structure for these that is proposed for (80).

(81) Gakusei-ga $[_{VP}$ ofisu-ni **futa-ri** kira].
student-NOM office-to two-CL came
'Two students came to the office.'

(82) Otoko-ga $[_{VP}$ baa-ni **futa-ri** haitta].
men-NOM bar-to two-CL entered
'Two men entered the bar.'

(83) Zyosei-ga [$_{VP}$ butai-ni **hito-ri** agatta].
woman-NOM stage-to one-CL went up
'One woman went up onto the stage.'

(84) Kyaku-ga [$_{VP}$ rokyan-ni **futa-ri** tuita].
guests-NOM inn-to two-CL arrived
'Two guests arrived at the inn.'

(85) Doa-ga [$_{VP}$ kono kagi-de **futa-tu** aita].
door-NOM this key-with two-CL opened
'Two doors opened with this key.'

These all have a theme subject, which, under the analysis we are pursuing, originates in the object position within the VP.

A crucial assumption behind the examples just presented is that the phrase that intervenes between the antecedent NP and its NQ, such as *kono kagi-de* 'with this key' in (85), is in the VP. (Cf. Section 3.3.1 concerning the same assumption for the 'by' phrase with the direct passive.) This is crucial because if the intervening phrase were outside the VP, dominated directly by the S node, the examples in (81)–(85) would have no bearing on the issue of unaccusative verbs. I justify this assumption because the intervening phrase semantically goes with the predicate of the sentence. Thus, for example, *kono kagi-de* 'with this key' in (85) denotes the instrument that made the action denoted by the verb *aita* 'open' possible. More importantly, while the instrumental PP *kono kagi-de* 'with this key' is fine in the unaccusative construction in (85), it cannot intervene between the subject and its NQ in the transitive counterpart.

(86) a. ?*Kodomo-ga kono kagi-de futa-ri doa-o aketa.[17]
children-NOM this key-with two-CL door-ACC opened

b. Kodomo-ga futa-ri kono kagi-de doa-o aketa.
children-NOM two-CL this-key with door-ACC opened
'Two children opened a door with this key.'

Based on the unaccusative hypothesis, (86a) is ungrammatical because the instrumental PP is in the VP, hence the NQ also is in the VP, thereby violating the mutual-c-command requirement. This violation occurs because, unlike the unaccusative constructions, there is no trace in the VP coindexed with the subject NP.

In contrast to unaccusative verbs, unergative verbs, which are intransitives with deep subjects (Perlmutter 1978), do not allow a NQ in the VP to take the subject as its antecedent NP.

(87) ?*Gakusei-ga [$_{VP}$ zibun-no kane-de futa-ri denwa-sita].
students-NOM self's money-by two-CL telephoned
(Intended: 'Two students telephoned using their own money.')

(88) *Kodomo-ga [$_{VP}$ geragera-to futa-ri waratta].
children-NOM loudly two-CL laughed
(Intended: 'Two children laughed.')

(89) ?*Kodomo-ga [$_{VP}$ wa-ni natte zyuu-nin odotta].
children-NOM circle become ten-CL danced
(Intended: 'Ten children danced in a circle.')

These sentences would be acceptable if the NQ occurred outside of the VP, where it can c-command the subject NQ.

A verb is categorized as unergative if it assigns an external thematic role, unlike the unaccusative verbs such as 'go' and 'arrive' that only assign an internal role that corresponds to the object NP. According to Burzio (1986), the property that separates these two types of one-argument verbs is case:

(90) Burzio's Generalization

A verb assigns an external thematic role if it can assign case.

The most straightforward manifestations of this generalization are the garden-variety transitive verbs such as *kill*; *kill* assigns the external thematic role of agent and it assigns case to its object. Likewise, unergative verbs such as *laugh*, which also assign an external thematic role, can assign case, according to Burzio, so they are able to take an object as in the following example:

(91) He laughed a laugh.

In (81) through (89), it was shown that a NQ within the VP can take the subject NP as its antecedent only if the verb is unaccusative. In the previous section, we saw the same thing for the direct passive. Unaccusative and passive verbs share the property of a surface subject that originates in the object position and moves to the subject position at S-structure, leaving behind a trace in the object position. It is this trace that c-commands, and is c-commanded by, the NQ in the VP, thus fulfilling the mutual-c-command requirement. As noted earlier, what is crucial in the examples is the assumption that what intervenes between the subject NP and the NQ is itself in the VP, so that the NQ that follows can likewise be understood to occur internal to the VP.

In summary, the mutual-c-command requirement imposed on NQs provides evidence for A-movement in passive and unaccusative constructions. Where there appears to be a violation of this requirement, the trace left by A-movement is what satisfies it.

2 Telicity, stranded numeral quantifiers, and quantifier scope

1 INTRODUCTION

In this chapter, I will give further support for two points found in the literature on Japanese:

> *Floating numeral quantifiers (NQs) in Japanese identify copies of A-movement.*
>
> (Chapter 1 of this volume; see also Ueda 1986)
>
> *Japanese is a scopally rigid language, but quantifier-scope ambiguity obtains (inverse scope is possible) if one quantifier is overtly moved over another quantifier.*
>
> (Kuroda 1971)

The first point is based on the idea that a NQ and its associate NP must observe strict locality, and when a floating NQ is allowed to occur, it is because there is a copy of the associated NP that meets the locality requirement. Often this copy occurs precisely where one expects the copy of A-movement to occur, which gives evidence for A-movement. In other words, floating NQs are really *stranded* NQs.

A number of counterexamples to strict locality between the associate NP and its NQ have been presented in the literature. Building on the work of Borer (2005), I will argue that many of the counterexamples fall under a particular aspectual interpretation—telic—and by making one assumption about the external argument for this aspectual interpretation, we can continue to uphold the approach to NQs that assumes strict locality. The evidence provides a particularly strong argument for the predicate-internal subject position, which is one of the most important concepts that distinguishes the Minimalist Program from the Government and Binding framework, but one for which evidence is hard to come by. What I will present also clarifies the relation that a stranded NQ has to the event expressed by the verbal predicate, something that has been noted but has not been given a formal analysis that is consistent with the local nature of NQs.

For the second point, that of scopal nonrigidity, we will see that here, too, telicity plays a crucial role. What I will show is that the widely held assumption of scopal rigidity—the assumption that quantifier scope that is the inverse of surface c-command relation is impossible in Japanese—does not hold in telic examples, something which has not been noticed before in any systematic way. I will demonstrate that the structure I propose for stranded NQs accounts readily for the surprising existence of inverse scope in telic sentences. What we will see is that the phenomenon is consistent with the observation by Kuroda (1971) that in Japanese, overt movement of a quantifier across another quantifier leads to scopal ambiguity. In Kuroda's work, the overt movement that induces inverse scope is scrambling, but in the telic examples, it is overt movement of the object quantifier to the domain of an aspect head, resulting in the object quantifier c-commanding the copy of the subject quantifier in Spec,*v*P.

I will begin with NQs.[1]

2 STRANDING OF QUANTIFIERS

Floating quantifiers have been an important source of empirical argumentation for identifying where copies of displaced elements lie. Sportiche (1988) notes that the distribution of floating quantifiers in French and English identifies the predicate-internal subject position.

(1) a. Tous les enfants ont vu ce film.
all the children have seen this movie

b. Les enfants ont tous ___ vu ce film.
the children have all seen this movie

(Sportiche 1988, 426)

On the assumption that the universal quantifier *tous* must be in a strictly local relation with the associated NP *les enfants*, (1b) indicates that there is a copy of the NP next to the floating (stranded) quantifier that fulfills the locality requirement, and this position corresponds to the predicate-internal subject position, an A-position that was not identified in Government and Binding but has come to play a critical role in the Minimalist Program era (Kuroda [1988] among others also independently proposed the predicate-internal subject position).

Floating NQs in Japanese, likewise, give evidence for the existence of copies left by movement. The following is the standard paradigm based on Haig 1980 and especially Kuroda 1980 (see Miyagawa and Arikawa 2007 for further discussion).

(2) Standard paradigm

a. Gakusei-ga san-nin sake-o nonda.
student-NOM three-CL_{Subj} sake-ACC drank
'Three students drank sake.'

b. *Gakusei-ga sake-o san-nin nonda.
student-NOM sake-ACC three-CL_{Subj} drank
(Intended: 'Three students drank sake.') (Haig 1980; Kuroda 1980)

c. Hon-o gakusei-ga go-satu katta.
book-ACC student-NOM five-CL_{Obj} bought
'Students bought five books.' (Haig 1980; Kuroda 1980)

In (2a) the NQ *san-nin* 'three' and the associated subject NP 'students' are adjacent to each other, but in (2b) the adjacency is violated because the object intervenes between the two. Example (2c) shows that, unlike the subject, the object can move away from its NQ and still meet adjacency, indicating that there is a copy of the moved object next to the stranded object-oriented NQ *go-satu* 'five', shown by the gap below.

(3) Hon-o gakusei-ga ___ go-satu katta.
book-ACC student-NOM five-CL_{Obj} bought
'Students bought five books.'

The generalization is that internal arguments may strand NQs when they undergo movement. In Chapter 1 of this volume and Ueda 1986, this line of argument is extended to the passive construction to demonstrate that the so-called direct passive involves movement; the following is from Chapter 1, example (66).

(4) Kuruma-ga_i doroboo-ni $\_\_\__i$ ni-dai nusum-are-ta. Passive
car-NOM thief-by two-CL steal-PASS-PAST
'Two cars were stolen by a thief.'

The subject-oriented NQ *ni-dai* 'two' is separated from the derived subject NP *kuruma-ga* 'cars' by the 'by' phrase, yet the sentence is perfectly grammatical because there is a copy of the subject next to the stranded NQ.

In Chapter 1, Section 4, I further show that the stranded NQ can distinguish between unaccusative and unergative constructions.

(5) a. Doa-ga_i kono kagi-de $\_\_\__i$ futa-tu aita. Unaccusative
door-NOM this key-with two-CL opened
'Two doors opened with this key.'

b. *Kodomo-ga geragerato san-nin waratta. Unergative
children-NOM loudly three-CL laughed
(Intended: 'Three children laughed loudly.')

Of the two types of intransitives, the unaccusative verb 'open' in (5a) allows a stranded NQ while the unergative 'laugh' in (5b) does not.[2] This together with the passive example shows decisively that NQ stranding is correlated with A-movement of arguments; thus, the NQ data from Japanese give evidence for copies left by A-movement.

However, one question that arises is, what about the predicate-internal subject position? In the ungrammatical member of the standard paradigm, (2b), and likewise in (5b), why doesn't the copy of the external argument in Spec,*v*P fulfill the locality requirement and enable stranding of a subject-oriented NQ?

At the time the observation was made that sentences like (2b) are ungrammatical (Haig 1980; Kuroda 1980), the theory did not include the notion of a predicate-internal subject position, but if this position indeed exists, we should see its effects in the stranding constructions. In Miyagawa and Arikawa 2007, we argued that, in fact, the lower copy of the external argument does play a role in some of the counter-examples to strict locality. In this chapter, I will extend that analysis by showing that the lower copy of the external argument is visible in telic aspect.

2.1 Intransitive verbs

A number of linguists have noticed that certain types of NQ stranding that are otherwise impossible are possible in a particular aspectual context, namely, in the *telic* aspect, in which there is an endpoint to the event expressed.[3] The first to note this was Tsujimura (1990b) in her study of unaccusative mismatches (Dowty 1991; Levin and Rappaport 1989; Levin and Rappaport Hovav 1995). She gives the following minimal pairs with the intransitive verbs 'run' and 'swim'.

(6) a. ?*Gakusei-ga kodomo-to san-nin hasitta.
student-NOM children-with three-CL ran
(Intended: 'Three students ran with the children.')

b. Gakusei-ga kooen-made san-nin hasitta.
student-NOM park-as far as three-CL ran
'Three students ran to the park.'

(7) a. ?*Gakusei-ga kodomo-to inukaki-de san-nin oyoida.
student-NOM children-with dog-paddling-by three-CL swam
(Intended: 'Three students swam with children by dog-paddling.')

b. Gakusei-ga kisi-made inukaki-de san-nin oyoida.
student-NOM shore-as far as dog-paddling-by three-CL swam
'Three students swam to the shore by dog-paddling.'

As Tsujimura (1990b, 269–270) notes, 'run' and 'swim' are typical unergative verbs, so that we would not expect them to allow stranding of NQ across PPs. The (a) examples demonstrate this, but, puzzlingly, the (b) examples allow stranding. According to Tsujimura, the addition of the goal phrase in the (b) examples "adds a specification of inherent direction as well as an *endpoint to the original meaning of the verb* and makes the verb function like [an unaccusative] verb" (emphasis added). Tsujimura, referring to Levin and Rappaport 1989 (see also Dowty 1991; Levin and Rappaport Hovav 1995), observes that with the goal phrase, these intransitive verbs behave like unaccusative verbs with inherent direction, such as 'arrive', 'come', 'go', 'depart', 'fall', 'return', and 'descend'.

In a later work, Mihara (1998) makes a similar observation based on his counterexamples to locality, such as the one given in (8a) below; in (8b) I have added a similar counterexample from Kuno and Takami 2003, 284, that demonstrates the same point.

(8) a. Gakusei-ga tosyokan-de go-nin benkyoosi-tei-ta.
student-NOM library-at five-CL study-PROG-PAST
'Five students were studying at the library.' (Mihara 1998, pt. 1, 89)

b. A: 'Is this new magazine selling well?'
B: Ee, kesa-mo gakusei-san-ga
Yes this morning-also students-NOM
[$_{VP}$ sore-o go-nin kat-te iki-masi-ta yo].
it-ACC five-CL buy-ing go-POLITE-PAST
'Yes, this morning also, five students bought it.'

In noting the counterexamples to locality, Mihara makes the observation that stranding of an NQ requires the sentence to have *aspectual delimitedness*, which is similar to the observation made earlier by Tsujimura. Note that in the example given by Kuno and Takami (for further discussion of which see Miyagawa and Arikawa 2007), the verb contains the motion verb 'go', which naturally leads to a telic interpretation.

The following minimal pair demonstrates in a direct fashion the importance of aspectual interpretation for stranding of NQs.

(9) a. *Tomodati-ga zyup-pun futa-ri odotta.
friend-NOM ten minutes two-CL danced
(Intended: 'Two friends danced for ten minutes.')

b. Tomodati-ga zyup-pun-no-uti-ni futa-ri odotta.
friend-NOM ten minutes-in two-CL danced
'Two friends danced (a dance) in ten minutes.'

This is a classic test of aspect found in Vendler 1967 that distinguishes between activities (X-ing for ten minutes) and accomplishments (X-ing in ten minutes), the former lacking an endpoint that bounds the event expressed, and the latter having such an endpoint. The judgment is crisp and clear: with an activity, which has atelic aspect, stranding of the NQ is entirely ungrammatical, while the telic aspect of an accomplishment makes NQ stranding totally acceptable.[4] There is nothing wrong with the meaning of the sentence in (9a), as shown by the fact that if the NQ is next to the subject, the example is perfectly fine.

(10) Tomodati-ga futa-ri zyup-pun odotta.
friend-NOM two-CL ten minutes danced
'Two friends danced for ten minutes.'

Furthermore, it has been noted that stranding of an NQ is ungrammatical with permanent/individual-level predicates (Harada 1976c; Fukushima 1991; Nishigauchi and Uchibori 1991; Ohki 1987), an observation that coincides with the idea that stranding of NQs is limited to telic expressions, since stage-level predicates are telic (see, e.g., Diesing 1992). The following is taken from Mihara 1998, pt. 3, 110–111 (see also Nakanishi 2008).

(11) a. Uti-no doobutuen-de-wa **kaba-ga** mada **san-too** genki-da.
my zoo-at-TOP hippo-NOM still three-CL healthy
'In my zoo, three hippos are still healthy.'

b. *Uti-no doobutuen-de-wa **kaba-ga** zannennakotoni **san-too** osu-da.
my zoo-at-TOP hippo-NOM unfortunately three-CL male
(Intended: 'In my zoo, unfortunately, three hippos are male.')

All of these examples of unexpectedly grammatical NQ stranding involve an external argument. The pattern that emerges is that stranding of a subject-oriented NQ by the external argument is possible in telic expressions.[5] How can we account for this? Whatever account we come up with will need to account for the unaccusative mismatch that Tsujimura observed: the addition of a goal phrase to an unergative construction creates the possibility of stranding a NQ. Although one option is to follow Tsujimura in assuming that the argument structure changes with the addition of the goal phrase, there is a sense that the predicate and the participant in the event are basically the same with and without the goal phrase, and that the difference is in the aspectual interpretation of the event.

What I suggest is the following:

(12) Telicity and the external argument (TEA)

Once the external argument moves to Spec,TP, its lower copy in the predicate-internal subject position is visible under telic interpretation.

It has been noted in the literature (e.g., Miyagawa 2001) that the lower copy of the external argument is not visible in Japanese. However, what TEA states is that the copy becomes visible under telic aspect. The reason is not clear, and it is beyond the scope of this chapter to try to come up with an account,[6] particularly because the relationship between the external argument and argument structure is, with few exceptions, uncharted territory. There are a handful of works that make observations concerning this relationship between the subject and telicity: see, for example, Folli and Harley 2005; Rappaport Hovav and Levin 2005; Rappaport Hovav 2008. Folli and Harley note a number of examples from English and Italian where there is a close link between the type of event in the verbal predicate and the type of external argument that is allowed, and often it is the aspect of the event that governs the type of the external argument that can occur.

TEA accounts for all of the examples above in which a subject-oriented NQ is successfully stranded; in the telic aspect, the lower copy of the subject meets the strict-locality requirement. We can in fact "repair" the ungrammatical example (2b) from the standard paradigm noted by Kuroda (1980) and see TEA at work.

(13) a. *Gakusei-ga sake-o san-nin nonda.
student-NOM sake-ACC three-CL_{Subj} drank
(Intended: 'Three students drank sake.')

b. Gakusei-ga sake-o **sudeni** san-nin nonda.
student-NOM sake-ACC already three-CL_{Subj} drank
'Three students already drank sake.'

While most speakers I have consulted agree with the judgment that (13a) is degraded, example (13b), which, because of the addition of 'already', has a telic interpretation, is perfectly acceptable. This is true whether 'already' is placed before the verb or even the subject.

The account according to TEA is particularly important for the notion of the predicate-internal subject position. Sportiche's (1988) examples from English and French of stranded quantifiers provided one of the strongest pieces of evidence for this notion. However, Bošković (2004) and Tada (1999), among others, argue that the position of the floating quantifier in English (and French, in Bošković's case) is not the original position of the subject, but is instead a derived, non-θ-marked position. If this is the case, we no longer have quantifier stranding in English and

French as empirical evidence for one of the most important notions distinguishing minimalism from Government and Binding. Instead, if our analysis of subject-oriented-NQ stranding in terms of TEA is correct, Japanese provides independent evidence for the predicate-internal subject position.

In presenting support for NQ stranding based on TEA, I will take into account observations made in the literature to the effect that a floating NQ not only modifies the associated NP, it also interacts with the event structure of the verbal predicate. Fujita (1994) argues that a NQ in the NP–NQ sequence (or likewise a stranded NQ) modifies its host NP through modification of the verbal predicate. Likewise, Nakanishi (2004, 2007a, 2007b) presents a semantic approach in which the floating NQ quantifies over events denoted by the verbal predicate as well as over individuals denoted by the host NP. What I will present is a stranding approach that makes explicit how the NQ can quantify over individuals denoted by the NP—which accounts for the agreement between the type of associated NP being counted and the classifier on the NQ—and at the same time can directly participate in the quantificational structure of telic events denoted by the verbal predicate.

2.2 Grammaticalizing telicity

The analysis I will present for NQs in the NP(-case)–NQ sequence and stranded NQs is based on an extension of Borer 2005. Borer argues that the telic aspect is structurally represented by an aspectual head, which she calls Asp_Q, where Q stands for *quantity*. This represents the notion that "telic events are quantities, in the sense that they involve quantification over event divisions" (74; see Link 1983, 1987; Bach 1989; Krifka 1989, 1992; see also Tenny 1987, 1994; among others). In contrast, "atelic events are homogeneous" and do not involve a quantitative aspectual head. In Borer's system, if Asp_Q occurs, an XP that provides the quantity is merged into the specifier of this head, and this XP then binds an operator position within an extended verbal projection.

(14)

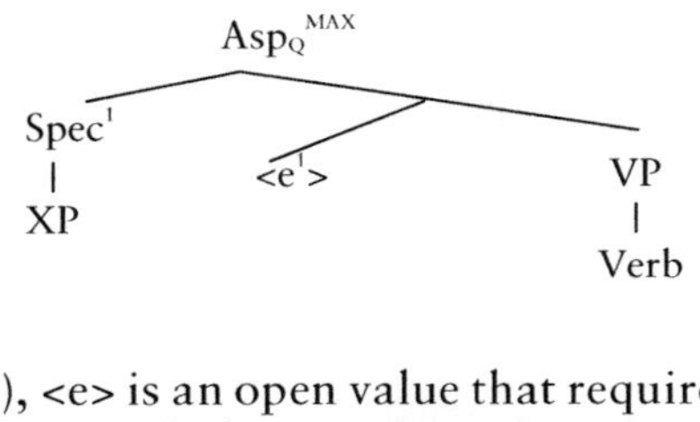

In (14), <e> is an open value that requires range assignment, and if bound by an XP with the property of quantity, it is given an appropriate range over event divisions. In an atelic event, there is no such structure. (Borer sometimes assumes a nonce projection for atelic events and at other times there is no such projection; I will make the latter assumption.)

I will extract from Borer's work the idea that telic events require a special aspectual head that has the property of quantity. Contrary to Borer, I am going to assume the standard analysis that arguments are merged in the complement position of verbs and in the specifier of *v*P. The aspectual head, when required to occur, is projected above *v*P, where other aspectual types are also represented; the following demonstrates this for the head-final structure of Japanese.

(15)

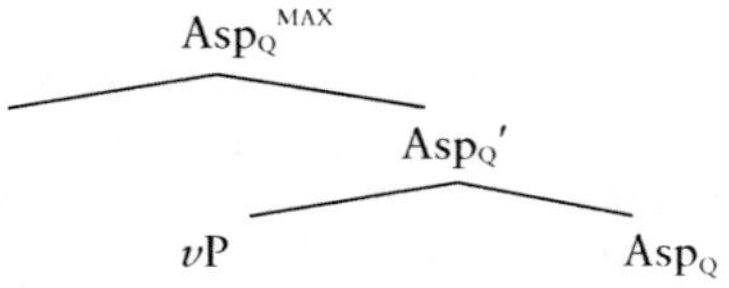

I will further assume that an XP—the direct object in the most typical case—can move into Spec,Asp_QP in order to implement the telic interpretation, making the derived structure similar to Borer's structure.

Let us again look at the minimal pair presented earlier.

(16) a. *Tomodati-ga zyup-pun futa-ri odotta.
friend-NOM ten minutes two-CL danced
(Intended: 'Two friends danced for ten minutes.')

b. Tomodati-ga zyup-pun-no-uti-ni futa-ri odotta.
friend-NOM ten minutes-in two-CL danced
'Two friends danced (a dance) in ten minutes.'

To begin with the grammatical (16b) example, this sentence has a telic interpretation because of the adverb 'in ten minutes'. The structure for this sentence before and after the movement of the external argument is given below.

(17)

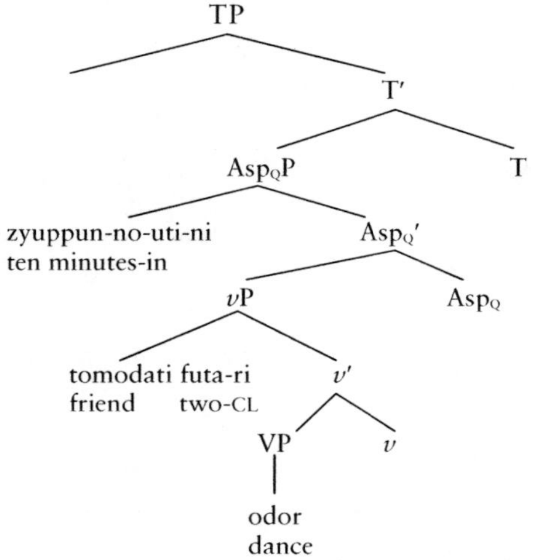

(18)

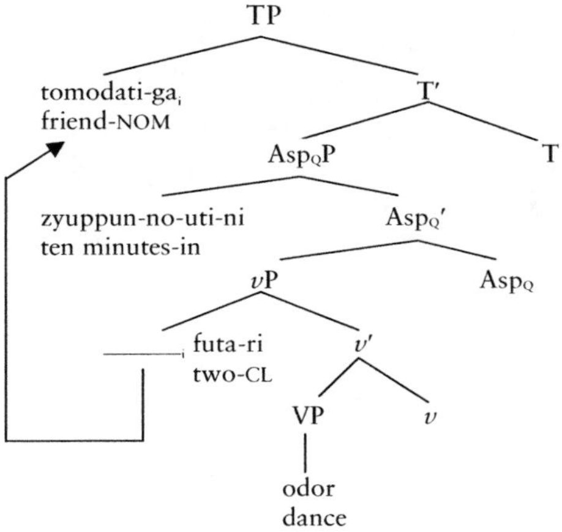

The adverb *zyuppun-no-uti-ni* 'in ten minutes' gives the sentence the telic interpretation, hence it occurs in Spec,Asp_QP.[7] The external argument 'friends' moves to Spec,TP, leaving behind a copy in the predicate-internal subject position. Because this is in telic aspect, this lower copy is visible by TEA and able to fulfill the locality requirement with the stranded NQ.

In the ungrammatical example, (16a), the aspect is that of an activity, which is atelic, so the lower copy is not visible under TEA and hence the stranded NQ violates locality.[8] If the subject NP and the NQ are moved together to Spec,TP, the NQ is local to its associate NP and the sentence is grammatical as expected.

(19) Tomodati-ga futa-ri zyup-pun odotta.
friend-NOM two-CL ten minutes danced
'Two friends danced for ten minutes.'

2.3 Subjects and objects

We have so far dealt mostly with intransitive constructions. Let us now turn to transitive constructions to see how they fit into the kind of aspect structure that I have proposed by extending Borer's (2005) work. I will assume that, contrary to Borer, even in a transitive construction, Asp_Q is merged above vP.

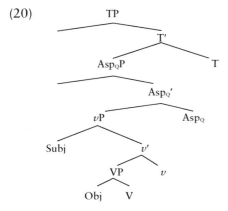

(20)

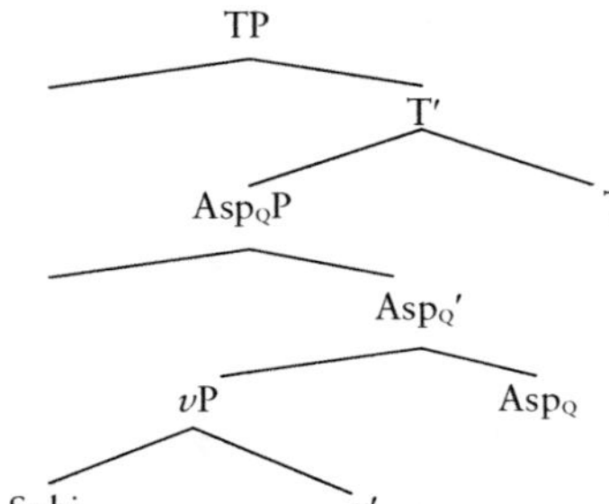

In a transitive construction, telicity is made possible by the object "measuring out" or "delimiting" the event (see, e.g., Tenny 1987, 1994). This means that, as Borer (2005) notes, the object, if it occurs, must occur in Spec,Asp$_Q$P. Unlike her approach, in which the object is merged directly into this position, I assume the structure in (20) above in which the object is merged as the complement of the verb, as is usually assumed. The object moves to Spec,Asp$_Q$P, leading to a structure essentially identical to Borer's original analysis, repeated below.

(21)

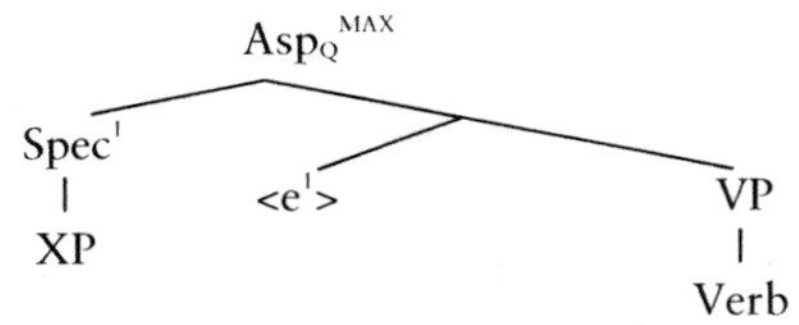

<e> is an open value that requires range assignment, and, on our analysis, it is created by moving the object to Spec,Asp$_Q$P. One immediate issue to face is locality. In the structure above in (20), the closest XP to Asp$_Q$ is the subject, and not the object, yet it is the object that must move into Spec,Asp$_Q$P. There are a number of ways to implement this. One possibility is that the agreement here is triggered by a feature called Quantity on Asp$_Q$, which agrees with the same feature on the object. This also would allow a nonobject, such as a goal PP, that has this feature to enter into agreement and move into Spec,Asp$_Q$P; we saw something like this with 'in ten minutes' in (17)–(18). There are other possibilities, such as case, but I will not pursue them here.

Let us now see what happens with the object NP–NQ grouping in which the NQ ends up stranded.

(22) Teeburu-o$_i$ Taroo-ga ___$_i$ mit-tu fuita.
table-ACC Taro-NOM two-CL wiped
'Taro cleaned three tables.'

Note that there are two possible positions for the stranded NQ, one in the object's original complement position in VP, the other in Spec,Asp$_Q$P above *v*P. The NQ may stay in situ while the NP moves out of VP, or the NP and NQ may move to Spec,Asp$_Q$P together and then the NP may move higher, stranding the NQ.

(23) a. $\ldots [_{\text{Asp}_Q\text{P}} \ldots [_{v\text{P}} \ldots [_{\text{VP}} \ldots \text{NQ} \ldots]]] \ldots$
b. $\ldots [_{\text{Asp}_Q\text{P}} \ldots \text{NQ} \ldots [_{v\text{P}} \ldots [_{\text{VP}} \ldots]]] \ldots$

The first possibility is demonstrated by the example below, in which there is subject-NQ stranding as well as object-NQ stranding.

(24) Teeburu-o$_i$ kodomo-ga$_i$ sakki ___$_i$ futa-ri, ___$_i$ mit-tu fuita.
table-ACC child-NOM a while ago two-CL three-CL wiped
'Two children cleaned three tables a while ago.'

The stranded subject NQ, *futa-ri* 'two', is in Spec,*v*P, which means that the stranded object NQ *mit-tu* 'three' is in VP, arguably in the original complement position.[9] The following illustrates the possibility in (23b), with the object NQ stranded in Spec,Asp$_Q$P.

(25) (?)Omotya-o$_i$ kodomo-ga$_i$ itizikan-no-uti-ni ___$_i$ mit-tu, ___$_i$
toy-ACC child-NOM one hour-in three-CL
futa-ri kowasita.
two-CL broke
'Two children broke three toys in one hour.'

Because of the crossing nature of the example, the sentence is mildly awkward, but most speakers I consulted accept it as a grammatical sentence. The object NQ *mit-tu* 'three' is arguably in Spec,Asp$_Q$P, above the stranded subject NQ *futa-ri* 'two', which is in Spec,*v*P. Note that the judgment changes if the sentence is atelic.

(26) *Sigoto-o$_i$ gakusei-ga$_i$ kotosi ___$_i$ mit-tu, ___$_i$ futa-ri site-iru.
job-ACC student-NOM this year three-CL two-CL do-ing
'Two students are working on three jobs this year.'

In this atelic example, there is no Asp$_Q$, hence there is no position above Spec,*v*P to strand the object NQ. The sentence improves considerably if it is made into a telic example with the insertion of 'already'.

(27) Sigoto-o$_i$ gakusei-ga kotosi ___$_i$ mit-tu, ___$_i$ sudeni futa-ri site-iru.
job-ACC student-NOM this year three-CL already two-CL do-ing
'Two students have worked on three jobs this year already.'

2.4 On nonstandard judgments

In Miyagawa and Arikawa 2007, we responded to a number of counterexamples to the standard paradigm, including examples such as those below in which the subject and its NQ are separated by the object.

(28) ?Gakusei-ga sake-o **imamadeni** san-nin nonda.
student-NOM sake-ACC so far three-CL$_{Subj}$ drank
'Three students drank sake so far.' (Gunji and Hasida 1998, 57)

(29) Gakusei-ga watasi-no hon-o **futa-ri-sika** kaw-anakat-ta.
student-NOM my-GEN book-ACC two-CL$_{Subj}$-only buy-not-PAST
'Only two students bought my book.' (cf. Takami 1998, pt. 1, 92)

One point that we noted is that in these examples, the subject NQ is prosodically separated from the object, so that the NQ cannot mistakenly be construed with the object. What we argued is that these "nonstandard-judgment" examples are cases of double scrambling in which the object first scrambles above the subject, then the subject moves above the object, stranding its NQ. We adopted the EPP analysis in Miyagawa 2001 in which the object moves to Spec,TP, although this is not so crucial for present purposes.

(30) [$_{TP}$ Subj [$_{TP}$ Obj [$_{vP}$ [t_{Subj} NQ$_{Subj}$] . . . t_{Obj} . . .]]]

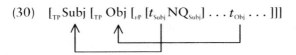

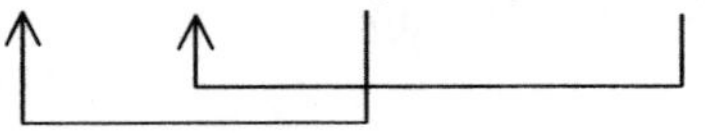

Based on the approach in this chapter, it is necessary to add that this "double scrambling" that strands the subject NQ is only possible under a telic interpretation. This is shown below.

(31) a. *Gakusei-ga sake-o yonzyuugo-fun san-nin nonda.
student-NOM sake-ACC forty-five minutes three-CL$_{Subj}$ drank
(Intended: 'Three students drank sake for forty-five minutes.')

b. Gakusei-ga sake-o yonzyuugo-fun-no-uti-ni san-nin nonda.
student-NOM sake-ACC forty-five minutes-in three-CL$_{Subj}$ drank
'Three students drank sake in forty-five minutes.'

2.5 Stranded NQs and modification of events

An interesting observation made by Fujita (1994) and Nakanishi (2004) is that a floating NQ not only modifies the associated NP but also the event represented by the verbal predicate. A particularly striking example is given by Nakanishi (2004, 67) to demonstrate this.[10]

(32) ?*/??Gakusei-ga kinoo san-nin Peter-o korosi-ta.
student-NOM yesterday three-CL Peter-ACC kill-PAST
(Intended: 'Three students killed Peter yesterday.')

Note that example (32) constitutes a potential counterexample to TEA: subject-NQ stranding should be allowed because 'kill' is telic, yet the sentence is judged odd. What Nakanishi observes is that the event of killing Peter is something that by nature can only occur once. The badness of (32) is explained if the NQ ranges over multiple events of killing Peter that distribute over each of the three students; this goes against the inherent uniqueness of an event of killing Peter. Nakanishi uses this interesting data to argue against the stranding analysis of floating NQs (see also Nakanishi 2008), arguing that the interpretative facts suggest that the NQ is an adverb.

This debate about the syntactic status of floating NQs in Japanese is a debate that has taken place for floating quantifiers in general: on one side it is asserted that all floating quantifiers are of the stranded kind (e.g., Cirillo 2009; Shlonsky 1991; Sportiche 1988) and on the other side, there are those who argue that floating quantifiers are either always adverbs or, perhaps, alternating between stranded quantifiers and adverbs depending on the context (see, e.g., Bobaljik 2003; Doetjes 1997; Fitzpatrick 2006; Fukushima 1991; Ishii 1998; Nakanishi 2004; Sag 1978). For Japanese, Nakanishi's example has been one of the most compelling pieces of empirical evidence given for the adverbial analysis of floating NQs (her analysis can be traced back to Ishii 1998, which in turn owes insights to Kitagawa and Kuroda 1992).

But there is no reason to consider (32) as a counterexample to a stranding analysis of floating NQs. The distributive reading can be generated by the analysis of transitives sketched in Section 2.4, without recourse to the adverbial analysis of the NQ. Given that the verb 'kill' clearly defines a telic event, the structure of (32) must contain Asp_Q. The stranded NQ 'three' c-commands the Asp_QP, thereby modifying the event subdivision of Asp_Q and giving the interpretation that there are three instances of the (subdivided) event. This accounts naturally not only for Nakanishi's (and Fujita's) observations, but it also accounts easily for the fact that the NQ, by virtue of its classifier, is closely associated with the associate NP, something that the adverb approach to stranded NQs fails to account for.

There is one type of example that argues against a Nakanishi-type adverb approach to floating NQs, and at the same time is consistent with the analysis we have presented.

(33) Gakusei-ga sakihodo san-nin teeburu-o motiageta.
student-NOM a while ago three-CL table-ACC picked up
'A while ago, three students picked up a table.'

This sentence is ambiguous between collective and distributive meaning, so that the students either together picked up a table once or they each individually picked up a table. The adverb analysis would only be consistent with the distributive meaning. But on the analysis we have presented, the NQ itself does not trigger event division; if the event itself can be collective because of the nature of the predicate, as in (33) above, the NQ does not force a distributed meaning. This is why a collective interpretation remains possible even with a stranded NQ; the distributed meaning is not a function of the NQ but simply an option that comes with the meaning of the verbal predicate.

2.6 Copy of A-movement in the VP

Let us conclude by revisiting Chapter 1. We have seen that the copy of A-movement left in Spec,*v*P is visible in telic aspect.

(34) Telicity and the external argument (TEA)

Once the external argument moves to Spec,TP, its lower copy in the predicate-internal subject position is visible under telic interpretation.

What about the copy of A-movement in VP that is found in passives and unaccusatives? Since TEA is a condition on the copy of A-movement in Spec,*v*P, we would not expect the copy inside VP to be subject to TEA or any other condition. Rather, as already shown in Chapter 1, NQ stranding with derived subjects is allowed generally and is not sensitive to the telicity of the predicate. We can see this in the passive example below.

(35) Kuruma-ga$_i$ doroboo-ni sanzyuppun ___$_i$ ni-dai untens-are-ta.
cars-NOM thief-by thirty minutes two-CL drive-PASS-PAST
'Two cars were driven by thieves for thirty minutes.'

This is an atelic-aspect example, as indicated by the temporal adverb 'for thirty minutes', yet the NQ stranding is possible, showing that the copy inside the VP is visible regardless of the kind of aspect that the sentence takes.

For unaccusatives, it is difficult to come up with an atelic example because unaccusative verbs are typically telic given that they represent change of state or position. However, a simple way to show that the copy inside VP is visible in atelic aspect is with existential examples like the following.

(36) a. Kodomo-ga$_i$ gakkoo-ni ___$_i$ san-nin iru.
child-NOM school-at three-CL exist
'Three children are at school.'

b. Hon-ga$_i$ teeburu-no-ue-ni ___$_i$ san-satu aru.
book-NOM table-on three-CL exist
'Three books are on the table.'

These are stative unaccusative predicates. As we saw earlier in (11), a stative predicate does not allow the copy of A-movement in Spec,*v*P to be visible. The fact that these examples are perfectly grammatical again indicates that the copy of A-movement within VP is visible regardless of the type of aspect found in the expression. These stranding examples with the passive and the unaccusative uphold the idea that there is a sharp line to be drawn between passives and unaccusatives on the one hand and transitives and unergatives on the other, as argued in Chapter 1.

The one addition I am making to my original analysis is that we now know that it is possible to strand a subject-oriented NQ under the telic aspect. A relevant example from Tsujimura 1990b is repeated below.

(37) Gakusei-ga kooen-made san-nin hasitta.
student-NOM park-as far as three-CL ran
'Three students ran to the park.'

The occurrence of the goal phrase 'to the park' furnishes an endpoint to the event, thereby making the aspect telic, and, by TEA, the copy of the external argument in Spec,*v*P is visible, allowing the stranding.

There is still a fundamental difference between this external argument and the internal argument of an unaccusative, even though a stranded NQ can occur with both kinds of subjects. As indicated in Miyagawa 1989, 97–100 (see also Tsujimura 1990a), a resultative phrase can only modify an internal argument (Simpson 1983).

(38) a. Taroo-ga sara-o konagona-ni watta.
Taro-NOM plate-ACC pieces-into broke
'Taro broke the plate into pieces.'

b. Sara-ga konagona-ni wareta.
plate-NOM pieces-into broke
'The plate broke into pieces.'

In both, the resultative phrase 'into pieces' modifies an internal argument within the VP. In contrast, the following shows that the external argument of an unergative verb cannot be modified by a resultative phrase.

(39) Kodomo-ga ni-san-nin-no guruupu-de/*-ni hasitta.
children-NOM two-three-CL-GEN group-in/-into ran
'The children ran in/*into two or three groups.'

We can see below that the Tsujimura-type example, which allows stranding, nevertheless disallows modification by a resultative phrase because what is visible is the copy of the external argument, not the internal argument.

(40) *Gakusei-ga kooen-made kutakutani hasitta.
student-NOM park-as far as tired ran
(Intended: 'Students ran to the park becoming tired.')

3 QUANTIFIER SCOPE

We now turn to the second thesis mentioned at the outset of this chapter. Since Kuroda 1971, it has been widely assumed that Japanese is a scopally rigid language (see also Hoji 1985).

(41) Dareka-ga dono-sensei-mo kiratteiru.
someone-NOM every teacher hates
'Someone hates every teacher.'

Unlike its English counterpart, in the Japanese example in (41), the surface-scope reading involving a particular person who loves everyone is strongly preferred; for most speakers, the inverse scope is out of the question. This has become one of the defining characteristics of Japanese.

However, a closer look at the data shows that this characterization of scopal rigidity as a general property of the language is incorrect. There are examples in which native speakers have an easier time getting an inverse-scope interpretation. Following are two such examples.[11]

(42) a. (Gozi-kan-no-uti-ni) dareka-ga dono-mado-mo aketa.
five hours-in someone-NOM every window opened
'Someone opened every window (in five hours).'

b. (Nizi-kan-no-uti-ni) dareka-ga dono-omotya-mo kowasita.
two hours-in someone-NOM every toy broke
'Someone broke every toy (in two hours).'

As we can see, these are clearly telic examples, suggesting that telicity has a role not just in licensing certain kinds of NQ stranding, but also scope inversion. Before turning to the analysis, the following minimal pair confirms that telicity is what is at work.

(43) a. Dareka-ga sanzi-kan-de dono-yama-mo nobotta.
someone-NOM three hours-in every mountain climbed
'Someone climbed every mountain in three hours.'
'someone' > 'every mountain', (?)'every mountain' > 'someone'

b. ??Dareka-ga sanzi-kan dono-yama-mo nobotta.
someone-NOM three hours every mountain climbed
'Someone climbed every mountain for three hours.'
'someone' > 'every mountain', *'every mountain' > 'someone'

Example (43a) has two pragmatically appropriate interpretations. One is surface scope in which a specific person climbed each mountain in three hours, obviously at different times. The other is that for each of the mountains, there is a different person who climbed it in three hours. Example (43b) is odd in that it has only surface scope, which makes the most prominent interpretation a single event in which someone climbed all the mountains for three hours, an unlikely state of affairs.

Finally, the following, pointed out to me by Toshiaki Inada and Hiroaki Tada, also demonstrates that telicity is relevant to scope relations.

(44) Dareka-ga dono-hon-mo yonde-iru.
someone-NOM every book read-ing
'Someone has read/is reading every book.'

The verbal inflection *-iru* can indicate progressive or resultative, the former representing activity and the latter accomplishment. In the progressive interpretation, this sentence is unambiguous, with only the surface scope being possible, but with the resultative interpretation, the inverse scope becomes possible, although surface scope is still preferred.

Why is it that inverse scope appears under the telic aspect? Let us begin by looking into how inverse scope is made possible in English. Johnson and Tomioka (1997) and Johnson (2000) argue that inverse scope in a sentence such as the following is possible thanks to the fact that the object quantifier *many of the questions on the exam* takes scope over the copy of the subject in Spec,*v*P.

(45) Some student or other has answered many of the questions on the exam.

(46) $[_{TP}$ Subject$_i$ $[_{vP}$ Object$_j$ $[_{vP}$ __$_i$ $[_{VP}$ V __$_j]$ . . .

In Johnson and Tomioka 1997, the reason why the object moves to *v*P is to correct type mismatch; in Johnson 2000 the movement of the object is covert scrambling. On either account, the analysis does not depend on the object undergoing Quantifier Raising to adjoin to TP, which is the classic analysis of inverse scope (May 1977). Johnson gives the following evidence to show that it is the copy of the subject in Spec,*v*P that is operative in inverse scope. First, we are reminded that the indefinite *some* cannot scope under negation.

(47) I have not met some student. some student > not

Johnson then notes the following example, which is the negative counterpart of the ambiguous sentence we saw in (45) above.

(48) Some student or other hasn't answered many of the questions on the exam.

This example fails to have the inverse scope in which *many questions on the exam* takes scope over the subject *some student or other*. We can understand this lack of inverse scope if negation keeps the subject indefinite *some student or other* from being interpreted in its original Spec,*v*P position. Without this copy available for interpretation, inverse scope becomes impossible, on the assumption that it is this copy that enters into the calculation of inverse scope.

Returning to Japanese, the surprising availability of inverse scope in telic sentences finds an explanation in our approach to stranding of NQs based on telicity, in a way that parallels the analysis of inverse scope in English just outlined. A telic example has the derived structure below.

(49) $[_{TP}$ 'someone'$_i$ $[_{Asp_QP}$ 'every window'$_j$ $[_{vP}$ —$_i$ $[_{VP}$ —$_j$ V] . . .

The object 'every window' has moved to Spec,Asp_QP, and from this position, it c-commands the copy of the subject 'someone', which is visible due to TEA.

Without Asp_Q, there is no reason for the object to move, and Japanese being a scrambling language, covert movement of the type Johnson (2000) posits for English is either not possible or strongly dispreferred (Miyagawa 2011b). This is consistent with the observation Kuroda (1971) made that scope ambiguity in Japanese obtains under overt movement, in his case, scrambling. Recall that the following is unambiguous.

(50) Dareka-ga dono-sensei-mo kiratteiru.
someone-NOM every teacher hates
'Someone hates every teacher.'

However, scrambling the object quantifier across the subject quantifier leads to scope ambiguity.

(51) Dono-sensei-mo dareka-ga kiratteiru.
every teacher someone-NOM hates
'Someone hates every teacher.'

The analogous overt movement in the case of the telic examples with inverse-scope readings in (42)–(44) is movement of the object (or some other appropriate quantifier) to Spec,Asp_QP, from where it is able to c-command the copy of the subject quantifier.

4 CONCLUSION

I demonstrated that a subject NQ can be stranded only under the telic aspect. The counterexamples that have been given in the literature to the analysis in Chapter 1 that requires strict locality between the NQ and its associate NP are, by and large, examples with telic interpretation. I suggested that the effect we are seeing with telicity is due to the fact that in this aspectual interpretation, the lower copy of the moved external argument is visible, and this lower copy fulfills the requirement of strict locality with the stranded NQ. We saw that this analysis can also account straightforwardly for the surprising cases of inverse scope in telic sentences.

3 Argument structure and ditransitive verbs in Japanese[1]

With Takae Tsujioka

1 INTRODUCTION

English ditransitive verbs often allow two distinct structures, the double-object construction (DOC) and the *to*-dative construction.

(1) DOC
John sent Mary a package.

(2) *To* dative
John sent a package to Mary.

What is the relationship, if any, between these two constructions? Not all ditransitive verbs permit both constructions, as, for example, in the case of *introduce*, which only allows the *to* dative. But when the verb does allow both, the two constructions have virtually the same meaning, which naturally suggests an analysis that derivationally relates the two. However, there are well-known barriers to relating the two derivationally. Simply put, the two constructions appear to be associated with distinct argument structures. One well-known fact pointed out by Oehrle (1976) is that the DOC, but not the *to* dative, may be associated with a causative meaning (cf. also Harley 1995b; Larson 1988; Pesetsky 1995; Pinker 1989; Gropen et al. 1989; Pylkkänen 2002; Richards 2001; among others).

(3) a. The article gave me a headache.
b. *The article gave a headache to me.

Example (3a) is interpreted as saying that my having read the article was responsible for *causing* my headache. Example (3b), the *to*-dative counterpart of (3a), cannot convey this causative meaning, so the sentence is odd (but see note 17). If the presence of the causative interpretation in the DOC, and its absence in the *to* dative, is viewed as reflecting the argument structure of the two constructions, one is led to an analysis in which they have distinct sources rather than being derivationally related.

Another difference has to do with the nature of the goal phrase. As noted by Bresnan (1978, 1982b), the goal phrase in the DOC is more restricted than in the *to* dative (cf. also Harley 1995b; Mazurkewich and White 1984; Pesetsky 1995; Pinker 1989; among others).

(4) a. I sent the boarder/*the border a package.
    b. I sent a package to the boarder/the border.

In the DOC example in (4a), the animate goal *the boarder* is fine but not the inanimate *the border*, while the *to* dative in (4b) allows both. This distinction arises from the requirement that the goal of the DOC be construed as the possessor of the theme, while in the *to* dative the goal is construed as locative (Mazurkewich and White 1984). As a possessor, the DOC goal is usually animate; if inanimate, there needs to be an understanding that animate entities are implied, as in the case of a country (*France gave some African countries humanitarian aid*). Such differences in argument structure have led some to postulate different underlying structures for the two constructions (e.g., Marantz 1993; Harley 1995b; Pylkkänen 2002). We will elaborate on this proposal shortly.

There is an entirely different consideration: what is the underlying structure of the two constructions from a purely hierarchical point of view? Take the DOC. In the absence of any additional assumption, one might postulate something like the following phrase structure.

(5)

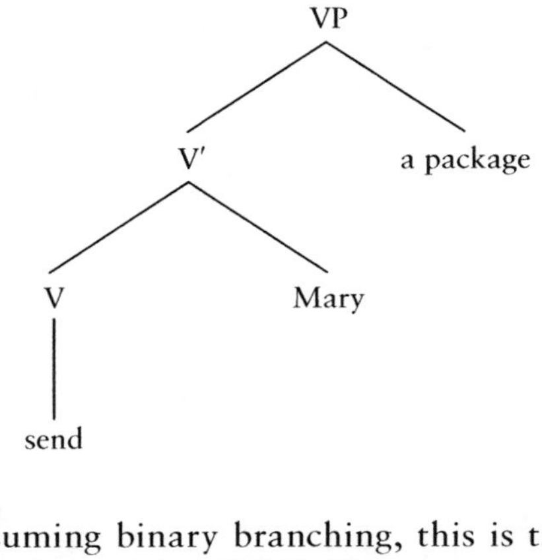

Assuming binary branching, this is the most obvious structure we can associate with a DOC. However, as argued convincingly by Barss and Lasnik (1986), in the DOC the goal phrase (*Mary*) asymmetrically c-commands the theme (*a package*). We can see this in anaphor binding.

(6) a. John showed Mary herself.
    b. *John showed herself Mary.

We can also see this with licensing of negative polarity items (NPIs).

(7) a. John sent no one anything.
b. *John sent anyone nothing.

Any, being an NPI, must occur in the scope of a negative element, in this case *no* X. In (7a) *anything* is c-commanded by *no one* while in (7b) the goal *anyone* fails to be licensed by the theme *nothing*, indicating that this goal phrase asymmetrically c-commands the theme.

This observation by Barss and Lasnik (1986) led Larson (1988) to make an important proposal for the DOC: the VP shell. The VP shell makes it possible for the goal to c-command the theme. A more recent approach by Marantz (1993), extended by Harley (1995b), Bruening (2001), and Pylkkänen (2002), builds on Larson's VP-shell idea. We will adopt this approach since it is able not only to capture the c-command relationship noted by Barss and Lasnik but at the same time to account for the argument-structure facts noted earlier.

Marantz (1993), taking a hint from Bantu languages that have applied arguments, argues that the DOC has the following structure.

(8)

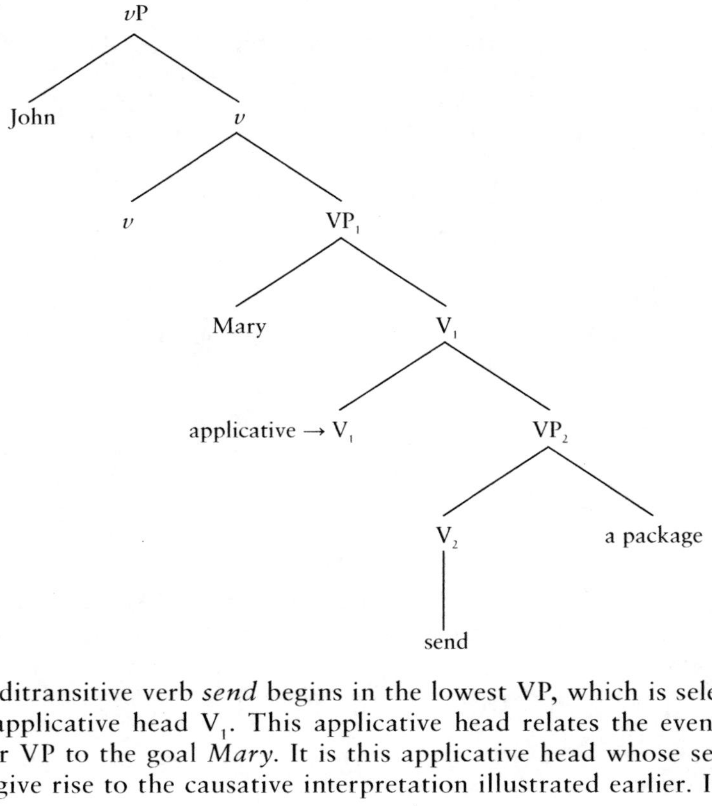

The ditransitive verb *send* begins in the lowest VP, which is selected by the applicative head V_1. This applicative head relates the event in the lower VP to the goal *Mary*. It is this applicative head whose semantics can give rise to the causative interpretation illustrated earlier. It is also its semantics that requires a possessive interpretation of the goal in the DOC. The interpretation is something like *send a package to the possession of Mary* (cf. Pylkkänen 2002). With this applicative structure for the DOC, we get both the argument-structure effects of causation and possession and also the hierarchical structure in which the goal asymmetrically c-commands the theme.

In contrast, the *to*-dative construction has a simpler structure, in which the applicative head is missing; as a result, the causative and the possessive interpretations do not arise. The following is adopted from Marantz 1993.

(9)

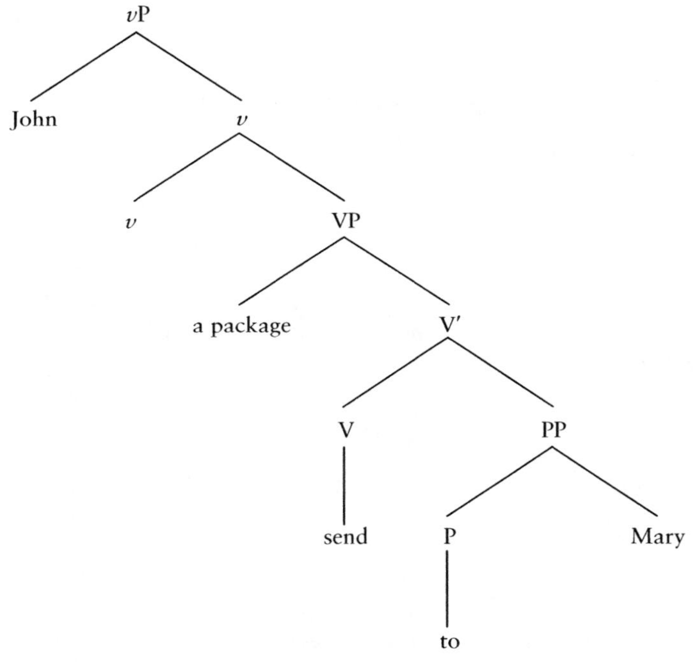

2 THE DITRANSITIVE CONSTRUCTION IN JAPANESE

Unlike English, Japanese does not have two different constructions for ditransitive verbs. The only variance is in the word order of the two internal arguments: goal–theme/theme–goal.

(10) a. Taroo-ga Hanako-ni nimotu-o okutta.
Taro-NOM Hanako-DAT package-ACC sent
'Taro sent Hanako a package.'

b. Taroo-ga nimotu-o Hanako-ni okutta.
Taro-NOM package-ACC Hanako-DAT sent

Japanese has scrambling, and the standard analysis of this word-order permutation is that it is a result of scrambling. Hoji (1985) proposed, based on quantifier-scope data and other facts, that the goal–theme order in (10a) is basic, and the theme–goal order in (10b) is derived by scrambling (cf. also Fukui 1993; Saito 1992; Tada 1993; Takano 1998; Yatsushiro 1998, 2003; among others). Hoji observes that if quantifiers occupy the VP-internal positions in the order goal–theme, the goal asymmetrically takes scope over the theme.

(11) Taroo-ga dareka-ni dono-nimotu-mo okutta.
Taro-NOM someone-DAT every package sent
'Taro sent someone every package.'
'some' > 'every', *'every' > 'some'

In contrast, in the theme–goal order, the scope is ambiguous.

(12) Taroo-ga dono-nimotu-mo$_i$ dareka-ni t_i okutta.
Taro-NOM every package someone-DAT sent
'some' > 'every', 'every' > 'some'

Hoji takes this scope ambiguity as evidence that movement has occurred.[2] As indicated by the trace, the theme 'every package' is proposed to have moved from its original complement position adjacent to the verb, leaving behind a trace, and it is this trace that makes the inverse scope (goal > theme) possible.[3] This leads him to the conclusion that the goal–theme order is the base word order and the theme–goal order is derived from it by scrambling the theme across the goal.

Hoji's analysis has become the standard approach in the field. When considered Japanese-internally, it is certainly a plausible analysis: Japanese has scrambling, and the case morphology appears to be invariant, with *-ni* for the goal and *-o* for the theme regardless of the word order. What is puzzling about this analysis is that it would make the ditransitive construction in Japanese fundamentally different from that in English. Unlike English, in Japanese there is only one structure associated with ditransitive verbs, and any variation is due to scrambling. Is this really correct?

This standard analysis predicts that, unlike in English, we should not find any argument-structure differences in Japanese ditransitive constructions because there is only one structure associated with ditransitive verbs. However, it turns out that this is incorrect. Recall that the quantifiers in the goal–theme order are scopally unambiguous. But if we change the quantifier slightly, ambiguity obtains more readily.

(13) Taroo-ga dokoka-ni[4] dono-nimotu-mo okutta.
Taro-NOM some place-to every package sent
'Taro sent every package to some place.'
'some' > 'every', 'every' > 'some'

We have consulted with a large number of native speakers, and for those who find the earlier example in (11) unambiguous, most find it easier to detect ambiguous scope in this example although some feel that it is a delicate judgment. The only difference between the two examples is in the animacy of the goal. In the earlier example the goal is animate (*dareka* 'someone'), but in the example here the goal is inanimate (*dokoka* 'some place'). This sentence is in the goal–theme order; it is also ambiguous in the other order of theme–goal. Why should an inanimate goal lead to scope ambiguity?

Recall that, as noted by Bresnan (1978, 1982b) and others, the DOC does not (usually) tolerate an inanimate goal because this goal must be interpretable as the ultimate possessor of the referent of the theme, but no such restriction occurs in the *to* dative. Suppose that, contrary to the standard analysis, Japanese has distinct structures corresponding to the DOC and the *to* dative. On this account, we would say that the example in (13) can only be a *to*-dative construction because the goal is inanimate. But does this solve the scope mystery? In fact, Aoun and Li (1989) pointed out that there is a scope difference between the two constructions, DOC and *to* dative.

(14) a. John sent some student every article.   *every > some

b. John sent some article to every student.   every > some

In the DOC, the two quantifiers are scopally unambiguous, limited only to the surface scope, while in the *to* dative, we get the inverse scope too. Marantz (1993) suggests that this difference arises from the fact that the DOC has a complex structure with an applicative head, with the goal QP outside of the VP that contains the theme QP. In this structure the theme QP cannot raise by Quantifier Raising (QR) over the goal QP. But in the *to* dative, which has a simpler structure in which both the theme and the goal are inside the same immediate VP, either the theme QP or the goal QP can raise first by QR, leading to ambiguity (cf. also Aoun and Li 1989; Bruening 2001). If we apply this analysis to Japanese, we get the right result. The DOC requires an animate goal; if the goal is inanimate, the structure is a *to* dative, which, in turn, makes scope ambiguity possible. This is what we have seen above.[5]

Let us look at another fact. In the DOC, the goal is a DP, but in the *to* dative it is a PP. This reflects the fact that in the DOC the goal is a possessor but in the *to* dative it is a location. If Japanese has these two constructions, as suggested by the quantifier-scope facts, we would expect this difference in categorial status, DP vs. PP, to arise. There is a way to test for this in Japanese. A numeral quantifier may float off its host only if the host is a DP (Shibatani 1978), as shown in (15a) below. If the host is a PP, it cannot float, as shown in (15b).

(15) a. Taroo-ga mati-o futa-tu otozureta.
Taro-NOM towns-ACC two-CL visited
'Taro visited two towns.'

b. *Hito-ga mati-kara futa-tu kita.
people-NOM towns-from two-CL came
(Intended: 'People came from two towns.')

Returning to the ditransitive construction, what we have observed with quantifiers is that if the goal is animate, it can be a DOC, which means that the goal is a DP that should allow quantifier float. However, if the goal is inanimate, it is in a *to*-dative construction, and the goal is a PP, which should block quantifier float. These predictions are borne out.

(16) Taroo-ga gakusei-ni futa-ri nimotu-o okutta.[6]
Taro-NOM students-DAT two-CL package-ACC sent
'Taro sent two students a package.' (Miyagawa 1989)

(17) *Daitooryoo-ga kokkyoo-ni futa-tu[7] heitai-o okutta.
president-NOM borders-to two-CL soldiers-ACC sent
(Intended: 'The President sent soldiers to two borders.')

The inanimate goal is fine with the numeral quantifier so long as there is no float, as shown below.[8]

(18) Daitooryoo-ga futa-tu-no-kokkyoo-ni heitai-o okutta.
president-NOM two-CL-GEN-borders-to soldiers-ACC sent
'The President sent soldiers to two borders.'

The quantifier-scope and numeral-quantifier-float facts converge to suggest that ditransitive verbs in Japanese have both the DOC and the *to* dative, just as in English. This means that, contrary to the standard analysis, the ditransitive construction in Japanese is associated with two distinct argument structures. This is not an entirely new idea. Some version of the distinct-underlying-structure analysis has already been proposed for Japanese by Harley (1995b), Kishimoto (2001b), Kitagawa (1994), Miyagawa (1995, 1997), and Watanabe (1996), among others. In the remainder of this article, we will further defend this distinct-underlying-structure analysis of the ditransitive construction.

3 TWO GOAL POSITIONS: HIGH AND LOW

In the previous section, we have shown that the quantifier-scope and numeral-quantifier facts suggest that Japanese, just like English, has two distinct structures for ditransitives, corresponding to the DOC and the *to* dative. A problem that arises with what we have observed so far is that, unlike in English, the difference between the DOC and the *to* dative in Japanese is not a function of word order. The order goal–theme may be the DOC if the goal is animate, but it must be the *to* dative if the goal is an inanimate that cannot be construed as the ultimate possessor of the referent of the theme. Is there a difference in structure between these two despite the shared word order? In particular, is there a difference of the sort proposed by Marantz (1993) between the DOC and the *to* dative? In fact, our idea is that Japanese and English are quite similar in an important respect: there are two dative positions, high and low; the DOC chooses one (high) while the *to* dative chooses the other (low).

3.1 Proposal

We propose that there are two goal positions, one higher than the other; the theme may occur before or after the low goal.

(19) a. high goal (possessive) . . . low goal (locative) . . . theme
b. high goal (possessive) . . . theme . . . low goal (locative)

The clearest evidence for the claim that there are two goal positions comes from the fact that, given an appropriate ditransitive verb, it is possible for both goals to appear in the same sentence. First recall that for ditransitive verbs such as *okuru* 'send', the *-ni*-marked goal can either be possessive (20a) or locative (20b).

(20) a. Taroo-ga Hanako-ni nimotu-o okutta.
Taro-NOM Hanako-DAT package-ACC sent
'Taro sent Hanako a package.'

b. Taroo-ga Tokyo-ni nimotu-o okutta.
Taro-NOM Tokyo-to package-ACC sent
'Taro sent a package to Tokyo.'

Given the right ditransitive verb, both the possessive and the locative goals can occur in the same sentence.[9] 'Send' is such a verb. Other verbs compatible with the two-goal construction include *todokeru* 'deliver', *kaesu* 'return', *kakeru* 'ring', *ataeru* 'give', *dasu* 'send', and *azukeru* 'entrust'.[10, 11]

(21) Taroo-ga Hanako-ni Tokyo-ni nimotu-o okutta.
Taro-NOM Hanako-DAT Tokyo-to package-ACC sent
'Taro sent Hanako a package to Tokyo.'

The meaning of this sentence is that Taro sent a package to Tokyo, which is a location, with the intention that Hanako will come to possess it. Hanako does not need to be in Tokyo; she could be in Boston, but Taro has the knowledge that sending the package to (some destination in) Tokyo will guarantee that Hanako will receive the package. The surface order here reflects the proposed hierarchy in (19): high goal–low goal.[12]

A surprising property of the two-goal construction is that the word order is quite rigid. As shown below, the low goal cannot precede the high goal.

(22) *Taroo-ga Tokyo-ni Hanako-ni nimotu-o okutta.
Taro-NOM Tokyo-to Hanako-DAT package-ACC sent
(Intended: 'Taro sent Hanako a package to Tokyo.')

Likewise, for many speakers it is not possible for the theme phrase to occur in front of the high goal.

(23) */?Taroo-ga nimotu-o Hanako-ni Tokyo-ni okutta.[13]
Taro-NOM package-ACC Hanako-DAT Tokyo-to sent
('Taro sent Hanako a package to Tokyo.')

On the other hand, it is possible for the theme to occur in front of the low goal.

(24) Taroo-ga Hanako-ni nimotu-o Tokyo-ni okutta.
Taro-NOM Hanako-DAT package-ACC Tokyo-to sent
'Taro sent Hanako a package to Tokyo.'

As far as we can tell, this permutation of low goal–theme/theme–low goal is the only word-order flexibility allowed in this two-goal construction.

We have seen that a sentence may have two goals, high and low. But what if a sentence has just one goal? Is it the high goal or the low goal? If the goal is inanimate, we know that it must be a low goal. But what if it is animate, as below?

(25) Taroo-ga gakusei-ni ronbun-o okutta.
Taro-NOM student-*NI* article-ACC sent
'Taro sent his students an article.'

This is in the goal–theme order; given what we have said so far, we cannot tell whether the goal is high or low. In the absence of something that would force one interpretation or the other (such as having another goal, or having an inanimate goal), the sentence is ambiguous. Now take the theme–goal order below.

(26) Taroo-ga ronbun-o gakusei-ni okutta.
Taro-NOM article-ACC student-*NI* sent

Here, the goal must be low. We learned as much from the two-goal construction, in which we saw that the theme cannot occur in front of the high goal, but it may before the low goal.

We can in fact confirm that if the goal follows the theme, it must be a low goal. The low goal is a locative, which means that it is a PP, not a DP. As noted by Miyagawa (1995, 1997) and Watanabe (1996), the following Japanese-internal distinction that Haig (1980) observes is consistent with the fact that a goal following a theme is a PP.

(27) a. Taroo-ga tomodati-ni futa-ri nimotu-o okutta.
Taro-NOM friends-*NI* two-CL package-ACC sent
'Taro sent two friends a package.'

b. ???Taroo-ga nimotu-o tomodati-ni futa-ri okutta.
Taro-NOM package-ACC friends-*NI* two-CL sent

Numeral-quantifier float is possible off the goal if the goal is in front of the theme; this is shown in (27a). This goal is the high goal, which is a DP, which makes the quantifier float possible. But in (27b), with the order theme–goal, the goal is a PP, which blocks quantifier float.

Thus, in both the two-goal construction and the single-goal construction, the high goal always appears before the theme while the low goal may appear either before or after the theme. This casts new light on the issue debated in the literature, namely, whether the word-order permutation in a ditransitive construction is derived by movement or whether the two word orders are base-generated. In the standard approach, the goal–theme/theme–goal permutation is characterized as free scrambling of the theme over the goal. Others have argued that the two word orders have different sources (Harley 1995b; Kishimoto 2001b; Kitagawa 1994; Miyagawa 1995, 1997; Watanabe 1996). Now, we can be more precise: *the permutation, whether it is derived by movement or by base generation, only happens with low goals.*

This conclusion relates to an interesting proposal by Takano (1998), who attempts to unify the analysis of English and Japanese. Takano argues, first, that in English the theme object in the *to* dative begins lower than the goal PP and undergoes overt short scrambling over the PP. (The idea that the theme starts low is found earlier in Pesetsky 1995.)

(28) John sent a book$_i$ to Mary t_i.

This captures directly the observation by Aoun and Li (1989) that in the *to* dative, the goal is able to be interpreted above the theme despite the surface word order. Thus, for example, we get scope ambiguity, as noted earlier in (14b). Backward binding is also possible (cf. Barss and Lasnik 1986).

(29) (?)Mary sent his$_i$ paycheck to every worker$_i$.

In Takano's theory, this movement is optional in itself. However, if it does not apply, the derivation crashes at LF because the theme (remaining in situ) cannot be attracted to the higher functional head for case checking due to the intervening goal phrase. In other words, only the derivation involving scrambling of the theme converges, thereby rendering the theme–goal order rigid in the English *to*-dative construction.[14]

In contrast, Takano argues that in Japanese, this movement is not necessary for convergence because case on the theme is licensed differently. Thus, in Japanese, we get both orders, goal–theme and theme–goal.

(30) a. Taroo-ga gakusei-ni ronbun-o okutta.
Taro-NOM student-*NI* article-ACC sent

b. Taroo-ga ronbun-o_i gakusei-ni t_i okutta.
Taro-NOM article-ACC student-*NI* sent

He thus upholds the standard analysis of Japanese but with an interesting twist about the correlation with English, with the difference captured by the nature of case marking.

Without ever mentioning the difference between high and low goals, Takano actually captures something we have observed: the word-order permutation in Japanese is found in a construction that corresponds to the English *to*-dative construction. The permutation thus involves only the low goal. This much we agree with. We also agree that there does appear to be a difference between the two languages in licensing of case on the object, along the lines Takano argues for. However, we will argue that the two orders in Japanese are base-generated, that one is not derivationally derived from the other. We will take up the movement/base-generation issue later in Section 5 and give evidence that the two orders are base-generated. As part of our discussion we will address issues raised by Yatsushiro (1998, 2003), who defends the standard approach against a base-generation approach.

Our analysis raises a question about scope judgment. Why is a goal–theme construction with an animate goal judged unambiguous? The example is repeated below.

(31) Taroo-ga dareka-ni dono-nimotu-mo okutta.
Taro-NOM someone-DAT every package sent
'Taro sent someone every package.'
'some' > 'every', *'every' > 'some'

Based on what we have said, the animate goal could be a possessor, in which case this construction would be a DOC, and the lack of ambiguity is expected. However, there is nothing to prevent interpreting this goal as locative, which would make this construction a *to* dative, identical to the construction with an inanimate goal. On this interpretation we should expect ambiguity, just as we saw with an inanimate goal. In fact, although in the minority, there are claims in the literature that examples such as this are ambiguous (Kuroda 1993b; Kitagawa 1994; Miyagawa 1997). This is what we expect based on our distinct-underlying-structure analysis of ditransitive constructions. If this is correct, then there is apparently just a preference (for many people, a strong one) to interpret an animate goal in the goal–theme order as the possessor and not the locative. We do not know why such a preference should exist, and we leave this as an open question.[15] Finally, if a numeral quantifier is associated with the goal, no ambiguity obtains, even for one of the authors who otherwise is able to detect the ambiguity even with an animate goal.

(32) Taroo-ga gakusei-ni futa-ri dono-ronbun-mo okutta.
Taro-NOM students-DAT two-CL every article sent
'Taro sent two students every article.'
'two' > 'every', *'every' > 'two'

This is expected because the numeral quantifier forces the goal to be a DP, thus a possessor. This construction can only be a DOC as a result, and we don't expect ambiguity to obtain.

3.2 The structure of high and low goals

We now turn to the structural representation of the high- and low-goal constructions. What type of structure can we postulate to account for these two constructions? Let us begin with the high goal. This goal is what emerges in the DOC. Marantz (1993) proposes that the structure of the DOC is the following.

(33)

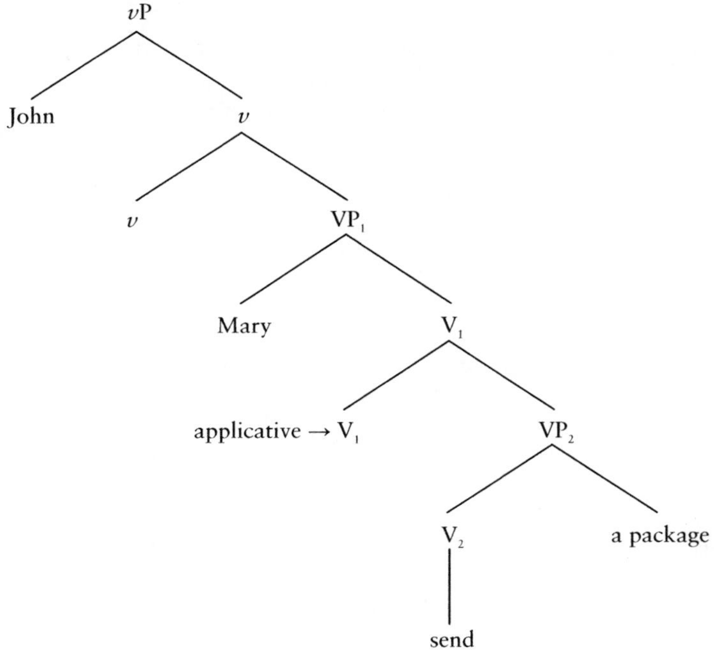

The applicative head, V_1, relates the high goal, *Mary*, to the event in VP_2, particularly, that the theme of this event, *a package*, ultimately comes into the possession of Mary. The *to*-dative construction is the following.

(34)

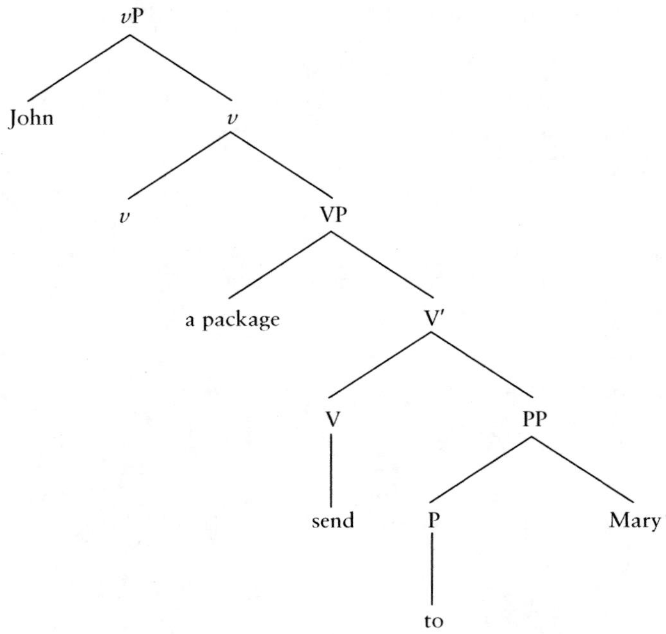

Building on Marantz's proposal, we propose that the two-goal construction is the following.[16] We give it in the Japanese order.

(35)

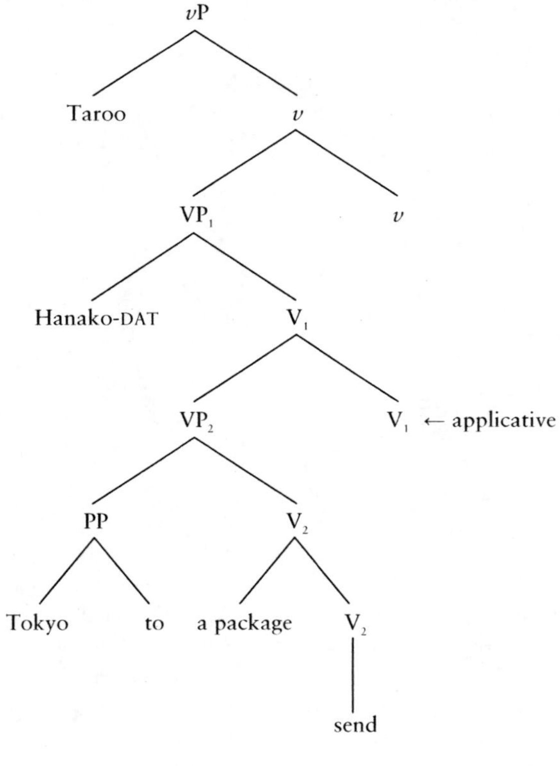

This sentence means that Taro sent a package to Tokyo, to the possession of Hanako. The specifier of the applicative head (V_1), *Hanako*-DAT, must be the possessor. The order of the PP and the theme in the lower VP (VP_2) may be generated in this order, or in the order theme–PP (cf. Marantz 1993 for relevant discussion).[17, 18]

4 EVIDENCE FOR HIGH AND LOW GOALS

In this section we will give several pieces of evidence for the various aspects of the structure we have proposed for the high and low goals.

4.1 Quantifier scope in the two-goal construction

One piece of evidence for the high and low goals comes from the quantifier-scope facts in the two-goal construction. In the canonical order, the high goal takes wide scope over both the low goal (36) and the theme (37).

(36) Taroo-ga dareka-ni subete-no-basho-ni nimotu-o okutta.
Taro-NOM someone-DAT all-GEN-place-to package-ACC sent
'Taro sent someone a package to every place.'
'some' > 'every', *'every' > 'some'

(37) Taroo-ga dareka-ni Tokyo-ni subete-no-nimotu-o okutta.
Taro-NOM someone-DAT Tokyo-to all-GEN-package-ACC sent
'Taro sent someone every package to Tokyo.'
'some' > 'every', *'every' > 'some'

In contrast, the locative goal allows inverse scope with the theme.

(38) Taroo-ga Hanako-ni dokoka-no-basho-ni subete-no-nimotu-o
Taro-NOM Hanako-DAT some-GEN-place-to all-GEN-package-ACC
okutta.
sent
'Taro sent Hanako every package to some place.'
'some' > 'every', 'every' > 'some'

This low goal–theme sentence is equally ambiguous in the theme–low goal order. We follow Marantz (1993) in assuming that QR can target either of the quantifiers if they are in the same immediate VP. This is the reason why, according to Marantz (1993), we get scope ambiguity in the *to* dative (cf. also Bruening 2001). In the English example *John sent some package to every boy*, the VP is *some package to every boy*, hence either quantifier can QR over the other. In contrast, in the DOC, the goal and the theme are not in the same immediate VP; the goal is in the specifier of the applicative head, which selects the VP containing the theme as its complement. Hence we get scope freezing.[19] What we saw above in (36)–(38) demonstrates exactly these characterizations. The high goal is in the specifier of the applicative head, hence it is outside the VP that dominates the low goal and the theme, so it always takes wide scope over either of these other phrases. But the low goal and the theme are in the same immediate VP, which correctly predicts scope ambiguity between these two.

4.2 Categorial status of the high and low goals

We can confirm the categorial status of the high goal and the low goal using passivization. While the high goal can be passivized, the low goal cannot.

(39) a. Taroo-ga nimotu-o okur-are-ta.
Taro-NOM package-ACC send-PASS-PAST
'Taro was sent a package.'

b. *Tokyo-ga nimotu-o okur-are-ta.
Tokyo-NOM package-ACC send-PASS-PAST
'*Tokyo was sent a package.'

The difference in the categorial status of high and low goals predicts this difference. The high goal is a DP that is assigned case, and under passivization this case may be absorbed. But the low goal is a PP, so there is no case to absorb, and passivization cannot apply. The English equivalents show that the same thing holds for English. The exact same pattern is observed in the two-goal construction.

(40) a. Taroo-ga Tokyo-ni nimotu-o okur-are-ta.
Taro-NOM Tokyo-to package-ACC send-PASS-PAST
'Taro was sent a package to Tokyo.'

b. *Tokyo-ga Taroo-ni nimotu-o okur-are-ta.
Tokyo-NOM Taroo-DAT package-ACC send-PASS-PAST
'*Tokyo was sent a package to Taro.'

We thus see that passivization helps to distinguish between the high goal, which is a DP, and the low goal, which is a PP.

The same point can be made by looking at the distribution of floated numeral quantifiers. The following is a minimal pair.

(41) a. Gakusei-ga$_i$ Taroo-ni t_i san-nin nimotu-o okur-are-ta.
students-NOM Taro-by three-CL package-ACC send-PASS-PAST
'Three students were sent a package by Taro.'
(cf. Kubo 1992; Miyagawa 1996)

b. *Gakusei-ga$_i$ Taroo-ni nimotu-o *t*$_i$ san-nin okur-are-ta.
students-NOM Taro-by package-ACC three-CL send-PASS-PAST
'Three students were sent a package by Taro.'
(Miyagawa 1996)

The only difference between these two examples is the position of the stranded numeral quantifier that is intended to modify the externalized goal 'students'. In (41a), it is in the position of the high goal, but in (41b), it is in the position of the low goal because it follows the theme. Remember that the goal can follow the theme only if the goal is low. By placing the numeral quantifier after the theme in (41b), we are forcing a PP interpretation of the goal 'students'. Because a PP is not associated with case, this cannot be an extraction site for passivization, hence there is no trace to support the stranded numeral quantifier. No such problem arises in (41a); the stranded numeral quantifier is in the position of the high goal, which is a DP.

We saw that the high goal is a DP, but the low goal is a PP. We can also see this readily by substituting the postposition *-e* 'to'. This is a true postposition, hence it can only occur where a PP occurs. Note that, in a two-goal construction, only the low goal may take this postposition.

(42) Taroo-ga Hanako-ni/*-e Tokyo-ni/-e nimotu-o okutta.
Taro-NOM Hanako-DAT/-to Tokyo-to/-to package-ACC sent

As shown below, the postposition *-e* may occur with an animate goal in either order, confirming that an animate goal may emerge as a low goal.

(43) a. Taroo-ga Hanako-e nimotu-o okutta.
Taro-NOM Hanako-to package-ACC sent
'Taro sent a package to Hanako.'

b. Taroo-ga nimotu-o Hanako-e okutta.
Taro-NOM package-ACC Hanako-to sent

Recall from the earlier discussion that if the goal is inanimate, scope ambiguity obtains even in the goal–theme order.

(44) Taroo-ga dokoka-ni dono-nimotu-mo okutta.
Taro-NOM some place-*NI* every package sent
'Taro sent every package to some place.'
'some' > 'every', 'every' > 'some'

We now know that this is because an inanimate goal cannot be a high goal, because it cannot take on the meaning of a possessor. Thus it is a low goal, which occurs in the same immediate VP as the theme. We predict that scope ambiguity should obtain even if the goal is animate, if this goal is marked with *-e* 'to'. Although the judgment is somewhat delicate, we believe that it is easier to get scope ambiguity with the following than with *-ni*.

(45) Taroo-ga dareka-e dono-nimotu-mo okutta.
Taro-NOM someone-to every package sent
'Taro sent every package to someone.'
'some' > 'every', 'every' > 'some'

This is predicted from our discussion of *-e*. This particle, being a postposition, only occurs on low goals regardless of whether they are animate or inanimate.

4.3 Locality and passivization

In the discussion earlier, we looked at the passivization possibility of the goal phrase. In this subsection we will look at the passivization of the theme. In English (for many dialects), and in many other languages, passivization of the theme is limited to the *to*-dative construction.

(46) a. The package was sent to Mary.
b. *The package was sent Mary.

The ungrammaticality of (46b) follows from locality: in a DOC, there are two DPs, and the operation responsible for externalizing an internal-argument DP must target the closer DP, which is the goal, not the theme. It is fine to passivize the goal in a DOC.

(47) Mary was sent a package.

What about Japanese? The following is an example in which the theme has passivized.

(48) Nimotu-ga Taroo-ni (yotte) Hanako-ni okur-are-ta.
package-NOM Taro-by Hanako-*NI* send-PASS-PAST
'The package was sent to Hanako by Taro.'

What is the nature of the *-ni* particle on the goal phrase in this example? If Japanese is like English, we expect the goal phrase here to be a PP, not a DP. If it were a DP, it would be the high goal, and it should interfere in the raising of the theme, which occurs below it.

We can again turn to the numeral quantifier to confirm that the goal is a PP (cf. Miyagawa 1996).

(49) *Nimotu-ga Taroo-ni (yotte) gakusei-ni futa-ri okur-are-ta.
package-NOM Taro-by students-*NI* two-CL send-PASS-PAST
(Intended: 'A package was sent to two students by Taro.')

The numeral quantifier *futa-ri* has a classifier that goes with an animate entity, in this case, 'students'. Nevertheless, as shown, this construal is impossible because the goal phrase containing 'students' is a PP.

One question about the above example is, where does the theme originate, above or below the low goal? In principle, either should be possible. Even if it starts out below the low goal, the low goal would not interfere since it is a PP, not a DP. We can see that such a derivation is possible.

(50) a. Nimotu-ga Taroo-ni (yotte) Hanako-ni futa-tu okur-are-ta.
package-NOM Taro-by Hanako-to two-CL send-PASS-PAST
'Two packages were sent to Hanako by Taro.'

b. Nimotu-ga Taroo-ni (yotte) futa-tu Hanako-ni okur-are-ta.
package-NOM Taro-by two-CL Hanako-to send-PASS-PAST

In (50a), the numeral quantifier that goes with the externalized 'packages' occurs after the low goal. In (50b), the stranded numeral quantifier occurs in front of the (PP) goal phrase.[20]

5 WORD-ORDER PERMUTATION: DERIVED OR BASE-GENERATED?

We now turn to the issue of the order of low goal and theme. As we have seen, these two may occur in either order.

(51) a. Taroo-ga Hanako-ni Tokyo-ni nimotu-o okutta.
Taro-NOM Hanako-DAT Tokyo-to package-ACC sent
'Taro sent a package to Hanako to Tokyo.'

b. Taroo-ga Hanako-ni nimotu-o Tokyo-ni okutta.
Taro-NOM Hanako-DAT package-ACC Tokyo-to sent

What we want to know is this: What is the relationship between these two orders? Are they derivationally related to each other, or are they base-generated? This is the same debate that is in the literature for the two possible orders, goal–theme and theme–goal, but now, it is recast as a debate about *low* goal and theme. We must consider whatever arguments given in favor of the standard approach or of a base-generation approach are still applicable. We will defend the base-generation approach (e.g., Miyagawa 1995, 1997) by first giving new evidence for it, then responding to Yatsushiro's (1998, 2003) argument for a movement approach.

5.1 Idioms

Ditransitive verbs occur in many idioms. Larson (1988) postulates that a phrasal idiom indicates that the parts of the idiom, for instance, goal and verb, must be base-generated adjacent to each other. On this assumption, we find evidence for the base-generation approach to the word-order variation involving low goal and theme. That is, we find idioms both of the goal–V type and the theme–V type, indicating that both goals and themes can be base-generated adjacent to the verb. The most interesting of these are idioms involving the same verb, with the two orders appearing in different idioms. These are given below. For all these idioms, the reverse order leads to disappearance of the idiomatic meaning. If no idiom is involved, all of these verbs readily allow both the goal–theme and the reverse theme–goal orders.

(52) *dasu* 'let out, send'

a. Goal–V idiom

Taroo-wa omotta koto-o **kuti-ni dasu.**
Taro-TOP thought thing-ACC mouth-to let out
'Taro says what's on his mind.'
??? . . . **kuti-ni** omotta koto-o **dasu**.

b. Theme–V idiom

Taroo-wa hito-no koto-ni **kuti-o dasu**.
Taro-TOP person-GEN business mouth-ACC let out
'Taro cuts in on someone else's business.'
* . . . **kuti-o** hito-no koto-ni **dasu**.

(53) *kakeru* 'hang'

a. Goal–V idiom

Taroo-wa sainoo-o **hana-ni kaketeiru**.
Taro-TOP talent-ACC nose-to hanging
'Taro always boasts of his talent.'
* . . . **hana-ni** sainoo-o **kaketeiru**.

b. Theme–V idiom

Taroo-wa sono giron-ni **hakusya-o kaketa**.
Taro-TOP that controversy-to spur-ACC hang
'Taro added fresh fuel to the controversy.'
* . . . **hakusya-o** sono giron-ni **kaketa**.

(54) *ireru* 'put in'

a. Goal–V idiom

Taroo-wa kuruma-o **te-ni** **ireta**.
Taro-TOP car-ACC hand-in put in
'Taro acquired a car.'
* . . . **te-ni** kuruma-o **ireta**.

b. Theme–V idiom

Taroo-wa genkoo-ni **te-o** **ireta**.
Taro-TOP draft-to hand-ACC put in
'Taro revised the draft.'
* . . . **te-o** genkoo-ni **ireta**.

(55) *ageru* 'raise'

a. Goal–V idiom

Taroo-wa itumo zibun-no sippai-o **tana-ni** **ageru**.
Taro-TOP always self-GEN mistake-ACC shelf-to raise
'Taro always shuts his eyes to his own mistakes.'
* . . . **tana-ni** zibun-no sippai-o **ageru**.

b. Theme–V idiom

Taroo-wa maajan-ni **timiti-o** **ageta**.
Taro-TOP mah-jongg-to blood vessel-ACC raise
'Taro was obsessed with mah-jongg.'
* . . . **timiti-o** maajan-ni **ageta**.

The standard analysis would predict that no goal–V idioms should exist, because under this approach the goal–V order is always derived by moving the theme across the goal. As we can see from the (a) examples above, this is clearly incorrect.[21, 22]

5.2 The Chain Condition

In order to maintain the base-generation hypothesis, we need to respond to an interesting challenge to it by Yatsushiro (1998, 2003). Although Yatsushiro was arguing for the standard approach, which does not distinguish between high and low goals, we can view it as also a movement approach to the word-order variation involving low goal and theme.

Yatsushiro's work is in part a response to Miyagawa 1995, 1997, in which Rizzi's (1986) Chain Condition is used to argue that the two orders, goal–theme and theme–goal, are base-generated. The Chain Condition is designed to capture the ungrammaticality of examples such as the following.

(56) *Gianni$_i$ si$_i$ èstato affidato t_i
Gianni to-himself was entrusted

The problem here is that *Gianni* crosses the clitic *si*. The Chain Condition is given below.

(57) Chain Condition (Rizzi 1986)

Chains: C = (x_i, . . . , x_n) is a chain iff, for 1 < i < n, x_i locally binds x_{i+1} (x locally binds x' iff it binds x' and there is no closer potential binder y for x')

Consider again the Italian example in (56). It has the form given below.

(58) XP_i . . . anaphoric $element_i$ . . . t_i

Rizzi's suggestion is that an anaphoric element enters into a chain by chain formation. By the Chain Condition, which imposes a strict locality on the members of a chain, there are only a handful of chain-formation possibilities for a structure like (58), all respecting the hierarchical ordering XP > anaphor > *t*. So, the XP and the anaphor form a chain, and the anaphor and the trace form a chain, and all three elements comprise the chain (XP, anaphor, *t*); but the XP and the trace do not form a chain to the exclusion of the anaphor.

Any ill-formed chain results in ungrammaticality. To see one illustration of how an ill-formed chain results, consider the three-member chain (XP, anaphor, *t*). The Chain Condition is satisfied because all nonhead members are locally bound. However, this results in a chain with two θ-roles (anaphoric element, *t*), violating the Theta Criterion. Other possibilities are equally bad for independent reasons.

Snyder (1992) and Koizumi (1995) showed that the Chain Condition applies to Japanese, using the reciprocal anaphor *otagai* 'each other'.

(59) ?*[John-to Bob]-o_i otagai-ga_i t_i nagutta.
John-and Bob-ACC each other-NOM hit
(Intended: 'John and Bob, each other hit.')

This structure parallels Rizzi's Italian example. If the reciprocal anaphor is embedded in a larger phrase, the Chain Condition problem disappears.

(60) [John-to Bob]-o_i [otagai-no_i hahaoya]-ga t_i nagutta.
John-and Bob-ACC each other-GEN mother-NOM hit
'John and Bob, each other's mothers hit.'

In this example, the reciprocal anaphor does not c-command the trace, making it possible for the antecedent 'John and Bob' and the trace to form a chain by themselves, leading to a well-formed chain with one θ-role and one case.

Based on this, it is noted in Miyagawa 1995, 1997 that the two orders in the ditransitive construction, goal–theme and theme–goal, must be viewed as base-generated. Neither order evidences a Chain Condition violation.

(61) a. Goal–theme
John-ga [Hanako-to Mary]-ni$_i$ otagai-o$_i$ syookaisita.
John-NOM Hanako-and Mary-*NI* each other-ACC introduced
'John introduced Hanako and Mary to each other.'

b. Theme–goal
(?)John-ga [Hanako-to Mary]-o$_i$ (paatii-de) otagai-ni$_i$
John-NOM Hanako-and Mary-ACC (party-at) each other-*NI*
syookaisita.
introduced
'John introduced Hanako and Mary to each other (at the party).'

The crucial example is (61b); as shown, the sentence is essentially fine despite the fact that this is a theme–goal order. According to the standard approach, this theme has been scrambled across the goal, but that should trigger a Chain Condition violation, specifically a locality violation (the scrambled theme does not locally bind the trace because there is a closer binder, the goal). The fact that the sentence is fine suggests that no such movement has occurred, in turn opening the door to the base-generation analysis.

Yatsushiro (1998, 2003) criticizes the use of the reciprocal anaphor *otagai* to establish the existence of the Chain Condition in Japanese. She gives several interesting arguments to show that *otagai* 'each other' does not always display a Chain Condition violation where one expects it.[23] Because we have already given evidence for the base-generation hypothesis using idioms, we will not attempt to respond to the issues she brought out for reciprocals, setting them aside for this chapter. More important to our present purpose is Yatsushiro's contention that the "reflexive anaphor" *kare-zisin* 'himself' is an anaphoric expression truly subject to the Chain Condition and that its behavior supports the standard movement-based analysis. We will respond to this argument that uses *kare-zisin*. The relevant data is given below.

First, as with *otagai* 'each other', *kare-zisin* 'himself' appears to show the problem triggered by the Chain Condition.

(62) *Taroo-o$_i$ kare-zisin-ga$_i$ t_i hometa.
Taro-ACC him-self-NOM praised
(Intended: 'Taro, himself praised.')

Yatsushiro then points out that *kare-zisin* is fine in the goal–theme order but not in the theme–goal order (we have changed the English translation of Yatsushiro's examples slightly; it has no bearing on the argument).

(63) a. ?Hanako-ga (kagami-o tukatte) Taroo-ni$_i$ kare-zisin-o$_i$ miseta.
Hanako-NOM (mirror-ACC using) Taro-*NI* him-self-ACC showed
'Hanako showed Taro himself (in the mirror).'

b. (*)Hanako-ga (kagami-o tukatte) Taroo-o$_i$ kare-zisin-ni$_i$
Hanako-NOM (mirror-ACC using) Taro-ACC him-self-*NI*
miseta.
showed
('Hanako showed Taro to himself (in the mirror).')

c. Hanako-ga (kagami-o tukatte) Taroo-o$_i$ [kare-zisin-no$_i$
Hanako-NOM (mirror-ACC using) Taro-ACC him-self-GEN
hahaoya]-ni miseta.
mother-*NI* showed
'Hanako showed Taro to his own mother (using a mirror).'

The example in (63a) is what we are calling the DOC. The antecedent 'Taro' in the goal position can be coreferential with the reflexive anaphor in the theme position. In contrast, in (63b), which is what we are calling the *to* dative, the reflexive anaphor in the goal position cannot be coreferential with the antecedent in the theme position. The asterisk in parentheses indicates that there are some speakers who did not judge this example as ungrammatical (Yatsushiro 2003), but rather as well formed. In (63c), which is the same construction as (63b), the reflexive anaphor is embedded in a larger phrase, presumably making it possible to avoid a Chain Condition violation.

While we find this new empirical discovery interesting, we believe that the conclusion that this reflexive anaphor gives evidence for the movement analysis is unwarranted. It is important to understand the details of Rizzi's Chain Condition: the Chain Condition is designed to allow chain formation that goes beyond the normal notion of chain—head and its traces—as defined in Chomsky 1981. In that work (332–333), a chain is defined as being formed from *links* (a_i, a_{i+1}), where a_i locally A-binds a_{i+1}. The head of the chain is "a lexical category, PRO, or a variable, and each non-head is a trace coindexed with the head" (332). Rizzi extends this notion of a chain by allowing an anaphor in the appropriate position to participate in the composition of a chain. The crucial point is that, as stated in the definition of the Chain Condition above (57), for an anaphor to so participate in chain formation, it must be locally *bound* by another member of the chain.

Based on this notion of chain, it is improbable that the so-called reflexive anaphor *kare-zisin* 'himself' would be subject to the Chain Condition. It is in fact misleading to call this item an "anaphor." This item is composed of the pronoun *kare* 'him' and the intensifier/reflexive *zisin* 'self'. An important property of *kare-zisin* is that it retains a well-known property of overt pronouns in Japanese, namely, that it cannot be a bound variable (Nakayama 1982; Saito and Hoji 1983).

(64) Taroo-ga$_i$/*dareka-ga$_i$ kare-no$_i$ kodomo-o sikatta.
Taro-NOM/someone-NOM him-GEN child-ACC scolded
'Taro/*someone scolded his child.'

It is fine for an R-expression to be the antecedent of the overt pronoun *kare* 'him', but not a quantifier such as 'someone'. This restriction carries over to *kare-zisin* (Aikawa 1995; cf. also Richards 1997).

(65) ?Taroo-ga$_i$/*dareka-ga$_i$ kare-zisin-o$_i$ hometa.
Taro-NOM/someone-NOM him-self-ACC praised
'Taro/*someone praised himself.'

The reason why the overt pronoun cannot be bound by an operator is that a pronoun such as *kare* in Japanese is always referential. It has a unique referential index so that any coreference between it and an NP is just that, coreference, and not binding.[24] Our point is this. Because *kare-zisin* is incapable of being bound, it cannot possibly become a member of a chain by chain formation. Chain formation requires binding, which *kare-zisin* does not allow, as we have seen. Suppose, for a moment, that, contrary to fact, *kare-zisin* becomes a part of a chain. The chain will automatically be ill formed because the chain would be associated with more than one referential index: the referential index of the head and the referential index of *kare-zisin*. The data on the clitic and reciprocal anaphors in Italian, which were the basis of Rizzi's original proposal, and the wider range of data on the Chain Condition explored by McGinnis (1998), all involve true anaphors that are referentially dependent on the head of the chain, hence they are bound.

Another way to look at the problem with *kare-zisin* is to think about it in the context of the copy theory of movement (cf. Chomsky 1993). Each link of a chain is a copy of the head. The intuition behind Rizzi's Chain Condition is that in certain special cases, such as a clitic, an element that is not internally merged, but instead externally merged, can nevertheless function as a link in a chain because it can function in effect as a copy of the head. But *kare-zisin* can't possibly function as such because it has a different referential index than the head of the chain, hence by no stretch of the imagination can it be a copy of the head of the chain.[25]

We can therefore set aside Yatsushiro's argument for the movement analysis. This still leaves a question as to why we get the pattern of grammaticality with *kare-zisin* described by Yatsushiro. We leave this problem open.[26]

6 THE HIGH GOAL AND THE WORD-ORDER RESTRICTION

We have seen that the theme cannot scramble across the high goal. The example is repeated below.

(66) */?Taroo-ga nimotu-o Hanako-ni Tokyo-ni okutta.
Taro-NOM package-ACC Hanako-DAT Tokyo-to sent
('Taro sent a package to Hanako to Tokyo.')

There are two questions to ask. First, why can't the theme adjoin to the applicative phrase?

(67) */?

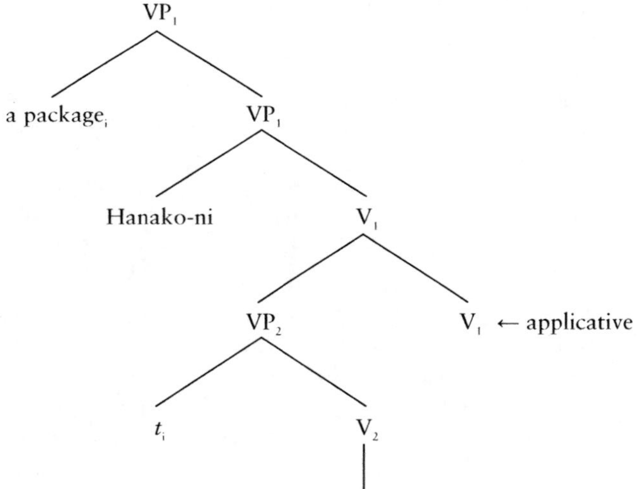

Second, why can't the theme move across the high goal to *v*P?

We will give an EPP-based explanation of both of these questions; we will show that our analysis is confirmed by facts Anagnostopoulou (1999, 2003) observes in Greek. As noted by McGinnis (2002), the applicative phrase may be a phase or not a phase in a particular language (cf. Chomsky 2001 for the notion of phase).[27] Miyagawa (2003b) suggests that the applicative phrase in Japanese is not a phase. What this means is that the applicative head would never be associated with an EPP feature. Hence, nothing could be attracted to it. This is the answer to the first question—why the theme cannot adjoin to the maximal projection headed by the applicative head. For the second question, we can simply appeal to locality. If the little *v* has an EPP feature, it should attract the closest phrase, which is not the theme but the high goal. The EPP-based explanation also accounts for why the low goal cannot occur above the high goal.

If our answers to the two questions are on the right track, they indicate that scrambling in Japanese behaves more like the common type of movement that is triggered by a feature (EPP) as defined in Chomsky 2001, something Miyagawa (1995, 1997, 2001) has argued for. Setting aside the issue of how one obtains locality of the object and the subject relative to T (by V raising, in Miyagawa 1997, 2001, or by moving the object to the edge of the phase, in Miyagawa 2003b), this contrasts with the prevailing view that scrambling is free movement without a triggering feature (Fukui 1993; Saito and Fukui 1998; etc.). Fukui, for example, proposes that scrambling in Japanese, which moves an element in the direction of the head projection (to the left), is "costless." What we have seen is that this is incorrect. The theme cannot move across the high goal, due to the combination of a lack of an EPP feature on the applicative head and locality that blocks its movement to the *v*P, whose head does contain an EPP feature. Where there appears to be free movement (low goal–theme/theme–low goal), we have evidence that the two orders are base-generated. Fukui's proposal, although interesting, is based on insufficient data, and his conclusion appears unwarranted.[28]

6.1 Greek

We turn to Greek (Anagnostopoulou 1999, 2003), which has a slightly different pattern of grammaticality. The Greek ditransitive construction parallels Japanese in many ways. Unlike Japanese, and like English, Greek has different markings for high and low goals.

(68) a. Estila tis Marias to vivlio.
sent-1SG the Maria-GEN the book-ACC
'I sent Maria the book.'

b. Estila to vivlio s-tin Maria.
sent-1SG the book-ACC to-the Maria
'I sent the book to Maria.'

Example (68a) is the DOC; in Greek, genitive and dative cases have merged, with the genitive generalizing to the dative. We can see that (68a) is a DOC by the fact that the genitive goal cannot be inanimate. No such restriction holds for the *to*-dative version, as expected.

(69) a. *Estila tis Gallias to vivlio.
sent-1SG the France-GEN the book-ACC
'*I sent France the book.'

b. Estila to vivlio s-tin Gallia.
sent-1SG the book-ACC to-the France
'I sent the book to France.'

Greek has scrambling similar to Japanese. One striking difference is that in Greek, it is apparently possible to scramble the theme across the high goal. The following is taken from Anagnostopoulou 2003.

(70) a. Fanerosa tis Marias tin alithia.
revealed-1SG the Maria-GEN the truth-ACC
'I revealed (to) Mary the truth.'

b. ?Fanerosa tin alithia tis Marias.[29]

The example in (70a) is the "normal" genitive–accusative (high goal–theme) order, and in (70b) the theme has scrambled across the genitive goal phrase. There is apparently some mild awkwardness in this movement, perhaps reflecting what in Japanese is ungrammatical for most speakers. An interesting point is that this movement in Greek is clearly A′-movement. This is shown by the following.

(71) a. ?Edhosa tu kathe fititi$_i$ tin ergasia tu$_i$.
gave-1SG the every student-GEN the paper-ACC his-GEN
'I gave every student his term paper.'

b. *?Edhosa to kathe tseki tu katochu tu$_i$.
gave-1SG the every check-ACC the owner-GEN its-GEN
(Intended: 'I gave every check (to) its owner.')

The example in (71a) is the basic order, with the universal quantifier in the goal position able to bind the pronoun inside the theme. In (71b), the order has been reversed, and as indicated, the theme, which precedes the goal, cannot bind into the goal. This is a typical A′-scrambling property: it does not create a new binder (Mahajan 1990). In Greek, then, there is an A′-position somewhere in the region of the *v*P, and a phrase can move into this position apparently without observing locality. What is the nature of this A′-position? It is possibly a focus position, something proposed in this location by Miyagawa (1997).

We noted earlier that even in Japanese, some speakers find scrambling of the theme across the high goal to be essentially fine with only a slight degradation. We surmise that these speakers have the "Greek" A′-position. We can see this from the fact that scrambling to this position does not make a new quantifier scope possible, a hallmark of A′-scrambling, as discovered by Tada (1993). In the example below, we have arbitrarily assumed the trace of the theme to occur after the low goal.[30]

(72) */?Taroo-ga dono nimotu-mo$_i$ dareka-ni Tokyo-ni t_i okutta.
Taro-NOM every package someone-DAT Tokyo-to sent
('Taro sent someone every package to Tokyo.')
*'every' > 'some', 'some' > 'every'

7 CONCLUDING REMARKS

In this article we explored the question of whether ditransitive verbs in Japanese are associated with the kinds of argument structures well attested in languages such as English. On the surface, it doesn't appear to be the case. Rather, the only variation we can see is word order, and, in fact, the standard analysis identifies one order (goal–theme) as basic and the other order as derived by the free application of scrambling (Hoji 1985). We gave ample evidence that this cannot be correct. We gave proof for different argument structures that parallel the DOC and the *to* dative. We also gave arguments against the most recent version of the standard approach (Yatsushiro 1998, 2003).

Our study also questions the notion of a completely free optional scrambling (e.g., Fukui 1993). What we observed is that scrambling within the VP is highly restricted, observing strict locality, which is a hallmark of a feature-driven operation rather than a triggerless, purely optional operation. There is, in fact, a question as to whether there is such a thing as purely free movement.

4 Nominalization and argument structure

Evidence for the dual-base analysis of ditransitive constructions in Japanese

1 INTRODUCTION

In the study of ditransitive constructions in Japanese, there is a debate that reflects a tension that often arises in linguistic study: the seeming conflict between focusing on what is unique about a particular language and asking what that language can tell us about universal grammar. These two perspectives do not always lead to divergent views, and, when they do diverge, taking one or the other approach by no means gives a better chance of emerging with the right analysis.

In the case of ditransitive verbs in Japanese, a distinctive feature of the Japanese language has molded the earliest and what we can consider even today the most influential analysis. This feature is scrambling, which sets Japanese apart from most Indo-European languages and many of the East Asian languages, and it is an operation that has garnered the attention of perhaps more generative linguists working on Japanese than any other property of the language. It is no surprise, then, that the earliest analysis of ditransitive verbs crucially depends on scrambling. Ditransitive verbs allow both the IO–O–V order and the O–IO–V order. Hoji (1985) argued—quite convincingly based on what we knew at the time—that the first word order (IO–O) is basic, and the second (O–IO) is derived by scrambling the O over IO. This is an entirely reasonable and even a compelling view, one that is certainly compatible with the evidence that Hoji presents; in this so-called standard analysis of the ditransitive construction we find yet another domain of Japanese grammar where scrambling plays a crucial role in making certain expressions possible.

However, in Miyagawa 1997 and in Chapter 3 of this volume (see also Miyagawa 1994), I abstracted away from the two word orders and scrambling, and looked at the ditransitive construction from another perspective, asking the question, can we detect in Japanese the two argument structures often shown to be associated with ditransitive verbs in other languages? Hoji's approach, in its simplest and most intuitive form, predicts that Japanese has only one argument structure associated with ditransitive verbs, the argument structure reflected in the IO–O word order, with the other word order, O–IO, being a derived form. This is the single-base analysis of ditransitive verbs. In Miyagawa 1997 and in Chapter 3, instead of the single-base analysis of Hoji, arguments are given for a dual-base analysis of ditransitives.[1]

In this chapter, I will give further evidence for the dual-base analysis based on nominalization, building on the important work of Kishimoto (2006). I will in particular show that, despite what appears to be a single argument structure associated with ditransitives, nominalization helps to tease apart the two argument structures often associated with ditransitive constructions in many other languages. Furthermore, what we can see in Japanese helps us to understand the right approach to the nominalization facts in other languages where differences have been detected between the two argument structures, showing that Pesetsky's approach based on Myers's Generalization makes the right prediction with regard to not only the similarities between English and Japanese, but also one sharp difference between the two languages. In the appendix, I will summarize two criticisms of the dual-base analysis, one that comes from sentence processing and the other from the study of idiomatization, and recent responses that neutralize or effectively argue against the criticisms.

2 THE *-KATA* CONSTRUCTION

In the *-kata* construction, the nominal element *-kata* 'way' attaches to the adverbial form of the verb.

(1) Taroo-no syokudoo-de-no piza-no tabe-kata
Taro-GEN cafeteria-in-GEN pizza-GEN eat-way
'Taro's way of eating pizza in the cafeteria'

This corresponds to the sentence in (2).

(2) Taroo-ga syokudoo-de piza-o tabe-ta.
Taro-NOM cafeteria-in pizza-ACC ate
'Taro ate pizza in the cafeteria.'

In the *-kata* construction in (1), the arguments—subject and object—which in (2) are marked with the nominative *-ga* and the accusative *-o* must bear only the genitive case marking *-no*. Adjunct PPs such as the locative must retain the postposition and the entire PP must bear the genitive case marking (Sugioka 1992; Ito and Sugioka 2002, 104; see also Hoshi 2006).

Kageyama argues that the *-kata* construction is formed in syntax, giving as evidence the fact that it may nominalize clauses containing arguably syntactic elements such as aspectual, causative, and passive morphemes (the following are taken from Kageyama 1993, 358).

(3) a. sake-no nomi-hazime-kata
sake-GEN drink-begin-way
'the way of starting to drink sake'

b. yom-ase-hazime-kata
read-CAUS-begin-way
'the way of making (someone) start to read'

c. (zidaigeki-de-no) akuyaku-no kir-are-kata
(period-play-in-GEN) villain-GEN cut-PASS-way
'villains' way of being cut (with a sword) (in period plays)'

These are compelling pieces of evidence for the syntactic analysis, and I will assume it. What is the process by which this nominalization appears in syntax? Kageyama (1993, 363) suggests that the adverbial form of the verb adjoins to the nominal *-kata*, rendering the verb into a nominal.

(4)
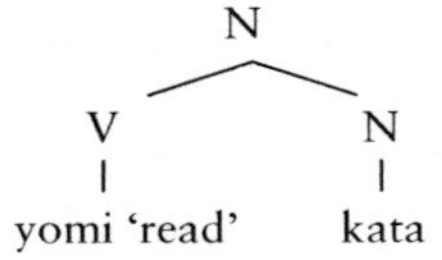

Later, I will return to this particular view of nominalization and show that it is compatible with recent developments in syntactic word formation.

3 KISHIMOTO 2006

Kishimoto (2006) explores a number of issues in syntax using the *-kata* construction. He provides a number of arguments to reinforce Kageyama's conclusion that this construction is syntactically based, and proposes an analysis that is consistent with the spirit of Kageyama's study, but with one major difference. Unlike the adjunction analysis (4) that Kageyama proposed, Kishimoto suggests (780) that *-kata* takes a *v*P complement. The following is for *John-no hon-no yomi-kata* 'John's way of reading books'.

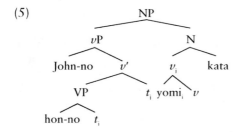

(5)
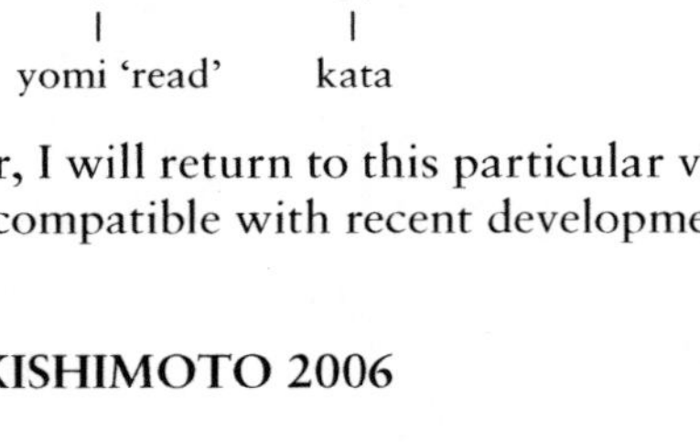

Just as with Kageyama (1993), there is adjunction to the nominal head *-kata*, but what adjoins is an amalgam of the verb in the adverbial form and the "small" *v*, the latter having been picked up by the verb when it raised to *v*.

Among the reasons Kishimoto gives for proposing that the *-kata* construction involves the *v*P is that the external argument can show up, as in the case of (5) (*John-no*), *v* being the head that introduces the external argument.

It is crucial in Kishimoto's analysis that *-kata* selects for *v*P, not TP. An obvious reason is that tense never shows up in this construction. Furthermore, the lack of T is tied to an important observation that Kishimoto makes, namely, that there is no scrambling in this nominal construction. The following is taken from Kishimoto 2006, 789.

(6) a. John-no hon-no yomi-kata
John-GEN book-GEN read-way
'John's way of reading books'

b. *hon-no John-no yomi-kata
book-GEN John-GEN read-way

Kishimoto argues, following a number of studies, that A-movement scrambling is triggered by the EPP feature on T (Kishimoto 2001a; Kitahara 2002; Miyagawa 2001; Tsujioka 2001). In Miyagawa 2001, for example, I argue for the following structures for the orders SOV and OSV.

(7) a. [$_{TP}$ Taroo-ga$_i$ [$_{vP}$ t_i hon-o yonda]].
Taro-NOM book-ACC read
'Taro read a book.'

b. [$_{TP}$ Hon-o$_i$ [$_{vP}$ Taroo-ga t_i yonda]].
book-ACC Taro-NOM read

In both, something is in Spec,TP: in (7a) it is the subject, while in (7b) the object has moved to this position, allowing the subject to remain in situ in Spec,*v*P, an idea inherited from Kuroda (1988).[2] I argued that this requirement that something must occupy Spec,TP receives a natural account under the assumption that T has an EPP feature, which forces T to have a specifier (Chomsky 1981, 1995; see Alexiadou and Anagnostopoulou 1998 for arguments for the universality of the EPP on T). This approach to scrambling presumes that (A-movement) scrambling can only occur in the presence of T, and, as Kishimoto notes, this leads to the prediction that in the *-kata* construction, there should be no scrambling, something confirmed by the minimal pair in (6) above. I will return to this point in the next section.

4 DITRANSITIVES

In this section, I will briefly summarize the arguments given in Chapter 3 for the dual-base analysis. In the literature, we find two different approaches to the ditransitive construction in Japanese. I will briefly introduce the issues, and in the sections to follow, we will look to see what the

-*kata* construction can tell us about ditransitives in particular and syntactic nominalization in general.

The so-called standard analysis assumes that there is only one underlying structure associated with ditransitives, and this underlying structure has the order goal–theme.

(8) Taroo-ga Hanako-ni tegami-o okutta.
Taro-NOM Hanako-DAT letter-ACC sent
'Taro sent Hanako a letter.'

The other order theme–goal, shown below, is, in this standard approach, the result of scrambling.

(9) Taroo-ga tegami-o Hanako-ni okutta.
Taro-NOM letter-ACC Hanako-DAT sent

Hoji (1985) gives arguments based on quantifier scope, variable binding, and other phenomena in favor of the standard analysis.

In contrast, in Chapter 3, Takae Tsujioka and I, based in part on Miyagawa 1997, propose that there are two distinct argument structures associated with ditransitive predicates. In one of the structures, the goal has a possessive meaning, which means that the referent of the goal is most naturally an animate entity, although an inanimate referent is possible if it can be interpreted as being composed of humans, as in the case of 'committee', 'company', and so forth. This "possessive" goal is a DP (or NP). The other type of goal is locative and, as such, there is no implication that it has to be animate. The category of this goal is PP. This possessive–locative bifurcation for the goal in ditransitives is commonly found among languages of the world, including in English, where we find the double-object and dative constructions (*John sent Mary a letter, John sent a letter to Mary*). As we note in Chapter 3, there are a number of parallels between the Japanese ditransitives and the English double-object and dative constructions. I will give two here.

The goal in a double-object construction is possessive in nature (see, e.g., Bresnan 1978, 1982b; Harley 1995b; Mazurkewich and White 1984; Pinker 1989). The following is taken from Bresnan 1978.

(10) a. I sent the boarder/*the border a package.
b. I sent a package to the boarder/the border.

The double-object example shown in (10a) only allows the animate *boarder* to occur in the goal position, while the dative example shown in (10b) allows either the animate *boarder* or the inanimate *border.* We can see that the goal in the double object is a DP while the goal in the dative is a PP (*to*). In Chapter 3, Section 2, Tsujioka and I note that the same distinction based on animacy is found in Japanese. We focus on this distinction as manifested in the phrasal type, DP or PP, using the numeral quantifier to establish the type of phrase. To set the stage, observe that, as noted by Shibatani (1978), floated numeral quantifiers are only possible off a DP.

(11) a. Taroo-ga mati-o futa-tu otozureta.
Taro-NOM town-ACC two-CL visited.
'Taro visited two towns.'

b. *Hito-ga mati-kara futa-tu kita.
people-NOM town-from two-CL came
(Intended: 'People came from two towns.')

In (11a), the object *mati-o* (town-ACC) is a DP, and it allows the numeral quantifier *futa-tu* (two-CL) to be in the floated position following it, while in (11b) *mati* is inside a PP, so that it cannot be construed with the floated numeral quantifier.

Returning to the ditransitive construction, note that animate and inanimate goals may occur in the same order relative to the theme.

(12) a. Taroo-ga gakusei-ni nimotu-o okutta.
Taro-NOM student-DAT package-ACC sent
'Taro sent the students a package.'

b. Daitooryoo-ga kokkyoo-ni heitai-o okutta.
president-NOM border-DAT soldiers-ACC sent
'The president sent soldiers to the border.'

These two examples appear to be completely parallel, but when we put them under the numeral-quantifier test, we can see that the phrasal category of the two goal phrases is different.

(13) a. Taroo-ga gakusei-ni futa-ri nimotu-o okutta.
Taro-NOM student-DAT two-CL package-ACC sent
'Taro sent two students a package.'

b. *Daitooryoo-ga kokkyoo-ni futa-tu heitai-o okutta.
president-NOM border-DAT two-CL soldiers-ACC sent
(Intended: 'The president sent soldiers to two borders.')

As we see in (13a), it is possible to have a floated numeral quantifier with an animate goal, but not with an inanimate goal (13b), clearly indicating that there are two kinds of goals, hence two distinct argument structures. There is nothing inherently wrong with the meaning of (13b), as we can see by the fact that if we change the goal's numeral quantifier to a nonfloated version (*futa-tu-no kokkyoo-ni* 'to two borders'), the sentence becomes fine.

Obviously, this means that the "dative" particle *-ni* has two existences, one a case marker, the other a postposition, a bifurcation noted earlier by Sadakane and Koizumi (1995).

The second parallel between Japanese ditransitives and the English double-object and dative constructions is quantifier scope. As Hoji (1985) and others have noted, in the goal–theme order, the scope of quantifiers is unambiguous, while the other order, theme–goal, leads to ambiguity.

(14) a. Taroo-ga dareka-ni dono-nimotu-mo okutta.
Taro-NOM someone-DAT every package sent
'Taro sent someone every package.'
'some' > 'every', *'every' > 'some'

b. Taroo-ga dono-nimotu-mo dareka-ni okutta.
Taro-NOM every package someone-DAT sent
'some' > 'every', 'every' > 'some'

What I wish to focus on is the lack of ambiguity in (14a) (see note 6 for a comment about the ambiguity of (14b)). Note that the goal here is animate, thus inviting an interpretation of possession. As we note, however, if the goal is changed to inanimate, the judgment changes (example (13) in Chapter 3).

(15) Taroo-ga dokoka-ni dono-nimotu-mo okutta.
Taro-NOM some place-to every package sent
'Taro sent every package to some place.'
'some' > 'every', 'every' > 'some'

This example, despite being in the goal–theme order, shows ambiguity of scope. This parallels English examples (see Aoun and Li 1989; Bruening 2001; Pesetsky 1995).

(16) a. Mary sent someone every book.
some > every, *every > some

b. Mary sent something to every student.
some > every, every > some

The double-object construction only allows surface scope, while scope ambiguity obtains in the dative construction. Just so are the Japanese examples, in which the animate-goal construction does not evidence ambiguity, while the dative construction, which is forced by the occurrence of the inanimate goal, leads to scope ambiguity.[3] I will not give the analysis for the lack/presence of scope ambiguity (see, for example, Bruening 2001; Marantz 1993; Pesetsky 1995; among others). I simply note that the scope facts in Japanese match the double-object and dative constructions in English, thereby giving further evidence for the dual-base analysis.

To account for these two argument structures, we adopted in Chapter 3 the applicative-head analysis of Marantz (1993) and Pylkkänen (2002). As originally noted by Marantz, the DP goal argument is an "added-on" argument; this sort of "extra" argument is typically found, in the languages of the Bantu, being introduced with an applicative head. For the DP goal argument, we gave the following structure from Marantz 1993, which we called the high goal.

(17)

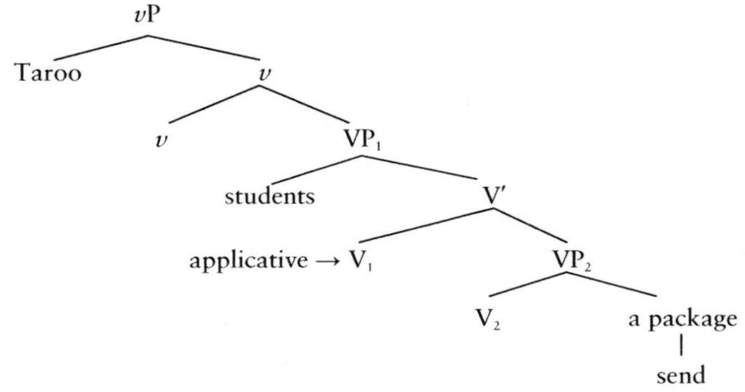

The high goal 'students' is introduced by the applicative head V_1, which in turn selects VP_2 (see Pylkkänen 2002 for a different structure). For the low PP goal, again, the structure is adopted from Marantz 1993 (see also Larson 1988 and Pesetsky 1995 for relevant discussion).

(18) *To* dative (Marantz 1993)

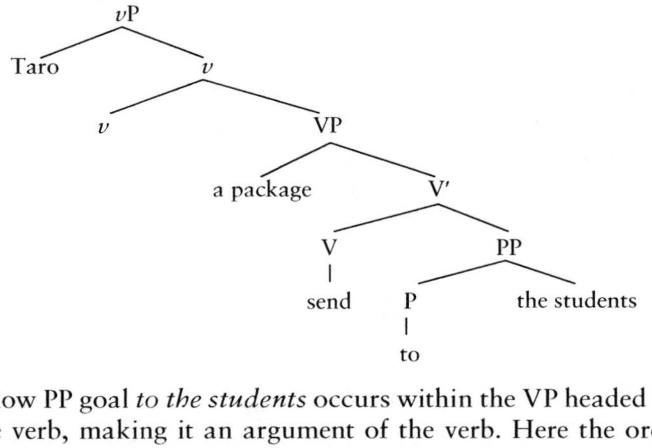

The low PP goal *to the students* occurs within the VP headed by the ditransitive verb, making it an argument of the verb. Here the order is theme–goal, but in Japanese, the order can also be goal–theme even for a low goal. In fact, the "controversy" between the standard approach (e.g., Hoji 1985)

and the dual-base approach (e.g., Chapter 3) is not about word order per se. While word order does come into play (see below for discussion of this), the principal difference is whether one recognizes a single base or dual bases.

As a demonstration of the two types of goals that exist in Japanese, we noted in Chapter 3 that, for some people at least, it is possible for both the high goal and the low goal to occur simultaneously. Some find it easier with *-e* instead of *-ni* on the low goal; also, having an element in the low goal that is coreferential with the high goal appears to improve the example, a point that Richard Larson noted to me.

(19) Taroo-wa Hanako-ni hon-o kanozyo-no-kenkyuusitu-ni
Taro-TOP Hanako-DAT book-ACC her-GEN-office-to
okutta.
sent
'Taro sent Hanako a book to her office.'

This sentence means that Taro sent a package to Hanako's office, with the intention that Hanako would come to possess it.[4] Hanako does not even need to be in her office. While not all speakers accept (19) (the same split in judgment is found among English speakers for the parallel English examples), many do accept it with varying degrees of hesitation, from "fine" to "awkward." One point that we note in Chapter 3, Section 3.1 is that even for those who accept (19), the following, in which the low goal occurs higher than the high goal, is unacceptable. (I have held constant the order of 'Hanako' and 'her' to avoid backward pronominalization.)

(20) *Taroo-wa Hanako-no-kenkyuusitu-ni kanozyo-ni hon-o okutta.
Taro-TOP Hanako-GEN-office-to her-DAT book-ACC sent
(Intended: 'Taro sent Hanako a book to her office.')

This indicates that the high DP goal occurs high in the structure, which, in the dual-base approach, means that it is introduced in that position by an applicative head, while the low goal occurs low in the structure. What (20) indicates is that this hierarchy cannot be violated even by something as common in Japanese as scrambling. In fact, the example remains bad even if the theme is moved higher than the high goal.[5]

(21) ?*Taroo-wa hon-o Hanako-ni kanozyo-no-kenkyuusitu-ni
Taro-TOP book-ACC Hanako-DAT her-GEN-office-to
okutta.
sent
(Intended: 'Taro sent Hanako a book to her office.')

This has an immediate consequence for word order. In a "normal" sentence with just one goal, the goal and the theme may occur freely in either order, goal–theme or theme–goal. In the goal–theme order, the goal is likely the high goal, unless it is inanimate. However, in the theme–goal order, the goal *must* be the low goal, because the theme cannot occur above the high goal. This is true regardless of whether this goal is animate or inanimate.[6] In the "normal" goal–theme/theme–goal examples, this point cannot be detected, but when we put both the high and low goals in the same sentence, we can see the restrictions on word order clearly. Thus, as we see below, for those who accept the two-goal construction, the order is: agent–high goal–(low goal)–theme–(low goal)–verb.

(22) Taroo-wa Hanako-ni (kanozyo-no-kenkyuusitu-ni) hon-o
Taro-TOP Hanako-DAT (her-GEN-office-to) book-ACC
(kanozyo-no-kenkyuusitu-ni) okutta.
(her-GEN-office-to) sent
'Taro sent Hanako a book to her office.'

This predicts that the goal in the theme–goal order is always a PP, something already argued in Miyagawa 1997.[7]

(23) a. Taroo-wa tomodati-ni go-nin CD-o okutta.
Taro-TOP friends-DAT five-CL CD-ACC sent
'Taro sent five friends a CD.'

b. ???Taroo-wa CD-o tomodati-ni go-nin okutta.
Taro-TOP CD-ACC friends-to five-CL sent

5 THE -*KATA* CONSTRUCTION AND DITRANSITIVES

Let us return to the -*kata* construction and see what it can tell us about the ditransitive construction. As noted earlier, one important observation that Kishimoto (2006) makes is that there is no scrambling in this construction, which means that whatever order we find in this construction is the base order.

With this assumption in mind, let us consider the ordering of the goal relative to the theme. We saw that, in finite clauses, the high goal must always occur to the left of the theme and low goal, a point we will take up below. But what about the low goal? As we saw in (22), the low goal is free to merge either before or after the theme. Now note the following pair from Kishimoto 2006, 807, which provides further evidence for this point from the -*kata* construction.

(24) a. koinu-e-no esa-no atae-kata
puppy-to-GEN food-GEN give-way
'the way of giving food to a puppy'

b. esa-no koinu-e-no atae-kata
food-GEN puppy-to-GEN give-way

The occurrence of the postposition *-e* on the goal in both ensures that we are dealing with a low goal, that is, a PP. The fact that in the *-kata* construction either order is possible suggests that the PP low goal may merge freely on either side of the theme.

Turning to the high goal, this is a DP argument, and as noted by Kageyama (1993), Sugioka (1992), and Ito and Sugioka (2002), as well as Kishimoto (2006), argument DPs in nominalization do not appear with case markers such as the nominative, dative, or accusative, but rather, they appear solely with the genitive marking.[8] The following pair is from Kishimoto 2006, 791; the judgments are as reported by Kishimoto.

(25) a. John-no koinu-no esa-no atae-kata
John-GEN puppy-GEN food-GEN give-way
'John's way of giving food to a puppy'

b. *John-no esa-no koinu-no atae-kata
John-GEN food-GEN puppy-GEN give-way

The ungrammaticality of (25b) is predicted. In this example the goal follows the theme, and this goal is marked solely with the genitive, which would make it a DP argument, a high goal. As we saw in (21)–(23), however, the goal that occurs after the theme can only be a low goal, thus, a PP, so that it must bear the postposition *-e* 'to' (not *-ni*; see note 8) along with the genitive marker. Example (25b) would be fine if the goal had *-e* as well as the genitive, as we already observed in (24b).

Example (25a) also appears to be in accordance with the analysis in Chapter 3: the goal precedes the theme and it is animate, both pointing to the possibility that this is a high goal, hence capable of occurring solely with the genitive marking given its DP status. But is (25a) actually grammatical? My reaction to it, and that of several native speakers I consulted, is that (25a) does not sound natural. Yoko Sugioka (personal communication) notes that there is one possible interpretation of (25a) that might render it grammatical, though still awkward. It is a reading where the "core meaning" is 'the way of giving food', and *koinu-no* (puppy-GEN) is in some modificational relation to this core meaning, with one possible relation being that the puppy is the recipient of 'way of giving food'. 'Puppy' here modifies the entire phrase, 'the way of giving food', and is not an argument of 'give'.

Whether one can perceive this special interpretation or not, (25a) as originally intended by Kishimoto appears to be ungrammatical. Other examples to confirm this are given below; the (a) examples give the high goal, while (b) provides the low-goal counterpart.

(26) a. *Hanako-no John-no MIT-no susume-kata
Hanako-GEN John-GEN MIT-GEN recommend-way

b. Hanako-no John-e-no MIT-no susume-kata
Hanako-GEN John-to-GEN MIT-GEN recommend-way
'Hanako's way of recommending MIT to John'

(27) a. *Itiroo-no Hanako-no nimotu-no okuri-kata
Ichiro-GEN Hanako-GEN package-GEN send-way

b. Itiroo-no Hanako-e-no nimotu-no okuri-kata
Ichiro-GEN Hanako-to-GEN package-GEN send-way
'Ichiro's way of sending a package to Hanako'

(28) a. *Setuko-no Ziroo-no nyuusu-no tutae-kata
Setsuko-GEN Jiro-GEN news-GEN convey-way

b. Setuko-no Ziroo-e-no nyuusu-no tutae-kata
Setsuko-GEN Jiro-to-GEN news-GEN convey-way
'Setsuko's way of conveying the news to Jiro'

To understand why a high goal is apparently not permitted in the *-kata* construction, let us look at English deverbal nominalization (Kayne 1984; Pesetsky 1995), which displays precisely the same pattern of grammaticality. In deverbal nominalization, the argument of the verb may surface inside an *of* phrase or as the genitive of the resulting NP. The following are taken from Kayne 1984.

(29) a. examine the problem ⇒
b. the examination of the problem
c. the problem's examination

The dative construction allows nominalization with the theme occurring inside an *of* phrase or as the genitive of the NP.

(30) a. present the ball to John ⇒
b. the presentation of the ball to John
c. the ball's presentation to John

However, the double-object construction resists nominalization in English, just as the high-goal construction resists *-kata* nominalization in Japanese.

(31) a. present John the ball ⇒
b. *the presentation of John of the ball
c. *John's presentation of the ball

Kayne concludes that the double-object construction involves a small clause that contains both the goal and the theme. This is based on his observation that the small clause also fails to nominalize.

(32) a. believe Thilo handsome ⇒
b. *the belief of Thilo handsome
c. *Thilo's belief handsome

Pesetsky (1995) gives an account of these nominalization facts by postulating an abstract preposition, which he calls *G* (for "Goal"), for the double-object construction, the counterpart of the overt preposition *to* in the dative construction.

(33) a. Double object (Pesetsky 1995, 155–156; I have labeled the nodes based on structures given on 126–127)

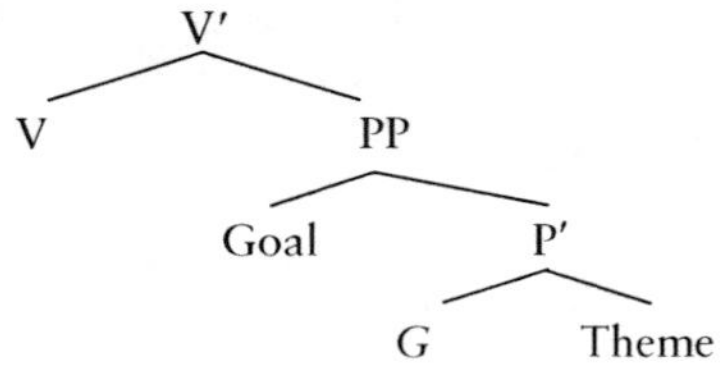

b. *To* dative (Pesetsky 1995, 174; slightly modified)

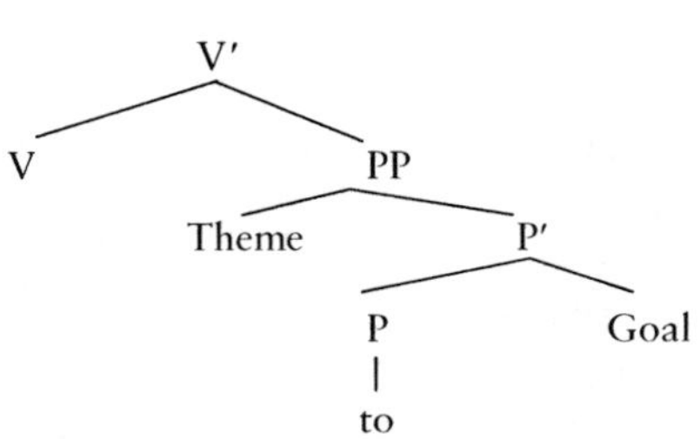

Pesetsky further assumes that *G* in the double-object construction undergoes incorporation into the verb, which is similar to the preposition incorporation we find in many languages (see, e.g., Baker 1988); the incorporation is triggered presumably by the fact that *G* is a dependent morpheme.

(34)

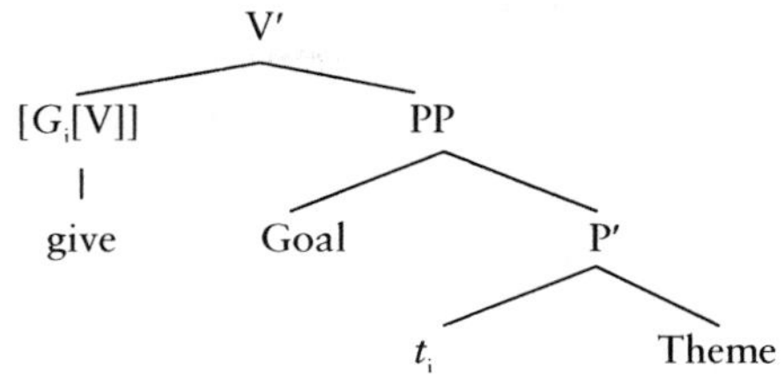

On this account, there are two different verbs derived in syntax, one for the double object, the other for the dative construction.[9]

(35) $give_1$ [*G*[V]]: double-object construction
$give_2$ [V]: dative construction

To explain the nominalization facts, Pesetsky invokes Myers's Generalization.

(36) Myers's Generalization (Myers 1984)
Zero-derived words do not permit the affixation of further derivational morphemes.

Because the double-object verb has undergone a derivation whereby the abstract *G* incorporates into it ([*G*[V]]), it is an instance of a zero-derived word, hence it cannot undergo further derivational processes such as nominalization. On the other hand, the dative-construction verb has no zero-morpheme that attaches to it in the normal course of derivation, hence there is nothing to prevent its nominalization.

Though somewhat different in structure, Pesetsky's approach to the two constructions associated with ditransitive verbs is comparable to the applicative-head approach in one crucial fact: in both, a phonologically null head (*G* in Pesetsky's approach, applicative V in ours) occurs in the double-object construction that introduces the goal, but in the dative construction there is no such null head. Just as with Pesetsky's *G*, the applicative approach assumes that the verb and the applicative head come together, by verb raising (Marantz 1993; Pyllkänen 2002), resulting in the verbal complex [[V] applicative], as opposed to simply [V] for the dative construction. We can see that Myers's Generalization can also explain the absence of the high-goal applicative structure in the *-kata* construction while allowing the low-goal dative construction.

The analysis based on Myers's Generalization does raise an issue with Kishimoto's approach to the *-kata* construction. Recall that in his approach *-kata* selects a *v*P.

(37)

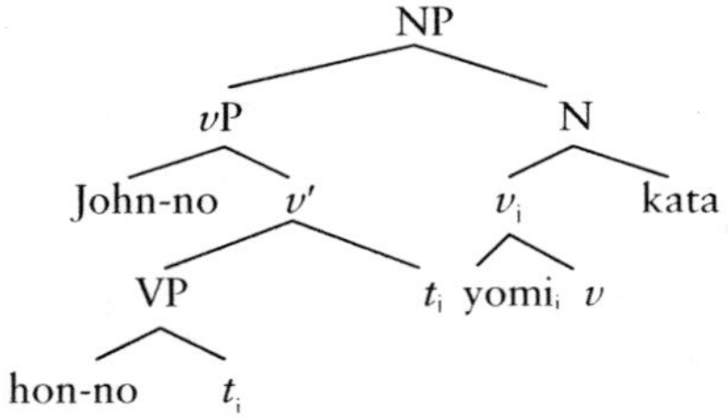

Strictly speaking, this is a violation of Myers's Generalization because the verb *yomi* picks up the phonologically null *v*. This null head should block further derivational processes such as nominalization. We will need to adjust Kishimoto's structure.

A possible problem with this objection to Kishimoto's proposal is that we find causative verbs built on structures that clearly have *v*, as in *tabe-sase-ru* (eat-cause-PRES), which presumably has the structure [[[*tabe*]*v*]*sase*]. This is affixation of *-(s)ase* to an item that contains the zero morpheme *v*. Pesetsky himself reinterprets Myers's Generalization in a way that does not always preclude affixation to a zero-derived item. He notes (76–77) that the agentive nominalizer *-er* and the adjectivizer *-able* are exceptions to the generalization. From this, Pesetsky proposes that Myers's Generalization is not a blanket restriction against affixation to zero-derived items. Instead, it is a restriction encoded on specific derivational affixes, such as *-ion*, that prohibits them from attaching to items with a zero morpheme (83–93). Unlike the nominalizer *-ion* in English—and *-kata* in Japanese—the causative morpheme *-(s)ase* in Japanese, like *-er* and *-able*, is not blocked from attaching to zero-derived items. Hence, while a nominalization construction with *-kata* or *-ion* cannot be built on an item that has a zero morpheme, *-(s)ase* can. Further evidence for this is that, while nominalization of a double-object ditransitive verb in Japanese is impossible, as we saw, such a ditransitive verb does allow causativization.

(38) Syatyou-wa Taroo-ni buka-ni futa-ri kaiko-tuuchi-o
president-TOP Taro-DAT subordinate-DAT two-CL dismissal notice-ACC
okur-ase-ta.
send-CAUS-PAST
'The president made Taro send two subordinates dismissal notices.'

The ditransitive verb *okuru* 'send' has been causativized; we can see that it is the double-object ditransitive because the goal appears with a floated numeral quantifier.

What is the structure of the *-kata* nominalization? Recall Kageyama's (1993, 363) original proposal that adjoins V to *-kata*.

(39)

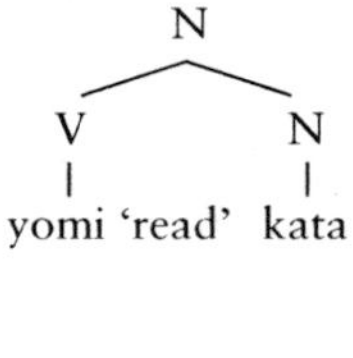

This is consistent with Myers's Generalization, since there is no zero morpheme that attaches to the verbal element *yomi* 'read'. However, Sugioka (1992, 60), who independently proposes V incorporation, gives convincing evidence that there is more than the V head involved in this nominalization; she proposes that *-kata* takes VP. The following is Sugioka's proposal for *tomodati-no hagemasi-kata* 'the way of encouraging friends'.

(40)

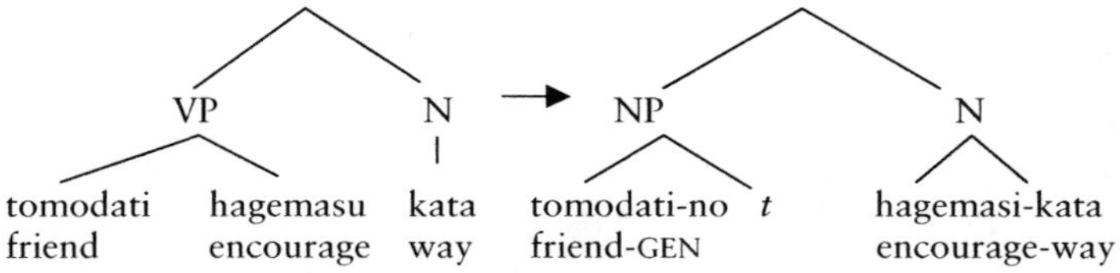

This is similar to Kishimoto's approach, except that what *-kata* selects is a VP, not a *v*P; Sugioka's analysis is still consistent with Myers's Generalization. The evidence that Sugioka (1992, 59) gives for her analysis is the fact that VP idioms can appear in the *-kata* construction.

(41) bouryokudan-kara-no asi-no arai-kata
gang group-from-GEN leg-GEN wash-way
'the way to cut connection from a gang group'

The VP idiom we see here is *asi-o arau* 'cut connection from' (lit. 'wash one's legs of'). I find this to be quite compelling, and I will assume it for the *-kata* nominalization, but with one exception.

As shown above in (40), according to Sugioka, the VP is turned into an NP (the right side) when the verbal head incorporates into *-kata*. To be fair to both Kishimoto and Sugioka, I should remind the reader that at the time that Sugioka was developing her analysis of *-kata*, small *v* had not made its way into the general theory, so *v*P would not have been even a possibility at the time. However, given Myers's Generalization, our prediction is that even today, *v*P would not be possible because *v* would constitute a zero morpheme, and *-kata* nominalization does not attach to zero-derived items. This means that the VP analysis of Sugioka's is the appropriate one even today.

This leaves the question of what to do with the "subject," which would be introduced by *v* if it were present.

(42) Hanako-no hon-no yomi-kata
Hanako-GEN book-GEN read-way
'Hanako's way of reading books'

One point that is important to note is that the "agent" here is strictly optional.

(43) a. Hon-o yomu.
book-ACC read
'(I/you/etc.) will read a book.'

b. hon-no yomi-kata
book-GEN read-way
'the way of reading books'

In the sentential example in (43a) without an overt subject, there is a clear sense that the subject is missing, but in the *-kata* construction in (43b), which is also missing the subject, the example sounds complete with nothing missing from it for full interpretation, a point that Kishimoto also notes. A number of linguists have observed this phenomenon of optionality of arguments (not just subjects) in nominals (Dowty 1989; Grimshaw 1990; Higginbotham 1983; among others). On this basis, one possible account of the "subject" is to view it as modifying the entire *-kata* clause.

(44)

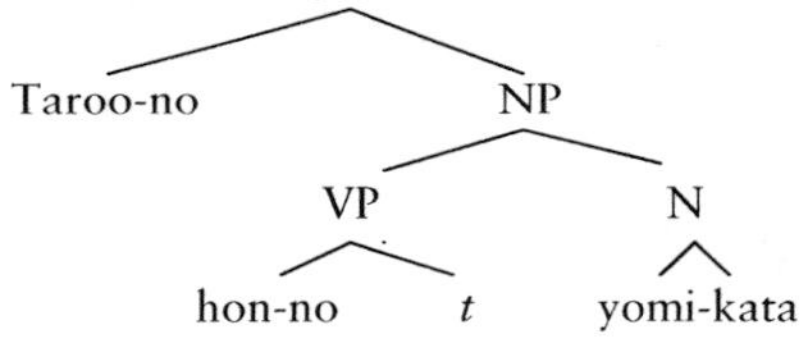

Under this analysis, this noun phrase means 'Taro's way of reading books'. 'Taro' is most naturally interpreted as the agent of 'read' (= 'the way that Taro reads books'), but on this analysis, that reading comes about indirectly by 'Taro' modifying 'way of reading books'. Without 'Taro', the phrase simply means 'the way of reading books'.

A challenge to the analysis just presented is that, as Kishimoto (2006, 776) notes, it is possible find subject honorification within the *-kata* construction. The following are examples with a plain form (no subject honorification) and subject honorification, the latter taken from Kishimoto's work.

(45) a. Suzuki-sensei-no hanasi-kata
Professor Suzuki-GEN speak-way
'Professor Suzuki's way of speaking'

b. Suzuki-sensei-no o-hanasi-ni-nari-kata
Professor Suzuki-GEN speak$_{\text{HONORIFIC}}$-way

Subject-honorification morphology *o- . . . -ni-nar* occurs, wrapped around the verb as in *o-hanasi-ni-nar* 'speak' above, when the subject of the verb is socially superior to the speaker (Harada 1976b). It presupposes the existence of such a subject in the structure, which suggests that in a structure such as (45b), 'Professor Suzuki' is the external argument introduced by the small *v*, entailing that in this structure *-kata* selects *v*P. This seemingly contradicts the analysis above that what *-kata* takes is a VP, not a *v*P, in order to respect Myers's Generalization. But is it a contradiction? There is one clear difference between *-kata* examples with and without subject honorification. Recall from our discussion earlier that the example below, repeated from earlier, does not necessarily imply the existence of an agent.

(46) hon-no yomi-kata
book-GEN read-way
'the way of reading books'

However, *-kata* nominals with subject honorification differ sharply in that there is a clear indication of an agent.

(47) hon-no o-yomi-ni-nari-kata
book-GEN read$_{\text{HONORIFIC}}$-way
'the way of reading books'

In this example there is a clear sense that an agent is being referred to who is socially superior to the speaker. This, in turn, indicates that in the subject-honorification example, *-kata* necessarily selects a *v*P, not a VP. But how is that possible given Myers's Generalization? A reasonable solution is to assume that the subject-honorification morphology itself spells out *v*, so that *v* is not a zero morpheme, and this enables the predicate to circumvent Myers's Generalization, an assumption that is further supported by the fact that the subject-honorification morphology appears inside tense in a sentence, hence it clearly occurs lower than T, plausibly as *v*.

(48) Suzuki-sensei-ga hon-o o-yomi-**ni-nat**-ta.
Professor Suzuki-NOM book-ACC read$_{\text{HONORIFIC}}$-PAST
'Professor Suzuki read a book.'

On the analysis we have seen, *-kata* may take either VP or, as Kishimoto argued, *v*P. This is in principle a free option, unless *v*P is forced by an external factor, as we saw with the occurrence of subject honorification.

6 FURTHER NOTE ON MYERS'S GENERALIZATION

I will close out the chapter by looking briefly at an additional point about Myers's Generalization and nominalization.

Pesetsky draws a parallel between the impossibility of nominalization of the double-object construction (Kayne 1984) and a similar fact about deverbal nominals noted by Chomsky (1970) in "Remarks on nominalization."

(49) a. John grew tomatoes (in his backyard).
  b. Tomatoes grew (in John's backyard).

As noted by Chomsky, only the unaccusative, (49b), allows nominalization.

(50) a. *John's growth of tomatoes
  b. the growth of tomatoes

Chomsky notes (25) that *the growth of tomatoes* "has the interpretation of *tomatoes grow* but not of *John grows tomatoes*," and gives (59) the following derivations for the examples in (49) above.

(51) John grows tomatoes: John [+cause, grow] tomatoes

(52) Tomatoes grow: [$_S$ tomatoes grow]$_S$

For the causative construction in (51), a natural way to conceive of the derivation is that it is syntactic word formation.

(53) John [+cause] [tomatoes grow]

This leads to two versions of *grow*, just as we saw that there are two versions of ditransitives, one with G (double object) and the other without G (dative).

(54) grow$_1$ [+cause, V] (lexical causative)
  grow$_2$ [V] (unaccusative)

What Pesetsky notes is that *grow*$_1$ contains the zero morpheme [+cause], which, under Myers's Generalization, would block further derivation such as nominalization. This accounts for the ungrammaticality of (50a).

However, when we turn to the *-kata* construction, we see that causative verbs can appear freely (Kageyama 1993, 358; I have changed the example to more directly demonstrate the point).

(55) yom-ase-kata
  read-CAUS-way
  'the way of making (someone) read'

This difference between English and Japanese is predicted: while [+cause] in English is represented by a phonologically null morpheme, which triggers Myers's Generalization under nominalization, in Japanese it is overtly manifested by the causative morpheme *-(s)ase*, which avoids the effect of Myers's Generalization, thereby allowing *-kata* nominalization to take place. This situation with the causative verb is different from the applicative construction, in which the applicative head is a zero morpheme in both languages, leading to a failure to nominalize in both languages.

7 CONCLUSION

In this chapter, I gave evidence from nominalization for the dual-base analysis of ditransitive verb constructions in Japanese. Using insights from Kishimoto's (2006) work as a starting point, what we saw is that the *-kata* nominalization can occur with the low-goal construction, which corresponds to the dative construction in English, while nominalization is blocked with the high-goal construction, which corresponds to the double-object construction in English. I argued that the analysis based on Myers's Generalization (Pesetsky 1995) makes the correct predictions for the array of data found in Japanese, and that this approach further predicts that the *-kata* construction may occur with a *v*P, as Kishimoto argued, but, alternatively, with a VP, as originally proposed by Sugioka (1992).

Appendix to Chapter 4
Challenges to the dual-base analysis of ditransitives

In this appendix, I will discuss two recent challenges to the dual-base analysis of ditransitive verbs in Japanese, one from processing (Koizumi and Tamaoka 2004) and the other from the study of VP idioms (Kishimoto 2008). For processing, I will report on work (Sato et al. 2009) that neutralizes Koizumi and Tamaoka's original criticism, and for the idioms, I will summarize a recent study by Tsujioka (2011) that shows that the intriguing observations made by Kishimoto can actually be analyzed as further evidence for the dual-base analysis.

1 PROCESSING: KOIZUMI AND TAMAOKA 2004

There is mounting evidence that the canonical *-ga -o* (NOM–ACC) order is easier to process than the scrambled *-o -ga* (ACC–NOM) order. We see this in plausibility-judgment tasks (Chujo 1983), data from aphasic patients (Hagiwara and Caplan 1990), fMRI studies (Koizumi 2005), and in self-paced-reading tasks and eye-tracking experiments (Mazuka, Itoh, and Kondo 2002). Extending this fact about scrambling and processing to ditransitive constructions, Koizumi and Tamaoka (2004) report that the reaction times to their plausibility tests are shorter for *-ni -o* (DAT–ACC) than for *-o -ni* (ACC–DAT) (see also Miyamoto and Takahashi 2002). They use this result to argue for the single-base analysis (*-ni -o*) and against the dual-base analysis of Miyagawa 1997 and Chapter 3 of this volume, claiming that the ACC–DAT order is the scrambled order. In Table A.1, taken from Koizumi and Tamaoka 2004, the reaction time for judging the plausibility of a sentence ("yes" or "no") is always less for the DAT–ACC order than for the ACC–DAT order.

The reason why *'pass' type* and *'show' type* are given as different categories is that Matsuoka (2003) argues that the 'pass' type of Japanese ditransitive verbs has the basic order of ACC–DAT while the 'show' type has the basic order of DAT–ACC. As we can see, the experiment did not discriminate between these two types, the result showing *-ni -o* (DAT–ACC) to always be faster than *-o -ni* (ACC–DAT) to process. It is a mystery of Koizumi and

Table A.1 Reaction Times and Error Rates for Correctness Decisions

Response type	*Type of verbs*	*Sentence type*	*Reaction time (ms)*		*Error rate (%)*	
			M	*SD*	*M*	*SD*
"Yes" responses	'Pass' type	Order DAT–ACC	1414	374	1.67	5.65
		Order ACC–DAT	1512	310	1.67	5.65
	'Show' type	Order DAT–ACC	1570	275	3.33	7.61
		Order ACC–DAT	1679	360	10.00	13.19
"No" responses	'Pass' type	Order DAT–ACC	1513	321	7.64	12.02
		Order ACC–DAT	1589	355	7.64	12.02

Note: M refers to mean; SD refers to standard deviation.
Source: Koizumi and Tamaoka 2004.

Tamaoka's work that their results do not distinguish between these two types of verbs, something that they themselves acknowledge.

As argued by Miyamoto and Nakamura (2005), Sato et al. (2009), and others, Koizumi and Tamaoka's results point to something other than evidence for the single-base hypothesis. Rather, they point to the fact that when native speakers encounter an accusative phrase, they typically expect it to be directly followed by the verb.[10] I elaborate on this alternative account of Koizumi and Tamaoka's data in the following subsection.

1.1 Problem with Koizumi and Tamaoka 2004

There is fairly clear evidence that a native speaker, when faced with the accusative NP-*o*, overwhelmingly expects the verb to follow, while such an expectation does not arise with NP-*ni*. The slower reaction time with -*o* -*ni* (ACC–DAT) in Koizumi and Tamaoka 2004 can be viewed as an indication that this expectation was violated when the subject encounters -*o* (ACC), then, instead of the expected verb, encounters -*ni* (DAT) instead, which forces the subject to reanalyze the structure at that point, leading to the longer reaction time. This alternative explanation neutralizes Koizumi and Tamaoka's argument in favor of the single-base analysis.

Sato et al. (2009), based in part on earlier work by Miyamoto and Nakamura (2005), report on two experiments they conducted that show that when a native speaker encounters an accusative NP (-*o*), there is an expectation that it will be followed directly by a verb, while such an expectation typically does not arise with the dative NP. I will briefly summarize the experiments; for details of the experimental design, see Sato et al. 2009.

In the first experiment, 24 native speakers of Japanese were asked to complete sentences of the following type.

(1) a. NOM–DAT
Sihatsu-no sinkansen-de butyoo-ga kakarityoo-ni ____.
first-GEN bullet train-by manager-NOM chief-DAT
'In the earliest bullet train, the manager ___ to the chief.'

b. NOM–ACC
Sihatsu-no sinkansen-de butyoo-ga kakarityoo-o ____.
first-GEN bullet train-by manager-NOM chief-ACC
'In the earliest bullet train, the manager ___ the chief.'

The results are shown in Table A.2. For the first type of stimulus, which ends with a dative phrase, speakers tended to add an accusative NP and then a verb, thereby forming a three-argument structure. In contrast, with the second type of stimulus, which ends with the accusative NP, they tended to complete the sentence with a verb, giving rise to a two-argument structure. This is similar to results reported earlier by Miyamoto and Nakamura (2005; also see Kamide, Altmann, and Haywood 2003; Muraoka 2006).

As Table A.2 shows, for the sentence fragment ending with a dative phrase, there were 71 instances in which the subject added no extra NP after it, and 168 instances when he or she did (147 cases of adding an NP and 21 cases where a clause was added). For the sentence fragment ending with an accusative phrase, 220 of the stimuli were directly completed with a verb, while there were only 20 instances in which an extra item other than the verb was added (19 instances of an NP and 1 instance of a clause). As Sato et al. note, this demonstrates a clear tendency to expect a verb to directly follow an accusative phrase, while such an expectation is not the norm after a dative phrase.

In Experiment 2, 23 native speakers participated in a reading experiment. Table A.3 gives examples of the two conditions that were the focus of this experiment. Both contain a relative clause (RC) with a causative verb. In the first, the object of the causative verb (secretary-ACC) precedes the verb, and the head of the RC (employee-TOP) corresponds to the causee, which normally would be marked by the dative. In the second, the causee (secretary-DAT) precedes the causative verb, and the head of the RC corresponds to the object of the causative verb. Figure A.1 shows the reading times for each element of the two stimuli.

Table A.2 Results of Sentence-Completion Task

		Extra argument added	
	No extra NP	*NP*	*Clause*
NOM–DAT	71	147	21
NOM–DAT	220	19	1

Source: Sato et al. 2009.

Table A.3 Example of Target Materials in Experiment 2

1	*2*	*3*	*4*	*5*	*6*
DAT RC					
Katyoo-ga	hisyo-o	kyooiku-sase-ta	syain-wa	syorui-o	nakusi-ta.
manager-NOM	secretary-ACC	train-CAUS-PAST	employee-TOP	document-ACC	lose-PAST
'The employee that the manager made train the secretary lost the document.'					
ACC RC					
Katyoo-ga	hisyo-ni	kyooiku-sase-ta	syain-wa	syorui-o	nakusi-ta.
manager-NOM	secretary-DAT	train-CAUS-PAST	employee-TOP	document-ACC	lose-PAST
'The employee that the manager made the secretary train lost the document.'					

Source: Sato et al. 2009.

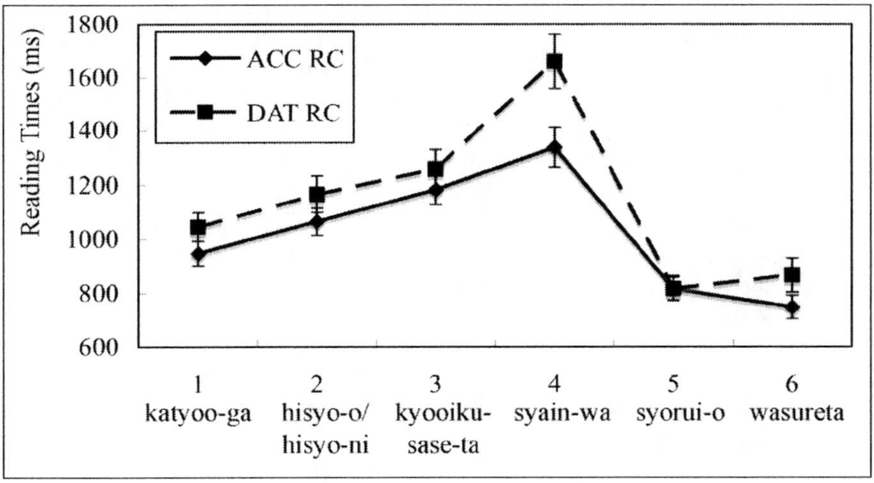

Figure A.1 Mean reading times from Experiment 2.
Source: Sato et al. 2009.

The reading time for both conditions is essentially the same until the subject encounters the head noun of the RC. As shown, for the "DAT RC," in which the NP preceding the verb is the accusative object phrase of the RC, the subject took longer to read the head noun (employee-TOP) corresponding to the causee (DAT) than for the "ACC RC," in which the NP preceding the verb is the dative causee phrase. Simply put, when the accusative NP occurs, there is no expectation that there is any additional NP, hence the appearance of the head noun corresponding to the dative is unexpected and leads to a lag in reading time. But when the phrase directly preceding the verb is the dative, there is no expectation that nothing occurs between it and the verb, and the head noun corresponding to the object phrase is read faster than in the other condition.

Both of the experiments in Sato et al. 2009 are consistent with the hypothesis that when the native speaker encounters the accusative NP, there is an expectation that nothing follows it except the verb. This would explain Koizumi and Tamaoka's (2004) experimental result that *-ni -o* is processed faster than *-o -ni*, and it also explains the fact that their results do not distinguish between the 'pass'-type and 'show'-type verbs.

2 IDIOMS

In Chapter 3, it is proposed that the goal phrase that occurs in a ditransitive construction may be the high goal or the low goal. A high goal is a DP that occurs high in the structure and has the meaning of "possessor," while a low goal is a PP that has the meaning of "location." Crucially, the word-order flexibility noted by Hoji (1985) and others involves only low goals: thus, in the order theme–goal, the goal is always the low goal; in the order goal–theme, the goal may be either the high goal or the low goal. In Chapter 3, idioms are given as evidence that the low goal may occur before or after the theme: we find idioms in which the idiom portion is ACC–V, and it is preceded by a dative phrase, which shows a base order of DAT–ACC; and we also find idioms in which the idiomatic part is DAT–V, and it is preceded by an accusative phrase, showing a base order of ACC–DAT. The crucial assumption here, taken over from Larson 1988, is that idioms require adjacency. The following pairs of examples show ACC–V and DAT–V idioms that use the same verb.

(2) a. Taroo-wa [hito-no koto]-ni **kuti-o dasu.**
Taro-TOP person-GEN thing-to mouth-ACC let out
'Taro cuts in on someone else's business.'

b. Taroo-wa [omotta koto]-o **kuti-ni dasu.**
Taro-TOP thought thing-ACC mouth-to let out
'Taro says what's on his mind.'

(3) a. Taroo-wa sono giron-ni **hakusya-o kaketa.**
Taro-TOP that controversy-to spur-ACC hang
'Taro added fresh fuel to the controversy.'

b. Taroo-wa sainoo-o **hana-ni kaketeiru.**
Taro-TOP talent-ACC nose-to hanging
'Taro always boasts of his talent.'

(4) a. Taroo-wa genkoo-ni **te-o** **ireta.**
Taro-TOP draft-to hand-ACC put in
'Taro revised the draft.'

b. Taroo-wa kuruma-o **te-ni** **ireta.**
Taro-TOP car-ACC hand-in put in
'Taro acquired a car.'

(5) a. Taroo-wa maajan-ni **timiti-o** **ageta.**
Taro-TOP mahjong-to blood vessel-ACC raise
'Taro was obsessed with mahjong.'

b. Taroo-wa itumo zibun-no sippai-o **tana-ni** **ageru.**
Taro-TOP always self-GEN mistake-ACC shelf-to raise
'Taro always shuts his eyes to his own mistakes.'

As shown below, these idioms lose their idiomatic interpretation when the order is reversed.

(6) a. *Taroo-wa **kuti-o** [hito-no koto]-ni **dasu.**
Taro-TOP mouth-ACC person-GEN thing-to let out

b. ???Taroo-wa **kuti-ni** [omotta koto]-o **dasu.**
Taro-TOP mouth-to thought thing-ACC let out

Idioms have been used to argue for the underlying structure of ditransitives. The following, taken from Larson 1988, shows that the verb and the theme are adjacent in the double-object construction (7a) while the verb and the PP are adjacent underlyingly in the dative construction (7b) (see also Richards 2001).

(7) Larson 1988, Richards 2001
a. Bill **gave** Mary **hell.**
b. Lasorda **sent** John **to the shower.**

The existence of idioms in both directions, *-ni -o* (DAT–ACC) and *-o -ni* (ACC–DAT), suggests that both of these orders are base orders, thus giving credence to the dual-base hypothesis.

Kishimoto (2008) challenges the use of idioms like those given above as support for the dual-base hypothesis. He agrees that there are two types of goals, high and low, but he argues that both types are base-generated above the theme, so that the base order for the Japanese ditransitive construction is always *-ni -o* (DAT–ACC). What we see in the idiom data involving the other order of *-o -ni* (ACC–DAT), according to Kishimoto, is a special construction in which *-ni* is base-generated in this order only in the case of idioms. That is, Kishimoto argues that the base order of *-o -ni* (ACC–DAT) only occurs if *-ni* (DAT) is part of an idiom. On the other hand, in an ordinary sentence, only the *-ni -o* (DAT–ACC) order is allowed in the base. His main argument is that the idiom data in (2)–(5) that we present as evidence for the base-generation of theme–goal and goal–theme orders cannot be extended to ordinary ditransitive sentences. To account for the *-o -ni* (ACC–DAT) base order, Kishimoto proposes a structural position that is reserved solely for the goal argument of goal–V idioms.

(8)

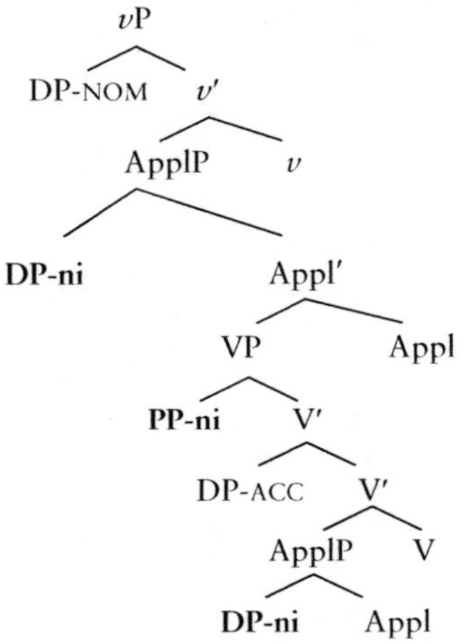

The relevant position is the lowest one, the sister of the lower Appl: it is reserved only for idioms, and it is characterized by obligatory *-ni* marking. As evidence, Kishimoto points out that while the goal in ordinary ditransitives (with a single goal) can be marked either with *-ni* or *-e*, as shown in (9), the goal in goal–V idioms cannot, as shown in (10).[11]

(9) Taroo-ga nimotu-o Hanako-ni/-e okutta.
Taro-NOM package-ACC Hanako-DAT/-to sent
'Taro sent a package to Hanako.'

(10) a. omotta koto-o kuti-ni/*-e dasu
thought thing-ACC mouth-DAT/-to let out
'say what's on his mind'

b. sainoo-o hana-ni/*-e kakeru
talent-ACC nose-DAT/-to hang
'boast of a talent'

Furthermore, Kishimoto makes intriguing observations based on *-sa* nominalization to argue for the special position reserved for idioms.

(11) a. Nimotu-o Hanako-ni okuri-yasu-i.
package-ACC Hanako-to send-easy-PRES
'It is easy to send a package to Hanako.'

b. nimotu-no Hanako-e-no okuri-yasu-sa
package-GEN Hanako-to-GEN send-easy-NL
'the easiness of sending a package to Hanako'

In (11a) we see a type of tough clause in which an adjectivizing morpheme *yasu* 'easy' or *niku* 'difficult' takes a verbal clause.[12] When the nominal suffix *-sa* is present as in (11b), *nimotu-o* is changed to *nimotu-no*, and *Hanako-ni* is changed to *Hanako-e-no*. That is, given the nominal nature of *-sa* clauses, the phrases within them are all marked with the genitive *-no*. When this happens, nominative (*-ga*) and accusative (*-o*) case markers are suppressed, while postpositions such as *-e* 'to' may co-occur with the genitive; for reasons that are not understood, the sequence **-ni-no* (DAT-GEN) is not allowed, so that the alternative *-e-no* (to-GEN) is used instead.

Now to Kishimoto's argument: he reports on a surprising phenomenon in *-sa* nominalization—the *-ni* marking may survive nominalization. His point is that this is only possible with idioms.

(12) a. omotta koto-no kuti-ni/*-e-no dasi-niku-sa
thought thing-GEN mouth-DAT/-to-GEN let out-difficult-NL
'the difficulty of saying what's on his mind'

b. zibun-no sainoo-no hana-ni/*-e-no kake-yasu-sa
self-GEN talent-GEN nose-DAT/-to-GEN hang-easy-NL
'the easiness of boasting of his own talent'

c. kuruma-no te-ni/*-e-no ire-niku-sa
car-GEN hand-DAT/-to-GEN put in-difficult-NL
'the difficulty of acquiring a car'

Independent of the controversy surrounding the base form or forms of the ditransitive construction, this is an important observation that is completely unexpected given what we know about nominalization in Japanese. Based on all cases of nominalization up to now, we expect every phrase within the nominal clause to be marked by the genitive.

As Tsujioka (2011) notes, there are problems with Kishimoto's analysis. First, with regard to the claim that goal–V idioms involve a special low-goal position with obligatory *-ni* marking, there are goal–V idioms that allow the *-ni/-e* alternation.

(13) a. kanzyoo-o omote-ni/-e dasu
emotion-ACC front-to/-to let out
'express one's emotion'

b. sono zizitu-o mune-ni/-e simau
that fact-ACC chest-to/-to put away
'keep the fact as a secret'

Whether the alternation is allowed or not appears to be a property of individual idioms.

Second, in response to Kishimoto's data involving *-sa* nominalization, Tsujioka (2011) shows that the unusual phenomenon of *-ni* marking in nominalization is not, in fact, limited to idioms. Furthermore, when *-ni* appears in a nonidiomatic context, either *-e* or *-e-no* is also possible. So not only is *-ni* possible in nonidiomatic contexts, *-ni* and *-e/-e-no* may also alternate in the immediate preverbal position.

(14) a. gakkoo-de-no toire-**ni/-e(-no)** iki-niku-sa
school-at-GEN toilet-to/-to(-GEN) go-difficult-NL
'the difficulty of going to the bathroom at school'

b. syoohin-no kago-**ni/-e(-no)** ire-yasu-sa
goods-GEN basket-to/-to(-GEN) put in-easy-NL
'the easiness of putting the goods in a basket'

c. bebiikaa-no tennai-**ni/-e(-no)** ire-yasu-sa
stroller-GEN inside shop-to/-to(-GEN) put in-easy-NL
'the easiness of putting a stroller inside the shop'

Unlike the *-sa* nominalization, in a "pure" nominal construction the genitive *-no* must always appear.

(15) a. [Taroo-to*(-no) sigoto]
Taro-with-GEN work
'work with Taro'

b. [ginkoo-kara*(-no) okane]
bank-from-GEN money
'money from the bank'

From this, Tsujioka deduces that the reason why both nominal marking (*-e-no*) and verbal marking (*-ni, -e*) may appear in (14) is due to the fact that a verbal structure is embedded inside the *-sa* nominalization. She assumes the structure in (16), in which *-sa* selects a clause headed by a tough adjective such as *yasu* 'easy'/*niku* 'difficult', which in turn selects a verbal structure (Sugioka 1984, 1992; Inoue 1978a).

(16)

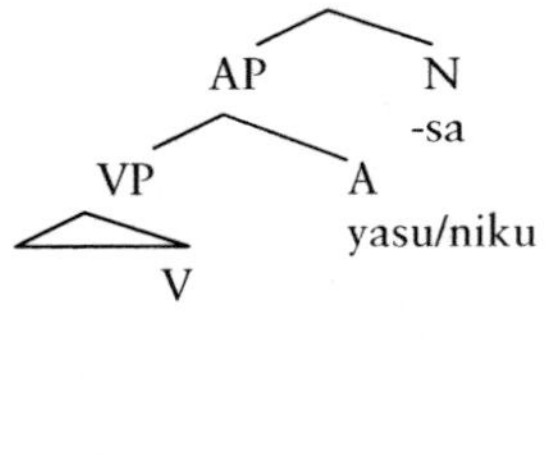

If V raises to A, and this V-A cluster raises to N, the entire clause is nominalized, and all phrases within it must bear the genitive marking *no*. If, however, V does not raise, the verbal structure stays intact, and what appears in the VP may bear verbal marking. As Tsujioka observes, on this account, the following are both predicted to be ungrammatical (cf. (14a)).

(17) a. *toire-**ni/-e** gakkoo-de-no iki-niku-sa
toilet-to/-to school-at-GEN go-difficult-NL
(Intended: 'the difficulty of going to the toilet at school')

b. *toire-e-no gakkoo-**de** iki-niku-sa
toilet-to-GEN school-at go-difficult-NL

The version in (17a) is bad because the goal, 'to the toilet', which is verbally marked, occurs to the left of the genitive-marked 'at school'. In other words, the verbally marked phrase is occurring outside the VP, which is illicit. In (17b), the problem is that 'to the toilet' is thematically close to the verb 'go', yet it occurs outside the locative 'at school', in fact outside the VP headed by 'go'.

Finally, the fact that examples such as (14b, c) exist, in which the *-ni*-marked goal actually follows the *-no*-marked theme, shows that cases exist where the goal is underlyingly closer to the verb than the theme. This gives credence to the analysis in Chapter 3, which holds that the low goal may be base-generated either in front of or after the theme phrase.

5 Genitive subjects in Altaic and specification of phases[1]

1 INTRODUCTION

Subjects may appear with the genitive case marker in certain instances. Three Altaic[2] languages exemplify this—Dagur (Mongolian; Hale 2002; Martin 1961), Japanese (Bedell 1972; Harada 1971), and Turkish (Kornfilt 1984).

(1) [**Mini** au-sen] mer^{y}-min^{y} sain. Dagur
1SG.GEN buy-PERF horse-1SG.GEN good
'The horse I bought is good.' (Hale 2002, 109)

(2) [**Watasi-no** katta] uma-wa ii. Japanese
me-GEN bought horse-TOP good
'The horse I bought is good.'

(3) [**Ben-im** al-dığ-ım] at iyi-dir. Turkish
me-GEN buy-NL$_{FACT}$-1SG horse good-is
'The horse I bought is good.' (Jaklin Kornfilt, personal communication)

In these examples, the subject of the relative clause (RC) is marked with the genitive case marker. Although genitive subjects are not limited to Altaic languages (see, for example, Hiraiwa 2001), in this article I will focus on these languages, with much of the discussion centering on Japanese.

I will address the question of how the genitive case marker is licensed in Altaic RCs and other constructions. Dagur and Turkish demonstrate that the licensing conditions are not uniform across languages.[3] Hale (2002), based on his own fieldwork and on Martin 1961, shows that the Dagur RC has the structure of an Aspect Phrase (AspP), a structure commonly found in prenominal modification (Krause 2001). AspP is smaller in structure than CP, and this reduced nature of the structure allows the nominal head, or more precisely the D associated with the nominal head, to license the genitive case marker inside the AspP. As we can see in (1), this D enters into agreement with the subject, clearly identifying the D head as the licensor. I will call this *D-licensing* of the genitive subject.

In contrast, Kornfilt (1984, 2003) shows that in Turkish, it is the nominalized form of C that licenses the genitive case marker on the subject; like the D licensor in Dagur, it also enters into agreement with the subject. I will call this *C-licensing* of the genitive subject.

For Japanese, both D-licensing and C-licensing have been proposed: D-licensing is represented by, for example, Bedell 1972; Miyagawa 1993, 2008; Ochi 2001; Saito 1983; while C-licensing is found in Watanabe 1996 and Hiraiwa 2001. Hiraiwa in particular draws attention to the fact that Turkish and languages like it C-license the genitive subject and argues that the Japanese genitive subject should be considered in parallel. Capturing cross-linguistic affinity in this way potentially enhances the strength of an analysis, and it is one reason why Hiraiwa's—and Watanabe's—proposal has been so influential. But when we look across languages, we see that another possible affinity that the Japanese genitive-subject construction may have is with Dagur, which involves D-licensing, not C-licensing.[4] I will give arguments to show that the Japanese construction better fits the Dagur model of D-licensing. Starting with the original work on genitive subjects in Japanese by Harada (1971), which contains a number of examples that cast doubt on the Watanabe–Hiraiwa C-licensing proposal, I will develop a D-licensing analysis based on Hale's (2002) study of Dagur. As we will see, the D-licensing approach I will present opens the door to exploring issues of aspect/tense marking, which has been largely ignored in the study of the genitive-subject construction. In addition, our analysis has consequences for specifying the nature of the phase. As we will see, the comparative study of these three languages leads us to a particular way to describe the notion of the phase (see, e.g., Chomsky 2001). I will argue that a phase is defined by case, not uninterpretable agreement features (Chomsky 2001); in particular, the appearance of a case-assigning head identifies it as a phase head. The three natural candidates are D, *v*, and C—not T but C, on the assumption that case, like ϕ-feature agreement, originates at C and is only inherited by T (Chomsky 2001, 2007, 2008).

2 DAGUR AND TURKISH: D-LICENSING VS. C-LICENSING

Why do we find the two heads, D and C, in Dagur and Turkish, respectively, emerging as the heads that license the genitive subject? Why not N or T, for example? What I suggest is that the presence of ϕ-feature agreement in these languages, as we saw in (1) and (3), is the key to understanding why D or C becomes the locus of licensing of the genitive subject (Miyagawa 2006, 2008). What is crucial is the notion that ϕ-feature agreement occurs at the phase level (Chomsky 2005; see also Boeckx 2003; Carstens 2003; Kornfilt 2003; Miyagawa 2005). The two phase heads most commonly noted are C and *v*; I will assume that D is also a phase head (see Chomsky 2001 for relevant discussion; also Hiraiwa 2005; Svenonius 2004; among others). Because D and C are phase heads, D-licensing and C-licensing are members of a natural set, the set of types of licensing we would predict based on this idea of a connection to ϕ-feature agreement. (v-licensing is another possibility, but v typically does not license embedded subjects, at least not in RCs. However, see the next chapter for a form of v-licensing of genitive in Japanese.) A phase head—C or D in this instance—is needed to host the ϕ-feature agreement. There is, then, a principled reason why D and C, rather than other heads, play the central role in licensing the genitive subject when there is ϕ-feature agreement.

For Dagur, I will follow Hale (2002), who, based on Krause 2001, postulates that the Dagur RC is AspP, thus a reduced structure. The reason for positing Aspect instead of a full CP is that the embedded verb does not carry any agreement. From our perspective the absence of C predicts exactly that—that agreement would not occur on the verbal inflection because there is no C to host the agreement to begin with. Also, the verb only carries aspectual marking (perfect, imperfect), not tense marking. The reduced nature of the RC in Dagur allows the ϕ-features on D to enter into agreement with the subject of the RC, as shown in (4b) (only the relevant portion of the structure from Hale 2002 is given, with some details changed).

(4) a. [[**Mini** au-sen] mer^{y}-**min**^{y}] sain.
1SG.GEN buy-PERF horse-1SG.GEN good
'The horse I bought is good.'

b.

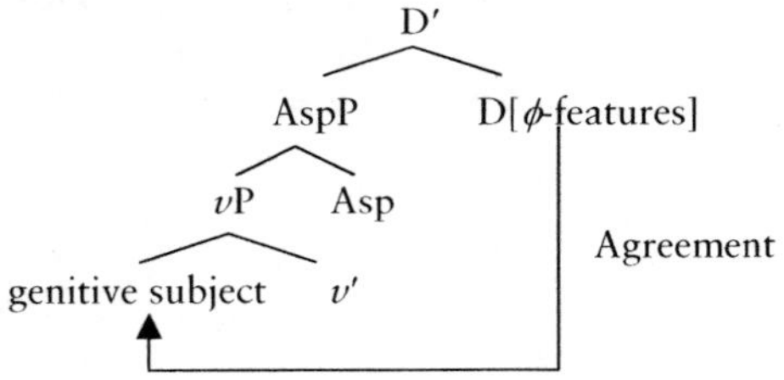

The probe in Dagur appears on the phase head, D, and it enters into an agreement relation with the genitive subject.[5] Hale also argues that the genitive subject undergoes movement to Spec,DP, in line with the assumption in earlier studies of agreement and case that required Spec–head agreement. I will not assume this movement and will return to the issue later.

For Turkish, I will assume the analysis in Kornfilt 2003, 2008, in which the nominal agreement resides at C. As in the example below, repeated from earlier, the agreement we see is in the nominal, and not the verbal, paradigm of agreement (genitive, not nominative), even though the head is C not D; this is because C is nominalized, a common assumption made for Turkish subordinate clauses (see, for example, Kornfilt 1984, 2003).

(5) [**Ben-im** al-dığ-ım] at iyi-dir.
me-GEN buy-NL$_{FACT}$-1SG horse good-is
'The horse I bought is good.'

In Turkish RCs, then, unlike Dagur RCs, C does occur and licenses the genitive case marking as well as agreeing in ϕ-features.

Kornfilt's argument that the agreement in Turkish is C-licensed is based on an asymmetry observed in the distribution of agreement depending on what is relativized (Kornfilt 2008 and references therein).

(6) a. Subject relativization
[[e_i dün bölüm-de ben-i destekle-**yen**] arkadaş-lar$_i$]
yesterday department-LOC me-ACC support-*(Y)AN* friend-PL
'the friends/colleagues who supported me in the department yesterday'
(No ϕ-feature morphology; special nominalization form on predicate)

b. Nonsubject relativization
[[*pro* dün bölüm-de e_i destekle-**diğ-im**] arkadaş-lar$_i$]
yesterday department-LOC support-NL$_{FACT}$-1SG friend-PL
'the friends/colleagues whom I supported in the department yesterday'
(ϕ-feature morphology and general indicative nominalization form on predicate)

In (6a), it is the subject that has undergone relativization, while in (6b) the target of relativization is the object. The important point to note is that the verb carries no agreement in the subject-relativization example, while there is full agreement in the nonsubject relativization. What Kornfilt suggests is that this asymmetry is parallel to the well-known *que–qui* complementizer alternation in French (Rizzi 1990), in which *que* is selected for nonsubject extraction while *qui* must occur if the subject is extracted. There is no question that *que/qui* is at C, and, with the parallel that Kornfilt draws, the agreement in Turkish must also be related to C. See Kornfilt's (2008) article for details of the analysis.

3 TWO APPROACHES TO THE GENITIVE SUBJECT IN JAPANESE (*GA–NO* CONVERSION)

Harada (1971) first brought to our attention the phenomenon of genitive subjects in Japanese—the fact, particularly, that in RCs and in noun-complement clauses, nominative *-ga* and genitive *-no* may alternate on the subject—although not in all cases. Instead of delving into the licensing condition for the genitive subject, he focused on the differences between the *-ga* and *-no* constructions, including idiolectal differences with respect to what later was termed the *transitivity restriction* (see Watanabe 1996; also

Harada 1976a), an issue we will take up in some detail below. In the literature on Japanese today, we find both competing approaches to the genitive subject, D-licensing and C-licensing. I will review the two approaches, and show that the C-licensing approach is open to question and that D-licensing not only appears to be the right approach, it also opens the door to interesting research topics heretofore largely ignored in the study of genitive subjects. One important observation that emerges from our study is that in Japanese RCs, two heads play a role in licensing case on the subject: D for genitive and C for nominative. Note that these are the same two heads that we saw licensing case on RC subjects in Dagur and Turkish, respectively, although in those languages we focused on genitive case marking and excluded nominative.

On the assumption that in Dagur and Turkish, respectively, D and C serve to license case on the RC subject *because* D and C, as phase heads, host ϕ-feature agreement, it is surprising that in Japanese, which does not have ϕ-feature agreement in the relevant sense, the same heads emerge to license case on the subject. If phase heads are somehow defined by the occurrence of ϕ-feature agreement (see, e.g., Chomsky 2007, 2008), this would be puzzling. I will argue that phases are, in fact, defined universally by case and not by ϕ-feature agreement.

3.1 The D-licensing approach

In Japanese, the genitive case marker occurs in the context of D (or N). The D-licensing approach takes advantage of this fact.

(7) [$_{DP}$ Hanako-**no** gakkai-de-**no** Taroo-**no** hihan]
Hanako-GEN conference-at-GEN Taro-GEN criticism
'Hanako's criticism of Taro at the conference'

In this example, two arguments and an adjunct within the noun phrase headed by the noun 'criticism' must all bear the genitive case marker. The D-licensing approach equates the genitive marking on the RC subject with this phenomenon of genitive in noun phrases. Within the D-licensing approach, we find two views of where the genitive subject ultimately resides. Bedell (1972), reflecting the spirit of the time, argued that the genitive subject occurs in Spec,DP (in contemporary terms). But Miyagawa (1993) argued that the genitive subject undergoes only covert movement to Spec,DP; "covert movement" could translate into today's framework as simply Agree without movement, which is the approach I will support. Such an approach is taken explicitly in Ochi 2001. The argument in Miyagawa 1993 is based on data from Nakai 1980. An adjunct belonging to the modifier clause may precede the genitive subject, as shown in (8) below and as diagrammed in (9) (this example is modeled after Nakai's example).

(8) [kyonen-made danro-**no** atta] heya
last year-until fireplace-GEN existed room
'the room where there was a fireplace until last year'

(9) $[_{DP}$ . . . $[_{TP}$ kyonen-made danro-no . . .] heya]

As Nakai (1980) notes, this militates against Bedell's assertion that the genitive DP occupies Spec,DP at overt syntax, because an adjunct belonging to the TP occurs to its left. The PP 'until last year' cannot directly modify the head 'room' ('the room until last year' is ungrammatical in Japanese: **kyonen-made heya*), so the PP must reside in the TP. The genitive subject therefore cannot be in Spec,DP. Rather, the best way to view the matter, under D-licensing, is that D directly licenses the genitive subject by Agree without requiring the subject to overtly move to Spec,DP.

3.2 The C-licensing approach

Drawing on his prior work (Watanabe 1993) on *wh*-agreement, Watanabe (1996) introduces a novel proposal for the analysis of *ga–no* conversion. He argues (391) that the genitive is a reflex of *wh*-agreement on a "subjunctive" C that occurs in RCs and nominal clauses. As evidence, he gives the following (394):

(10) John-wa [Mary-**no** yonda yori] takusan-no hon-o yonda.
John-TOP Mary-GEN read than many-GEN book-ACC read
'John read more books than Mary did.'

The 'than' construction here evidently has no nominal head, which arguably excludes D-licensing for its genitive subject. *Wh*-movement of the comparative operator licenses the genitive under *wh*-agreement. *-ga* and *-no* are free alternants under this agreement (399–400).

Hiraiwa (2001) takes over Watanabe's C-licensing analysis and demonstrates its applicability to a variety of languages. He abstracts away from Watanabe's notion of *wh*-agreement and specifically allocates the responsibility for the licensing of the genitive to what he calls the *C-T amalgam* that results from movement of T to C, and this C-T combination forms what he calls, following Watanabe, subjunctive.[6] Hiraiwa likewise assumes that this subjunctive morphology licenses both the genitive and the nominative, the two being entirely free alternants of the same case licensed by the subjunctive (72–73, 115).

3.3 Problems with the Watanabe–Hiraiwa C-licensing approach

Watanabe (1996, 399–400) argues that the subjunctive C that licenses the genitive also licenses the nominative, so that the *ga–no* alternation is a completely free alternation. Hiraiwa (2001, 72–73, 115) also makes this claim. However, it has been known since Harada's (1971) article that *-ga* and *-no* differ, the latter typically more limited in its range of acceptability than the former. Harada notes (80) the following minimal pair involving the distance of the subject from the embedded verb.

(11) a. kodomotati-ga minna-de ikioi-yoku kake-nobotta kaidan
children-NOM together vigorously run-climb up stairway
'the stairway that those children ran up together vigorously'

b. *kodomotati-no minna-de ikioi-yoku kake-nobotta kaidan
children-GEN together vigorously run-climb up stairway

Harada's generalization is that if there is more than one element intervening between the subject and the verb, the genitive is not tolerated on the subject, while the nominative raises no problem. I will return to this issue of intervening elements below. We will see that it is not just any intervening element that degrades acceptability. Certain distinctions are apparently idiolectal, being limited to Harada's "Speaker B," but there are many pairs that he provides where every speaker finds a difference in grammaticality, such as the pair we see above in (11). He also gives the following (see his work for others).

(12) a. Taroo-ga Hanako-ni kasita (Ziroo-no) hon
Taro-NOM Hanako-DAT lent (Jiro-GEN) book
'the book (of Jiro's) that Taro lent Hanako'

b. *Taroo-no Hanako-ni kasita (Ziroo-no) hon
Taro-GEN Hanako-DAT lent (Jiro-GEN) book

Later, I will show that there are different reasons for the contrasts in grammaticality in the minimal pairs in (11) and (12).

The Watanabe–Hiraiwa approach is based on the idea that the "subjunctive" morphology on the verb licenses the case on the subject, and this case may freely alternate between *-ga* and *-no*. It is, in fact, the most interesting aspect of their approach that they deal with *ga–no* conversion literally as a free alternation between nominative and genitive. But the existence of minimal pairs such as those noted by Harada above, which clearly distinguish between the nominative and genitive subjects—and there are many other examples of this sort, some of which I will take up below—opens this otherwise interesting proposal to question. Harada's examples show that the choice of *-ga* or *-no* has consequences, and his observations hint at a structural difference, which we will take up below.[7] In Hiraiwa 2005, Hiraiwa does draw one distinction between nominative and genitive case markings: to license the genitive, he proposes that the verbal complex, which includes T and C in his analysis, is in what he calls the Predicate Adnominal form, and this form is nominalized. However, structurally, he draws no distinction between the two case markings, so that there is no clear way in which his proposal could account for the kinds of differences between the nominative and the genitive observed by Harada.

This still leaves the problem noted by Watanabe (1996) that there are constructions where the genitive subject is licensed despite the apparent absence of a nominal head. The example is repeated below.

(13) John-wa [Mary-**no** yonda yori] takusan-no hon-o yonda.
John-TOP Mary-GEN read than many-GEN book-ACC read
'John read more books than Mary did.'

Hiraiwa provides additional examples such as this (example (14b) below without the additional overt nominal is from his work); see Chapter 6 for evidence that (13) is in fact an instance of the D-licensed genitive. Maki and Uchibori (2008) point out that these examples, which ostensibly do not have a nominal head, in fact can be viewed as having a phonetically null nominal head (see also Sudo 2009 for a similar point, although his analysis differs fundamentally from Maki and Uchibori's).[8]

(14) a. Taroo-wa [Hanako-**ga/-no** yonda-**teido/-no** yori] takusan-no
Taro-TOP Hanako-NOM/-GEN read-degree/-NO than many-GEN
hon-o yonda.
book-ACC read
'Taro read more books than Hanako did.'

b. Taroo-wa [ame-**ga/-no** yamu **toki/zikan** made] ofisu-ni ita.
Taro-TOP rain-NOM/-GEN stop time/time until office-at was
'Taro was at his office until the rain stopped.'

As Maki and Uchibori note, the meaning of ostensibly headless constructions like (13) is best captured by positing a phonetically null head that has the appropriate meaning, analogous to *teido* 'degree' or *toki* 'time' in (14). There is, then, an explanation for the evidence given for the C-licensing hypothesis that is consistent with the D-licensing hypothesis.[9]

We saw earlier that there is evidence drawn from Harada 1971 that the nominative and genitive RC subjects belong to different structures. The only way, then, to enable C-licensing to remain as a possible contender is to entertain the idea that C-licensing holds only when there is a genitive subject. When there is a nominative subject, some other licensing is operative. Although it is a weaker version of C-licensing, hence less attractive, it is a possibility that we need to address. We will see that when the genitive subject occurs, the structure that licenses it is smaller than when there is a nominative subject. This structure when the genitive subject occurs cannot possibly be a CP, in other words, but what we will see is that it is similar to Hale's AspP for Dagur; I will actually argue that it is a TP. This makes even the weak version of C-licensing difficult to uphold. From here on, I will assume the D-licensing approach to genitive subjects in Japanese RCs. I note, however, that in developing the particular D-licensing analysis below, despite its incompatibility with C-licensing, I nevertheless draw on some important insights and ideas particularly from Watanabe's (1996) version of the C-licensing approach.

4 GENITIVE SUBJECTS IN RCS: D-LICENSING

In the remainder of this chapter, I will develop a D-licensing analysis of the genitive subject in Japanese. In so doing, I will be informed by Hale's (2002) D-licensing analysis of Dagur. There are two points from his analysis that I wish to focus on. The first is that, in order to allow D-licensing, the modificational clause (RC) that contains the genitive subject must be sufficiently small to allow the D to "reach in" and license the genitive subject. I will argue that the clause that contains the genitive subject is a TP without a CP above it. This differs from Hale's analysis, since he postulates an AspP for Dagur. In the end, the Japanese case may be the same (see Miyagawa 2008 for such an analysis), but since in Japanese the predicate of the RC can inflect for tense, as shown below, it makes sense to assume that TP is present.

(15) ame-no hur-u/hut-ta hi
rain-GEN fall-PRES/fall-PAST day
'the day it rains/rained'

This structure fits one of several nominalization structures that Borsley and Kornfilt (2000) propose based on Grimshaw's (1991, 2000) idea of mixed projections. The second point is that the inflection on the verb is in many cases aspectual inflection, not tense. I will take up these points in this order in this and the following section.

4.1 Size of the clause

Sakai (1994, 187) points out that the nominative and genitive structures differ relative to Condition B of the binding theory.

(16) a. Mary-no$_i$ [kanozyo-ga$_i$ kik-anakat-ta] hihan
Mary-GEN her-NOM hear-NEG-PAST criticism
'Mary's criticism that she did not hear'

b. *Mary-no$_i$ [kanozyo-no$_i$ kik-anakat-ta] hihan
Mary-GEN her-GEN hear-NEG-PAST criticism

Example (16a) contains a pronominal nominative subject in the RC, and this pronoun may be coreferential with the possessor R-expression 'Mary' in Spec,DP; 'Mary' here is the possessor of the noun 'criticism'. Due to the pro-drop nature of Japanese, having the overt pronoun as in (16a) naturally invites a contrastive interpretation; coreference is nevertheless possible with such interpretation. In contrast, as indicated in (16b), when the subject is genitive, coreference becomes difficult, if not impossible. If we replace the pronoun with an R-expression like *Taroo* (*Mary-no [Taroo-no kik-anakat-ta] hihan* 'Mary's criticism that Taro didn't hear'), or if we interpret 'she' in (16b) as disjunct from Mary, there is no problem.[10]

This suggests (17).

(17) The clause containing the genitive subject is smaller than the clause containing the nominative subject.

A reasonable way to think about the "small" nature of the clause containing the genitive subject is that it contains no case-assigning head that would intervene between D and the genitive subject. What I suggest is that the clause containing the genitive subject is a TP. In Miyagawa 2003a, I suggested that when the genitive subject occurs, it is because the T is defective and therefore is unable to assign (nominative) case. The notion of defective T shows up in the analysis of the ECM construction in English, where the lower clause is only a TP, and *v* from the higher clause reaches into the TP and marks the subordinate subject as accusative.

(18) I expect **him** to win.

Chomsky (2001) suggests that the defectiveness of T in the ECM construction naturally follows from the idea that probes, including case, appear on phase heads such as C, and lower by inheritance (to T, for example). In the ECM construction, because the lower clause is a TP to begin with, so that there is no phase head to host a probe or case, this lower clause naturally would not contain agreement or case, forcing its external argument to seek case from *v* in the higher clause. We can account for the defective nature of T in the genitive-subject construction in the same way: the genitive-subject RC is a TP, not a CP, so that T cannot license (nominative) case. Because T is not a case licensor, it does not intervene to prevent D from licensing case on the subject. We can see below that the defective T does not count as a binding domain in the ECM construction, which is consistent with Sakai's observation for the genitive-subject construction in (16b) above.[11]

(19) *John$_i$ expects him$_i$ to win.

On this view, the D-licensing of subjects is simply another instantiation of ECM, with the following structure.[12]

(20)

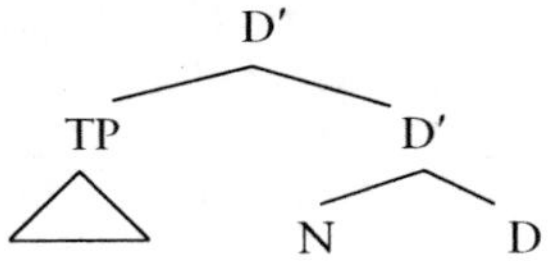

On the other hand, if T assigns nominative, it must be that it is in a larger clause, namely, CP (I omit the N head below).

(21)

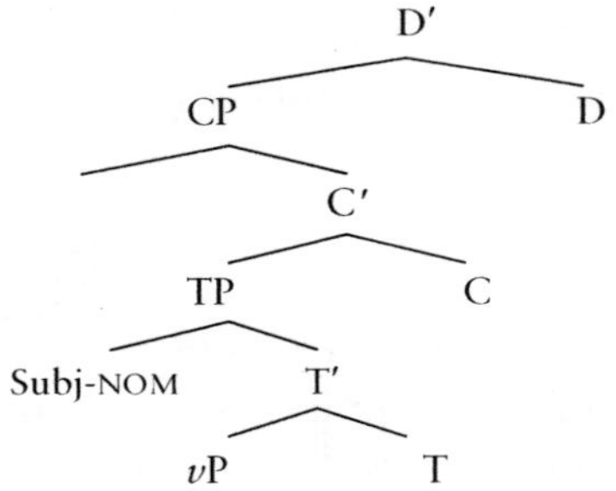

CP is a phase, so C blocks D from licensing case on the subject. The CP also functions as a binding domain, as we saw from Sakai's data earlier in (16).

Scope facts provide corroborating evidence for the reduced nature of the structure for genitive subjects. In English, Quantifier Raising (QR) is not possible out of a tensed clause, as we can see in (22) (May 1977).

(22) Someone thinks that every student failed the test.

Example (22) only has the surface-scope reading, *someone* > *every student*. However, if the subordinate clause is an infinitive, inverse scope is possible (see, e.g., Johnson 2000).

(23) Someone wants to order every item in the catalog.
someone > every item, every item > someone

The clause that contains *every item in the catalog* is a TP, and this reduced nature of the clause allows the universal quantifier to QR outside of it.[13] We find the same difference in scope between nominative and genitive subjects. In a noun-complement construction, this scope difference appears between the subject and the head noun (Miyagawa 1993; see also Ochi 2001).

(24) a. [[Taroo-ka Hanako]-ga kuru] riyuu-o osiete.
Taro-or Hanako-NOM come reason-ACC tell me
'Tell me the reason why either Taro or Hanako will come.'
'reason' > 'Taro or Hanako', *'Taro or Hanako' > 'reason'

b. [[Taroo-ka Hanako]-no kuru] riyuu-o osiete.
Taro-or Hanako-GEN come reason-ACC tell me
'Tell me the reason why Taro or Hanako will come.'
'reason' > 'Taro or Hanako', 'Taro or Hanako' > 'reason'

The nominative subject in (24a) solely takes narrow scope relative to the head 'reason', which is expected since the nominative subject is inside the CP, which contains a fully tensed TP, and we would not expect it to QR outside of this domain. In contrast, the genitive subject in (24b) may take scope over the head noun, 'reason', so that, on one reading, the speaker is seeking either the reason why Taro is coming or the reason why Hanako is coming, as opposed to the other reading involving the reason why either Taro or Hanako, but not both, is going to come. This is shown below (the noun head is excluded).[14]

(25)

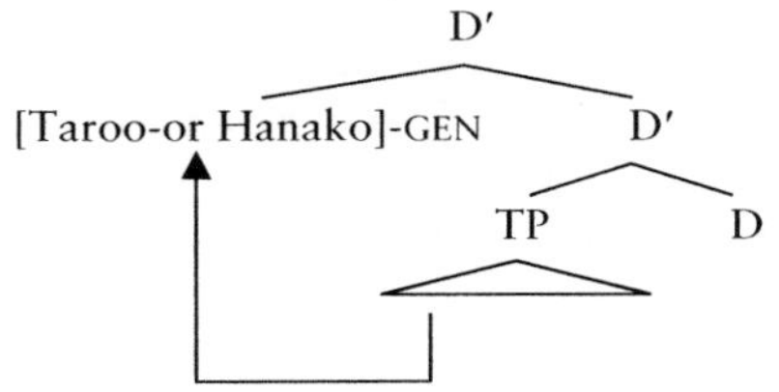

On the assumption that the genitive subject is contained in a reduced clause, TP, these examples in (24) parallel what we observed for quantifier scope in English. This parallelism gives further credence to the idea that while the nominative subject is contained in a full CP, the genitive subject is contained in TP.[15]

Further evidence for the CP–TP/*ga–no* distinction comes from the types of adverbials that may occur. Cinque (1999) holds that speech-act, evaluative, and evidential adverbials ('honestly', 'unfortunately', 'evidently') occur in the CP region, while, for example, "modal" adverbials such as 'probably' occur lower, possibly in the TP region. Note the following (thanks to Heizo Nakajima for these observations).

(26) a. [saiwai-ni Taroo-ga/*-no yomu] hon
fortunately Taro-NOM/-GEN read book
'the book that Taro will fortunately read'

b. [kanarazu Taroo-ga/-no yomu] hon
for certain Taro-NOM/-GEN read book
'the book that Taro will read for certain'

In (26a), we see that with the CP adverbial 'fortunately', only the nominative subject is possible, suggesting that there is no CP structure with the genitive subject, while in (26b), with the TP adverbial 'probably', either the nominative or the genitive subject is possible.[16]

The CP–TP distinction also addresses in the most direct way an observation that Hiraiwa (2005, 142) makes, namely, that the genitive subject only occurs if the complementizer is covert; if there is an overt complementizer, the genitive subject is blocked. From our perspective, the "covert" complementizer is simply an absent complementizer, because the clause that allows the genitive subject is a TP.

We thus have strong evidence that in Japanese, the head that licenses case on the RC subject is D when the RC is a reduced clause (TP), and C when there is a full CP (the relevant feature being inherited by T). This is a combination of what we saw in Dagur and Turkish: D and C respectively license the case associated with the RC subject. In those two languages, the same head also agrees with the subject. In Chomsky 2001, it is suggested that one purpose of the probe (uninterpretable feature) is to specify the phase head and close off the phase, but in the data he looks at, principally English, it is not clear whether it is the uninterpretable agreement feature or the concomitant case feature that thus serves to identify the head of a phase. The same could be said of Dagur and Turkish. The fact that in Japanese we see the same phase behavior as in Dagur and Turkish despite the apparent lack of agreement strongly suggests that it is case, not agreement, that serves to specify the phase head.

(27) Case identifies phase heads.

This makes sense because many languages lack ϕ-feature agreement while all languages presumably have case in some fashion. Since phases are part of the universal architecture of narrow syntax, it is only natural that case is invoked to specify a phase.

4.2 Intervening elements

As mentioned earlier, Harada (1971) observed that one major difference between the nominative- and genitive-subject constructions is that in the latter, placing items between the genitive subject and the predicate sometimes leads to degradation in grammaticality. I repeat the examples.

(28) a. kodomotati-ga minna-de ikioi-yoku kake-nobotta kaidan
children-NOM together vigorously run-climb up stairway
'the stairway that those children ran up together vigorously'

b. *kodomotati-no minna-de ikioi-yoku kake-nobotta kaidan
children-GEN together vigorously run-climb up stairway

While Harada's point here is that two or more intervening elements lead to ungrammaticality, many speakers find even one intervening phrase to be awkward.[17]

(29) ??kodomotati-no minna-de kake-nobotta kaidan
child-GEN together run-climb up stairway
(Intended: 'the stairway that those children ran up together')

Setting aside the degrees of difference, what could be the source of this degradation in naturalness? It has been one of the main puzzles in the analysis of genitive subjects in Japanese. I will propose an analysis based on economy.

It has been argued that in Japanese, T is associated with the EPP feature, so that something—most typically the subject—must raise to Spec,TP (Kishimoto 2001a; Kitahara 2002; Miyagawa 2001). However, in Miyagawa 2010, I give arguments to show that, universally, when T lacks any formal grammatical features as a result of not being selected by C, it does not trigger movement; hence there is no EPP on T in, for example, infinitival clauses in English, including ECM constructions. The genitive-subject construction should, then, have the same property of not requiring movement.

(30)

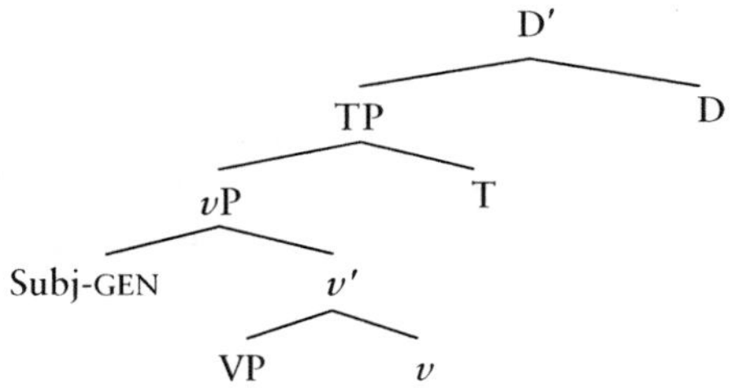

Given that T here is not selected by C, so that it fails to inherit any formal grammatical features, we would not expect it to trigger movement of the subject (or any other element).[18] On this account, the awkwardness associated with intervening elements is due to the fact that movement takes place without any motivation. In other words, in order for the genitive subject to occur to the left of an adverb, for example, the subject must undergo movement from its original position in Spec,*v*P to a higher position, with its landing site depending on the nature of the intervening element. In order to occur to the left of the intervening element, the genitive subject must have undergone movement, and this movement, being unmotivated, is flagged as uneconomical, hence the degradation in grammaticality.

Finally, if the intervening element is something that does not require the genitive subject to move, we predict that the construction should be grammatical. The following is a sentence taken from the novel *Koibumi* by

Renjo Mikihiko (see next section for discussion of a corpus study that used this and other novels).

(31) Koozi-no mattaku sir-anai kakudo
Koji-GEN at all know-NEG angle
'an angle that Koji doesn't know at all'

The genitive subject occurs to the left of the adverb *mattaku* 'at all', which is a VP adverb that can be viewed as directly modifying the VP and sits lower than Spec,*v*P; hence the genitive subject need not have moved.

4.3 The transitivity restriction

Harada (1971) observed another phenomenon involving a particular type of intervening element between the genitive subject and the predicate. This is the restriction that forbids accusative objects from occurring in structures that have the genitive subject; if the subject is nominative, there is no problem with such an object.[19] The following is taken from Watanabe 1996, 389, with one addition to show that nominative case marking is fine.

(32) [John-ga/*-no hon-o kasita] hito
John-NOM/-GEN book-ACC lent person
'the person to whom John lent a/the book'

To account for this transitivity restriction, Watanabe offers an analysis couched in early minimalism. He assumes that while the genitive subject does not move to Spec,TP at overt syntax, it must undergo movement at LF. This is shown below.

(33) [$_{CP}$ [$_{Agr_SP}$ Agr [$_{TP}$ Tns [$_{Agr_OP}$ Agr [$_{VP}$ John-no hon-o kasita]]]]]

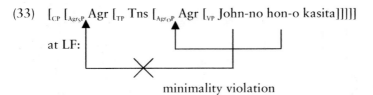

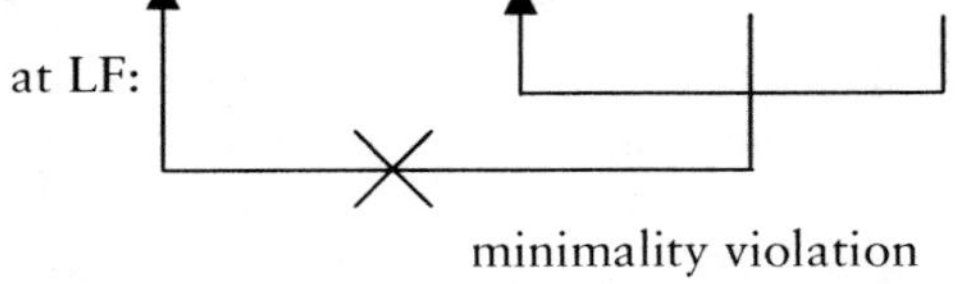

At LF, the genitive phrase—which for Watanabe is simply nominative pronounced as the "genitive" *-no*—must move to Spec,Agr$_S$P to have its case feature licensed at LF. Likewise the accusative case marker must move to Spec,Agr$_O$P. The problem arises after the accusative object moves to Spec,Agr$_O$P, and the genitive subject tries to move to Spec,Agr$_S$P. This movement is blocked by locality because the closest potential landing site is Spec,Agr$_O$P. If the subject is nominative, it undergoes movement at overt syntax, so no minimality violation occurs at LF for licensing the accusative object.

While this analysis that assumes LF movement is intriguing, there are alternatives to that assumption found in the more recent version of the theory, and these alternatives do not similarly account for the transitivity restriction. For example, under certain assumptions, the object only needs to enter into an Agree relation with the small *v* without movement. The small *v* would be below the genitive subject, so that the genitive subject would not intervene in this *v*–accusative relation.

How then can we account for the transitivity restriction?[20] As it turns out, we can find fragments of another solution in Watanabe's (1996) article, one that he does not fully implement himself. Two fundamental points from his article are: (i) the genitive subject stays in Spec,*v*P in overt syntax; (ii) the transitivity restriction in the genitive-subject construction in Japanese resembles a similar restriction found in French stylistic inversion (SI). Alexiadou and Anagnostopoulou (A&A; 2001, 2007) provide a broader theory of case that incorporates both of these points; I will adopt their analysis and extend it to another observation made by Harada (1971).

A&A propose the following generalization (this formulation is from A&A 2007).

(34) The subject-in-situ generalization (SSG)

By Spell-Out, *v*P can contain only one argument with an unchecked case feature.

The "case" here is structural case, and it typically receives its valuation from *v* (accusative) or T (nominative) under Agree; the case feature is, then, deleted (checked) at the point of Spell-Out, which occurs after the next higher phase is constructed (Chomsky 2000, 2001; see also Collins 2003). A typical case of the SSG is found in a construction where both the subject and the object can stay in situ in *v*P; if both have structural case, the sentence is ungrammatical. A&A (2001) demonstrate the SSG with data from a variety of languages such as Arabic, Celtic, English, Icelandic, Greek, and French, the last of which I will summarize.

SI in French (Kayne and Pollock 1978, 2001; Déprez 1990; Collins and Branigan 1997) occurs in *wh*-questions, RCs, and subjunctive complements. The examples below are from Déprez 1990 (cited in A&A 2001).

(35) a. Je me demande quand partira Marie.
I wonder when will leave Mary
'I wonder when Mary will leave.'

b. les resultats que nous donnent ces experiences
the results that us give these experiments
'the results that these experiments give us'

See Déprez 1990 for evidence that the subject in SI stays in situ in *v*P.

The observation that demonstrates the SSG is that SI is impossible if the *v*P contains a direct object (Kayne and Pollock 1978; Voalis and Dupuis 1992; Collins and Branigan 1997; among others).

(36) *Je me demande quand acheteront les consommateurs les pommes.
I wonder when will buy the consumers-NOM the apples-ACC

There are three ways to "save" this construction, all having to do with the object: (i) *wh*-extract it; (ii) cliticize it; (iii) have it surface as a PP (the last point is due to Collins and Branigan [1997], citing Kayne 1976). These are illustrated below.

(37) a. Que crois-tu que manquent un grand nombre
What believe-you that be absent from a great number
d'etudiants?
of students
'What do you think a great number of students are absent from?'

b. Tes cours, a quelle occasion les ont manques
your courses at which occasion them have been absent from
un grand nombre d'etudiants?
a great number of students
'On what occasion were a great number of students absent from your courses?'

c. ?Quand ecrira ton frere a sa petite amie?
when will write your brother to his little friend
'When will your brother write to his little friend?'

A&A (2001) point out that the SSG can account for the transitivity restriction in Japanese if we assume, following Watanabe (1996), that the genitive subject, but not the nominative subject, stays in situ in Spec,*v*P. Both the subject and the object would then receive case within *v*P before Spell-Out in violation of the SSG. A&A (2001) note correctly that this account is neutral as to D-licensing vs. C-licensing; so long as we assume that the genitive subject stays inside the *v*P, the SSG can account for the restriction.

Given this, let us return to another example given by Harada (1971), repeated below.

(38) *Taroo-no Hanako-ni kasita (Ziroo-no) hon
Taro-GEN Hakako-DAT lent (Jiro-GEN) book
(Intended: 'the book (of Jiro's) that Taro lent Hanko')

Sadakane and Koizumi (1995) argue that the particle *-ni* may be either a case marker or a postposition. Miyagawa (1997) and Miyagawa and

Tsujioka (Chapter 3 of this volume) provide further evidence for this, and Miyagawa and Tsujioka point out that the distinction between case and postposition is sensitive to animacy. If the goal phrase in a ditransitive construction is inanimate, *-ni* is necessarily a postposition, while *-ni* with an animate goal such as *Hanako* in (38) tends to be interpreted as case (although it needn't be). To force the *-ni* to be case, we can insert a floated numeral quantifier, which co-occurs with case-marked DPs but not with PPs. Note the contrast below (see Miyagawa 2003a for further discussion).

(39) a. *Taroo-no gakusei-ni san-nin okutta (Ziroo-no) hon
Taro-GEN student-*NI* three-CL sent (Jiro-GEN) book
(Intended: 'the book (of Jiro's) that Taro sent three students')

b. Taroo-no daigaku-ni okutta (Ziroo-no) hon
Taro-GEN university-*NI* sent (Jiro-GEN) book
'the book (of Jiro's) that Taro sent to the university'

On the surface these examples differ only in the animacy of the goal phrase (and the floated numeral quantifier in (39a)); as a consequence, in (39b) *-ni* must be a postposition while in (39a) it is case, as permitted by the animacy of 'students' and forced by the floated numeral quantifier. For (39a) and Harada's example in (38), we can impose the SSG account: there are two cases in *v*P in (38) and (39a), in violation of the SSG, but not in (39b), which has a postposition for the goal. Finally, we can presume that speakers who do not find (38) as bad as Harada are interpreting *-ni* as a postposition, an option even with an animate goal so long as there is no floated numeral quantifier to force *-ni* to be a case marker as in (39a).

In the original analysis of *ga–no* conversion, Harada, who discovered the transitivity restriction, noted that this restriction does not hold if the object is relativized.

(40) [Taroo-no e_i katta] hon_i
Taro-GEN bought book
'the book that Taro bought'

What is the nature of the empty element in the object position? If the SSG is responsible for the transitivity restriction, and the SSG has to do with case, it means that in (40) the empty element does not have case. What would be the identity of the empty element if there is no case? One possibility is to postulate an empty *pro* (see Murasugi 1991 and Hiraiwa 2001 for relevant discussion) and adopt Baker's (1996) suggestion that an empty *pro* does not require case. This is speculative, and there may be other possibilities, but I will not attempt to develop a more articulated analysis.[21]

Finally, we predict that Turkish should not evidence any transitivity restriction because the clause that contains the genitive subject is a full (nominalized) CP. This is shown below (see Hiraiwa 2001; thanks to Jaklin Kornfilt for the example).

(41) [Sen-**in** bilgisayar-da makale-ler-in-i yaz-acağ-mi]-ı
you-GEN computer-LOC article-PL-2SG-ACC write-FUT-2SG-ACC
duy-du-m.
hear-PAST-1SG
'(I) heard that you will write your articles on the computer.'

This is because in Turkish the genitive subject behaves essentially the same as a nominative subject in entering into agreement with the probe at C (which is inherited by T), so it would be reasonable to assume that the genitive subject moves to Spec,TP and avoids an SSG violation.

5 DEFECTIVE T AND INTERPRETATION

What consequence does the defectiveness of T in the genitive-subject construction have for interpretation? In English, infinitival clauses, which arguably contain a defective T, are known to have severe restrictions on tense interpretation (see, e.g., Stowell 1982). What I suggest is that in the (D-licensed) genitive-subject construction, the defectiveness of T also imposes a restriction on its interpretation. In particular, it appears that this construction is aspectually limited to stative interpretations, where stative may be the actual *Aktionsart* of the predicate or the result of an eventuality.[22]

A good way to begin is to look at a recent corpus study by Kim (2009). Kim looked at four novels from the 1970s to the 1990s,[23] and from these works she identified 1,143 examples of subjects in RCs or noun-complement clauses. Of these, 572 were genitive subjects and 571 were nominative subjects, so half were genitive and half were nominative, a result that by itself does not directly shed light on our question of the interpretation of clauses containing a genitive subject. However, when she broke down the examples into the types of predicates that occurred in the clause—adjective, unaccusative, and transitive/unergative—a striking pattern emerged. The following gives the percentage of genitive subjects for each of the predicate types.

(42) Adjective: 91%
Unaccusative: 56%
Transitive/unergative: 17%

As shown, 91% of the relevant occurrences of adjectives are associated with a genitive subject as opposed to a nominative subject.[24] Adjectives are by nature stative. Below is an example from Kim 2009 of an adjective taking a genitive subject.

(43) kami-no nagai hito
hair-GEN long person
'a person whose hair is long'

We can surmise that when the *Aktionsart* of the predicate is purely stative, as in the case of adjectives, the predicate appears in unmarked cases with the genitive subject because the genitive-subject construction itself has an inherently stative meaning. Although a nominative subject is also possible, it clearly is the case that the genitive is favored (91%), and the nominative, which must be licensed by a T selected by C, would presumably carry special meaning such as contrast or focus. The following is the nominative-subject counterpart of (43).

(44) kami-ga nagai hito
hair-NOM long person
'a person whose hair is long'

In reality, there is no obvious difference in meaning between this and the genitive-subject counterpart, most likely because an adjective, being purely stative, only has this aspectual meaning whether it occurs in a defective TP or a full CP. However, as we will see below, with verbs, we can detect differences between the two cases.[25]

As noted in (42), Kim (2009) found that 56% of the subjects of unaccusatives in RCs/noun-complement clauses are genitive. This is a smaller percentage than adjectives but far greater than unergatives/transitives (17%). The following are two examples.

(45) [tokutyoo-no aru] kao-tuki
distinctive-GEN exist face-expression
'a facial expression that is distinct'

(46) [kaze-no fuku] sakamiti
wind-GEN blow hill
'a hill where the wind blows'

Unaccusative constructions appear to be associated with at least two different kinds of stative interpretations. The first is the purely stative interpretation that we see in (45), in which there is no eventuality contained in the meaning of the sentence, so that it is the same as adjectives in its aspectual meaning. Example (46) is different in that it contains the event of wind blowing, but because it is a habitual/generic statement, it too is straightforwardly stative.[26]

The following example, pointed out to me by Yasuaki Abe, differs from (45) and (46) and provides an example of the second kind of stativity associated with unaccusatives that take a genitive subject.

(47) [Simi-no tuita syatu]-o kiteiru.
stain-GEN had shirt-ACC is wearing
'He's wearing a shirt that has sustained a stain.'

Here there is clearly an event—the shirt getting stained—but the clause containing the genitive subject refers to the *result* of this eventuality. A natural interpretation is that the shirt is still stained, in other words, although one could imagine a situation where this result held sometime in the past. So the difference between adjectives and unaccusatives such as (45) on the one hand and (47) on the other is like the difference between adjectives and resultative participles (e.g., verbal/adjectival passives) in English. For example, Kratzer (1994) distinguishes the pure stative *cool* from the resultative participle *cooled* as follows.

(48) a. cool: $\lambda x \lambda s[\text{cool}(x)(s)]$
b. cooled: $\lambda x \lambda s \exists e[\text{cool}(x)(s) \wedge s = f_{\text{target}}(e)]$

With *cooled*, there is an event, and the adjectival passive expresses the result of this event.

An important point about (47) above is the use of the "past tense" *-ta* on the unaccusative predicate. This verbal inflection *-ta* is known to lack a tense interpretation in certain RCs (see, e.g., Teramura 1982; Abe 1993; Kinsui 1994; Ogihara 2004). An example often given to demonstrate this is the following.

(49) [yude-ta] tamago
boil-PAST egg
(i) 'the egg that (I) boiled' (eventive reading)
(ii) 'the boiled egg' (stative reading)

The first reading contains the event of having boiled the egg, and *-ta* here is used as past tense to indicate that this event occurred prior to the utterance time. The second reading is often described as a stative modifier in which the state holds at the time of utterance, so that *-ta* here does not indicate past tense. However, even in the second interpretation, the event of having boiled the egg is contained in the meaning of the sentence, so that, following Kratzer's analysis, the perceived lack of tense is probably due to the focus of this second interpretation on the *state* that holds at the time of the utterance as a result of a past eventuality (see Ogihara 2004 for a different analysis). To further explore this idea of resultant states, let us compare (47), repeated here as (50b), with the nominative-subject counterpart.

(50) a. [Simi-ga tuita syatu]-o kiteiru.
stain-NOM had shirt-ACC is wearing
'He's wearing the shirt that sustained a stain.'

b. [Simi-no tuita syatu]-o kiteiru.
stain-GEN had shirt-ACC is wearing
'He's wearing the shirt that has a stain.'

In (50a), which has the nominative case marker, the RC indicates that there was an event of the shirt getting stained; the RC is ambiguous about whether the result is being made prominent. In (50b), while the event of staining is included in the meaning, the focus is on the result of this eventuality, and the most natural interpretation is that the shirt being worn has a stain at the time of the utterance. The latter is stative in aspect due to the focus on the resultative meaning. We can see the stative as opposed to eventive nature of the genitive-subject clause by the fact that it is odd with an adverb emphasizing the event as opposed to the result (thanks to Masayuki Wakayama for the data).

(51) [Totuzen simi-ga/*-no tuita syatu]-o misete kudasai.
suddenly stain-NOM/-GEN had shirt-ACC show me please
'Please show me the shirt that was suddenly stained.'

The adverb 'suddenly' puts focus on the event of the shirt getting stained, and is in conflict with the meaning of the genitive-subject construction as stative. As we can see, this adverb is fine with the nominative subject.

Finally, the smallest number of genitive subjects in Kim's (2009) corpus is found with transitives and unergatives, as expected (17%).[27] According to Kim (personal communication), many of these involve psychological predicates, which, by virtue of lacking an agent, are amenable to a stative interpretation. The following are two such examples.

(52) kare-no sinziteiru kami
he-GEN believe God
'the god that he believes in'

(53) Koozi-no mattaku sir-anai kakudo
Koji-GEN at all know-NEG angle
'an angle that Koji doesn't know at all'

There are, however, instances in which the predicate appears to have an agent, as exemplified by the following.

(54) tuma-no tukatta mono
wife-GEN used thing
'the thing that my wife has used'

Up to now the examples have all involved nonagentive predicates—adjective, unaccusative, psych—which are amenable to a stative interpretation of some sort, either because the predicate itself has this *Aktionsart* or because the focus is placed on the result of an eventuality. In (54), we have what appears to be a genuine agent of an event, 'wife'. Is this the correct interpretation? The transitive verb here has the "past" inflection *-ta*, but because the verb is not unaccusative but a straightforward transitive verb, this *-ta* is likely not the aspectual inflection we saw earlier. What I speculate is that the *-ta* form here indicates what is equivalent to perfect tense, which "is said to describe (or focus on) a state that follows from a prior eventuality" (Iatridou, Anagnostopoulou, and Izvorski 2001, 154; see their article for the references). There are several different kinds of perfect tenses, but the one that appears to be consistent with all that we have observed is the experiential perfect demonstrated below (Iatridou, Anagnostopoulou, and Izvorski 2001, 155).

(55) I have read *Principia Mathematica* five times.

On the experiential-perfect interpretation, (55) states that "I have the experience of having read *Principia Mathematica* five times." For (54), a similar experiential-perfect interpretation would give it the meaning of "the thing that my wife has the experience of having used." While it is difficult to tease apart the difference between this and the nominative-subject counterpart, which presumably lacks this experiential meaning, we can find evidence elsewhere for the stative nature of the genitive-subject construction.

(56) Wazato kodomo-ga/?*-no kowasita kabin-o misete kudasai.
intentionally child-NOM/-GEN broke vase-ACC show me please
'Please show me the vase that the child broke intentionally.'

The adverb *wazato* 'intentionally' goes with an agent, so that in this example, it puts the focus on the actual event of breaking the vase instead of on the result or the experience of having broken the vase. As shown, while the nominative subject is fine, the genitive subject is highly degraded, if not ungrammatical. One possible way to view (56) is that the genitive-subject construction does not allow agents but only experiencers for external arguments. On this interpretation, (56) without the agentive adverb 'intentionally' would mean, with the genitive subject, that there is a vase that the child has the experience of having broken. These suggestions are all speculative at best, and I will have to leave the topic without a more definitive analysis.

6 CONCLUDING REMARKS

In this article, I showed that there are two ways in which Altaic languages license genitive case marking on the subject: D-licensing is found in Dagur while C-licensing is what is operative in Turkish. I gave evidence that the *ga–no* conversion in Japanese, where the genitive is allowed on the subject of RCs and noun-complement clauses, best fits the D-licensing model of Dagur. This is a counterproposal to the analysis by Watanabe (1996) and Hiraiwa (2001), who have put forth a C-licensing analysis for Japanese. They specifically argue that both the nominative *-ga* and the genitive *-no* are a reflex of the same case feature licensed by C with "subjunctive" inflection, which is ostensibly found in environments in which the genitive subject occurs. However, data from the earliest work on the topic, by Harada (1971), gives clear indication that the nominative and genitive subjects must be treated differently. In Japanese, the key heads are C for the nominative and D for the genitive. C and D are phase heads, and their projections emerge in all three Altaic languages—and in all other languages, presumably—as phases, which, we argued, are defined not by uninterpretable agreement features but by case.

6 The genitive of dependent tense in Japanese and its correlation with the genitive of negation in Slavic

1 INTRODUCTION

In Japanese, the subject of relative clauses (RCs) and noun-complement clauses may be marked by the nominative case marker or, in some instances, by the genitive case marker.

(1) [**Watasi-ga/-no** yonda] hon-wa omosiroi.
 me-NOM/-GEN read book-TOP interesting
 'The book I read is interesting.'

While it is generally assumed that T licenses the nominative case marker (Takezawa 1987), there is lively debate as to what licenses the genitive case on the subject. In the D-licensing approach (e.g., Bedell 1972; Miyagawa 1993, 2008, Chapter 5 of this volume; Ochi 2001; Saito 1983), this genitive is licensed by the D head that takes the RC/noun-complement clause. In contrast, in the C-licensing approach (Watanabe 1996; Hiraiwa 2001, 2002, 2005), it is the "subjunctive" C of the RC/noun-complement clause that makes the genitive marking possible.

In Chapter 5, I give arguments for D-licensing of the Japanese genitive subject. One point that I note is that, contrary to the prediction made by the C-licensing approach, which portrays the choice between nominative and genitive as optional, meaning that there should be no real difference resulting from choosing one over the other (Watanabe 1996, 399–400; Hiraiwa 2001, 72–73, 115), there are, in fact, substantial differences. Many of these differences were first noted by Harada (1971) in the first comprehensive study of the genitive-subject construction. As Harada observed, while nominative marking virtually always leads to a grammatical sentence, that is not the case with the genitive subject, which has a narrower range of grammatical possibilities. In Chapter 5, following Hale's (2002) work on Dagur genitive subjects, I argue that at least some of what Harada noted can be accounted for by the fact that the clause containing the genitive subject is *smaller* than the one containing the nominative subject; the compact nature of the genitive-subject clause allows the D that selects the clause to reach in and license the genitive on the subject.

We can see the difference in the size of the clauses in the different range of adverbs that are possible with them (see Chapter 5). Cinque (1999) holds that speech-act, evaluative, and evidential adverbials ('honestly', 'unfortunately', 'evidently') occur in the CP region, while, for example, a "modal" adverb such as 'probably' occurs lower, possibly in the TP region. We can see below that while a CP-level adverb is possible when the nominative case marker occurs, this is not the case with the genitive subject (thanks to Heizo Nakajima for this point). No such difference occurs with an adverb that occurs lower in the structure.

(2) a. Kore-ga [saiwai-ni Taroo-ga/?*-no mituketa] yubiwa desu.
this-NOM fortunately Taro-NOM/-GEN found ring COP
'This is the ring that Taro fortunately found.'

b. Kore-ga [kitto Taroo-ga/-no mituketa] yubiwa desu.
this-NOM probably Taro-NOM/-GEN found ring COP
'This is the ring that Taro probably found.'

This difference suggests that when the nominative subject occurs, the structure is a full CP, while the genitive subject is contained in a smaller clause, which I argue in Chapter 5 to be a TP. The following structures illustrate the difference (I have left out the RC head). Note that the genitive subject stays in *v*P, a suggestion made earlier in Watanabe 1996.

(3) Nominative

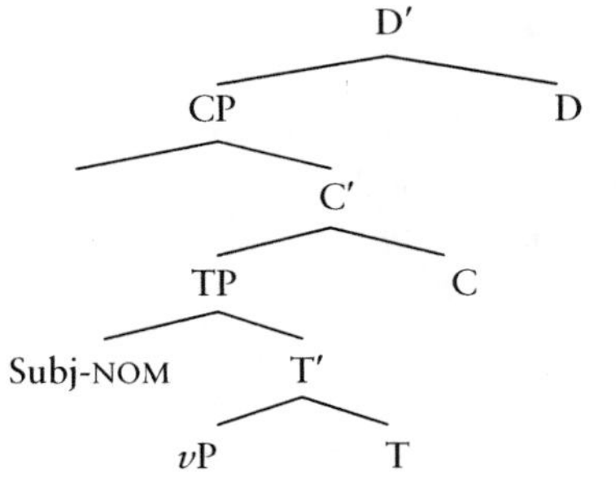

(4) Genitive

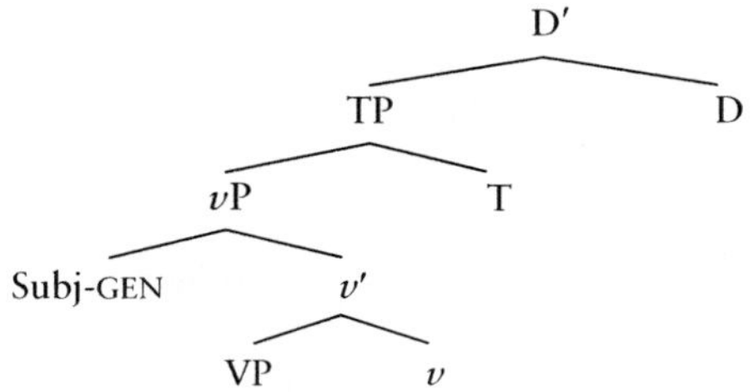

Why does the nominative subject in (3) move to Spec,TP, while the genitive subject in (4) doesn't? In (3), a full CP occurs, and T inherits formal features from C, including the (nominative) case feature, in turn triggering movement of the nominative subject. In contrast, in (4), there is no CP, so that the T does not end up with relevant formal features, which makes movement of the subject unnecessary.[1] This difference solves a problem noted by Harada (1971, 80): that there is a difference between the nominative and the genitive subject when it comes to elements that may intervene between the subject and the verb.

(5) a. kodomotati-ga minna-de ikioi-yoku kake-nobotta kaidan
children-NOM together vigorously run-climb up stairway
'the stairway that those children ran up together vigorously'

b. *kodomotati-no minna-de ikioi-yoku kake-nobotta kaidan
children-GEN together vigorously run-climb up stairway

I argued in Chapter 5 that in (5b), the genitive subject violates economy because it has to have moved—presumably to Spec,TP—although nothing requires it to do so. This analysis further predicts that an adverb may occur between a genitive subject and the verb if it is a low adverb that does not require the genitive subject to move from its original position of Spec,*v*P.

(6) Koozi-no mattaku sir-anai kakudo
Koji-GEN at all know-NEG angle
'an angle that Koji doesn't know at all'

The genitive subject occurs to the left of the adverb *mattaku* 'at all', which is a VP adverb that can be viewed as directly modifying the VP and sits lower than Spec,*v*P, hence the genitive subject need not have moved. As further evidence, Nambu (2010) points out that in two large corpora that he examined, there are 34 cases of a phrase occurring between a genitive subject and the verb, and all 34 are either VP adverbs or PPs, the latter presumably also occurring within the VP.

Further evidence for the difference in the size of the clause comes from Sakai's (1994, 187) observation based on binding theory, specifically Condition B.

(7) a. Mary-no$_i$ [kinoo kanozyo-ga$_i$ yatotta] gakusei
Mary-GEN yesterday her-NOM hired student
'Mary's student whom she hired yesterday'

b. ??Mary-no$_i$ [kinoo kanozyo-no$_i$ yatotta] gakusei
Mary-GEN yesterday her-GEN hired student

As Sakai notes, if we put a possessor phrase in Spec,DP, it is possible to have a pronoun in the subject position of the embedded structure that is coreferential with the possessor phrase, but only if the subject pronoun is marked by the nominative case. This again suggests that the clause that contains the nominative subject is larger than the one that contains the genitive subject. As noted above, I argue in Chapter 5 that, while the nominative subject is contained in a CP, the clause that contains the genitive subject is a TP without a CP above it. Because the structure that contains the nominative subject is a CP, and the C selects the T, it is a "full" structure with an active T, and this allows the CP/TP to act as a governing category. But in the case of the clause that contains the genitive subject, there is no CP, only a TP, so that this T is not selected by C and therefore is defective, and this TP fails to constitute a governing category, very much like the cases of the infinitive that we see in English constructions such as ECM.

One way in which the T here is defective is that, being unselected by C, it cannot assign nominative case. This allows the D that takes the TP to license the genitive on the subject because T is not a case assigner, so there is no minimality violation. I also gave evidence that the clause with the genitive subject, having a defective T, is limited to the interpretation of "stative," where the stativity may be the actual *Aktionsart* of a predicate or the result of an eventuality, which typically has a stative interpretation (see, e.g., Kratzer 1994; Iatridou, Anagnostopoulou, and Izvorski 2001). So, there is ample evidence that the genitive case on the subject is licensed by D, and what makes this possible is that the clause that contains this subject is smaller—a TP and not a full CP.

In this chapter, I will look at an entirely different phenomenon of genitive marking on the subject in Japanese, one that apparently does not depend on the occurrence of D; rather, it appears to be licensed by a certain type of *v* in combination with dependent tense. As we will see, the distribution of this genitive virtually matches the genitive of negation in Slavic, the only difference arising from the fact that it is licensed in part by dependent tense, which only occurs in subordinate structures, while the genitive of negation in Slavic may occur freely in matrix as well as subordinate clauses.

2 CHALLENGES TO THE D-LICENSING APPROACH

Watanabe (1996) drew our attention to examples that ostensibly show that genitive subjects may occur in contexts where there is no D, which, he argued, gave credence to the idea that the genitive is licensed by some other means than D—for him, C. Extending this line of analysis, Hiraiwa (2002) gave the examples below, one of which is taken from Watanabe, that seem to further demonstrate that the genitive case marking on the subject is not dependent on the occurrence of D.

(8) a. John-wa [Mary-**ga/-no** yonda yori] takusan-no
John-TOP Mary-NOM/-GEN read.PAST.ADN than many-GEN

hon-wo yonda.
books-ACC read-PAST

'John read more books than Mary did.' (Watanabe 1996, 396)

b. John-wa [ame-**ga/-no** yamu made] office-ni
John-TOP rain-NOM/-GEN stop.PRES.ADN until office-at

i-ta.
be-PAST

'John was at his office until the rain stopped.'

c. [Boku-**ga/-no** omou-ni] John-wa Mary-ga
me-NOM/-GEN think.PRES.ADN-DAT John-TOP Mary-NOM

suki-ni-tigainai.
like-must-PRES

'I think that John likes Mary.'

d. Kono atari-wa [hi-**ga/-no** kureru nitsure(-te)]
around here-TOP sun-NOM/-GEN go down.PRES.ADN(-as)

hiekondeku-ru.
get colder-PRES

'It gets chillier as the sun goes down around here.'

e. John-wa [toki-**ga/-no** tatsu-to tomoni]
John-TOP time-NOM/-GEN pass.PRES-ADN with as

Mary-no koto-wo wasurete-itta.
Mary-GEN fact-ACC forget-go.PAST

'Mary slipped out of John's memory as time went by.'

Maki and Uchibori (2008) argue that these are not counterexamples to D-licensing; they propose that these examples all have a silent nominal head, something analogous to *teido* 'degree' for (8a) or *toki* 'time' for (8b), so that these structures actually do have a D head that licenses the genitive marking. However, Takahashi (2010) shows that this cannot be entirely true because examples with and without such an overt head behave differently; we will see how in the next section. If every example without an overt nominal head really did have a covert head, we would not expect any variation in the examples. Nevertheless, we will see some evidence that supports the type of approach suggested by Maki and Uchibori.

An important point that Takahashi notices about Hiraiwa's examples is that three of them, (8b), (8d), and (8e), contain an unaccusative verb. Although Takahashi does not provide an analysis, she notes that unaccusatives have been observed to behave in a special fashion in the context of genitive subjects (Fujita 1988; Miyagawa 1989, 103–105). What I will argue is that the examples from Hiraiwa that contain an unaccusative verb are, just as Hiraiwa and Watanabe argue, genitive case markings licensed in the absence of D. But contrary to Hiraiwa and Watanabe, I will show that this special instance of genitive marking is similar to the genitive of negation found in Slavic languages, which occurs only on internal arguments, including the subject of the unaccusative. I will show that the genitive in these examples is licensed by the "weak" *v* in combination with dependent tense. For (8a) and (8c), I will give arguments to show that these are cases of D-licensing with an empty nominal head, along the lines of Maki and Uchibori 2008. The type of genitive licensing that is the focus of this chapter must be dealt with separately from the D-licensed kind, the latter strictly dependent on the occurrence of the D head.

3 TEMPORAL CLAUSE: CP OR DP

In Miyagawa 1989, 103–105, I reported on Fujita's work (1988) that identified a type of genitive subject that, from the perspective of today's D- vs. C-licensing debate, is puzzling under either approach; Fujita's work is an extension of Terada's (1987) original insights. I will begin with examples that clearly fall under the D-licensing approach, then move onto the puzzling examples.

In a temporal clause headed by a phrase such as *toki* 'time', only the nominative case is possible, with one exception that I will discuss later.

(9) [Kodomo-ga/*-no waratta toki], tonari-no heya-ni ita.
child-NOM/-GEN laughed when next-GEN room-in was
'When the child laughed, I was in the next room.'

Here the 'when' clause is a temporal adjunct. However, as Fujita noted, if the temporal clause occurs as an argument, the genitive subject becomes possible. This is shown below.

(10) [Kodomo-ga/-no waratta toki]-o omoidasita.
child-NOM/-GEN laughed time-ACC recalled
'I recalled the time when the child laughed.'

For the adjunct-clause effect in (9), in which the genitive subject is excluded, I will adopt a suggestion of Whitman (1992), who, upon examining this data, proposed that an adjunct clause headed by a word such as *toki* 'time' (or *koto* 'matter') is a CP, so that *toki* in this construction is itself a C ('when'). This is comparable to a 'when' adjunct clause such as the following in English.

(11) When the kids laughed, I was in the next room.

Given that there is no D, we would not expect the genitive subject to be possible, and this is what we find, at least with examples such as (9) above. When this temporal clause occurs in an argument position as in (10), the clause takes on a DP structure, with *toki* 'time' occurring as an N head instead of as a C head (Whitman 1992), which is evident from the fact that the accusative case marker occurs on it. One can also find the nominative, as shown below (Miyagawa 1989, chap. 3). The first example is an instance of the temporal clause functioning as an adjunct; in the second example it is functioning as an argument, with the nominative *-ga* marking attached to the subordinate structure.

(12) a. [Minna-ga/?*-no odotta toki], nigiyaka-ni natta.[2]
all-NOM/-GEN danced when lively became
'When everyone danced, it became lively.'

b. [Minna-ga/-no odotta toki]-ga itiban nigiyaka datta.
all-NOM/-GEN danced time-NOM most lively was
'The time when every danced was very lively.'

3.1 Genitive of dependent tense

We saw that genitive subjects are impossible in temporal adjunct clauses. However, there is an exception to this prohibition. Note that the verbs in the ungrammatical examples in (9) and (12a) above are unergative ('laugh', 'dance'). As Fujita (1988) observed (see Miyagawa 1989, 104–105), genitive subjects are in fact allowed in this environment if the predicate is unaccusative.

(13) [Kodomo-ga/-no kita toki], tonari-no heya-ni ita.
child-NOM/-GEN came when next-GEN room-in was
'I was in the next room when the child came.'

(14) [Kaze-de doa-ga/-no aita toki] daremo kizukanakatta.
wind-by door-NOM/-GEN opened when no one noticed
'When the door opened due to wind, no one noticed.'

Though not as natural as the nominative, the genitive in these examples is certainly within the range of ready acceptability. Given our assumption that these temporal adjunct clauses are CPs, with no relevant D in the structure, the occurrence of the genitive is completely unexpected. Clearly, it is licensed by something other than D.

We can in fact show that the genitive found in (13)–(14) is fundamentally different from the D-licensed genitive that we have been looking at up to now. The D-licensed genitive occurs in a defective TP, which allows the D selecting the TP to reach inside the TP and license the genitive. In contrast, in (13)–(14), the adjunct clause that contains the genitive subject is a CP because the temporal word *toki* 'when' is C. To show this, recall that in a typical case of the D-licensed genitive subject, a CP adverb such as 'fortunately' is infelicitous because the structure only has a TP.

(15) Kore-ga [saiwai-ni Taroo-ga/?*-no mituketa] yubiwa desu.
this-NOM fortunately Taro-NOM/-GEN found ring COP
'This is the ring that Taro fortunately found.'

However, with the genitive subject involving an unaccusative, the situation is different.

(16) [Saiwai-ni ame-no yanda toki], minna kooen-de asonda.
fortunately rain-GEN stopped when everyone park-in played
'When the rain fortunately stopped, everyone played in the park.'

(17) [Saiwai-ni seki-no aita toki], Hanako-wa obaasan-ni
fortunately seat-GEN opened when Hanako-TOP grandmother-DAT
osiete-ageta.
let know
'When a seat fortunately opened up, Hanako let her grandmother know.'

Given that passives, like unaccusatives, involve a subject that starts out as an internal argument, we expect the subject of passives to also allow the genitive in the adjunct clause, and this is indeed the case.

(18) Watasi-wa [kodomo-no home-rare-ta toki] hontouni uresii
me-TOP child-GEN praise-PASS-PAST when really happy
kimoti datta.
feeling was
'When my child was praised, I was really happy.'

As with the genitive of the unaccusative, the genitive of the passive occurs in CP.

(19) Watasi-wa [saiwai-ni kodomo-no erab-are-ta toki],
me-TOP fortunately child-GEN choose-PASS-PAST when
hotto simasi-ta.
relieved was
'When my child was fortunately chosen, I was relieved.'

What is the nature of this genitive marking that is allowed, in spite of the absence of D, on the subject of unaccusatives and passives but not of transitives and unergatives? I suggest that this unusual genitive is similar to the genitive that occurs in the context of negation in Slavic languages such as Russian (Babby 1980; Pesetsky 1982; Bailyn 1997; Babyonyshev 1996; etc.). What is of interest is that the Slavic genitive of negation only occurs on internal arguments—the "subject" of passives and unaccusative and the direct object of transitives, not the subject of unergatives or transitives. The following examples taken from Pesetsky 1982, 40–50, demonstrate this point.[3]

Direct objects:

(20) a. Ja ne polučal pis'ma.
I NEG received letters.ACC.PL

b. Ja ne polučal pisem.
I NEG received letters.GEN.PL

Subjects of passives:

(21) a. Ni odna gazeta ne byla
not one newspaper.FEM.NOM.SG NEG was.FEM.SG
polučena.
received.FEM.SG

b. Ni odnoj gazety ne bylo
not one newspaper.FEM.GEN.SG NEG was.NEUT.SG
polučeno.
received.NEUT.SG

Unaccusative subjects:

(22) a. Griby zdes' ne rastut.
mushrooms.NOM here NEG grow.3PL

b. Gribov zdes' ne rastët.
mushrooms.GEN here NEG grow.3SG

(23) a. Otvet iz polka ne prišël.
answer.NOM from regiment NEG arrived.MASC.3SG

b. Otveta iz polka ne prišlo.
answer.GEN from regiment NEG arrived.NEUT.3SG

Unergative subjects:

(24) a. V pivbarax kul'turnye ljudi ne p'jut.
in beerhalls cultured people.NOM NEG drink.3PL

b. *V pivbarax kul'turnyx ljudej ne p'ët.
in beerhalls cultured people.GEN NEG drink.3SG

(25) a. Ni odin rebënok ne prygnul.
not one child.MASC.SG.NOM NEG jumped.MASC.SG

b. *Ni odnogo rebënka ne prygnulo.
not one child.MASC.SG.GEN NEG jumped.NEUT.SG

Transitive subjects (regardless of their agentivity):

(26) a. Studenty ne smotrjat televizor.
students.NOM NEG watch.PL TV

b. *Studentov ne smotrit televizor.
students.GEN NEG watch.SG TV

In Japanese a similar genitive is apparently licensed by *v*, specifically, a "weak" *v* in the sense of Chomsky (1995, etc.), in combination with dependent tense. I will call it the *genitive of dependent tense* (GDT). In fact, as Takahashi (2010) notes, some of the examples that Hiraiwa (2002) gives as counterexamples to D-licensing are the Fujita-type examples involving an unaccusative verb. Following is one such example, drawn from Hiraiwa 2001.[4]

(27) John-wa [ame-ga/-no yam-u made] office-ni ita.
John-TOP rain-NOM/-GEN stop-PRES until office-at be-PAST
'John was at his office until the rain stopped.'

This is a type of adjunct clause headed by the temporal head *made* 'until', which Hiraiwa points out is not associated with D. As Takahashi (2010) notes, this temporal-adjunct construction becomes ungrammatical with the genitive subject if the verb is unergative.

(28) John-wa [oogoede Mary-ga/?*-no wara-u made] odotteita.
John-TOP loudly Mary-NOM/-GEN laugh-PRES until was dancing
'John was dancing until Mary laughed loudly.'

Thus, Hiraiwa's example in (27) is a demonstration of the genitive marking that occurs with *v* (and dependent tense), but it is not a demonstration of an overall phenomenon of genitive subject marking in Japanese as he assumed.

But is there evidence that *v* is indeed responsible for licensing the GDT? Takahashi (2010) makes an interesting observation in this regard. First, as noted in Miyagawa 1993 (see also Ochi 2001), there is a scope difference between nominative and genitive case markings. The genitive subject in (29b) is the D-licensed kind we have seen before.

(29) a. [[Taroo-ka Hanako]-ga kuru] riyuu-o osiete.
Taro-or Hanako-NOM come reason-ACC tell me
'Tell me the reason why Taro or Hanako will come.'
'reason' > 'Taro or Hanako', *'Taro or Hanako' > 'reason'

b. [[Taroo-ka Hanako]-no kuru] riyuu-o osiete.
Taro-or Hanako-GEN come reason-ACC tell me
'Tell me the reason why Taro or Hanako will come.'
'reason' > 'Taro or Hanako', 'Taro or Hanako' > 'reason'

The nominative subject in (29a) only takes narrow scope relative to the head 'reason', so that this sentence is asking for the single reason why Taro or Hanako will come. In (29b), there is this reading, but also, there is a reading in which the genitive subject takes wide scope relative to 'reason', and on this latter reading, the speaker is asking to be told either the reason why Taro will come or the reason why Hanako will come. I argued in Chapter 5 that because the clause containing the genitive subject is a TP, not a CP, there is no barrier to having the genitive subject undergo Quantifier Raising (QR) to the higher D projection, allowing the wide-scope reading that we see.

(30)

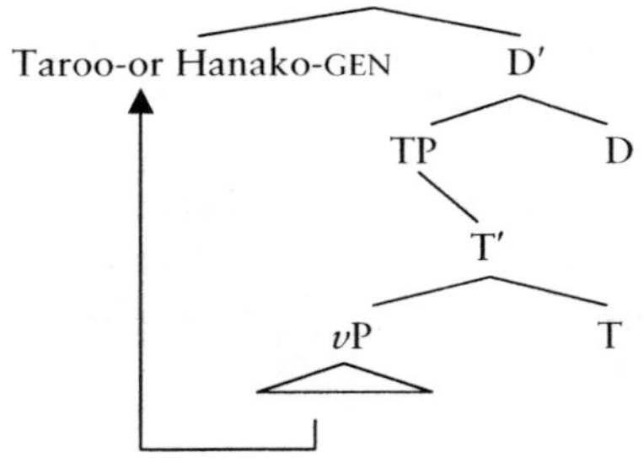

This is similar to the observation that QR in English, which is known to be clause-bound (May 1977), may nevertheless extract a quantifier out of an infinitival clause, that is, a TP (Johnson 2000; Miyagawa 2011b).

(31) Someone wants to order every item in the catalog.

This sentence readily admits the inverse-scope interpretation, *every item* > *someone*.

Takahashi (2010) observes that in the temporal adjunct clause, scope relations are fundamentally different from what we find in RCs and noun-complement clauses.

(32) a. [[John-ka Mary]-**ga** kuru made] mati-masyou.
John-or Mary-NOM come until wait-let us
(i) 'Let's wait until the time when John or Mary comes.'
(ii)*'Let's wait either until John comes or until Mary comes.'

b. [[John-ka Mary]-**no** kuru made] mati-masyou.
John-or Mary-GEN come until wait-let us
(i) 'Let's wait until the time when John or Mary comes.'
(ii) *'Let's wait either until John comes or until Mary comes.'

In (32a), with the nominative case, the subject only takes narrow scope, which is what we expect. What is surprising is that in (32b), the genitive subject does not lead to scope ambiguity as we saw earlier. Although Takahashi does not give a reason for this difference, an analysis based on Chapter 5 together with the assumption that *v* (and dependent tense—see below) assigns the genitive case in (32b) provides a possible account. In Chapter 5, I argue that phases are specified by case (or whatever formal statement one prefers for case): if a head has case to assign, that head is designated as a phase head. I also suggested that QR is limited in its local domain to the phase in which the quantifier occurs (see Miyagawa 2011b for exceptions and other relevant discussion of QR). If we assume that *v* (in combination with dependent tense) licenses the genitive case marking on the internal argument of the unaccusative verb, *v* is designated as a phase head, and it would block the genitive subject from raising by QR beyond it. This blocks the wide-scope reading of the genitive subject relative to 'until'.[5] As Takahashi also notes, if we change (32) so that there is an overt nominal head, scope ambiguity returns with the genitive subject.

(33) a. [[John-ka Mary]-**ga** kuru **zikan**-made] mati-masyou.
John-or Mary-NOM come time-until wait-let us
(i) 'Let's wait until the time when John or Mary comes.'
(ii)*'Let's wait either until John comes or until Mary comes.'

b. [[John-ka Mary]-**no** kuru **zikan**-made] mayi-masyou.
John-or Mary-GEN come time-until wait-let us
(i) 'Let's wait until the time when John or Mary comes.'
(ii) 'Let's wait either until John comes or until Mary comes.'

This is clear evidence that when an overt nominal heads the clause, D may license the genitive; the clause containing the genitive subject being a TP, the genitive subject can raise above the TP and take scope over the head. As Takahashi (2010) notes, this fact is a counterexample to Maki and Uchibori's (2008) argument that when there is no overt nominal head, there is a covert one. If Maki and Uchibori were right, we should not detect any difference between the expressions with and without an overt nominal head. See Takahashi 2010 for other interesting facts that parallel the scope observation. I will return to the idea of covert heads later, showing that Maki and Uchibori are correct in certain instances.

An immediate question that arises with this *v*-licensed genitive in Japanese is, why doesn't it ever occur in the matrix clause? Given that it isn't dependent on the occurrence of D, we should, in principle, expect it to occur everywhere, but, in fact, it does not.[6]

(34) *Ame-no futta.
rain-GEN fell
'It rained.'

The reason why this genitive does not occur in root environments is due to the fact that its licensing is dependent not only on weak *v*, but also on the occurrence of a certain type of tense, dependent tense, which only occurs in subordinate clauses.

Tense in subordinate contexts, including temporal clauses of the type we have been looking at, is often not a fully specified tense. Ogihara (1994, 256) points out that the semantic content of tense in the subordinate clause is determined "in relation to structurally higher tenses." The following example demonstrates this.

(35) a. [Hanako-ga te-o ageta toki] kore-o watasite
Hanako-NOM hand-ACC raised when this-ACC give
kudasai.
please
'Please hand this (to her) when Hanako (lit.) raised her hand.'

b. [Hanako-ga te-o ageru toki] kore-o watasite
Hanako-NOM hand-ACC raise when this-ACC give
kudasai.
please
'Please hand this (to her) when Hanako (lit.) raises her hand.'

In (35a), the inflection on the verb within the adverbial clause is that of past tense, yet the event it refers to occurs at a future time. The past inflection simply indicates a sequence in which first Hanako raises her hand and then an event of giving something to her should take place. In (35b), the verb within the temporal clause has the "present" inflection, but again denotes a future event. In this sentence, it simply refers to an event of Hanako raising her hand either after or at the same time as an event of giving something to Hanako. Ogihara (1994, 257) points out that "a present tense morpheme in a temporal adverbial clause shows that the episode described in it is simultaneous with (or is subsequent to) the event or state described in the matrix clause." What we see, then, is that in these temporal constructions, the subordinate tense is somehow not fully specified as tense in the sense that it is dependent on the higher tense for semantic determination.

We therefore have the following generalization for genitive subjects in general, whether they are licensed by D or by weak *v*.

(36) Genitive subjects in Japanese are contained in a TP headed by a T that is not fully specified as independent tense.

Although we can state the generalization in (36) to cover all instances of genitive subjects in Japanese, there is clearly a difference between the D-licensed type and the type licensed by weak *v*. The former occurs in a TP clause without a CP, which allows D to license the genitive in Spec,TP without violating minimality. We can see that lack of CP in a variety of ways, including the fact that a CP-level adverb cannot occur in a D-licensed genitive environment. On the other hand, the genitive licensed by weak *v* occurs within a CP, as indicated by the fact that a CP-level adverb occurs without a problem. We know that the D-licensed genitive is licensed by the D head. What about the genitive that is licensed by the weak *v*? It cannot just be any weak *v* since there is the additional condition that the T that takes the *v*P must be dependent tense. It appears, then, that this genitive is licensed by a combination of a weak *v* and dependent tense. Let us stipulate the following.

(37) Genitive of dependent tense
The combination of weak *v* + dependent tense licenses genitive case in Japanese.[7]

Presumably, this combination is implemented by *v* raising to T. Though merely a stipulation that needs to be derived from independent assumptions, (37) captures the fact that subjects with the GDT occur only in subordinate clauses, unlike what we see in Slavic, because dependent tense never occurs in the main clause. In Slavic, we can imagine a similar stipulation, not with dependent case, but with negation.

(38) In Slavic, the combination of weak *v* + negation licenses genitive case.[8]

Since both weak *v* and negation occur in root clauses as well as subordinate clauses, in Slavic the genitive may occur in root clauses.

In the remainder of this chapter, I will give further evidence for (37).

4 TEMPORAL ADJUNCTS VS. OTHER TYPES OF ADJUNCTS

We saw that the genitive subject is licensed within temporal adjuncts that clearly do not contain a D. These include 'when' and 'until'.

(39) Hanako-no kaeru toki/made, uti-ni ite-kudasai.
Hanako-GEN come home when/until home-at be-please
'When/until Hanako comes home, please be at home.'

The tense in all these temporal adjuncts may be dependent. We saw this for *toki* 'when' in (35) above; the following shows it for *made* 'until', which requires the preceding predicate to be in the present form.

(40) [Taroo-ga/-no kuru made] matte-ita.
Taro-NOM-GEN come until wait-PAST
'I waited until Taro came.'

I suggested that the GDT is licensed by a combination of weak *v* and dependent tense. This predicts that if a subordinate clause does not contain dependent tense, genitive should be impossible. The reason clause and *nara* conditionals are exactly such adjunct clauses. The tense marking on the subordinate verb is deictic, thus has independent tense reference based on time of speech.

(41) Hanako-ga kekkon-suru/*kekkon-sita kara/nara,
Hanako-GEN marry/married because/if
kanozyo-no kekkonsiki-ni de-tai.
her-GEN wedding-DAT attend-want
'Because/if Hanako is getting married/*got married, I'd like to attend her wedding.'

As predicted, the GDT cannot occur in either the reason clause or *nara* conditionals.[9]

(42) a. Hanako-ga/*-no kuru kara, uti-ni ite-kudasai.
Hanako-NOM/-GEN come because home-at be-please
'Because Hanako will come, please be at home.'

b. Ame-ga/*-no futta kara, miti-ga nurete-iru.
rain-NOM/-GEN fall because street-NOM wet-is
'Because it rained, the streets are wet.'

(43) a. Hanako-ga/*-no kuru nara, uti-ni ite-kudasai.
Hanako-NOM/-GEN come if home-at be-please
'If Hanako is coming, please be at home.'

b. Ame-ga/*-no furu nara, dekake-na-i.
rain-NOM/-GEN fall if go out-NEG-PRES
'If it rains, I won't go out.'

5 OBJECTS AND THE GENITIVE CASE

We have seen that the GDT is clearly different from its D-licensed counterpart. There is one issue that I have not focused on concerning the licensing condition for these two types of genitives, namely, is there a difference in the status of T in the two cases? In the D-licensing environment, because T is not selected by C, T is defective, and it cannot assign nominative case. That is the reason why the D that selects the TP can reach inside the TP and license the genitive case of the subject. What about the T involved in the GDT? The TP that contains this genitive is selected by C, as we saw from the fact that CP-level adverbs occur easily, so, we predict that unlike in the case of T for the D-licensed genitive, the T for GDT should be able to assign the nominative case. We will see that this prediction is borne out.

I drew a parallel in Section 3.1 between the GDT in Japanese and the genitive of negation in Slavic, showing that the internal argument of unaccusatives and passives may be licensed by weak *v* + dependent case in subordinate environments. There is so far one gap in this parallel, mentioned in note 8, namely that while the genitive of negation in Slavic may place genitive case on the direct object of transitive verbs, such a construction in Japanese is impossible.

Direct objects:

(44) a. Ja ne polučal pis'ma.
I NEG received letters.ACC.PL

b. Ja ne polučal pisem.
I NEG received letters.GEN.PL

(45) *[Hanako-ga tegami-no okutta] hito
Hanako-NOM letter-GEN sent person
'the person to whom Hanako sent a letter'

Is this a gap in the otherwise close parallel between the two types of genitive? As it turns out, there exists a parallel with the genitive of negation even here, in that, although objects of transitive verbs such as 'send' above cannot bear the genitive case marker, objects of stative predicates may do so. What is involved is an alternation between nominative and genitive case marking on stative objects. Objects of stative predicates in independent clauses are (optionally or obligatorily) marked as nominative, rather than accusative.

(46) Hanako-ga eigo-ga hanas-e-ru.
Hanako-NOM English-NOM speak-can-PRES
'Hanako can speak English.'

When we put this in a temporal adjunct clause, the following pattern of judgment emerges.

(47) a. [Ziroo-ga eigo-ga wakar-anakat-ta toki]
Jiro-NOM English-NOM understand-NEG-PAST when
Hanako-ga tasuke-ta.
Hanako-NOM help-PAST
'When Jiro didn't understand English, Hanako helped out.'

b. *[Ziroo-no eigo-ga wakar-anakat-ta toki]
Jiro-GEN English-NOM understand-NEG-PAST when
Hanako-ga tasuke-ta.
Hanako-NOM help-PAST

c. ?*[Ziroo-no eigo-no wakar-anakat-ta toki]
Jiro-GEN English-GEN understand-NEG-PAST when
Hanako-ga tasuke-ta.
Hanako-NOM help-PAST

d. [Ziroo-ga eigo-no wakar-anakat-ta toki]
Jiro-NOM English-GEN understand-NEG-PAST when
Hanako-ga tasuke-ta.
Hanako-NOM help-PAST

In (47a), both the subject and the object have nominative case, just as in (46), and there is no problem. In the ungrammatical (47b) and (47c), the subject has the genitive case; just as with Slavic, we do not expect the genitive on the subject of a transitive predicate. The striking example is (47d). In this example the subject has the nominative case and the object has the genitive case. This example is predicted to occur on our analysis because it is an instance of the GDT, and this genitive occurs with T that is selected by C. Though it is dependent tense, being selected by C, this T is capable of licensing the nominative on the subject. The *v* here is weak because the entire predicate is stative and the *v* does not assign accusative case. This *v*, in conjunction with the dependent tense, can license the genitive on the object.

Let us now look at the same construction, but in an environment where the genitive may be D-licensed. Unlike the GDT case above, all four possibilities are essentially fine (Miyagawa 1993).[10]

(48) a. Hanako-ga furansugo-ga hanas-e-ru koto NOM–NOM
Hanako-NOM French-NOM speak-can-PRES fact
'the fact that Hanako can speak French'

b. Hanako-no furansugo-ga hanas-e-ru koto GEN–NOM
Hanako-GEN French-NOM speak-can-PRES fact

c. Hanako-no furansugo-no hanas-e-ru koto GEN–GEN
Hanako-GEN French-GEN speak-can-PRES fact

d. Hanako-ga furansugo-no hanas-e-ru koto NOM–GEN
Hanako-NOM French-GEN speak-can-PRES fact

While transitive stative predicates mark their object with the nominative case, for complex statives like 'can speak' in (48) the object may alternatively be marked as accusative (see, e.g., Kuno 1973). However, Miyagawa (1993) assumes that the alternation on the object in (48) is strictly nominative–genitive and not accusative–genitive, because, as we saw earlier, an object that can only be marked by the accusative cannot bear the genitive case instead.

As we can see in (48), in the environment of a noun-complement clause whose predicate is a transitive stative, all four possible case combinations exist: the nominative case marking may alternate with the genitive on both the subject and object phrases. Assuming that the genitive on the subject is D-licensed—this is the only option, because, like in Slavic, the GDT does not occur on the subject of transitive predicates—what we want to know is the licensing mechanism for the genitive on the object.

Let us begin by asking about the size of the RC in each case. What we predict is that in those examples in which the subject is marked with the genitive, the RC is a TP, not a CP, because the genitive on the subject of a transitive predicate must be D-licensed. We can see that this prediction is borne out.

(49) a. saiwai-ni Hanako-ga furansugo-ga NOM–NOM
fortunately Hanako-NOM French-NOM
hanas-e-ru koto
speak-can-PRES fact
'the fact that Hanako fortunately can speak French'

b. *saiwai-ni Hanako-no furansugo-ga GEN–NOM
fortunately Hanako-GEN French-NOM
hanas-e-ru koto
speak-can-PRES fact

c. *saiwai-ni Hanako-no furansugo-no hanas-e-ru koto GEN–GEN
fortunately Hanako-GEN French-GEN speak-can-PRES fact

d. saiwai-ni Hanako-ga furansugo-no hanas-e-ru koto NOM–GEN
fortunately Hanako-NOM French-GEN speak-can-PRES fact

The relative clauses in examples (49b) and (49c), which contain a genitive subject, are not compatible with CP-level adverbs, while in (49a) and (49d), which have a nominative subject, the clause is demonstrably a CP.

Let us look at (49d), which has a nominative subject and a genitive object. The relative clause here is a CP, so the T is selected by C, and this gives T the ability to license the nominative on the subject. This is exactly the same construction as (47d), again showing that the T that enters into licensing of the genitive with the weak *v* may assign nominative, so that the only requirement on this T is that it be dependent tense, which it clearly is (Ogihara 1994). We can thus maintain the licensing condition given in (37) intact; it is repeated below.

(50) Genitive of dependent tense
The combination of weak *v* + dependent tense licenses genitive case in Japanese.

The examples in (48c) and (48b) raise questions that I will indicate here but will not attempt to answer. In (48c), both the subject and the object are marked with genitive case. We know that the genitive on the subject is D-licensed, but what about the genitive on the object? There are two possibilities, and I will simply list them. First, the genitive on the object may also be D-licensed under multiple agreement with the D head; we know that such multiple agreement occurs in Japanese (see, for example, Hiraiwa 2005). The other possibility is that the genitive on the object is the GDT kind, since the licensing condition is met (weak *v* + dependent tense). We have to account for the fact that the structure is TP, not CP, as shown by the fact that 'fortunately' is not possible.

In (48b), the subject is marked with the genitive case while the object has the nominative case. This example challenges the most straightforward analysis of the object nominative, namely, that it is licensed by T just like the subject nominative (Koizumi 1994; Ura 1999; Kishimoto 2001a; see also Takezawa 1987). One piece of evidence given for this analysis is that when the nominative alternates with the accusative on the object, the two case markers give rise to different scope interpretations (Sano 1985; Tada 1992). See Koizumi 2008 for a summary of the different approaches; the following is taken from his work, which, in turn, uses data from several previous works including Tada 1992.

(51) a. Kiyomi-wa migime-dake-o tumur-e-ru.
Kiyomi-TOP right eye-only-ACC close-can-PRES
'Kiyomi can close only his right eye.'
'can' > 'only' (Kiyomi can wink his right eye)

b. Kiyomi-wa migime-dake-ga tumur-e-ru.
Kiyomi-TOP right eye-only-NOM close-can-PRES
'Kiyomi can close only his right eye.'
'only' > 'can' (Kiyomi can't close his left eye)

As we can see in (51a), when the accusative case occurs on the object, this object takes scope low in the structure, presumably in its original position, but when the object has the nominative case as in (51b), it takes scope wider than the higher predicate 'can', suggesting that the nominative object raises to a position in the TP region. This would be consistent with the idea that the nominative is licensed by T. However, what we saw in (48b), which has a genitive subject and a nominative object, is an instance in which the T cannot assign nominative—because of the lack of C in this structure, as we know from the minimally different (49b)—yet the nominative shows up on the object. This may indicate that the T that cannot license the nominative on the subject may nevertheless somehow license nominative on the object; or, that the nominative object is somehow licensed differently, albeit by some high functional head, something that would be consistent with Tada's (1992) analysis. I will leave this question open.

Let us return to the main point of this chapter, namely, the phenomenon of the GDT. We saw in the transitive-stative-predicate construction that the examples in which a genitive object occurs with a nominative subject, such as (49d), are necessarily instances of the GDT. I will give further evidence for this analysis. Recall that one hallmark of the GDT is that the genitive phrase is unable to take scope above *v*P. In this regard, we can find in Miyagawa 1993 evidence that the genitive on the object in (49d) is the GDT. The following are taken from that work.

(52) a. Taroo-ga [tenisu-ka sakkaa]-ga dekiru riyuu NOM–NOM
Taro-NOM tennis-or soccer-NOM can reason
'the reason why Taro can play tennis or soccer'
'reason' > 'tennis or soccer', *'tennis or soccer' > 'reason'

b. Taroo-no [tenisu-ka sakkaa]-ga dekiru riyuu GEN–NOM
Taro-GEN tennis-or soccer-NOM can reason
'the reason why Taro can play tennis or soccer'
'reason' > 'tennis or soccer', *'tennis or soccer' > 'reason'

c. Taroo-no [tenisu-ka sakkaa]-no dekiru riyuu GEN–GEN
Taro-GEN tennis-or soccer-GEN can reason
'the reason why Taro can play tennis or soccer'
'reason' > 'tennis or soccer', 'tennis or soccer' > 'reason'

d. Taroo-ga [tenisu-ka sakkaa]-no dekiru riyuu NOM–GEN
Taro-NOM tennis-or soccer-GEN can reason
'the reason why Taro can play tennis or soccer'
'reason' > 'tennis or soccer', *'tennis or soccer' > 'reason'

In these examples, there is a disjunctive phrase ('tennis or soccer') in the object position, and in all but (52c), this phrase is incapable of taking scope over the head noun 'reason'. The reason why this object phrase can scope over the head noun is because both the subject and the object bear the genitive case, and, as noted earlier for (48c), there is an analysis available in which both genitive cases are licensed by D. At LF both can raise by QR outside of the TP and above the head noun in the absence of a CP projection.

(53)

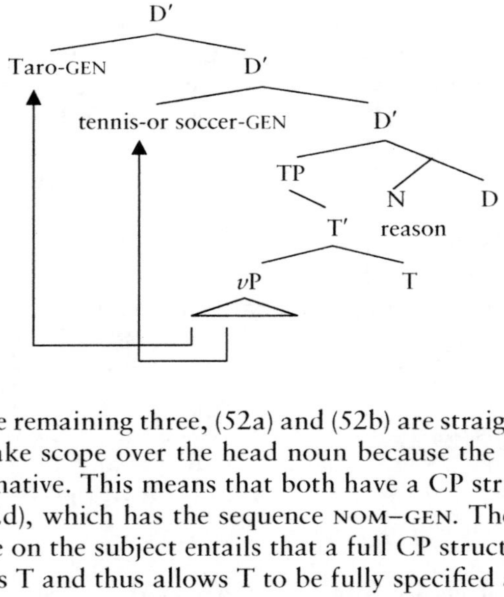

Of the remaining three, (52a) and (52b) are straightforward: the object cannot take scope over the head noun because the object is marked with the nominative. This means that both have a CP structure. Let us look finally at (52d), which has the sequence NOM–GEN. The occurrence of the nominative on the subject entails that a full CP structure exists, in which the C selects T and thus allows T to be fully specified and assign the nominative case. This account forces the analysis of the genitive on the object to be the GDT kind, not one that is D-licensed; consistent with this, as Takahashi (2010) observes, this object does not take scope over the head noun.

6 TWO REMAINING EXCEPTIONS

Watanabe (1996) cites the phenomenon of genitive subjects with comparatives as a counterexample to the D-licensing approach.

(54) John-wa [Mary-ga/-no yonda yori] takusan-no
John-TOP Mary-NOM/-GEN read-PAST-ADN than many-GEN
hon-o yonda.
books-ACC read-PAST
'John read more books than Mary did.' (Watanabe 1996, 396)

What is noteworthy is that the predicate that goes with the genitive subject in this example is a transitive verb, and hence it is not an instance of the GDT. What the comparative must represent, then, is an instance where there is a covert nominal head, as argued by Maki and Uchibori (2008) and from a different, semantic point of view by Sudo (2009). A piece of evidence for this covert-nominal analysis is that there are speakers who do not find Watanabe's example fully grammatical with the genitive. However, it becomes grammatical even for these speakers if the nominalizer *-no* is inserted (thanks to Hisako Takahashi for this point).

(55) John-wa [Mary-no yonda-**no** yori] takusan-no
John-TOP Mary-GEN read-PAST-ADN-*NO* than many-GEN
hon-o yonda.
books-ACC read-PAST
'John read more books than Mary did.'

This *-no* represents an overt nominal head, thus allowing D-licensing of the genitive. One way to view Watanabe's example is that what is covert is this nominal head *-no*, or some such semantically consistent head, an analysis that is consistent with Maki and Uchibori's (2008) approach. Furthermore, the comparative clause cannot host a CP adverb, which is predicted if D-licensing of the genitive is the only option.

(56) John-wa [saiwaini Mary-ga/?*-no yatotta(-**no**) yori]
John-TOP fortunately Mary-NOM/-GEN hire-PAST-ADN(-*NO*) than
takusan-no gakusei-o yato-e-nakat-ta.
many-GEN students-ACC hire-can-NEG-PAST
'John was unable to hire more students than Mary fortunately hired.'

This leaves the following counterexample (Hiraiwa 2002).

(57) [Boku-ga/-no omou-ni] John-wa Mary-ga
me-NOM/-GEN think.PRES.ADN-DAT John-TOP Mary-NOM
suki-ni-tigainai.
like-must-PRES
'I think that John likes Mary.'

The occurrence of the dative case marker suggests that this structure is a DP despite the fact that there is no indication of a nominal head. If so, this would be, like the comparative construction, an instance of a covert nominal head, as argued by Maki and Uchibori (2008). The subject is an external argument (subject of 'think'), hence the genitive case can only be the D-licensed kind based on all that we have seen.

7 CONCLUSION

In this chapter I gave evidence for a form of genitive case marking, the GDT, that is not licensed by D but rather by a combination of weak *v* and dependent tense. While this licensing condition itself must be derived from other assumptions, what we have been able to capture are similarities and differences between this genitive and the genitive of negation in Slavic. In both cases, the genitive occurs on the internal argument of a predicate—unaccusative subjects, passive subjects, and direct objects (in Japanese, only of stative predicates). In Slavic, the licensing condition for this type of genitive is, informally, a combination of weak *v* and negation, and since both of those things may occur in root clauses as well as subordinate clauses, the genitive of negation is not restricted to one or the other. In contrast, in Japanese, due to the fact that one element of the licensing condition is dependent tense, which only occurs in subordinate clauses, this type of genitive is restricted to subordinate clauses. Finally, we gave ample evidence that the GDT is different from the D-licensed genitive, which also occurs in Japanese, but with a clearly different distribution from the GDT.

7 Blocking and Japanese causatives[1]

1 INTRODUCTION

At an earlier stage in the development of generative grammar, when morphology was largely ignored, the lexicon was simply viewed as an unstructured list of lexical items (Chomsky 1965). However, the Lexicalist Hypothesis (Chomsky 1970) brought about a renewed interest in word formation, and it is now clear that the lexicon has a rich internal structure. Much of the recent work on morphology has focused on the principles governing the internal structure of words and the relationship of this to syntax (e.g., Aronoff 1976; Lieber 1980; Williams 1981b). A related and equally important issue that has not received as much attention is the question of how lexical items, both simple and complex, are actually listed in the lexicon. Are lexical items simply listed without regard to shared features, or are there organizing principles that group some items together? One observation, made by Aronoff (1976), indicates that lexical items are organized in the lexicon according to their meaning. Aronoff notes that when a morphologically complex word potentially shares the same *semantic space* as a simple one (e.g., **gloriosity*, *glory*), the former is *blocked* from occurring in the language. Clark and Clark (1979) have observed the same phenomenon (they name it *preemption*) with a wide range of denominal verbs. The idea of blocking presupposes a lexicon that is structured into groups of semantic slots. The slots grouped together share a significant semantic feature, and all lexical items that receive an entry must find an appropriate slot to enter. When a morphological derivative is produced from a base belonging to group X, the derivative must find a slot in X to enter in order for it to receive an entry; if the appropriate slot is already filled, the derivative is blocked from occurring in the language.

In this paper we will investigate how verbs are organized in the lexicon. It will be proposed that verbs are organized according to their meaning and the number of arguments they require. Every verb that receives an entry in the permanent lexicon must enter a slot in what we will term the Paradigmatic Structure (PDS); each PDS consists of three slots, Intransitive, Transitive, and Ditransitive. The PDS slots are first filled by verb stems, which are morphologically the simplest form of the verb; at this point, a PDS can have one, two, or all three slots filled depending on the existence of verb stems that share the appropriate meaning. To this are added morphological derivatives made up of a verb stem plus one or more derivational suffixes. A morphological derivative can receive entry in the permanent lexicon if it is able to enter a PDS slot; such a slot, if vacant, is in the same PDS as the base (verb stem) of the derivative. If the appropriate slot is already filled by a verb stem, the derivative is blocked, and will never enter the permanent lexicon. The PDS thus acts as a filter for the permanent lexicon, letting some derivatives in while blocking others.

The PDS will be motivated on the basis of the causative construction in Japanese. There are two dependent causative morphemes in Japanese, *-sas* and *-sase*. We will show that the complex causative verb built from either *-sas* or *-sase* manifests effects of blocking. Unlike previously noted cases of blocking, however, blocked causative verbs occur freely in the language, they just behave differently from unblocked ones. A causative verb that is not blocked by the existence of a corresponding verb stem enters a PDS slot. When this happens, the unblocked causative verb manifests characteristics normally associated with simple verb stems, thereby leading us to characterize the PDS as a filter for the permanent lexicon. The data we provide on causatives give a much more convincing argument for blocking than Aronoff's; our data are more comprehensive, and even within the small set of data used by Aronoff, there are some disagreements in judgment (cf. note 4).

This chapter is organized as follows. In Section 2, relevant data involving the *-sas* causative verb are given to motivate the PDS and to demonstrate effects of blocking. Data from Mitla Zapotec are also given for cross-linguistic evidence for the PDS. In Section 3, we turn to the other causative morpheme, *-sase*. It is shown that *-sase* causatives likewise participate in the PDS unless blocked. Those that enter the PDS exhibit lexical behavior commonly associated with simple verbs, thereby suggesting that the PDS acts as a filter for the permanent lexicon. Because both the *-sas* and *-sase* causatives can potentially enter the PDS, they are always competing for the same slot. The consequences of this are investigated in Section 4. In Section 5, we turn to the syntax of causatives. Previous accounts postulate a complex underlying structure, with the *-sase/-sas* morpheme as the "higher" verb. We propose instead that the causative verb is formed in the lexicon, because of its clearly lexical characteristics vis-à-vis the PDS. To also account for the "complex structure" behavior of this verb, we present an argument that a causative verb is associated with parallel structures, one simplex, the other complex, both projected directly from the lexicon.

2 THE CAUSATIVE CONSTRUCTION WITH *-SAS*

-sas and *-sase*, the two causative morphemes in Japanese,[2] attach to a verb stem or a complex verb to form a complex causative verb. We will refer to

such verbs as V-*sas* and V-*sase*. (-*sas* and -*sase* appear as -*as* and -*ase* when attached to a consonant-ending verb; the vowel *i* is inserted after -*sas* when a consonant-initial morpheme follows.)

(1) a. Taroo-ga Hanako-ni hon-o yom-**asi**-ta.
Taro-NOM Hanako-DAT book-ACC read-CAUS-PAST
'Taro made/let Hanako read the book.'

b. Taroo-ga Hanako-ni hon-o yom-**ase**-ta.

Both morphemes are highly productive, and in many cases they have the analytical meaning of 'cause X to V'. When they do not share this meaning, it is usually because -*sas* has a lexical-causative interpretation in addition to the analytical interpretation, while -*sase* only has the analytical interpretation.

2.1 V-*sas* and V-*sase*

While many V-*sas* are synonymous with their corresponding V-*sase*, cases exist in which identity of meaning does not obtain. The following are taken from Shibatani 1973, 346–347.

(2) a. Taroo-ga isu-o ugok-**asi**-ta.
Taro-NOM chair-ACC move-CAUS-PAST
'Taro moved the chair.'

b. *Taroo-ga isu-o ugok-**ase**-ta.

(3) a. Taroo-ga yu-o wak-**asi**-ta.
Taro-NOM (hot) water-ACC boil-CAUS-PAST
'Taro boiled the water.'

b. *Taroo-ga yu-o wak-**ase**-ta.

In these examples, V-*sas* has a straightforward transitive (lexical-causative) interpretation. The unacceptability of *ugok-ase* and *wak-ase* is due to the fact that the causee in the analytical causative must be animate and self-propelled (Shibatani 1973). The difference between the lexical-causative and analytical-causative interpretations becomes clear if we replace *isu* 'chair' in (2) with an animate noun, making both causative morphemes possible.

(4) a. Taroo-ga boo-o tukatte Ziroo-o ugok-**asi**-ta.
Taro-NOM stick-ACC using Jiro-ACC move-CAUS-PAST
'Taro moved Jiro using a stick.'

b. Taroo-ga boo-o tukatte Ziroo-o ugok-**ase**-ta.
'Taro made Jiro move using a stick.'

Example (4a) has the interpretation that Taro physically moved Jiro with a stick, but (4b) implies that Taro used the stick to direct Jiro to move. Shibatani gives the following pair that also illustrates the lexical–analytical distinction.

(5) a. Eiga kantoku-ga motto umaku zyoyuu-o odorok-**asi**-ta.
movie director-NOM better actress-ACC surprise-CAUS-PAST
'The movie director surprised the actress better.'

b. Eiga kantoku-ga motto umaku zyoyuu-o odorok-**ase**-ta.
'The movie director made the actress be surprised better.'

The sentence in (5a) is interpreted to mean the movie director literally surprised the actress, for example, by sneaking up on her. Example (5b), on the other hand, has the director directing the actress to act surprised more convincingly.

2.2 Verbal paradigm and blocking

We have seen V-*sas* with a lexical-causative meaning that distinguishes it from the analytical V-*sase*. But there are many instances in which V-*sas* has only the analytical interpretation, making it indistinguishable from V-*sase*. Is there a way to predict when a V-*sas* has the lexical interpretation?

V-*sas* has the lexical meaning when there is no corresponding monomorphemic verb stem (Shibatani 1973, 348).[3] Take the intransitive verb *odorok* 'be surprised' in (5). This verb lacks a simple transitive form. As a result, the V-*sas*, *odorok-as*, acts as its transitive counterpart and is associated with the lexical-causative meaning. The intransitive verbs *ugok* 'move' in (2) and *wak* 'boil' in (3) likewise lack a unique transitive counterpart, allowing *ugok-as* and *wak-as* to be associated with the lexical-causative interpretation. To capture this, let us suppose that a verb stem is associated with a PDS of the type illustrated below for *odorok* 'be surprised'.

(6)

INTR	TR	DITR
odorok		

Because the transitive slot for this verb is vacant, the V-*sas*, *odorok-as*, fills this slot and acquires the straightforward "transitive" interpretation of a lexical causative. We will assume that each and every stem has to fit into such a PDS.

2.2.1 Blocking

Let us now see what happens to the interpretation of V-*sas* if a corresponding simple transitive verb does exist. The transitive–intransitive pair *agar* 'rise' and *age* 'raise' is comprised of two "unique" verbs in the sense that one cannot be morphologically derived from the other in any principled way. The PDS for this pair is given in (7).

(7)

INTR	TR	DITR
agar	age	

If we attach *-sas* to the intransitive *agar*, the resulting V-*sas* can only be associated with the analytical interpretation. Examples (8) and (9) illustrate this.

(8) a. Taroo-ga boo-o tukatte kodomo-o hako-no ue-ni
Taro-NOM stick-ACC using child-ACC box-GEN top-on
age-ta.
raise-PAST
'Taro raised the child onto the box using a stick.'

b. Taroo-ga boo-o tukatte kodomo-o hako-no ue-ni agar-**asi**-ta.
'Taro made the child get up on the box using a stick.'

(9) a. Taroo-ga hon-o atama-no ue-ni age-ta.
Taro-NOM book-ACC head-GEN top-on raise-PAST
'Taro raised the book above his head.'

b. *Taroo-ga hon-o atama-no ue-ni agar-**asi**-ta.
(Intended: 'Taro made the book rise above his head.')

In (8a), the simple transitive verb *age* 'raise' has the lexical-causative interpretation, implying that a stick was used to physically raise the child onto the box. The sentence in (8b), with *agar-as* 'cause to rise', can only be associated with the analytical-causative meaning; hence, the stick was used to direct the child onto the box. Example (9a), with the simple transitive, is fine with the inanimate causee *hon* 'book'. However, an inanimate causee is unacceptable with *agar-as* 'cause to rise' as in (9b), again showing that the V-*sas* here is associated with only the analytical interpretation, which requires an "animate and self-propelled" causee.

We will characterize the inability of *agar-as* to be associated with the lexical-causative meaning as a case of blocking. A V-*sas* is blocked from filling a PDS slot if a simple verb stem already occupies that slot. As a result, the V-*sas* is incapable of taking on the lexical-causative interpretation, leaving it with the analytical interpretation identical to V-*sase*.

Aronoff (1976) originally proposed the concept of blocking to explain certain gaps in English morphological derivatives. The following is taken from Aronoff 1976.

(10)

X*ous*	Nominal	+*ity*
various	*	variety
curious	*	curiosity
glorious	glory	*gloriosity
furious	fury	*furiosity

The +*ity* suffix attaches to a X*ous* adjective to form a nominal. While *variety* and *curiosity* occur, **gloriosity* and **furiosity* do not because they are blocked by the existence of the simple nominals *glory* and *fury*. Aronoff thus assumes that a blocked item is a nonoccurring item that otherwise follows a regular morphological rule.[4]

Our examination of V-*sas* shows that the process of blocking does not always entail nonoccurrence. A V-*sas* is blocked if it is unable to enter a PDS slot due to the existence of a simple verb stem already occupying that slot. Unlike **gloriosity* and **furiosity*, the blocked V-*sas* does occur, but it is incapable of taking on the lexical-causative meaning. A universal characterization of blocking is then that it is a process by which one item is barred from entering a semantic slot due to the existence of another item already occupying that slot. Whether or not a blocked item will actually occur in the language is an independent issue, one that should not be included as a necessary part of the definition of blocking. Indeed, within one language, one finds both occurring and nonoccurring blocked items. While **gloriosity* does not arise in English, *cooker* does occur even though it is blocked from having the predicted agentive meaning due to the existence of *cook*; *cooker* as a result "shifts" to have the meaning of a cooking implement (Kiparsky 1982).

2.3 Further evidence

The establishment of the verbal PDS together with the universal characterization of blocking predicts precisely when a V-*sas* is associated with the lexical-causative interpretation. We now present data from Mitla Zapotec that give further support for the PDS.

In Mitla Zapotec, the causative prefix *s-* attaches to an intransitive verb such as *niʔ* 'move' to form the transitive *s-niʔ* 'move'; this *s-* can also attach to a transitive verb to form a ditransitive verb, as in *gidza* 'scold', *s-gidza* 'cause to scold'. This is a productive morphological process, but there are gaps in the occurrence of the derived causative verbs, gaps that are consistent with the PDS and blocking.[5]

(11) a. niʔ 'move$_{\text{INTR}}$'
b. s-niʔ 'move$_{\text{TR}}$'

(12) a. gidza 'scold'
b. s-gidza 'cause to scold'

(13) a. riʔ 'come/go out'
b. *s-riʔ
c. Læʔ 'take out'

(14) a. yabtaʔ 'fall down'
b. *s-yabtaʔ
c. zæltaʔ 'knock down'

(15) a. dauch 'eat'
b. *s-dauch
c. yaæn 'feed'

The *s-* derivatives occur in (11) and (12). But they do not in (13)–(15); in their place is a corresponding unique verb stem. The existence of the simple verb thus blocks the *s-* derivative, resulting in its nonoccurrence. The PDSs for these verbs are illustrated below.

	INTR	TR	DITR
(16)	niʔ 'move'	s-niʔ 'move'	
(17)		gidza 'scold'	s-gizda 'cause to scold'
(18)	riʔ 'come/go out'	Læʔ 'take out'	
		*s-riʔ (blocked)	
(19)	yabtal 'fall down'	zaeltaʔ 'knock down'	
		*s-yabtaʔ (blocked)	
(20)		dauch 'eat'	yaæn 'feed'
			*s-dauch (blocked)

Unlike the Japanese V-*sas*, a blocked *s*-V in Mitla Zapotec does not occur in the language. This is probably because *s-* itself only carries the lexical-causative meaning; the analytical causative is expressed by a periphrastic construction. Consequently, when *s*-V is blocked, it is prohibited from being associated with the only possible meaning it can have, and the derivative thus fails to occur in the language. V-*sas* on the other hand has the analytical-causative meaning to "fall back on" when it is blocked from a slot that would allow its association with the lexical-causative interpretation.

3 THE CAUSATIVE CONSTRUCTION WITH -*SASE*

The PDS has been proposed to deal with the two possible interpretations of V-*sas*, a strictly analytical-causative interpretation and a lexical-causative interpretation. We will now look at the other causative morpheme, -*sase*. It will be shown that this causative verb also participates in the PDS. Because a V can usually take either -*sas* or -*sase*, this leads to the conclusion that a V-*sas* and the corresponding V-*sase* are always competing for the same PDS slot. We take up this problem in Section 4. The lexical behaviors exhibited by V-*sase* vis-à-vis the PDS give further indication that the PDS functions as a filter for the permanent lexicon. We begin our discussion with the PDS.

3.1 The PDS

The PDS is a hypothesis about how verbs are organized in the lexicon. According to this hypothesis, verbs are arranged in the lexicon according to the meaning and the number of arguments they take. The PDS has three slots, "Intransitive," "Transitive," and "Ditransitive"; one verb, either simple or complex, may be placed into each slot. A verb stem, being the morphologically simplest form, automatically enters a PDS slot. Before morphological derivation takes place, all PDS slots that are filled are filled only by verb stems. At this point, a PDS may have only one of its slots filled, for example, the "Intransitive" slot, as in the case of *odorok* 'be surprised', which has no simple transitive counterpart, or just the "Transitive" slot filled, as in the case of *tabe* 'eat'; some PDSs may have two slots filled, as in *ak* 'open$_{\text{INTR}}$' and *ake* 'open$_{\text{TR}}$', or the Mitla Zapotec case of *dauch* 'eat' and *yaæn* 'feed'. These possible PDSs are illustrated below.

		INTR	TR	DITR
(21)	a.	hasir 'run'		
	b.		tabe 'eat'	
	c.	ak 'open'	ake 'open'	
	d.		dauch 'eat'	yaæn 'feed'

Henceforth, we will refer to any verb that occupies a PDS slot as having *PDS status*.

All verb stems by nature are part of the permanent lexicon; by virtue of this, they are always available for any pertinent lexical processes such as semantic drift or nominalization. Verb stems are also automatically given PDS status since they are the morphologically simplest form of the verb. We propose that this relationship between the permanent lexicon and PDS is not an accident, but rather is a necessary condition. The PDS is a filter that allows some but not all lexical items to enter the permanent lexicon. If a lexical item attains PDS status, it then becomes a candidate for the permanent lexicon, but if it is blocked by the existence of another lexical item, it will never become a member of the permanent lexicon unless another slot is found into which it can enter (cf. *cooker* in English). In the case of verbs, only one potential slot is available. Consequently, if a verb is blocked, it will never attain PDS status, in turn failing to enter the permanent lexicon. Languages differ on how they treat blocked items: in Mitla Zapotec, blocked *s*-V causative verbs simply do not occur, but in Japanese a blocked causative verb may occur in the language. What we observed for V-*sas* is that a V-*sas* that has PDS status may be associated with the lexical-causative interpretation, but a blocked V-*sas* can only be associated with the analytical interpretation 'X cause Y to V'. The lexical-causative interpretation is most commonly found among simple transitive verbs, as in *tome* 'stop$_{\text{TR}}$' and *age* 'raise'. A V-*sas* that attains PDS status is thus used to fill a gap in the paradigm of verb stems. In so doing, the V-*sas* is treated as a simple verb, one that can enter the permanent lexicon.

3.2 The causative morpheme -*sase*

We now turn our attention to the other causative morpheme in Japanese, -*sase*. We will give three arguments to demonstrate that a V-*sase* receives PDS status unless blocked by a simple verb or by V-*sas*. In so doing, we will give further support to the idea that the PDS is a filter for the permanent lexicon.

3.2.1 Nominalization

There are a large number of nominals that use a simple verb stem in their formation. The nominal may simply be a nominalized verbal infinitive, as in *hare* 'clear weather' (*hare* 'to clear up'), *tanomi* 'request' (*tanom* 'to request'), and *amari* 'remainder' (*amar* 'to remain'); or it can be a compound composed of a verbal infinitive and a noun, as in *tabe-mono* 'food' (*tabe* 'to eat', *mono* 'thing'), *nori-mono* 'vehicle' (*nor* 'to ride'), and *tate-mono* 'building' (*tate* 'to build'). Since all verb stems automatically receive PDS status, we can hypothesize based on the large number of these nominals that nominalization is a process available only to verbs that enter the PDS and are hence in the permanent lexicon.

Based on this, we can show that V-*sase* participates in the PDS if we find nominals based on a V-*sase*. There are in fact such nominals:

(22)	a. sir-**ase**	'notice'	(sir 'to know')
	b. aw-**ase**	'garment lining'	(aw 'to fit')
	c. asob-**ase**-uta	'children's song'	(asob 'to play', uta 'song')
	d. kuw-**ase**-mono	'fake'	(kuw 'to receive harm', mono 'thing')
	e. iya-gar-**ase**	'harassment'	(iya-gar 'to be bothered')

In each of these, the V-*sase* does not have a corresponding simple verb; for instance, there is no simple transitive counterpart of *aw* 'to fit' or *asob* 'to play'. The last nominal given above, *iya-gar-ase* 'harassment', is especially noteworthy. The V to which -*sase* attaches here is made up of an adjective/adjectival nominal (*iya*) and the verbalizer -*gar*. As shown in (23), this verbalizer regularly attaches to "psych" adjectives/adjectival nominals to form a verb, as in *tanosi* 'fun', *tanosi-gar* 'to enjoy'; *uresi* 'happy', *uresi-gar* 'to be happy'. Now, along with the nominal *iya-gar-ase* 'harassment' we find *uresi-gar-ase* 'flattery' (*uresi-gar* 'to be happy'), but not **kanasi-gar-ase* (*kanasi-gar* 'to be sad') or **tanosi-gar-ase* (*tanosi-gar* 'to enjoy'). The PDS hypothesis predicts the gaps because of the existence of a simple intransitive form corresponding to *kanasi-gar* and *tanosi-gar*; no such corresponding simple forms exist for *iya-gar* or *uresi-gar*.

(23)	Adjective/ adjectival nominal	Verb	V-*sase*	Nominalized V-*sase*
	iya 'bothersome'	iya-gar 'to be bothered'	iya-gar-ase	iya-gar-ase 'harassment'
	uresi 'happy'	uresi-gar 'to be happy'	uresi-gar-ase	uresi-gar-ase 'flattery'
	kanasi 'sad'	kanasi-gar 'to be sad'	kanasi-gar-ase	*kanasi-gar-ase
		kanasim 'to be sad'	kanasim-ase	
	tanosi 'fun'	tanosi-gar 'to enjoy'	tanosi-gar-ase	*tanosi-gar-ase
		tanosim 'to enjoy'	tanosim-ase	

Note that, in the "Verb" column, the first two verbs, *iya-gar* 'to be bothered' and *uresi-gar* 'to be happy' lack a corresponding simple verb; and, as shown in the "Nominalized V-*sase*" column, the V-*sase* counterparts of these occur in a nominal. The last two, *kanasi-gar* 'to be sad' and *tanosi-gar* 'to enjoy', on the other hand do have corresponding simple verbs, *kanasim* and *tanosim*. According to the PDS scheme, *kanasi-gar* and *tanosi-gar* are blocked from entering a PDS slot by the existence of the simple verbs. Since neither *kanasi-gar* nor *tanosi-gar* attains PDS status, their V-*sase* counterparts likewise fail to enter a PDS slot, leading to the prediction that no nominal exists that exhibits these V-*sase*. This is shown in the "Nominalized V-*sase*" column. The paradigm in (23) thus gives credence to the assumption that a V-*sase* does enter a PDS slot unless it is somehow blocked. While the causative verbs *iya-gar-ase* and *uresi-gar-ase* enter a PDS slot, making them available for nominalization, *kanasi-gar-ase* and *tanosi-gar-ase* do not (even though they do occur in the language) because *kanasi-gar* and *tanosi-gar* are blocked by the existence of corresponding simple verbs *kanasim* and *tanosim*. It is noteworthy that these simple verbs appear in nominals, namely *kanasimi* 'sadness' and *tanosimi* 'pleasure', the existence of which gives further evidence that these, but not the corresponding *-gar* verbs, enter the PDS.

3.2.2 Verb-phrase idioms

The second piece of evidence that V-*sase* is subject to the PDS involves one type of idiomatic expression. A large number of idioms exist that are composed of a transitive verb and direct-object NP. Most of these VP idioms contain a simple verb, but there are some that contain a V-*sase*. Zenno (1983) points out a clear pattern in the distribution of simple verbs and V-*sase* in idioms: when a simple verb occurs, the corresponding V-*sase* is never a possible replacement, and conversely, when a V-*sase* does occur, it is always the case that the corresponding simple transitive verb is nonexistent. Examples (24) and (25) exemplify this distribution.

(24) VP idioms with a simple transitive verb

a. iki-o nuk/*nuke-**sase**
breath-ACC pull/be pulled-CAUS
'to relax'

b. ago-o das/*de-**sase**
chin-ACC push out/come out-CAUS
'to give up'

c. me-o toos/*toor-**ase**
eye-ACC go through$_{TR}$/go through$_{INTR}$-CAUS
'read through'

d. tenoura-o kaes/*kaer-**ase**
back of hand-ACC return$_{TR}$/return$_{INTR}$-CAUS
'to betray'

(25) VP idioms with V-*sase*

a. hana-o sak-**ase**
flower-ACC bloom-CAUS
'to succeed'

b. hara-o her-**ase**
stomach-ACC decrease-CAUS
'to be hungry'

c. haba-o kik-**ase**
width-ACC be effective-CAUS
'to make one's influence felt'

d. hana-o ugomek-**ase**
nose-ACC wiggle-CAUS
'to try to sniff'

e. kao-o aw-**ase**
face-ACC meet-CAUS
'to meet'

None of the V-*sase* in (25) has a corresponding simple transitive verb.

An idiom by definition is associated with a meaning that cannot be derived from the composition of its parts. In each of the examples in (24) and (25) the phrase as a whole has undergone semantic drift to be associated with the noncompositional meaning; the idiom as a whole must thus be listed in the permanent lexicon with the noncompositional meaning. The point of interest for us is the complementary distribution of simple verbs and V-*sase*: a simple transitive in an idiom cannot be replaced by V-*sase*, and, more importantly, when a V-*sase* does appear, it always lacks a corresponding simple verb. This is a straightforward PDS effect: a V-*sase* in an idiom is one that attains PDS status, making it a member of the permanent lexicon, in turn making it available for idiomatization/ semantic drift.

3.2.3 Adversity causatives

Oehrle and Nishio (1981) point out that a simple transitive verb in Japanese has (at least) two interpretations, as shown in (26).

(26) Taroo-ga ie-o yai-ta.
Taroo-NOM house-ACC burn-PAST
(i) 'Taro burned his house (intentionally or otherwise).'
(ii) 'Taro's house burned, and he was adversely affected by this event (he did not cause the burning, intentionally or otherwise).'

They call this second interpretation the "adversity causative." They point out that a V-*sase* can also be associated with the adversity-causative interpretation, but there is a condition: a V-*sase* has this interpretation only if it lacks a corresponding simple transitive verb (Oehrle and Nishio 1981, 168). For example, ***kusar-ase*** 'cause to rot' can be associated optionally with the adversity interpretation because there is no corresponding simple transitive for ***kusar*** 'rot'.

(27) Taroo-ga yasai-o kusar-**ase**-ta.
Taroo-NOM vegetable-ACC rot-CAUS-PAST
(i) 'Taro caused the vegetable to rot.'
(ii) 'The vegetable rotted on Taro.'

But *sizum-ase* 'cause to sink', which has the corresponding simple transitive *sizume* 'sink$_{TR}$', only has the analytical reading.

(28) a. Taroo-ga hune-o sizume-ta.
Taroo-NOM boat-ACC sink-PAST
(i) 'Taro sank the boat.'
(ii) 'The boat sank on Taro.'

b. Taroo-ga hune-o sizum-**ase**-ta.
(i) 'Taro caused the boat to sink.'
(ii) *'The boat sank on Taro.'

We conclude that the adversity-causative interpretation for V-*sase* is governed by the PDS.

Nominalization, semantic drift (idiomatization), and the adversity-causative reading are common phenomena observed for simple verbs. These are, in other words, phenomena commonly associated with verbs with PDS status, which are members of the permanent lexicon. The fact that, for example, a verb has undergone semantic drift, either by itself or in an idiomatic phrase, demonstrates that the verb is a member of the permanent lexicon. If it is not listed as such, it cannot take on the additional, noncompositional meaning. A V-*sase* can also be associated with the same set of phenomena, but only if it has PDS status, that is, if it is not blocked. This demonstrates that the PDS is a filter for the permanent lexicon, letting the unblocked V-*sase* through and, in turn, making it available for processes associated with the verbs of the permanent lexicon.

4 V-*SAS* AND V-*SASE*

We have evidence to show that both V-*sas* and V-*sase* can enter the PDS unless blocked. Because -*sas* and -*sase* attach to virtually any V, this leads us to conclude that V-*sas* and V-*sase* with the same V compete for the same transitive PDS slot; the one that successfully enters the PDS blocks the other from doing so. We will see that this is indeed the case. However, there are some cases in which both appear to have PDS status. This would be in violation of what we have been assuming all along, that only one item is allowed per slot. For these cases, we show that in fact only V-*sase* enters the PDS, and the -*sas* here is a free morphological variant of -*sase*. This -*sase*/-*sas* morphological alternation is governed by the PDS in that only V-*sase* with PDS status can freely alternate with -*sas*. This -*sas* is simply an allomorph of -*sase*, and is to be differentiated from the -*sas* we examined in Section 2, which is a full-fledged morpheme.

4.1 Where V-*sas* and V-*sase* compete

We now present evidence that either the V-*sas* or the V-*sase*, but not both, can have PDS status. If V-*sas* has entered the PDS, its existence blocks V-*sase*, and vice versa.

4.1.1 VP idioms

There are VP idioms that contain V-*sas* but do not allow the corresponding V-*sase*. (The reverse generalization does not hold: see (35) and (36).) The data is taken from Zenno 1983.

(29) fuhei-o nar-**as/*-ase**
complaint-ACC sound out-CAUS
'to complain'

(30) mimi-o sum-**as/*-ase**
ear-ACC clear-CAUS
'to try to listen'

(31) saku-o megur-**as/*-ase**
fence-ACC circle-CAUS
'to plan carefully'

(32) himitu-o mor-**as/*-ase**
secret-ACC leak-CAUS
'to tell a secret'

In these cases, only V-*sas* has PDS status, which allows it to undergo idiomatization. The V-*sase* is blocked from entering the PDS by the existence of the V-*sas*.

4.1.2 Nominalization

We saw in the previous section that nominalization is a process associated with PDS-status verbs. When we look at the various nominals that exhibit the causative morpheme, we note that they have either V-*sas* or V-*sase*; no nominal exists in which both V-*sas* and V-*sase* are possible. Example (33) gives nominals that exhibit V-*sas*; (34) gives nominals with V-*sase*.

(33) Nominals with V-*sas*

a. o-sum-**asi** 'clear soup'	*o-sum-**ase**	(sum 'to clear')
b. megur-**asi**-bumi 'palindrome'	*megur-**ase**-bumi	(megur 'to circle', bumi 'sentence')
c. waraw-**asi** 'a funny thing'	*waraw-**ase**	(waraw 'to laugh')
d. wak-**asi**-tugi 'welded connection'	*wak-**ase**-tugi	(wak 'to boil', tugi 'connection')
e. odorok-**asi** 'threat, scare'	*odorok-**ase**	(odorok 'to be surprised')

(34) Nominals with V-*sase*

a. iya-gar-**ase** 'harassment'	*iya-gar-**asi**	(iya-gar 'to be bothered')
b. aw-**ase** 'garment lining'	*aw-**asi**	(aw 'to fit')
c. sir-**ase** 'notice'	*sir-**asi**	(sir 'to know')
d. asob-**ase**-uta 'children's song'	*asob-**asi**-uta	(asob 'to play')
e. kuw-**ase**-mono 'fake'	*kuw-**asi**-mono	(kuw 'to receive damage')

In (33), only the V-*sas* has attained PDS status, but not the V-*sase*, making it possible to undergo nominalization. In contrast, (34) gives cases where V-*sase* has PDS status, thus blocking V-*sas* from appearing in a nominal.

It is noteworthy that the V-*sas* in (33a), *sum-as*, and the one in (33b), *megur-as*, also appear in idioms that do not allow V-*sase* (cf. (30) and (31)). This is not surprising, and in fact predicted, since a V-*sas* with PDS status is subject to any process that applies to verbs in the permanent lexicon, including nominalization and idiomatization. What we do not expect to find is a nominalized V-*sas* and its corresponding V-*sase* appearing in an idiom (or vice versa). If we find a V-*sas* in a nominal, this indicates that it has PDS status, and its existence blocks the corresponding V-*sase*. This V-*sase* would never appear in an idiom or with any other phenomenon associated with the permanent lexicon. We have not found any cases that counterexemplify this prediction made by the PDS.

4.2 Two types of *-sas*

There are cases in which both V-*sas* and V-*sase* appear to have PDS status in violation of the "one-item-per-slot" assumption. For example, the VP idiom in (35) tolerates either *-sase* or *-sas*.

(35) me-o kagayak-**ase/-as**
eye-ACC shine
'to look with envy'

Based on the assumption that a V-*sas* or V-*sase* can undergo idiomatization only if it has PDS status, we are here faced with the problem of having to admit both V-*sase* and V-*sas* into the same PDS slot. Once we allow this, however, our entire theory of PDS and blocking is put on questionable ground: if more than one item can enter a PDS slot, why aren't the "blocked" cases of V-*sase*/V-*sas* in our previous discussions allowed to enter the PDS along with the corresponding simple verb? What we propose instead is that cases such as (35) illustrate a second type of *-sas*, one that is different from the regular dependent morpheme *-sas*. This second type is simply an allomorph of *-sase*, but there is a condition on when this allomorph can appear. The *-sase* in V-*sase* can freely alternate with the allomorph *-sas* only if the V-*sase* has PDS status. This then is another manifestation of the PDS effect. According to this, only the V-*sase*, *kagayak-ase*, in (35) enters the PDS, its existence thus blocking the corresponding V-*sas*; the *-sas* form that is also possible is the result of morphological alternation available to a V-*sase* with PDS status. By this analysis, we are able to maintain the "one-item-per-slot" assumption for the PDS.

Let us look at VP idioms again. We know that there are idioms that allow only V-*sas*. We have also seen idioms that contain a V-*sase*. What is crucial to note here is that, when a V-*sase* appears in an idiom, *-sas* is *always* possible as an alternate form. Thus all of the V-*sase* idioms in (25) can be expressed with *-sas* as well.

(36) a. hana-o sak-**ase/-as** 'to succeed'
b. hara-o her-**ase/-as** 'to become hungry'
c. haba-o kik-**ase/-as** 'to make one's influence felt'
d. hana-o ugomek-**ase/-as** 'to try to sneeze'
e. kao-o aw-**ase/-as** 'to meet'

These idioms mean exactly the same whether V-*sase* or V-*sas* is used. Consequently, we can postulate one of the forms to be basic and the other as a morphological variant. The question is, which is the basic form, V-*sase* or V-*sas*?

We propose that the basic form is V-*sase*. First of all, there are idiomatic phrases with V-*sas* that do not allow V-*sase* as an alternative (examples are in (29)–(32)). If V-*sas* were the basic form, then we would expect V-*sase* to also be possible. In contrast, when a V-*sase* does appear in an idiom, -*sas* is always possible as well. Secondly, some of the instances of V-*sase* that alternate freely with -*sas* also appear in nominals.

(37)	V-*sase*	Nominal	
a.	aw-**ase/-as** 'to join'	aw-**ase** 'garment lining'	*aw-**asi**
b.	sir-**ase/-as** 'to notify'	sir-**ase** 'notice'	*sir-**asi**
c.	asob-**ase/-as** 'to make/let play'	asob-**ase**-uta 'children's song'	*asob-**asi**-uta
d.	iya-gar-**ase/-as** 'to harass'	iya-gar-**ase** 'harassment'	*iya-gar-**asi**

All of the -*sase/-sas* alternating verbs lack a corresponding simple verb, making them candidates for the PDS; what we find in every case is that a nominal exhibits V-*sase,* but not V-*sas*. Since nominalization is a sign of PDS status, we conclude that the V-*sase*, but not the V-*sas*, has attained this status. We further conclude that -*sas* is an allomorph of -*sase* for V-*sase* with PDS status, and that this verbal allomorphy does not carry over to the nominalized form.

We can add this -*sase/-sas* alternation to the list of phenomena associated with PDS-status V-*sase*. We also predict that this phenomenon should be found among simple verbs in the same manner as idiomatization, nominalization, and the adversity-causative interpretation. There are in fact two verb stems, *nek-ase/-as* 'make/let sleep' and *mak-ase/-as* 'entrust', that allow either -*sase* or -*sas* in their form without changing meaning. These are simple verbs because they cannot be derived from any regular morphological rule: the intransitive of *nek-ase/-as* is *ne* 'sleep'; *mak-ase/-as* lacks an intransitive in modern Japanese. Based on our previous discussion, we can conclude that *nekase* and *makase* are the basic forms listed in the lexicon; the -*sas* forms arise from the morphological alternation available to all PDS status verbs that exhibit -*sase*.

5 DERIVATION OF V-*SASE*

In this section we will propose that V-*sase* is associated with dual syntactic structures.

5.1 The standard analysis

Since Kuroda 1965, a great deal of work has been done on the causative construction in Japanese. Virtually all of the research has focused on the

-sase construction, in part on the wrong assumption that *-sas* is *only* a morphological alternant of *-sase*. With few exceptions, the various analyses regard *-sase* as an independent verb, thereby postulating a complex underlying structure. A rule of Predicate Raising (Kuno 1973) collapses this structure to derive the surface form.

(38)

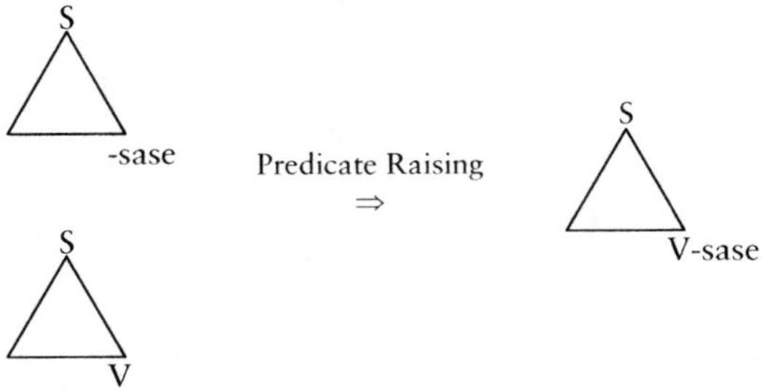

Among its merits, the analysis appropriately captures the highly productive nature of *-sase*: there are only a handful of verbs to which *-sase* cannot attach. Also, the analysis receives syntactic support from facts about reflexivization. The antecedent of the reflexive, *zibun*, is almost always a subject NP; the antecedent need not be in the same S as *zibun*. In the simplex sentence in (39), *zibun* only refers to the subject NP, but in the bisentential example in (40) it has ambiguous reference (cf. Kuroda 1965; Kuno 1973).

(39) Hanako-ga$_i$ Ziroo-o$_j$ zibun-no$_{i/*j}$ uti-de mi-ta.
Hanako-NOM Jiro-ACC self-GEN house-at see-PAST
'Hanako saw Jiro at her/*his house.'

(40) Hanako-ga$_i$ Ziroo-ga$_j$ zibun-o$_{i/j}$ mi-ta-to omot-ta.
Hanako-NOM Jiro-NOM self-ACC see-PAST-COMP think-PAST
'Hanako thought that Jiro saw her/himself.'

The V-*sase* behaves as a complex structure in allowing ambiguous interpretation of *zibun*, as shown below.

(41) Hanako-ga$_i$ Taroo-o$_j$ zibun-no$_{i/j}$ uti-e ik-ase-ta.
Hanako-NOM Taro-ACC self-GEN house-to go-CAUS-PAST
'Hanako made/let Taro go to her/his house.'

The complex-structure hypothesis easily accommodates this by allowing for two subject NPs at some appropriate level of abstraction.

5.2 Kuroda's (1981) proposal

However, what we have observed in this paper about V-*sase* (and V-*sas*) suggests an alternative approach, a nonsyntactic one in which V-*sase* is formed in the lexicon by a word-formation rule.[6] Phenomena such as nominalization, semantic drift, and morphological alternation are associated with simple verbs. That is, they are phenomena on the word level, not the level of syntax. If we are to account for these lexical facts about V-*sase* as part of an overall analysis of the causative construction, which surely we must, then a word-formation approach becomes a prime candidate, though we must of course explain the syntactic nature of V-*sase* in some fashion compatible with this approach. The single most crucial piece of evidence for a word-formation approach is that V-*sase* exhibits PDS effects. It is crucial because the PDS is a hypothesis about the lexicon, in particular, the permanent lexicon.

The PDS effects of V-*sase* need not necessarily lead us to a word-formation analysis, given some modification in the theoretical apparatus. Indeed, Kuroda (1981) has proposed an alternative syntactic approach that addresses both the PDS effects and the syntactic behavior of V-*sase*. Central to his approach is his rejection of a clear line of demarcation between the lexicon and the syntactic component. In essence, Kuroda proposes that "words" produced in the syntax via Predicate Raising can return to the lexicon as input to lexical processes. He proposes two types of "words," "S(urface) S(tructure)" words and "L(exicon)" words (Kuroda 1981, 117–118). SS-words are those that are produced only after the syntactic operation of Predicate Raising applies. Based on this distinction, he proposes the following principle, which he calls "SS-W:LW."

(42) Any word is a potential candidate for a new L-word, whatever its "generative" characteristics may be.

Kuroda cautions us that this principle is possibly too general: "there must be some constraints as to what SS-words can become L-words . . . [but] . . . this is a good way to start, or even the right way to start." Whatever these constraints turn out to be, the proposal does account for the PDS effects exhibited by V-*sase* and still maintains a syntactic account of the complex verb, by allowing V-*sase* to reenter the lexicon after it becomes an SS-word in the syntactic component.

5.3 Parallel structure

Kuroda's proposal, however tentative, addresses for the first time a basic fact about V-*sase*: the verb exhibits both wordlike and syntactic characteristics. It is wordlike because of the observable PDS effects; it behaves as a syntactic entity because, for example, it allows ambiguous interpretation of the reflexive *zibun*. Kuroda attempts to capture both by suggesting that the division between the lexicon and the syntactic component is not always clear-cut.

We will take this suggestion as a starting point, but from it develop a proposal different from Kuroda's. We will continue to assume that V-*sase* is produced in the lexicon, to account for its clearly lexical nature. To also accommodate its syntactic behavior, we propose that a V-*sase* is associated in the syntax with parallel structures, one simplex, one complex.[7] Central to this parallel-structure hypothesis is the assumption that the D-structure is projected directly from the lexicon according to universal-grammar principles, most notably the X-bar theory and the Projection Principle (Chomsky 1981, 1982; Stowell 1981). The X-bar theory ensures that all projected phrases are appropriately headed, and the Projection Principle requires that all thematic roles relevant to the predicate be categorially represented. The D-structure is thus in part a direct projection of the subcategorization feature of a predicate. An intransitive verb will not have an NP under VP; a transitive verb, by its subcategorization, will have an NP that it governs under VP.

Let us suppose that a V-*sase* is always associated with two subcategorization features, one with only NPs, the other having an S in addition. Let us further suppose that both of these subcategorization features are projected into the syntax, one resulting in a simplex structure, the other complex.

(43)

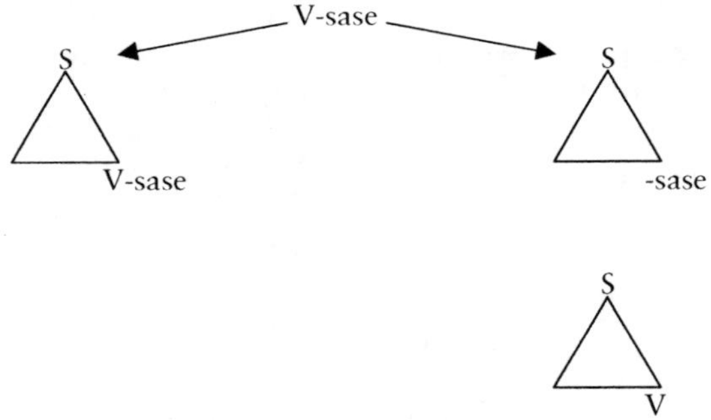

The parallel-structure hypothesis can account for both the PDS effects and the syntactic behavior of V-*sase*. It is worthwhile noting that there is a one-to-one correspondence between this approach and the one proposed by Kuroda. The simplex structure on the left in (43) reflects what Kuroda calls L-words; the complex structure on the right is comparable to his SS-words. The difference of course is that: (i) in our approach V-*sase* is produced in the lexicon; (ii) once a lexical item leaves the lexicon, it cannot "return" to the lexicon for further lexical processes. The two approaches share the view that the division between the lexicon and the syntactic components is not always clear-cut. In Kuroda's proposal, this is reflected in allowing SS-words to enter the lexicon; in our approach, it is reflected in the assumption that a complex syntactic structure can be directly projected from the lexicon. Our approach has the advantage that it allows us to maintain the traditional assumption that the syntax cannot produce inputs into lexical rules. What follows is an argument to support the hypothesis that a V-*sase* is simultaneously associated with both simplex and complex structures.

The argument involves Condition B of the binding theory (Chomsky 1981) and subject honorification.

5.3.1 Condition B

We begin by showing that Condition B must apply after Predicate Raising, or, in the more recent terminology, "restructuring." This condition pertains to pronouns, and in particular, to disjoint reference.

Condition B (Chomsky 1981, 188)
A pronominal must be free in its governing category.

I have elsewhere shown, using the purpose-expression construction, that Condition B must apply after restructuring in Japanese (Miyagawa 1984b). Below, I will show that the same holds with causative constructions.

It has been noticed that a pronoun in the object position of V-*sase* can be coreferential with the subject NP (Inoue 1976a; Oshima 1979).

(44) Taroo-ga$_i$ Hanako-ni$_j$ [$_{S'}$ PRO$_j$ kare-o$_i$ hihans]-ase-ta.
Taro-NOM Hanako-DAT him-ACC criticize-CAUS-PAST
'Taro$_i$ made Hanako criticize him$_i$.'

Let us suppose that S′ is a governing category in Japanese. In (44) the pronoun, *kare* 'him', can be coreferential with *Taroo* because this coreference leaves the pronoun free within the governing category of S′. This is evidence that the V-*sase* in (44) must be associated with a complex syntactic structure. Now, the fact that Condition B must apply *after* restructuring is illustrated in (45).

(45) Taroo-ga$_i$ Hanako-ni kare-**ga**$_{*i/j}$ hihans-**ase-rare**-ta.
Taro-NOM Hanako-DAT him-NOM criticize-CAUS-can-PAST
'Taro$_i$ was able to make Hanako criticize him$_{*i/j}$.'

The addition of the dependent desiderative morpheme -*(rar)e* optionally allows the direct object to be marked with the nominative -*ga*. However, this -*ga* is possible only if the object NP and -*(rar)e* are in the same clause. Hence, in (45), the object NP, *kare(-ga),* must be in the same clause as *(hihans-ase)-rare,* that is, the sentence must have undergone restructuring. But restructuring has the effect of obliterating the lower S′, and if Condition B does apply after restructuring, then the pronoun in the object position can no longer be coreferential with the matrix-subject NP. We see that this is indeed the case. It is the presence of the nominative -*ga* in (45) that signals restructuring, in turn making it impossible for *kare* and *Taroo* to be coreferential. On the other hand, if the accusative -*o* appears with the object NP, there is no reason to believe that restructuring has taken place, hence *kare* and *Taroo* need not be disjoint in reference. This is shown below.

(46) Taroo-ga$_i$ Hanako-ni kare-**o**$_i$ hihans-**ase**-rare-ta.
Taro-NOM Hanako-DAT him$_i$ criticize-CAUS-can-PAST
'Taro$_i$ was able to make Hanako criticize him$_i$.'

The occurrence of the accusative -*o* is not dependent on restructuring, but rather is what we expect because of the transitive embedded verb *hihans* 'criticize'. Based on these observations, we conclude that Binding Condition B applies after restructuring. This is schematized in (47).

(47)

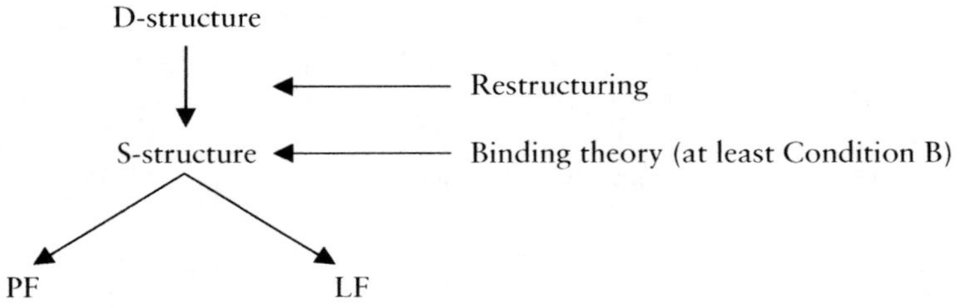

5.3.2 Subject honorification and Condition B

We now turn to subject honorification (SH). While Condition B gives evidence for a complex syntactic structure for V-*sase*, as shown in the previous section, SH requires V-*sase* to be associated with a simplex structure at some relevant level (Harada 1976b). When we combine SH with Condition B, we are faced with a paradox: SH requires simplex structure, but Condition B requires complex structure. We propose to resolve this paradox via the parallel-structure hypothesis.

SH is made by adding the prefix *o*- and -*ni-naru* to the verb; the verb in this construction is turned into an infinitive. The SH construction, *o*-V-*ni-naru*, is appropriate if the subject of the verb is socially superior to the speaker (Harada 1976b).

(48) Tanaka-sensee-ga hon-o **o**-yomi-**ni-naru.**
Professor Tanaka-NOM book-ACC read$_{\text{HONORIFIC}}$
'Professor Tanaka will read a book.'

(49) *Watakusi-ga hon-o **o**-yomi-**ni-naru.**
(Intended: 'I will read a book.')

The SH can be placed on complex predicates such as the V-*sase*, but only if the subject of the complex predicate as a whole is socially superior.

(50) Tanaka-sensee-ga watakusi-ni hon-o **o-yom-ase-ni-nat-ta.**
Professor Tanaka-NOM me-DAT book-ACC $\text{read}_{\text{HONORIFIC}}$-CAUS-PAST
'Professor Tanaka made me read the book.'

Here, the SH is appropriate because *Tanaka-sensee* is the subject of V-*sase*; in other words, SH can apply only after restructuring makes V and *-sase* into a surface constituent (Harada 1976b).

SH on V-*sase* thus indicates that the sentence has undergone restructuring. Given what we have said about Condition B already, we would thus expect disjoint reference for a pronoun in the object position when SH occurs. However, this is not the case.

(51) Tanaka-sensee-ga_i boku-ni kare-o_i adana-de
Professor Tanaka-NOM me-DAT him-ACC nickname-by

o-yob-ase-ni-natta.
$\text{call}_{\text{HONORIFIC}}$-CAUS-PAST
'Professor Tanaka_i made me call him_i by his nickname.'

In (51), the fact that SH is possible shows that the sentence must have undergone restructuring, but, paradoxically, the pronoun can be coreferential with the matrix subject. The sentence is slightly awkward because the formality of SH is incompatible with the use of *kare*, which is informal. There are, however, no grammatical problems in construing the pronoun with the subject NP. This paradox cannot be resolved by postulating a complex structure to which first restructuring applies, then SH. This would correctly predict that the SH is appropriate since it applies after V-*sase* becomes a "word" with *Tanaka-sensee* as its subject; however, because Binding Condition B applies after restructuring, it would incorrectly predict disjoint reference between the pronoun and the subject NP.

This paradox is solved if we assume that a V-*sase* is associated simultaneously with parallel structures, one simplex, one complex, both projected directly from the lexicon. The complex structure meets the condition for pronominal coreference under Condition B, and the simplex structure allows SH on the V-*sase*. We can readily see that this analysis also accommodates facts about reflexivization: the ambiguous interpretation arises for *zibun* because a complex as well as a simplex structure is projected from V-*sase*.

5.4 *-sas*

With the exception of the *-sase/-sas* morphological alternation attributed to special cases of V-*sase*, *-sase* and *-sas* have independent existence in the lexicon. Now, if the parallel-structure hypothesis is correct for V-*sase*, is it also correct for V-*sas*? The answer here must be "yes" because they often share the analytical-causative meaning and behave in the same manner in the syntax, for example, in allowing ambiguous interpretation of the reflexive *zibun*. The one problem is that for some V-*sas*, it is difficult to detect any complex-structure traits.

(52) Taroo-ga kodomo-o ugok-asi-ta.
Taro-NOM child-ACC move-CAUS-PAST
(i) 'Taro moved the child.'
(ii) ??'Taro made/let the child move.'

(53) Taroo-ga$_i$ kodomo-o$_j$ zibun-no$_{i/??j}$ heya-de ugok-asi-ta.
Taro-NOM child-ACC self-GEN room-in move-CAUS-PAST
'Taro$_i$ moved the child$_j$ in his$_{i/??j}$ own room.'

The causative verb here lacks a corresponding simple verb, and thus is able to attain PDS status, in turn becoming a candidate for the permanent lexicon. Indeed, the primary reading of *ugok-as* is intuitively as a simple verb ('move$_{TR}$'). On the basis of this observation, we can explain (52) and (53) in the following way. *Ugok-as*, having PDS status, has entered the permanent lexicon, in effect becoming a simple verb. Consequently, this "simple" verb now occupies the transitive slot in the PDS that contains *ugok* 'move$_{INTR}$' in the intransitive slot. From this "simple" transitive verb is projected only a simplex structure, just like any other simple transitive verb. It is this lone simplex structure associated with the lexicalized V-*sas* that we can observe in (52) and (53). In addition to this, however, the word-formation rule that attaches -*sas* to virtually any V can attach the causative morpheme to *ugok* 'move', thereby producing a second *ugok-as*. This *ugok-as* is blocked (recall that blocking does not necessarily prevent a word from occurring, only from entering a PDS slot) by the occurrence of the lexicalized *ugok-as*. The prediction for this second *ugok-as* is that: *(a)* it is only associated with the analytical-causative interpretation; *(b)* the parallel structures, one simplex, one complex, are projected from it. There is nothing to prevent these predictions from being realized, hence we must assume that both hold for the second *ugok-as*, despite the effect that we observe in (52) and (53). To account for that effect, we suggest the following (informal) principle.

(54) Given two homophonous and potentially synonymous lexical items, one a member of the permanent lexicon, the other a product of a regular word-formation process, the one in the permanent lexicon has primacy over the other.

Primacy here simply means that the lexical item in the permanent lexicon tends to overshadow any traits of the other item. We see just this in (52) and (53). In (52), the analytical-causative interpretation for *ugok-as* is shown to be very awkward, but the point is that it is not impossible. Likewise, in

(53), it is difficult to construe *zibun* as referring to the object NP, but, again, it is not impossible. The upshot of this is that *ugok-as* is associated with three structures, one directly projected from the lexicalized *ugok-as* and the other two projected from the regular *ugok-as*.

(55)

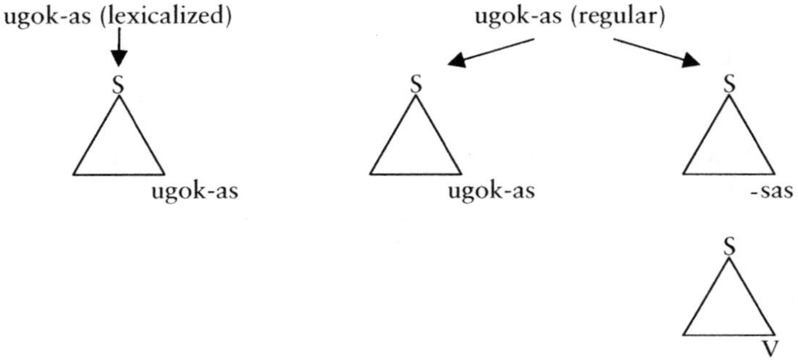

We conclude that it is grammatical to associate an analytical interpretation with *ugok-as,* and to recognize an ambiguous interpretation of *zibun* with this verb. The reason why both are difficult to detect is an independent issue: the lexicalized *ugok-as,* which does not share the traits of the regular *ugok-as*, virtually suppresses these characteristics because of its primacy due to its membership in the permanent lexicon. This "primacy" looks very much like another case of blocking. However, we will not attempt to reduce it to such in this paper.

6 SUMMARY AND CONCLUSION

It has been proposed in this paper that the PDS organizes verbs within the lexicon according to their meaning and the number of arguments they require. In so doing, the PDS acts as a filter for the permanent lexicon, in effect letting only "simple" verbs into the permanent lexicon. Verb stems are morphologically the simplest form of the verb, and are automatically given PDS status and entry in the lexicon. With morphologically complex verbs, only those that can attain PDS status are given entry; when they do, they behave very much like a verb stem in being associated with processes normally reserved for simple verbs. Those that fail to attain PDS status are still bona fide words, but nothing unpredictable can be observed in their behavior; hence, not only are they not listed in the lexicon, there is no reason to do so. Some of these blocked words occur in the language while others do not. We can predict to some extent whether a blocked item will actually occur. For example, the Japanese causative morpheme *-sas* can be associated with both lexical- and analytical-causative interpretations; if it is blocked, the lexical interpretation is impossible, but it has the analytical interpretation to "fall back on," and a blocked V-*sas* will freely occur in the language with the latter interpretation. On the other hand, the causative prefix *s-* in Mitla Zapotec can only be associated with the lexical interpretation, so if it is blocked from taking this interpretation, the *s*-V will not occur. In the case of the English nominal *cooker*, even though it is blocked by the occurrence of $cook_N$ from taking on the predicted agentive interpretation, the word has managed to fit into another semantic slot, namely the slot for 'instrument to carry out V'. It remains to be seen if we can always predict whether a blocked item will occur. One thing that is certain is that this issue of occurrence is independent of the actual process of blocking.

The fact that the causative verb in Japanese manifests PDS effects led us to the parallel-structure hypothesis. The problem addressed by this hypothesis is that V-*sase* and V-*sas* manifest both wordlike and syntactic characteristics. While this evidence can potentially also be used to support Kuroda's L-/SS-word hypothesis, the parallel-structure hypothesis allows us to maintain the traditional assumption that a syntactic rule cannot produce inputs to lexical rules. One interesting consequence of our hypothesis is that a V-*sase* or V-*sas* can appear in different forms and through different derivations. It always starts out as a complex word in the lexicon, but the PDS, parallel structure, and restructuring determine what structure or structures it projects: (1) if it attains PDS status, it in essence becomes a simple verb, hence only a simplex syntactic structure is projected from it; (2) parallel structures, one simplex, one complex, may be projected, resulting in both "lexical" and "syntactic" structures attributed to V-*sase*; (3) restructuring can optionally apply to the complex structure, reconverting the V-*sase* into a "word" at S-structure. There are, hence, some redundancies, but it is important to point out that the redundancies arise from "modular" components that are independently needed, namely the PDS, parallel structure, and restructuring. In a modular model of grammar, in which independent components work together to define the core grammar of a language, it would in fact be surprising not to find some redundancies such as those we have just observed. So long as each component is well motivated, the theory should tolerate some redundancy in the output. The PDS and restructuring are, I believe, well motivated; that leaves the parallel-structure hypothesis as a relatively "weak link." Kuroda proposed his L-/SS-word hypothesis with the qualification that major problems must still be solved, but that nevertheless it was the "right" way to proceed. We propose the parallel-structure hypothesis in the same spirit. It faces some of the problems faced by Kuroda's proposal, but it is, I believe, a promising approach, one that must be verified through further research.

8 Blocking and causatives revisited

Unexpected competition across derivations

1 INTRODUCTION

The Japanese causative verb is formed by attaching the causative morpheme *-sase* to a verb: *tabe-sase* (eat-CAUS) 'make eat, feed', *ik-(s)ase* (go-CAUS) 'make go, let go'; the initial *s* drops if the verb stem ends in a consonant. In the 1980s and 1990s, fierce debate arose about the exact nature of the causative form. Should it be analyzed as being formed in syntax, or does it belong to the lexicon where it is formed by some process of word formation? One piece of evidence in favor of the "lexical" analysis was the phenomenon of *blocking*, in which synthetic (monomorphemic) verbs were shown to block V-*sase* verbs from taking on a particular meaning (see Chapter 7). Given the standard assumption that synthetic verbs belong to the lexicon, the fact that they interact with the V-*sase* causative verb gave credence to the notion that the V-*sase* causative verb also belongs to the lexicon. In the last ten years or so, a similar debate has taken place over the analysis of certain inflectional and derivational forms in English (past, perfect, comparative, etc.) and other Indo-European languages, with blocking playing a central role (see, e.g., Embick and Noyer 2001; Embick 2007; Embick and Marantz 2008; Kiparsky 2005; Stump 2001). In this chapter, I will review the original arguments for blocking in Japanese causatives, then explore a recent proposal to analyze both the synthetic (lexical-causative) and the analytical V-*sase* verbs syntactically. I will then look at implications of this analysis for the acquisition of Japanese causatives and for the analysis of English causatives. I will end with a discussion on the nature of blocking, concluding that we don't need the filter-based approach advocated by Kiparsky (2005) and McCawley (1978).

2 LEXICAL AND ANALYTICAL CAUSATIVES

Lexical causatives in Japanese have irregular and nonproductive forms. The following are examples taken from Jacobsen 1992.

(1)

Class	Unaccusative	Lexical causative
(i) -ar-/-e-	ag-**ar**-u 'rise'	ag-**e**-ru 'raise'
(ii) -re-/-s-	hazu-**re**-ru 'come off'	hazu-**s**-u 'take off'
(iii) -ri-/-s-	ta-**ri**-ru 'suffice'	ta-**s**-u 'add, supplement'
(iv)-e-/-as-	kog-**e**-ru 'become scorched'	kog-**as**-u 'scorch'
(v) -i-/-os-	ok-**i**-ru 'get up'	ok-**os**-u 'wake (someone) up'
(vi) ∅/-as-	nar-u 'ring$_{INTR}$'	nar-**as**-u 'ring$_{TR}$'
(vii) ∅/-e-	ak-u 'open$_{INTR}$'	ak-**e**-u 'open$_{TR}$'
(viii) -e-/∅	kir-**e**-ru 'be cut'	kir-u 'cut'
(ix) -ar-/∅	matag-**ar**-u 'sit astride'	matag-u 'straddle'

Others: (x) -r-/-s-, (xi) -i-/-as-, (xii) ∅/-se-, (xiii) -or-/-e-, (xiv) -are-/-e-, (xv) -e-/-akas-, (xvi) "miscellaneous."

As we can see in (1), there are 16 different classes of unaccusative–lexical causative pairs, and these forms, which are irregular, must be learned, hence best viewed in the traditional model as being listed in the lexicon. Further evidence for the lexical nature of lexical causatives is that they undergo semantic drift, a property typically associated with listed items.

(2) Semantic drift

hone-o or-u (Class viii)
bone-ACC break-PRES
'exert oneself'

Furthermore, they appear in nonproductive nominal forms.

(3) Nonproductive nominalization

Lexical causative	Nominalization
fusag-u 'to obstruct' (Class ix)	fusagi 'closing, plug'
hasam-u 'to catch between' (Class ix)	hasami 'scissors'

Intuitively, then, lexical causatives are listed in the lexicon.

Unlike the lexical causatives, analytical causatives are fully productive and regular in form, with the suffix *-sase* attaching to a verb stem (simple or complex verb).

(4) a. Hanako-ga kodomo-o/-ni ik-(s)ase-ta.
Hanako-NOM child-ACC/-DAT go-CAUS-PAST
'Hanako made/let the child go.'

b. Hanako-ga kodomo-ni hon-o yom-(s)ase-ta.
Hanako-NOM child-DAT book-ACC read-CAUS-PAST
'Hanako made/let the child read a book.'

Sentence (4a) is an example of an analytical-causative verb formed by attaching *-sase* to an intransitive verb; as shown, the causee 'child' may be marked by the accusative or the dative case marker. In (4b) the causative morpheme attaches to a transitive verb; the causee in this construction must be marked by the dative, and not by the accusative—the so-called Double-*o* Constraint (Harada 1973).

A reasonable view of the two types of causatives, lexical and analytical, is that while lexical causatives belong to the lexicon, analytical causatives are formed in syntax. This is the standard analysis as seen, for example, in Kuroda 1965 and Shibatani 1973. The standard view of the two causatives makes a clear prediction.

(5) Prediction of the standard analysis

Analytical causatives and lexical causatives should not interact in any way—derivationally, semantically, etc.

Regardless of the particular model of generative grammar that one assumes (Standard Theory, Government and Binding, Minimalist Program), this prediction still applies, because in all generative theories what occurs within the lexicon is partitioned off from any forms that are constructed in syntax.

3 BLOCKING

Contrary to this prediction of the standard analysis, facts of blocking militate against a simple lexicon–syntax compartmentalization of lexical causatives and analytical causatives. The modern notion of blocking appears in Aronoff 1976, where Aronoff notes that certain *-ity* nouns do not occur due to the existence of a simple noun.

(6) Blocking (Aronoff 1976)

Adjective	Noun	Blocked
curious	curiosity	—
glorious	glory	*gloriosity

While the adjective *curious* has the *-ity* noun *curiosity*, the adjective *glorious* does not have an *-ity* counterpart due to the occurrence of the simple noun *glory*, which blocks **gloriosity* from occurring.

Blocking is found with causatives. The key observation is that the V-*sase* causative verb, which is always analytical in nature, *may also behave as a lexical causative in some cases.* It is blocked from behaving as a lexical causative if there is a corresponding synthetic lexical-causative verb to begin with (McCawley 1978; Miyagawa 1980, 1984a [= Chapter 7 of this volume], 1989). I will illustrate this with the double-causative test and also with idiomatization.

When a sentence has a double-causative meaning, two instances of the analytical *-sase* causative morpheme cannot co-occur; they are instead reduced to a single occurrence of *-sase* (Martin 1975; Kuroda 1993a).

(7) a. *Sensei-ga Hanako-ni kodomo-o yukkuri
teacher-NOM Hanako-DAT child-ACC slowly

taore-**sase-sase**-ta.
fall down-CAUS-CAUS-PAST

b. Sensei-ga Hanako-ni kodomo-o yukkuri
teacher-NOM Hanako-DAT child-ACC slowly

taore-**sase**-ta.
fall down-CAUS-PAST

'The teacher made Hanako make the child fall down slowly.'

Example (7b) has the double-causative meaning of the teacher *making* Hanako *make* the child fall down slowly, and if it weren't for the constraint against two instances of *-sase* emerging in the same verbal complex, we would expect the double *-sase* in (7a). Instead, the two occurrences of *-sase* must be reduced to one, and, despite the single occurrence of the causative morpheme, the sentence carries the double-causative meaning, as we can see in (7b).

Importantly, Kuroda (1993a) notes that a double-causative meaning with two causative morphemes is fine if the first causative is a lexical causative.

(8) Hanako-ga Taroo-ni doa-o ak-**e**-**sase**-ta.
Hanako-NOM Taro-DAT door-ACC open-CAUS-CAUS-PAST
'Hanako made Taro open the door.'

Here, we again have double causatives, but the first is the lexical causative represented by the morpheme *-e* attached to the unaccusative *ak* 'open', and it is fine for the analytical *-sase* to attach to this lexical causative. So, the double-causative prohibition is actually a prohibition against doubling of the analytical causative.

The double-causative test demonstrates that in certain cases, a V-*sase* verb acts as a lexical causative.

(9) Hanako-ga Taroo-ni yotei-o aw-(s)**ase**-**sase**-ta.
Hanako-NOM Taro-DAT schedule-ACC match-CAUS-CAUS-PAST
'Hanako made Taro match the schedule.'

(10) Intyoo-sensei-wa Taroo-ni tuuzyoo-yori nagaku byooin-ni
chief physician-TOP Taro-DAT usual-than longer hospital-at

hahaoya-o i-**sase**-**sase**-ta.
mother-ACC be-CAUS-CAUS-PAST

'The chief physician made Taro make his mother stay in the hospital longer than usual.'

What is the difference between **taore-sase-sase* in (7a), on the one hand, and *aw-(s)ase-sase* 'cause to match$_{\text{TR}}$' in (9) and *i-sase-sase* 'cause to make stay' in (10), on the other? The generalization is that a V-*sase* verb may function as a lexical causative (in addition to functioning as an analytical causative) if there is no corresponding synthetic lexical causative.

(11) Blocking (Miyagawa 1980; Chapter 7)

A V-*sase* that does not have a lexical-causative counterpart may function as a lexical causative (as well as an analytical causative).

This is shown in the following paradigms for *taore-sase* and *aw-(s)ase*.

(12)

Unaccusative	Lexical causative	Analytical causative
taore 'fall down'	tao-s 'push down'	taore-sase 'make fall down'
aw 'match$_{\text{INTR}}$'	aw-(s)ase 'match$_{\text{TR}}$'	aw-(s)ase 'make match$_{\text{INTR}}$'

The unaccusative *taore* 'fall down' has the synthetic lexical causative *tao-s* 'push down', and this lexical causative blocks the V-*sase* verb formed from the unaccusative *taore* from taking on a lexical-causative meaning. In contrast, *aw* 'match$_{\text{INTR}}$' does not have a synthetic lexical causative, so that the V-*sase* verb, *aw-(s)ase* (match$_{\text{INTR}}$-CAUS), is able to take on the lexical-causative function as well as being an analytical causative. The same holds for *i* 'be' in (10). If we use the lexical causative *tao-s* 'push down' as the first of the two causatives, we get a grammatical double-causative sentence as predicted, unlike (7a).

(13) Sensei-ga Hanako-ni kodomo-o yukkuri
teacher-NOM Hanako-DAT child-ACC slowly

tao-**s**-(**s**)**ase**-ta.
fall down-CAUS-CAUS-PAST

'The teacher made Hanako make the child fall down slowly.'

We saw at the outset that lexical causatives may undergo semantic drift to form idioms. What we find with V-*sase* is that idiomatization is only possible with unblocked V-*sase* (Miyagawa 1980; Chapter 7), showing again that an unblocked V-*sase* functions as a lexical (as well as an analytical) causative.

(14) a. Taroo-ga zisyoku-o niow-(**s**)**ase**-ta.
Taro-NOM resignation-ACC smell-CAUS-PAST
'Taro hinted resignation.' (Lit. 'Taro made resignation smell.')

b. *Zisyoku-ga nio-u.
resignation-NOM smell-PRES
'*Resignation smells.'

c.

Unaccusative	Lexical causative	Analytical causative
niow 'smell'	niow-(s)**ase** 'make smell; hint'	niow-(s)**ase**

The unaccusative *niow* 'smell' does not have a corresponding synthetic lexical causative, so that *niow-(s)ase* (smell-CAUS) takes up the lexical-causative role, and has undergone semantic drift to take on the noncompositional meaning of 'hint'. An example similar to this is the following.

(15) kazoku-o tabe-**sase**-ru
family-ACC eat-CAUS-PRES
'take care of the family'

The verb *tabe* 'eat' here is intransitive—as in *kazoku-ga tabe-ru* (family-NOM eat-PRES) 'the family eats' (cf. transitive *kuw* 'eat' in (17a))—and it does not have a synthetic transitive counterpart, a fact that allows the V-*sase* verb *tabe-sase* 'make eat, feed' to fill the lexical-causative role and acquire the meaning 'take care of'.

Two other examples of idioms with unblocked V-*sase* are given below, as well as two examples of idioms where blocking does occur.

(16)

Unaccusative	Lexical causative	V-*sase*
a. her-u 'lessen$_{INTR}$'	—	her-(s)**ase**-ru 'lessen$_{TR}$'
hara-ga her-u stomach-NOM lessen 'become hungry'		hara-o her-(s)**ase**-ru stomach-ACC lessen-CAUS 'wait for a meal'
b. hikar-u 'shine'	—	hikar-(s)**ase**-ru 'make shine'
me-ga hikar-u eye-NOM shine 'be under a watchful eye'		me-o hikar-(s)**ase**-ru eye-ACC shine-CAUS 'keep a watchful eye'
c. hair-u 'come in'	ire-ru 'put in'	hair-(s)**ase**-ru 'make come in'
kiai-ga hair-u spirit-NOM come in 'be full of spirit'	kiai-o ire-ru spirit-ACC put in 'put spirit into'	*kiai-o hair-(s)**ase**-ru
d. ore-ru 'break$_{INTR}$'	or-u 'break$_{TR}$'	ore-**sase**-ru 'make break$_{INTR}$'
hone-ga ore-ru bone-NOM break 'require hard work'	hone-o or-ru bone-ACC break 'exert oneself'	*hone-o ore-**sase**-ru

(from Zenno 1985; see Miyagawa 1989)

Examples (16a, b) involve unaccusative verbs that do not have a synthetic lexical causative, which allows the corresponding V-*sase* to take on idiomatic meaning. These are examples of V-*sase* functioning as a transitive lexical causative and occurring in an idiom. Examples (16c, d) involve unaccusative verbs that have a synthetic lexical causative; this lexical causative is what participates in idiomatization, and its occurrence blocks the corresponding V-*sase* from taking on noncompositional meaning. There are instances of V-*sase* that are ditransitive and likewise occur in idioms; they are also predicted by blocking since they do not have a synthetic ditransitive counterpart.

(17) a. binta-o kuw-ase-ru
slap-ACC eat-CAUS
'give (someone) a slap on the cheek'

b. yaruki-o das-ase-ru
desire-ACC put out-CAUS
'motivate (someone)'

c. saihu-o ake-sase-ru
wallet-ACC open-CAUS
'make (someone) pay'

Examples (14)–(15) show that semantic drift may involve just the V-*sase* causative verb, as in *niow-(s)ase* 'hint', while examples (16)–(17) show that it may involve the entire VP.

4 THE ONE-COMPONENT HYPOTHESIS OF LEXICAL AND ANALYTICAL CAUSATIVES

The blocking effect clearly demonstrates that lexical and analytical causatives interact at some level, so that these two types of causatives must be accessible to each other at some point in their derivation. A reasonable analysis based on the blocking effect is the One-Component Hypothesis (Miyagawa 1994, 1998), whereby both causatives are derived in the same component of the grammar. There are two possibilities for this component, the lexicon or syntax, and in the literature that adopts the One-Component Hypothesis, we find both possibilities:

Lexicon: Farmer 1980; Manning, Sag, and Iida 1999; Miyagawa 1980, 1984a (= Chapter 7), 1989

Syntax: Hale and Keyser 1993; Harley 1995a, 1995b, 2008; Miyagawa 1994, 1998; Pylkkänen 2002

There are other theories that would allow the lexicon–syntax distinction to stay intact and at the same time address the blocking effect. Kitagawa (1986) presents an analysis in which the V-*sase* is created in the lexicon and inserted as a unitary word into the syntactic tree, and at LF, -*sase* is excorporated to form a complex syntactic structure. Kuroda (1981, 116–121), who is one of the chief proponents of the standard analysis, suggested that the blocking facts point to the possibility that once V-*sase* is created in syntax, it is allowed to loop back into the lexicon, where it is compared to counterparts in the lexicon to see if blocking should prohibit it from taking on the lexical-causative function. More recently, Kiparsky (2005) has argued that blocking between lexical and syntactic elements (or between any two semantically relevant expressions) is a matter of a filter on the generative output—choose the simpler and more expressive expression. This is similar to McCawley's (1978) cooperative principle, which favors a simpler form for optimally expressing the meaning of causation at hand. I will return to McCawley's and Kiparsky's proposals in Section 7.

I will pursue the version of the One-Component Hypothesis in which both types of causatives are located in syntax (contra Miyagawa 1980, 1984a [= Chapter 7], 1989). This means that lexical causatives are syntactic in nature, something that has been argued for in a number of works, including an early work by Chomsky (1970), where he makes the following observations.

(18) a. John grew tomatoes (in his backyard).
     b. Tomatoes grew (in John's backyard).

Only the unaccusative allows nominalization.

(19) a. *John's growth of tomatoes
     b. the growth of tomatoes

Chomsky notes that *the growth of tomatoes* "has the interpretation of *tomatoes grow* but not of *John grows tomatoes*," that is, the derived nominal *growth* has only the unaccusative meaning. The following derivations for (18a, b) are given by Chomsky (for relevant discussion, see Marantz 1997; Pesetsky 1995; among others).

(20) John grows tomatoes: John [+CAUSE, grow] tomatoes

(21) Tomatoes grow: [$_S$ tomatoes grow]$_S$

The important point to note is that the lexical causative *grow* is decomposed syntactically into the unaccusative *grow* plus CAUSE, which in English is not pronounced. This CAUSE is a syntactic entity, and the reason Chomsky gives for why the lexical causative fails to nominalize is that the notion of CAUSE is inherently a syntactic one and does not belong in nominals.

I will adopt a modern version of the syntactic analysis of lexical and analytical causatives, as proposed by Hale and Keyser (1993). Introducing the notion of "small *v*," Hale and Keyser argue that the causative meaning emerges when this *v* selects an XP. If the selected XP is a VP (or AP, PP), we have a lexical causative, and if the XP is something larger—IP, in their analysis—we have an analytical causative.

(22) Hale and Keyser 1993

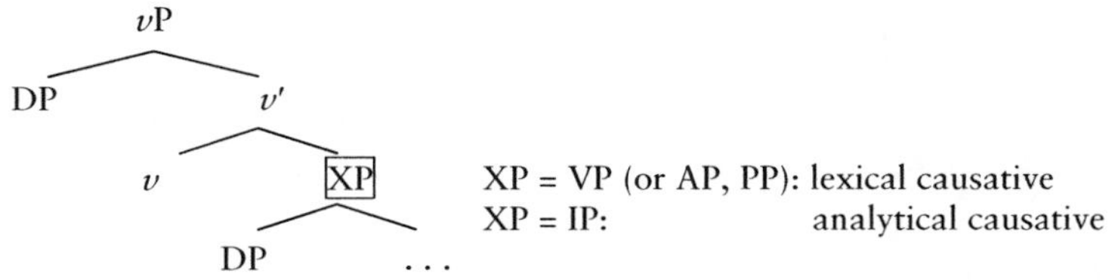

I will differ from Hale and Keyser in assuming *v*P rather than IP for the analytical causative (see, e.g., Harley 1995a, 1995b; Murasugi, Fuji, and Hashimoto 2008).

On this account, the lexical-causative sentence *John opens the door* has the following underlying structure (I am omitting the structure above the *v*P).

(23) Lexical causative

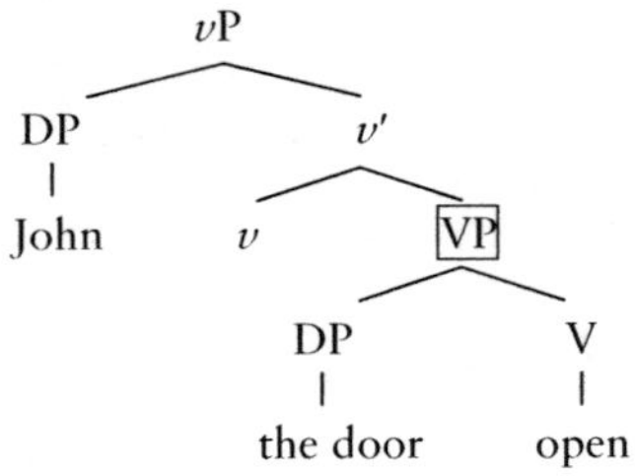

V raises to *v* to derive the final word order.

For Japanese, let us suppose that *v* is pronounced, and where *-sase* is unblocked, allowing it to function as both a lexical causative and an analytical causative, it has the following structure, essentially the same as in (22). (To maintain parallelism with the Hale–Keyser structure, I am artificially using the head-initial order instead of the default Japanese order.)

(24)

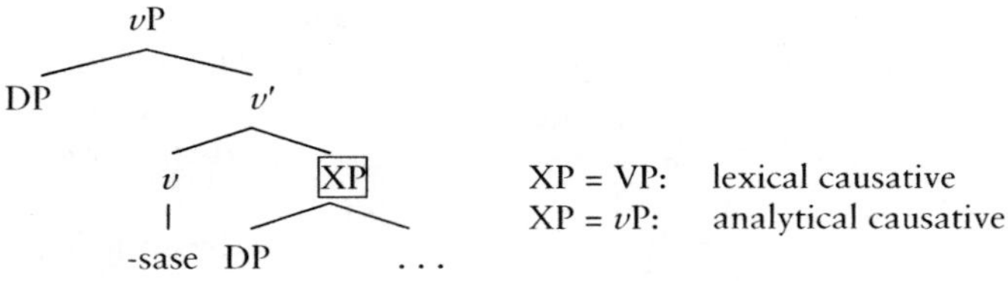

How can we distinguish between *-sase* and the irregular (synthetic) lexical-causative morphology we saw at the outset of this paper? I will assume the basic tenets of Distributed Morphology (Halle and Marantz 1993; Marantz 1997), which allows pronounced items such as *-sase* to be inserted after the syntactic structure is built and certain abstract morphological processes have taken place. A simple way to analyze the lexical causative in Japanese is to postulate CAUSE under *v* (this is different from the Hale–Keyser approach to *v*: see Hale and Keyser 1993). Under its complement V, a verb is inserted that carries a designation of its class (e.g., (i), (iii), (viii)).

(25)

The small v here selects the V. If, for example, the Class i stem *ag* 'rise' is inserted under V, this V is selected by v and raises to v, so that we have the structure $V_{ag(i)} + v_{CAUSE}$.[1] This is an instruction to insert the causative morpheme *-e* after the V to pronounce CAUSE, leading to the lexical causative *ag-e* 'raise'. We can do this for all sixteen classes from Jacobsen's (1992) list. Given a particular designation for a lexical causative (e.g., formed from a Class i verb), the speaker must know that a specific form arbitrarily corresponds to that designation. This is the meaning of the notion that the irregular synthetic causatives must be learned.

When does *-sase* get inserted? A simple way to describe its environment is to say that it is the environment where the verb under V does not have any specification with regard to the causative; that is, if a verb is inserted that does not belong to any of Jacobsen's classes, hence carries no specific information on how to pronounce the causative, *-sase* is inserted to pronounce the causative. This is the notion "elsewhere causative."

(26) *-sase* as an elsewhere causative

If there is no specific instruction for pronouncing CAUSE, *-sase* is inserted.

(Miyagawa 1998; see also Harley 2008)

The notion "elsewhere" is introduced in Kiparsky 1973, although the concept is found as early as Pāṇini's grammar of Sanskrit: when there are two potential candidates for the same position, choose the more specific form—one that has a larger set of relevant features for the slot. Thus, in the lexical causative *ak-e* 'open$_{TR}$', the causative morpheme *-e* is selected in the environment $V_{(vi)}$ + __. This is more specific than the other choice, *-sase*, which is not specified for any particular verb class. We can see that the elsewhere approach to *-sase* automatically captures blocking: *-sase* is blocked from being inserted if there is a specific form required for pronouncing CAUSE; a specific form results in a synthetic lexical causative.

The elsewhere designation of *-sase* also captures in a straightforward manner the fact that *-sase* is the only choice in an analytical causative. In an analytical causative, there is no structural sense in which the causative v selects the lower V in the way that it demonstrably does for lexical causatives. Due to locality, the causative v_1 would not be able to select beyond the v_2 in its complement v_2P. As a result, no instruction can be given to pronounce CAUSE under v_1 in some fashion conditioned by v_2, hence the elsewhere *-sase* is always inserted. This also makes the right prediction that in environments where no specification is given for pronunciation of CAUSE, *-sase* is ambiguous between lexical and analytical causatives. Matsumoto (2000) argues that V-*sase* is always ambiguous in this way, but he does not take into account the blocking facts, where blocked V-*sase* is unable to function as a lexical causative.

With regard to idiomatization, the analysis captures the fact that only lexical-causative V-*sase* may be associated with noncompositional meaning. Marantz (1997) argues that idiomatization is possible up to the external argument. If we look at the structures for lexical and analytical causatives, we see that while the lexical causative does not contain an external argument, the analytical causative does because *v* selects for *v*P, and this *v*P contains an external argument. Thus, only the lexical causative allows idiomatization (see also Kratzer 1996 for relevant discussion). Another way to look at this data, if we assume following Marantz (1997) that small *v* furnishes the lexical category for a root, is that idiomatization can only occur up to the root of the verbal head. Thus, a *v* selecting VP is fine because the root "verb" under V does not get its categorial designation until it raises to *v*. But in the case of *v* selecting a *v*P, the root under V already has its lexical category designated by the lower *v*, so that this *v*P cannot undergo idiomatization when selected by the causative *v*.

5 ACQUISITION

If *-sase* is the elsewhere causative, how does it emerge in language acquisition? According to the literature, analytical causatives with V-*sase* emerge around the age of five (Murasugi, Fuji, and Hashimoto 2008; hereafter, MFH). Interestingly, based on several longitudinal studies, MFH observe that V-*sase* does appear earlier, although not in great numbers. Crucially, these early occurrences of the causative verb are limited to the lexical-causative usage. They often take the form of a request, as in the following from MFH (see also Shirai et al. 2001).

(27) Akkun-ni tabe-**sase**-tee. (Akkun, 3;6)
Akkun-DAT eat-CAUS-REQ
'(Please) feed Akkun (me) (with food).'

This is an instance of a ditransitive verb, and, according to MFH, the context indicates that it is used as a lexical causative ('feed', not 'make eat'). We have already seen in (17) cases of ditransitive V-*sase* functioning as a lexical causative.

There are intriguing cases of V-*sase* prior to age five that are suggestive of how the acquisition of *-sase* as an elsewhere causative takes place. The following are from Ito 1990, 68.

(28) a. kutu-o hake-**sase**-te (Adult form: hak-ase-te) (4;0)
shoes-ACC put on-CAUS-REQ
'put on shoes (on a doll)'

b. toma-**sasi**-te (Adult form: tomar-ase-te) (3;6)
stop-CAUS-REQ (Adult form: tome-te 'stop$_{TR}$')
'stop (it)'

c. ori-**sase**-te (Correct form: orosi-te 'put (me) down')
lower-CAUS-REQ (4;0)
'put (me) down'

In (28a), instead of the "normal" *hak-ase* 'put on', the child inserts the vowel *e* at the end of the verb stem, which leads to *-sase* appearing as a full form. We see a similar phenomenon in (28b), in which the verb 'stop', which has the consonant-ending stem form of *tomar-*, is truncated to *toma*, again allowing the causative morpheme—in this case the allomorph of *-sase*, *-sasi*—to appear in its full form. We can speculate that the child at this stage knows that *-sase/-sasi* is the elsewhere causative for forming lexical causatives, but has not learned that the initial *s* drops if the verb stem ends in a consonant. If the stem is consonant-ending, either a vowel is inserted or the final consonant is deleted, in either case resulting in *-sase* or its allomorph emerging in its full form. In (28c), we again see *-sase* in its full form, but the verb stem happens to be vowel-ending, so no adjustment has been made to allow *-sase* to appear with the initial *s* intact. What is of interest is that, separate from this V-*sase* verb, there is the synthetic lexical causative, *oros-u* 'put (one) down'; either the child has not acquired that lexical causative yet, or simply uses *-sase* as the default morpheme for all lexical causatives.

There are other reported instances in which a child apparently has mastered the morphophonemics of *-sase* early on—being able to drop the initial *s* in the environment of a consonant-ending stem.

(29) Kii (1;6–2;0)

a. toor-**ase**-n (7 tokens) (too-s 'pass$_{TR}$')
pass-CAUS
'(I will not) let you pass'

b. kabur-**ase**-te
put on-CAUS-REQ
'let me put (it) on'

(Miyata 1998; Yokoyama 1991; cited in Shirai et al. 2001)

Assuming that these are also cases of lexical causatives, there are a couple of observations to make. In (29a), the child is using the elsewhere *-sase* to form the lexical causative instead of using the "normal" synthetic causative *too-s* 'pass$_{TR}$'. Either the child has not acquired the synthetic lexical causative, or there is, at this point in acquisition, a tendency to privilege the simpler elsewhere causative, a possibility we also saw in (28). Example (29b) is another instance of a ditransitive lexical causative with *-sase*. We can see that this is a lexical causative because the context is that of putting something on the head of a doll. There is no synthetic ditransitive lexical causative, so the elsewhere *-sase* is appropriate.

Finally, MFH report on what they characterize as overgeneration.

(30) Kuruma-o too-**s**-i-**sase**-ru. (Adult form: too-s-(r)u) (Taatyan, 3;10)
car-ACC pass-CAUS-CAUS-PRES
Intended: '(I'll) pass the car through.'

As MFH note, "the transitive verb [*too-s* 'pass'], which is a causative verb . . . is erroneously associated with an additional causative morpheme *sase*." The adult form would simply call for the transitive *too-s* 'pass' without the need for *-sase*. One way to interpret this overgenerated form is that, despite the selection of the transitive form *too-s*, the child, in order to express the meaning of lexical causation, is compelled to insert the elsewhere *-sase*, again suggesting that *-sase* is privileged for creating a lexical causative. See MFH for an interesting discussion of this example.

More work is required for us to understand the process of acquisition of elsewhere causatives, but this handful of examples is suggestive of the direction of future research.

6 THE ENGLISH CAUSATIVE

McCawley (1978) has made an observation about English causatives that is similar to what we have observed about blocking in Japanese causatives. According to him, where there is a synthetic lexical causative, the analytical causative only has its characteristic meaning of *indirect causation*, as opposed to the direct causation that characterizes lexical causatives.

(31) a. He caused the sheriff to die.
b. He killed the sheriff.

McCawley (1978, 249) notes, "[(31a)] would be an inappropriate thing to say if the person in question shot the sheriff to death, since there is an alternative available [(31b)] involving a less complex surface structure." The point is that on the simplest assumption about what transpired (the sheriff's death being brought about by someone), namely that the causation was direct, one would use the lexical causative to indicate that explicitly, but if the death was caused in some indirect way, (31a) may be chosen.

McCawley (1978, 250) also notes that the analytical (or periphrastic) causative may express the lexical-causative meaning if there is no synthetic lexical causative: "Periphrastic causatives can be used for direct causation in cases where there is no lexical causative." I will return to McCawley's description of (31) in Section 7.

6.1 The elsewhere causative in English

English appears to be different from Japanese in having two elsewhere causatives, with the choice between them unclear and sometimes both being possible. This unusual situation arises in part from the fact that one of the elsewhere causative morphemes, which is null, is limited to lexical causatives (like an elsewhere version of the lexical-causative classes in (1)), while the other, *make*, can function as either a lexical or an analytical causative, similar to *-sase*. This description does not explain why two elsewhere causatives exist, and I will not be able to offer an explanation. However, this unusual situation allows us to test a fundamental property of elsewhere causatives.

In English, unaccusative–lexical causative pairs typically, though not always, are comprised of words that are homophonous.

(32) $\text{open}_{\text{INTR}}/\text{open}_{\text{TR}}$

Based on the fact that there are a large number of pairs like these, a reasonable assumption to make is that there is a null causative morpheme that creates a lexical causative from unaccusative verbs. On this account, a lexical causative like $\textit{stop}_{\text{TR}}$ contains the null elsewhere causative morpheme.

The other elsewhere causative morpheme in English is more like *-sase* in being compatible with either analytical or lexical causatives. The verb *make* embeds another verb to form a complex predicate. In its typical use, it forms an analytical causative.

(33) Mary made John wash the windows.

The existence of a lexical causative formed from the null causative morpheme sometimes appears to block an analytical causative from functioning as a lexical causative. We can see this in the idiom data below.

(34) a. stop the rot
b. #make the rot stop (likewise: #cause the rot to stop)

While (34b) is interpretable, it only has the literal meaning of arresting physical decay, and not the idiomatic meaning in (34a) of doing something to prevent a situation from getting worse. Following are other examples.

(35) a. Henry killed time reading a novel.
b. #Henry made time die reading a novel.

(36) a. John's confession moved me.
b. #John's confession made me move.

However, in some contexts, *make* does function as a lexical causative. The following are examples of idioms formed with *make*, showing that the *make* causative is liable to semantic drift (some of these are taken from Marantz 1997 and Ruwet 1991).

(37) *Make* in idioms
a. make ends meet
b. make (someone) tick
c. make your mouth water
d. make oneself scarce
e. make (someone) over
f. make headway

The idioms in (37a–c) are examples of *make* selecting a VP. Just as we saw with Japanese idioms (cf. (14) and 16)), in some cases the noncausative counterpart also functions as an idiom (*ends didn't meet, my mouth watered*—thanks to Beth Levin for these examples), while in others only the causative constitutes an idiom (*#he ticked, #he became/was scarce, #he became/was over*).

The presence of two elsewhere causatives is certainly unusual, and we can only speculate as to how this situation came about historically. At the same time, the double elsewhere causative allows us to test a fundamental prediction of the elsewhere notion. While a basic property of an elsewhere item is that it is allowed to occur if and only if nothing blocks it in derivation, conversely, an elsewhere item itself would not block another item from occurring, not even another elsewhere item. We can see this in English. Unlike Japanese *-sase*, which is always blocked from functioning as a lexical causative in the presence of a synthetic lexical causative, English *make* apparently coexists with the null causative morpheme as another elsewhere causative. For example, the verbs $boil_{\text{INTR}}/boil_{\text{TR}}$ are a typical unaccusative–lexical causative pair, in which the null elsewhere causative morpheme functions to create the lexical causative. Yet there exists the idiom, *make X's blood boil*. This idiom is made up of the unaccusative construction *X's blood boils* and the elsewhere causative *make*. The synthetic lexical causative *boil* does not occur in the same idiom (*#something boiled my blood)*, which simply indicates that the *make* version has been picked out for semantic drift. The important point is that the *make* elsewhere causative is not blocked from functioning as a lexical causative by the existence of the null elsewhere causative.

We would further predict that there ought to be cases where both elsewhere causatives have undergone semantic drift, since one does not block the other, and what is picked to undergo idiomatization is a matter of idiosyncratic choice. Indeed, there are cases of idiom doublets involving *come/bring* (thanks to Beth Levin for the following).

(38) a. make him come to his senses/bring him to his senses
b. make it come to light/bring it to light

There is, in principle, nothing to prevent a language from having two (or more) elsewhere causatives, although one would hope that they are something like allomorphs whose occurrences are governed by the context. The fact that both can occur in the same context, as we can see in (38), makes this problem complex. I will leave it open.

6.2 Historical development of the null elsewhere causative[2]

We saw that English is in the unusual situation of having two elsewhere causatives, *make* and the null causative. Of these two, *make* behaves the same as *-sase* in functioning to pronounce CAUSE regardless of whether it is lexical or analytical, and I take this form to be the more natural type of elsewhere causative. This is so because, under Hale and Keyser's (1993) theory, there is no difference in the CAUSE that occurs in lexical and analytical causatives, hence we would expect the elsewhere causative not to distinguish between them. In contrast, the null causative is limited to lexical causatives, so its scope of elsewhereness is more narrow. We were able to take advantage of this unusual situation to demonstrate one predicted property of elsewhereness: an elsewhere item would not block any other item, because, by definition, an elsewhere item emerges when there is nothing more specific to block it. But how did English manage to develop two elsewhere causatives, when one is all that is required to fulfill the role of pronouncing CAUSE in the absence of a more specific form?

The null causative that is responsible for creating the lexical-causative member of intransitive–transitive doublets did appear in Old English (OE), but its occurrence was limited to a relatively small number of verbs. In post-OE, the null causative spread throughout the language, and this proliferation was due to a variety of factors. According to Visser (1963, chap. 2), based on his study of *Oxford English dictionary* volumes, there were over 220 verbs that were purely intransitive in OE, without the transitive companion. During the same era, there were only about 50 intransitive–transitive doublets. Of the 220 verbs that were purely intransitive in OE, only 58 or so remain as such in present-day English. Hence the proportion of those that are purely intransitive to those that form intransitive–transitive doublets essentially reversed over time: in OE the verbs in the purely intransitive category substantially outnumbered those that formed doublets, but in modern-day English it is the doublets that substantially outnumber the purely intransitive verbs.

We can see a snapshot of this change in a study by Kitazume (1996), who investigated when the members of intransitive–transitive doublets first appeared according to the *OED*. Of the approximately 100 doublets that she found, only a handful were those in which both members appeared around the same time; below I give these and the years in which they appeared. Kitazume does not distinguish between unaccusatives and unergatives, and some of her doublets are not the unaccusative–lexical causative pairs that concern us; I have limited the list to those whose intransitive member we can reasonably analyze as unaccusative. For each, the first date given is for the intransitive and the second is for the transitive.

(39)	break	1000	1000
	hang	1000	1000
	open	1000	1000
	end	975	1000

In contrast, there are a large number of doublets where the lexical causative first appears later—in some cases much later—than the unaccusative. The following is a sample.

(40)	melt	900	1000
	sink	975	1300
	burn	1000	1200
	boil	1000	1320
	drop	1000	1340
	rise	1000	1425
	float	1100	1586
	enter	1250	1362

7 ON THE NATURE OF BLOCKING

There are two general and competing approaches to blocking in the literature. In one view, blocking arises during the course of derivation, where two *derivations* compete and one wins based on the Pāṇini principle that the more specific form wins over the more general one. Distributed Morphology is a framework that is designed to capture these instances of blocking (e.g., Halle and Marantz 1993; Embick and Marantz 2008). The other approach, modeled on Optimality Theory, is to consider paired (or grouped) expressions that are equivalent/similar in meaning as competing *expressions*, and to place filters on the output of the generative component to let the simpler of the competing forms through (Kiparsky 2005).[3] Which view of blocking is correct, the one based on competing derivations or the one based on competing expressions, or do we need both approaches in different contexts? I will argue that we only need the derivation-based notion of blocking for the range of data in this paper, including the comparative construction, discussed below. On this view, there is no special notion of blocking, which instead is just an informal description for the result of derivations favoring a more specific form, presumably a universal characterization of derivation in human language. For expository purposes, I will continue to refer to these effects as blocking.

The most straightforward cases of derivation-based blocking are found with irregular forms in paradigms—*swam* as the past-tense form of *swim*, for example, where the combination *swim* + PAST comes with the instruction to pronounce it as *swam* and not as the elsewhere form **swimmed*. In such cases, the blocked elsewhere form simply fails to occur in the language. There is no context where *swimmed* may occur in English (see McCloskey and Hale 1983 for similar examples from Irish).

More interesting cases are those we observed with the elsewhere *-sase*. The assumption behind the analysis I presented is that CAUSE is identical across lexical and analytical causatives, and, in the absence of anything to block it, *-sase* may occur in both constructions. It is blocked in the course of the derivation of a lexical causative if there is a more specific form associated with a particular verb stem + CAUSE. In that case, *-sase* may not occur as a lexical causative, but may occur as an analytical causative. We saw a similar phenomenon in English, although more complex. English apparently has two elsewhere causatives, the null causative morpheme, which occurs only in lexical causatives, and *make*, which, like *-sase*, may occur in lexical and analytical causatives. What is intriguing is that the null causative morpheme and *make* may coexist even with the same unaccusative verb, as in the pair *make someone come to his senses–bring someone to his senses*, instead of one blocking the other. It is not clear if there are contexts that dictate the use of one elsewhere causative rather than the other for forming a lexical causative.

A morpheme similar to *-sase* is English *-er*, which can create an agentive nominal (e.g., *(dog) catcher*) or an instrument (e.g., *(fly) catcher*). In the presence of a more specific form for one or both of these uses, *-er* is blocked from that use, as with *cooker*, which is blocked from the agentive use by the occurrence of the nominal *cook* and thus limited to the instrument meaning (Aronoff 1976). Just as with *-sase*, we can consider the agentive use of *cooker* to be blocked in derivation because *cook* + AGENT comes with the specific instruction to pronounce it as *cook*.

A different type of blocking is found in cases where the base has two distinct meanings, as with *bad*, which has the conventional meaning as well as the meaning 'tough, mean' (Kiparsky 2005). The comparative of the conventional meaning is the synthetic form *worse*; but *worse* does not also mean 'tougher, meaner'. The comparative with this latter meaning is the elsewhere form *badder*, as in *badder than bad*. The fact that morphology distinguishes between the two meanings may be an indication that there are two distinct words, *bad*$_1$ and *bad*$_2$, an argument I will not pursue here. A similar phenomenon where a morphological process picks out one meaning of a polysemous verb is found in Japanese (Miyagawa 1989, chap. 3).

While all of the cases above are amenable to a derivation-based explanation, there are others noted in the literature that cannot readily be so explained. A well-known case is noted by Poser (1992).

(39) a. smarter, *more smart
 b. *intelligenter, more intelligent

Where the Adj-*er* form is possible, as in *smarter*, the analytical form *more* Adj is often blocked. The condition that dictates whether the *-er* form is possible is phonotactic: one-syllable adjectives allow the *-er* form while trisyllabic ones do not; disyllabic ones are variable, some allowing both forms.

The data in (39) on comparatives appear to show a case where a synthetic form blocks an analytical form and there is no ready derivational connection between the two forms. Kiparsky (2005) argues that these examples provide evidence for a different approach to blocking, one based on Optimality Theory, in which a filter is placed on the output of the generative component. This filter evaluates both syntactic and lexical items, selecting the simplest form (structurally simplest, presumably) that most closely expresses the intended meaning. If this approach is correct, it would also cover all cases of derivation-based blocking. We can see right away that the double occurrence of the elsewhere causative discussed above is potentially a problem for this filters-based approach.

Embick and Noyer (2001) argue that even cases such as (39) can be analyzed as an instance of derivation-based blocking. They assume that comparatives have a structure in which the comparative *-er* occurs in the position where *more* occurs in the analytical form—in a high position, in other words. This *-er* must lower to the adjective, producing the Adj-*er* form. The adjective is somehow marked for whether the *-er* comparative is possible; where it is not possible, the form with *-er* in the original high position is selected, and to this *-er*, *mo-* is attached, producing *more*.

Embick (2007) also notes (as does Kiparsky 2005) that *more smart* may occur in a different context.

(40) John is more smart than handsome.

This is what Embick calls a metalinguistic comparison, and he gives an analysis of it based on Bresnan's (1973) study. The crucial point is that the structure of this metalinguistic comparison is such that *-er* in the original high position cannot lower to the adjective *smart*, thereby always forcing the analytical form for this particular construction. See Kiparsky 2005 for criticism of this approach; see Embick 2007 for response. I will assume that the derivation-based approach is feasible.

Another type of example where a filters-type approach has long been suggested is with analytical causatives in English (examples (41b, c) are from McCawley 1978).

(41) a. John opened the door/John made the door open.
 b. John killed the sheriff/John caused the sheriff to die.
 c. John stopped the engine/John caused the engine to stop.

The periphrastic analytical causative *make the door open* requires a reasonably rich context compared to the conventional event of directly opening the door, the latter expressed by the synthetic lexical causative *open the door.* In all of the periphrastic cases in (41), the meaning implies some special method that was employed to indirectly bring about the eventuality being referred to. For example, in (41c), while *stop the engine* simply suggests that John turned off the engine with the key, *cause the engine to stop* implies some unconventional method, such as jamming the engine with a crowbar (see McCawley 1978). McCawley suggests that when there is a corresponding synthetic lexical causative, the analytical causative must have this kind of special meaning, which he chalks up to indirectness of causation. He proposes a Gricean approach based on a "cooperative principle" that obliges the speaker, unless expressing something out of the ordinary, to use the simpler form (the synthetic causative) if it exists. This is similar to Kiparsky's (2005) approach, in that it too puts the burden of the blocking effect on a filter on the output of the generative component.

But is McCawley's description of the examples correct, particularly the analytical examples? When one inspects them, those that behave as in (41) and require some special context for the indirect causation all contain an unaccusative verb (*open, die, stop*). Those he cites that do not require a special interpretation all involve verbs with an external argument, either an agent or an experiencer (*laugh, drop, drop*: McCawley 1978, 250). Unaccusative verbs by nature do not have agency or some inherent force associated with an experiencer. In causative structures, very generally, external agents or forces cause eventualities to take place. In the "special" examples in (41), given the lack of agency in the lower clause, the only external force is supplied by the external argument of *make*, which is an indirect causer according to the ordinary meaning of the analytical causative. This indirect causation cannot simply be in the form of, for example, ordering/directing an embedded agent/force to do something. Rather, one must employ some special method for indirectly bringing about the event. On this analysis, there is nothing special about the analytical-causative forms in (41); they are precisely what we expect of an analytical causative built on an unaccusative verb, and there is no reason to treat them in some special manner.

8 CONCLUSION

The causative forms in Japanese give support to the idea that both lexical and analytical causatives share a common syntactic frame, where a causative *v* selects a maximal projection: *v*P, VP, PP, AP, NP. If v_{CAUSE} selects a *v*P, the result is an analytical causative, while any of the other XPs results in a lexical causative (Hale and Keyser 1993). We saw that this v_{CAUSE} may be pronounced by the same morpheme in both the lexical causative and the analytical causative: *-sase* in Japanese and *make* in English. Where there is a specific (synthetic) lexical causative, it blocks V-*sase* from being identified with the lexical causative, so that it cannot participate in any lexical-causative processes such as idiomatization and the double-causative construction. While these cases of causatives in English and Japanese are amenable to a derivation-based approach to blocking, there are cases in the literature that have been analyzed on a filter-based approach. We saw that these, too, are compatible with a derivation-based analysis, making the filter-based approach to blocking unnecessary.

9 Historical development of the accusative case marker[1]

1 INTRODUCTION

In modern Japanese, the postpositional particle *-o* marks the accusative case on direct objects.

(1) Hanako-ga kuruma-**o** katta.
Hanako-NOM car-ACC bought
'Hanako bought a car.'

Aside from a handful of exceptions that are easily explained, the requirement in modern Japanese that the accusative marker *-o* must accompany a direct object is inviolable.[2] As I showed in Miyagawa 1989, chap. 5, the accusative case marking is licensed by the case-assigning feature on the verb.

In this chapter, I trace the historical development of the accusative case marker from the earliest written records to the present. Unlike in modern Japanese, it is well known that in the Japanese of the eighth and ninth centuries, which I call "Old Japanese" (OJ), word order commonly marks the accusative case without any case particle. The particle *-o* appears occasionally on direct objects, but its infrequent occurrence led traditional grammarians to claim that in OJ, *-o* does not function as a true accusative particle, or, at best, this function is unstable. Its clearest usage is as an emphatic marker, which is thought by traditional grammarians to be the source of the accusative particle.

I argue here that the OJ *-o* can be clearly established as the accusative case marker. Using case theory (Chomsky 1981, 1982; Stowell 1981), I show that the distribution of *-o* as a case marker is predictable and falls in line with the universal principle pertaining to case marking. Moreover, this analysis of OJ *-o* provides a straightforward account of the linguistic change that transformed OJ, which required the accusative marker *-o* on only some occasions, into modern Japanese, which requires the particle on all direct objects (with the exceptions noted in note 2). In other words, for the accusative case, our analysis explains why OJ is "semicaseless," whereas modern Japanese is fully cased.

The earliest written record in OJ that I draw from is the *Man'yōshū* (Collection of a myriad of leaves), which is the oldest of the Japanese anthologies compiled during the latter half of the eighth century. The anthology consists of more than four thousand poems distributed among twenty books, and it reflects life in both the city and the countryside in the seventh and eighth centuries. The versification mainly consists of the *tanka,* a verse form that epitomizes Japanese national poetry; its basic form is five lines of five or seven syllables each, 5–7–5–7–7. The *tanka* constitutes over 90 percent of the poems in the *Man'yōshū,* with the rest being other combinations of lines of five or seven syllables. For example, the next most prevalent form, the *chōka* ('long poem'), "consists of alternate lines of 5 and 7 syllables, finishing with an extra 7-syllable line" (Nippon Gakujutsu Shinkōkai 1965). Unless otherwise noted, the *Man'yōshū* examples are from Takagi et al. 1957, 1962, and most of the English translations are from Pierson 1931. I follow the common practice in traditional studies of identifying the examples by *Kokka taikan* (*KT*) number, which is given next to the examples.[3] In addition, I draw data from the early tenth-century works the *Kokinshū* and the *Tosa diary.* Later in the chapter, I also present data from the *Tale of the Heike,* which is a tale of warrior romance originally written around the thirteenth century. The authoritative text was written in 1371. I compare this text to a later version, the *Amakusa Heike,* written in the late sixteenth century. Overall, the data presented in this chapter, from the *Man'yōshū* in the eighth century to the *Amakusa Heike* in the late sixteenth century, span a period of nearly one thousand years. I also comment on the modern Japanese *-o* from the perspective of my analysis of its historical development.

This chapter addresses a major historical change in Japanese that transformed the "semicaseless" language of the eighth century into the fully cased language of today. In looking at this change, I attempt to demonstrate the following: historical change is constrained in the same way that synchronic variations among contemporary languages are constrained. The same theory of universal grammar that accounts for synchronic variation can also account for diachronic variation of the type examined here. In brief, we can state the following.

(2) Diachronic and synchronic variation

From the perspective of universal grammar, diachronic variation within a language (of the sort examined here) and synchronic variation among contemporary languages are, in principle, *nondistinct.*

According to this proposal, two distinct historical stages of a language might differ precisely in the same way that two contemporary languages differ. I am of course referring not to the entire language but rather to particular, isolable properties of a language. Specifically, I shall show that the difference between OJ and modern Japanese with regard to accusative case is identical to the difference that one can observe between modern Japanese and modern English. We can diagram this as follows, with *X* representing some property pertaining to the accusative case with respect to which these languages fundamentally differ:

(3) Old Japanese, modern Japanese, and modern English
Old Japanese ← *X* → modern Japanese ← *X* → modern English

What (3) indicates is that OJ and modern Japanese differ with regard to property *X*, and that the same difference distinguishes modern Japanese and modern English. To be more explicit, OJ and modern English are identical with regard to property *X*.

The idea that the principles of synchronic grammar impose restrictions on diachronic change is not new. Joseph (1980, 346) uses the same assumption in his historical study of the loss of the infinitive form in Greek when he says that "universal constraints which hold in synchronic grammars are used to explain the direction taken by certain changes in syntax." In the same vein, Lightfoot (1979, viii) states that the formulation of "a possible grammar will provide the upper limits to the way in which a given grammar may change historically, insofar as it cannot change into something which is not a possible grammar." He further notes, correctly I might add, that this approach to diachronic change has not met with much success in the past because we had a poor understanding of what constitutes a possible synchronic grammar. In recent years, a great deal of progress has been made toward this end within the Government and Binding theory. The most pertinent feature of the theory for our purpose is the idea that a language emanates from a set of universal principles, which are, in the terminology of the Standard Theory, substantive universals (Chomsky 1965), with some principles parameterized to account for variation among different languages. As I show, this idea of parameterization plays a key role in the analysis of the historical development of the accusative case marker.[4]

An adequate account of historical change based on the principles of universal grammar would have an important and highly desirable consequence: the sharp limitation of possible historical changes that a language can undergo. This effort to constrain historical change is consistent with how the field of generative grammar has attempted to limit the possible core grammars of human languages (Chomsky 1965, 1981), an effort that has met with considerable success especially in the last ten years. Indeed, it is possible to see that the application of universal principles to historical change is a natural extension of the theory. Each historical stage of a language is governed by the principles of universal grammar. Any change from one stage to the next must be within the confines of universal grammar.

From this perspective, we can surmise that a possible type of change would involve "resetting" a parameter. For example, one can imagine a language that changes from a head-final language into one that is head-initial, a variation intrinsically allowed in the theory of phrase structure (cf. Chomsky 1981, 1982, 1986a, 1986b; Stowell 1981). I argue that the dearth of *-o* in OJ and its increasing occurrence in post-OJ are together an example of a language taking advantage of the options inherent in universal grammar. The particular universal principle involved is case theory. I begin our discussion with a brief sketch of this principle.

2 CASE THEORY

Case theory requires every overt NP to have case. The intuitive reasoning here is that to understand a sentence, the function of every NP must be identified. This idea is formalized into what is known as the case filter, one version of which is given in (4).

(4) Case filter (Chomsky 1981, 49)
*NP if NP has phonetic content and has no case.

By this principle, a sentence containing an overt NP that lacks case is ungrammatical. An NP can receive case in two possible ways.

(5) Case assignment (Chomsky 1981, 1982; Stowell 1981)
 (i) Overt case marking
 (ii) Abstract case assignment

Overt case marking simply means that a case marker, such as the Japanese *-o*, actually appears with a NP. The second method, abstract case assignment, is possible only if the NP is governed by and is adjacent to a case assigner. A verb is a common case assigner.[5]

Modern Japanese represents the first means of assigning case because it has overt case particles. These particles meet the requirement that every overt NP must have case. Because the case itself is overt, the NP need not be adjacent to the verb.

(6) Taroo-wa **hon-o** kinoo katta.
Taro-TOP book-ACC yesterday bought
'Taro bought a book yesterday.'

As shown, the direct object with *-o* need not occur adjacent to the verb. English exemplifies the second means of assigning case. Because the assigned case is abstract, the NP must occur adjacent to the verb.

(7) a. Taro bought **a book** yesterday.
b. *Taro bought yesterday **a book**.

Example (7a) is grammatical, but, in (7b), the sentence is ungrammatical because the adverb *yesterday* intervenes between the caseless object NP and the verb.[6]

Old Japanese is like English in that the direct object commonly lacks overt case marking.

(8) Ware-wa imo __ omou. (*KT* 133)
I-TOP wife think
'I think of my wife.'

Here, we assume that the object NP *imo* 'wife' receives abstract case from the verb. In our data, every instance of a "bare" object NP occurs immediately adjacent to the verb as predicted by the adjacency condition on abstract case assignment.

As stated earlier, I intend to exploit historical data on the Japanese accusative case in order to argue that historical change is highly constrained because it occurs within the boundaries of the options made available in universal grammar. I can now be more specific. I shall show that the change in accusative case from OJ to modern Japanese is one in which the language has moved from abstract case marking of the direct object in OJ to the overt case marking of today. This is precisely the difference we see today between Japanese and English, a difference allowed by the options given in universal grammar—the same options that allowed the change from OJ to modern Japanese in the way the accusative case is marked.

3 DISTRIBUTION OF OJ PARTICLE -*O*[7]

Examples such as (8) that lack the particle -*o* are predominant in OJ (Matsuo 1938), but occasionally the particle does occur. At first glance, its occurrence appears arbitrary, to the point that one grammarian comments that the particle in OJ may have been inserted at the whim of the author (Hirohama 1966). I show here that the -*o* that marks the accusative case has a clear distributional property. But, first, let us look at another usage of -*o* that is truly arbitrary in distribution.

3.1 Exclamatory and emphatic -*o*

Before -*o* became a case particle, its sole function was exclamation or emphasis (Hashimoto 1969; Kobayashi 1970). This -*o*, which is common in OJ, attaches to any segment of a sentence, including the whole sentence (examples (9) and (10) are from Kobayashi 1970, 247).

(9) Kaganabete yo ni wa kokonoyo hi ni wa tooka-**o**.
total days nights nine nights days ten days-EMPH
'The number of days is, of nights, nine, and of days, ten.'

(10) Yaegaki tukuru sono yaegaki-**o**.
many fences build that many fences-EMPH
'I build a multiple-fenced palace; ah, that multiple-fenced palace!'

(11) kono tosi goro-**o** (*KT* 192)
this year-EMPH
'during this (mourning) year'

(12) Imo-ga ie mo tugite mimasi-**o**, Yamamoto
sweetheart-GEN house continually want to see-EMPH Yamato
naru Oosima-no ne-ni ie mo aramasi-**o**. (*KT* 91)
in Oshima-GEN top-in house hope to stand-EMPH
'To be able to see continually the surroundings of my love's house, oh, might my house stand on the top of Oshima in Yamato.'

This usage of -*o* does not represent any relationship between the -*o*-marked segment and the predicate as it would if -*o* were the accusative marker. It occurs any time the need for exclamation or emphasis arises, hence its distribution is syntactically arbitrary. Traditional grammarians generally view all occurrences of -*o* in OJ as embodying a sense of exclamation or emphasis, thus rejecting the idea that OJ -*o* can function purely as the accusative case (e.g., Hashimoto 1969; Kobayashi 1970). According to them, the exclamatory/emphatic sense gradually faded, giving rise to the use of -*o* as a pure case marker in the post-OJ era.

3.2 Distribution of nonemphatic -*o*

Traditional grammarians do not reject the idea that some occurrences of -*o* reflect the accusative case, but they are in virtual agreement that every occurrence of -*o*, accusative or not, embodies emphasis or exclamation. One might say that the ostensibly random occurrence of -*o* in OJ is simply owing to the fact that -*o* occurs only when there is emphasis, hence its distribution cannot be syntactically predicted. A close inspection, however, reveals that the particle indeed has a syntactic distribution. Although the particle rarely occurs in matrix clauses, such as (8), repeated here as (13), its occurrence is virtually obligatory in subordinate clauses, as exemplified in (14) and (15) (the latter cited in Zenno 1987, from the *Tosa diary*). I have enclosed the relevant subordinate clause with square brackets in (14) and (15).

(13) Ware-wa imo __ omou. (*KT* 133)
I-TOP wife think
'I think of my wife.'

(14) [sima-**o** miru] toki (*KT* 178)
island look when
'when I look upon the island'

(15) Yo-no naka-ni omoiyaredomo [ko-**o** kouru] omoi ni masaru
world's inside-at ponder child miss feeling surpass

omoi naki kana.
feeling not exist

'Ponder as we may the sorrows of this bleak world, we find none more sharp than the grief a parent feels mourning the loss of a child.'

In both (14) and (15), the particle *-o* attaches to an object NP in a subordinate clause. In a set of 249 sentences examined in the *Man'yōshū* (Takagi et al. 1957, 145–227), 36 have a transitive subordinate clause with an overt object NP. Of these 36, fully 32 have the particle *-o* on the subordinate object (Matsunaga 1983). The remaining 4 do not have the particle, hence they are apparent exceptions, though 2 of them might be described as idioms or as compounds (Matsunaga 1983).[8]

Leaving aside the possible exceptions, the data reveal the following distribution:

(16) Distribution of OJ *-o*
(i) In a matrix clause the particle *-o* need not occur.
(ii) In a subordinate clause it must occur.

Why is there this difference between matrix and subordinate clauses? Earlier, I suggested that the absence of the particle in matrix clauses is licensed by abstract case assignment by the verb, very much like the direct object in modern English. This implies that the subordinate clause takes the other option available in universal grammar—case is assigned overtly. In other words, OJ subscribes to *both* abstract case assignment and overt case assignment, the former implemented in the matrix clause and the latter in the subordinate clause. Both are dependent, of course, on the case-assigning feature on the verb. As demonstrated shortly, this is indeed an accurate picture, although the actual split is not between matrix and subordinate clauses. Rather, the distinction arises from a difference in the verbal inflection of these clauses.

3.3 Conclusive and attributive forms

The inflectional morphology of OJ verbs justifies the distinction posited between the case-assignment properties of matrix and subordinate verbs. In modern Japanese, there is no difference in shape between matrix and subordinate verbs.

(17) a. Sakana-o **taberu.**
fish eat
'(I) eat fish.'

b. **taberu** sakana
'the fish (that I) eat'

But in OJ, verbs are inflected differently in matrix and subordinate clauses (there are some exceptions, discussed later). The examples in (18) are OJ versions of (17).

(18) a. Sakana(-o) **tabu.** Conclusive form
b. **taburu** sakana Attributive form

As shown, matrix verbs take the *conclusive* form while subordinate verbs take the *attributive* form.[9] We thus have the following generalization:

(19) Accusative case assignment in OJ
The conclusive form assigns abstract case while the case-assigning feature of the attributive form must be manifested overtly as *-o*.

It is not just in the case-assigning property that these two verbal inflections differ. The conclusive is the "true verb form, used in principal sentences to predicate an action, property, or state" (Sansom 1928, 130). As a "pure" verb, we can surmise that it has all of the properties of a verb, including the capability to assign abstract case. In contrast, the attributive inflection shifts the lexical property of the "pure" verb (conclusive) into one with "substantive" properties. The following example from Sansom 1928, 136, illustrates two substantive properties of the attributive form.[10]

(20) hito-no **mitogamuru**-o sirazu
people blame not know
'not knowing that others blamed them'

First, the attributive form *mitogamuru* 'blaming' has a substantive interpretation similar to that of the English gerund. Second, the particle *-o* attaches to it to make the phrase an apparent argument of the verb *sirazu* 'not know'. These two qualities make the attributive form appear nominal in nature. It would be incorrect, however, to identify it as a pure nominal, because it has verbal and adjectival properties as well. For example, it is able to modify a noun without the prenominal genitive particle *-no*. In (17b), for example, if the attributive form *taburu* were a pure nominal, we would expect the prenominal modification particle *-no* between it and the relative head. The genitive particle *-no* does appear in the relative clause, but only on the subject, as exemplified in

(20), in which *-no* attaches to the subordinate subject *hito* 'people'. The same particle never arises on the object, indicating that the attributive verb is not a nominal. The attributive form appears to belong to the same category as the gerund in English—it is both verblike and nounlike. It may be that this ambiguous identity contributes to the requirement that the case-assigning feature be manifested as the overt case marker *-o*.[11]

4 FURTHER EVIDENCE

The evidence so far for the existence of *-o* as a pure accusative marker in OJ has been limited to the matrix–subordinate distinction: in a matrix clause, with the conclusive form, the particle need not occur, but, in a subordinate clause, with the attributive form, the particle must occur. In this section, I provide further evidence that the distinction between abstract and overt case arises from the distinction in verbal morphology between conclusive and attributive forms.

4.1 Subordinate conclusive form

Although I have only given examples of the conclusive form that appear in matrix clauses, it is by no means limited to matrix clauses. It can appear, for example, in a subordinate clause with the "quotative" complementizer *to*. In the following example from the *Tosa diary* (Zenno 1987), the subordinate transitive verb in the *to* complement assigns abstract case to its object.

(21) Kono hito, uta __ yoman to omou kokoro arite
this person poem compose-intend COMP think mind exist
narikeri.
COP
'This person had the intention to compose poems.'

Although *yoman* is in a subordinate clause, it is a conclusive form. Hence it is able to license the occurrence of the object NP *uta* 'poems' without an overt case marking by assigning it abstract case.

4.2 *Kakarimusubi*

In the same way that the conclusive form is not limited to matrix clauses, the attributive form is not limited to subordinate clauses. The attributive form appears in a matrix clause that has undergone a rule called *kakarimusubi*. This rule, which is triggered by a *kakari* particle occurring sentence-internally, requires that the matrix verb be in the attributive form instead of the conclusive form. The sentences in (22), taken from Sansom 1928, illustrate this rule for the *kakari* particles *zo* and *ya*. (*Zo* is used for emphasis, something akin to 'indeed', whereas *ya* is commonly used for rhetorical questions.)[12]

(22) a. Isi-wa kawa-ni otu. Conclusive
rock-TOP river-in fall
'Rocks fall into the river.'

b. Isi **zo** kawa-ni **oturu.** Attributive

c. Isi **ya** kawa-ni **oturu.** Attributive

From a set of 208 examples in the *Man'yōshū* (Takagi et al. 1962, 55–109), 34 are *kakarimusubi* constructions with a transitive verb and an overt object NP. All 34 are matrix clauses, and, significantly, the particle -*o* marks the object NP without exception (cf. Matsunaga 1983). The following construction exemplifies this:

(23) Kimi-ga mi-fune-**o** itu to ka matamu. (*KT* 3707)
you-GEN fine boat when KAKARI wait$_{\text{ATTRIB}}$
'When may we await your fine boat back?'

The following *Shoku Nihongi* example from Sansom 1928 illustrates the same point.

(24) Ware hitori ya wa tootoki sirusi-**o** uketamawamu?
I alone KAKARI precious token receive$_{\text{ATTRIB}}$
'Shall I alone receive the precious token?'

Example (24) is significant in that the object NP taking the particle is adjacent to the matrix verb, a condition that would allow abstract case assignment if the verb were not in the attributive but instead the conclusive form.

What we have seen about *kakarimusubi* based on data from the eighth century can also be seen in the texts of the early tenth century. As pointed out by Zenno (1987), both the *Kokinshū Kanazyo* and the *Tosa diary* texts contain a number of transitive *kakarimusubi* constructions that support the hypothesis that the case particle -*o* must occur when the verb is in the attributive form even in matrix clauses. The following examples are from Zenno's work ((25) and (26) are from *Kokinshū*; (27) and (28) are from the *Tosa diary*):

(25) Aru-wa, haru natu aki fuyu-ni mo iranu,
some-TOP spring summer fall winter-in even not included

kusagusa-no uta-**o** **nan** **erabasetamaikeru.**
various poems KAKARI choose.CAUS.PAST.HONORIFIC$_{\text{ATTRIB}}$

'(The emperor) had ordered (someone) to choose some miscellaneous compositions unsuited to seasonal categories.'

(26) Iki to si ikeru mono, izure **ka** uta-**o** yomazarikeru.
all the living things which KAKARI poem compose-NEG-exist$_{\text{ATTRIB}}$
'Every living creature sings.'

(27) Te kirukiru tundaru na-**o** oya **ya** **maboruran,**
hand cut-cutting picked herb parent KAKARI eat-must$_{\text{ATTRIB}}$
siutome ya kufuran.
mother-in-law KAKARI must eat
'Is an old man wolfing them now? Is an old mother-in-law eating them now? Those tender greens I picked (while the young miscanthus), cut my hands.'

(28) Hitobito umi-**o** nagametutu **zo** **aru.**
people sea looking KAKARI exist$_{\text{ATTRIB}}$
'People stared absently at the sea.'

These *kakarimusubi* constructions show that the distribution of the particle *-o* cannot be predicted from just the type of clause, matrix or subordinate. The distinction between abstract and overt case is due to the difference between the lexical properties of conclusive and attributive forms.

4.3 Particles that require the attributive form

As a final piece of evidence that the attributive form requires the overt object marker *-o* on the direct object, I turn to a point noted by Zenno (1987). He states that two sentential particles, the exclamation *kana* and the conjunctive *ni,* require the preceding verb to be in the attributive form, just like *kakarimusubi.* As predicted from our hypothesis, when these particles appear with a transitive verb, the object NP is accompanied by the particle *-o,* as illustrated by the *Tosa diary* examples that Zenno cites.

(29) Sao sasedo sokoi mo siranu
oar put in bottom even not know
watatumi-no fukaki kokoro-**o** kimi-ni **miru** **kana.**
sea's deep heart you-in see$_{\text{ATTRIB}}$ EXCL
'As when a boatman seeks in vain to plumb the sea, thrusting with his oar, even so do we behold the boundless depths of your hearts.'

(30) Kono uta-wa, tokoro-**o** **miru** **ni,** **emasarazu.**
this poem-TOP place see$_{\text{ATTRIB}}$ however surpass-NEG
'The poem was not the equal of the scene.'

The last example is especially instructive: the object NP is adjacent to the transitive verb, yet the overt particle appears because the verb is incapable of assigning abstract case.

5 OTHER VERBAL FORMS

I have so far dealt with the two verbal forms the conclusive and attributive. In OJ, there are four other forms, namely, perfect (*izen*), conjunctive (*ren'yoo*), imperfect (*mizen*), and imperative (*meirei*). Of these, Zenno (1987) demonstrates in the perfect and conjunctive forms properties relevant to this discussion on case.

5.1 Perfect

The perfect form, which exists in OJ but not in modern Japanese, "conveys the idea of the definite completion of the act or state described by the verb" (Sansom 1928, 43). The perfect form has three common uses: (i) it occurs with the conditional *-ba*; (ii) it occurs with *-do* or *-domo* to mean 'although'; and (iii) it participates in *kakarimusubi* constructions when the *kakari* particle is the emphatic *koso*. These three uses are illustrated in the following *Tosa diary* examples from Zenno 1987:

(31) umi-**o** **miyare**-ba
sea-ACC look across$_{\text{PERF}}$-*BA*
'gazing out across the sea'

(32) Kyoo-wa aouma-**o** **omoe**-do, kai nasi.
today-TOP festival of blue horse-ACC think$_{\text{PERF}}$-*DO* effect not exist
'People thought in vain about the White Horse Banquet being held that day.'

(33) Kagami-ni kami-no kokoro-**o** **koso** wa **miture.**
mirror-in god's mind-ACC *KAKARI* seen$_{\text{PERF}}$
'I saw the god's heart clearly in the mirror.'

As Zenno observes, the accusative marker *-o* is required when the verb is in the perfect form, just as we saw for the attributive form. Although Zenno does not give an account of this, one possible reason is the compound nature of the perfect form. As argued by Aston (cited in Sansom 1928, 142), the perfect form is a contraction of a verb in the conjunctive form and the verb *aru* 'exist'. For example, the perfect form *yuke* 'go' is a contracted compound form of the two verbs *yuki* (conjunctive form of the verb) and *ani*. We can speculate that this process of compounding somehow takes away the capability of the original transitive verb to assign abstract case, a speculation that naturally must be substantiated with data that is not available at present.

5.2 Conjunctive

The conjunctive form is used to conjoin sentences, and it occurs most commonly with the particle *te*. The interesting point noted by Zenno is that this form appears to *optionally* assign abstract case, since we find that both the overt *-o* and the bare NP occur fairly commonly with this form. The following examples from the *Tosa diary* are cited in Zenno 1987:

(34) Te __ **arai**, rei no kotodomo __ **si**-te, hiru ni narinu.
hand wash$_{\text{CONJ}}$ usual things do$_{\text{CONJ}}$-*TE* noon became
'It was around noon by the time people had washed their hands and performed the usual offices.'

(35) Kore-**o** nomi **itagari**, mono-**o** nomi **kui**-te, yo
this-ACC only appreciate$_{\text{CONJ}}$ things-ACC only eat$_{\text{CONJ}}$-*TE* night
fukenu.
fell
'They uttered words of praise and kept on eating, (and it became late).'

In (34), the direct-object NPs of the conjunctive forms appear without *-o*, whereas those in (35) appear with *-o*, indicating that the conjunctive verb optionally assigns abstract case.

Another point noted by Zenno is that when there are two coordinate sentences, each with a direct object, as we see in (34) and (35), either *both* of the direct objects have the overt particle or *neither* of them has the particle. That is, with a conjunctive form, a parallelism must obtain in the two clauses with regard to case: if one object NP lacks *-o*, then the other must not have it either, as we see in (34), but if one has the particle, then both must have it, as we see in (35). The former type observes adjacency because the direct-object NP receives abstract case from the verb, just as in the case of the conclusive form. But in the latter type—the overtly cased type—the object NP with *-o* is free to occur away from the verb.

6 WORD ORDER

The analysis of the OJ accusative case based on case theory makes the following predictions:

(36) Word order
  (i) An object NP without the particle *-o* must occur immediately adjacent to the verb.
  (ii) If the object NP is overtly cased, it is free to occur virtually anywhere within the clause.

Both predictions are borne out in our data. The caseless object NP occurs immediately adjacent to the conclusive form, but with the *-o*-marked object NP that occurs with the attributive, the perfect, and some conjunctive forms, the tendency is for the overtly cased NP to appear away from the verb, as shown in the following *Man'yōshū* examples:

(37) miyako-**o** Nara-ni utusisi noti (Title of poem no. 260)
capital-ACC Nara-to move$_{\text{ATTRIB}}$ after
'after (the emperor) moved the capital to Nara'

(38) Hizikata-no otome-**o** Hatuse-yama-ni (Title of poem no. 428)
Hijikata lady-ACC Mount Hatsuse-at
yakihaburu toki
cremate when
'on the occasion of the cremation of Lady Hijikata at Mount Hatsuse'

In both examples, an adverbial phrase intervenes between an attributive verb and the overtly cased NP.

Along with these two possibilities, there is a third. From time to time, the particle *-o* appears on the object NP of a conclusive form. The following *Man'yōshū* examples are from Sansom 1928:

(39) Nao si negaitu, titose-no inoti-**o.**
still EMPH pray thousand-GEN life
'I still do pray one thousand years of life.'

(40) Tugeyaramu . . . tabi-no yadori-**o.**
will proclaim travel-GEN lodge
'I will proclaim my stopping place.'

Note that the word order of these sentences is not the normal kind but rather the inverted kind. That is, the object NP, which normally occurs preverbally, appears instead in the postverbal position. Because of this inversion, the object NP does not occur in the position adjacent to and governed by the verb, so the verb cannot directly assign abstract case to it. One way, then, to account for the occurrence of *-o* in these examples is to view it as accusative case marking that appears on the NP because the NP cannot receive abstract case directly from the verb. By this account, the object NP begins in the normal preverbal position and is moved to the postverbal position, as illustrated in (41) for the sentence in (40).

(41) [[t_i tugeyaramu] tabi-no yadori-o$_i$]
will proclaim travel-GEN lodge

This is similar to the analysis of scrambling in modern Japanese, in which an object NP, for example, that occurs to the left of the subject NP is viewed as having originated in the normal preverbal position but moved to the sentence-initial position by the rule of Move *α* (cf. Saito 1985; see also Harada 1977).

(42) [Nani-o$_i$ [Taroo-ga t_i katta no]]?
what-ACC Taro-NOM bought Q
Lit. 'What$_i$, Taro bought t_i?'

One point about the scrambling cases such as (42) that is relevant to our discussion of OJ *-o* is the phenomenon of "case drop." Under certain conditions, the accusative *-o* in modern Japanese can be dropped, leaving a "bare" object NP (cf. note 2). This is very much like the OJ phenomena that we have observed in this chapter, though in modern Japanese the absence of the case marker is rare, unlike the language of the OJ era. As Saito (1983, 1985) notes, the optimal environment for this case drop is under adjacency. Thus, although the *-o* in (42) cannot drop because the object NP has been scrambled out of the position adjacent to the verb, the same particle can drop in the following example:

(43) Nani __ katta no?
what bought Q
'What did you buy?'

This suggests that even in modern Japanese, a transitive verb is able to (optionally) assign abstract case if the object NP is adjacent to it structurally.[13] If adjacency fails to obtain, as in (42), the particle must occur. As we can see, precisely the same can be said about the occurrence of *-o* with the conclusive verb in the *Man'yōshū* examples in (39) and (40). The case particle occurs on the object NP despite the fact that the verb takes the conclusive form because the object NP has been moved from the position adjacent to the verb, hence it is incapable of directly receiving abstract case. I resume the discussion of the modern accusative case later in this chapter.

7 LANGUAGE CHANGE

We have seen that in OJ texts such as the *Man'yōshū,* the object NP is more commonly marked by word order than by the particle -*o*. Beginning in the tenth century, this pattern begins to reverse until virtually every object NP is marked by the particle. This change occurred over a period of some five hundred years, during which time a number of other major changes occurred as well, together transforming the language into one that closely resembles modern Japanese. This change in the early stages is documented by Matsuo (1938), who investigated the number of occurrences of the object NP with and without -*o* in the *Man'yōshū* and in several texts written in the tenth century. In (44), the relevant portions of his findings are summarized.

(44) Increase in the frequency of -*o* from the eighth century to the tenth century

	Object NP with -*o*	Without -*o*
Man'yōshū (Book 17)	51	96
Tales of Ise	294	204
Tosa diary	254	231

As shown, in the *Man'yōshū,* compiled in the late eighth century, there are almost twice as many object NPs without -*o* as those marked by the particle. But in the *Tales of Ise* and the *Tosa diary*, both written in the early tenth century, the particle occurs on the object more frequently than not. Some of the occurrences of -*o* counted by Matsuo could be instances of the emphatic particle -*o* (see Section 3.1). Because he does not give the actual examples from these works, we cannot tell what proportion of each total represents the emphatic -*o,* but I believe that these proportions should be quite small. Hence, the figures in (44) indicate a trend toward increased usage of the accusative marker -*o,* a trend well recognized in traditional studies of the language (e.g., Koreshima 1966; Matsuo 1969).[14]

7.1 Traditional grammarians' explanation

The hypothesis put forth by traditional grammarians for this increased usage of -*o* is based on a literary tradition called *kanbun kundoku,* translated as 'a Japanese way of reading Chinese text' or 'reading Chinese text for meaning'. (I refer to this tradition as *kanbun* for short.) Around the sixth century, the Japanese seriously began to absorb elements of Chinese culture. The primary motive behind this importation of Chinese culture was the desire to learn Buddhism, and Japanese scholars avidly studied Buddhist texts in Chinese. The *kanbun* tradition finds its origin in the endeavor to grapple with Chinese, a language remote in structure from Japanese. Several subtraditions of *kanbun* arose to meet the diverse needs of the reading audience, but all share the feature of adding special "reading" markings to the original Chinese text. Two *kanbun* markings are illustrated in (45) for a simple Chinese SVO sentence.

(45) Subject–verb$^{(\rightarrow)}$–object$_{(\text{-}o)}$

The arrow superscripted to the verb directs the reader to read the verb after the object, thus transforming the SVO word order of Chinese into the SOV word order of Japanese. The particle *-o* subscripted to the object indicates that this is the object. The Japanese thus read (45) as: Subject–object-*o*–verb. Moreover, because the Chinese sentence is written in Chinese characters that embody meaning, it is possible to read the sentence completely in Japanese by using Japanese words with the same meaning. This is a rough and simplified description of *kanbun,* but it suffices for our purpose.[15]

In *kanbun,* the particle *-o* appears on the object NP without exception; it is never omitted (Matsuo 1938). This is natural because the function of the particle in *kanbun* is to identify the object NP in the Chinese language for Japanese speakers; it is the only distinctively Japanese way of marking the object. Traditional grammarians theorize that *kanbun,* with its ever-present *-o* on the object NP, influenced the Japanese language toward an increased use of *-o* (Hirohama 1966; Matsuo 1938). This is a plausible hypothesis especially in view of the fact that the Chinese language (like Chinese culture) was highly esteemed, so much so that Japanese officials were required to use it in writing.[16]

7.2 An alternative account

Although *kanbun* surely had an impact on the Japanese language, it is inconceivable that this literary tradition alone transformed OJ into the fully cased language of later years. Following Matsunaga (1983), I argue here that a linguistic change involving the verbal system is primarily responsible for the transformation.

Recall that the accusative *-o* occurs in OJ with the attributive form of the verb (and also the perfect). The attributive occurs in subordinate clauses and also in matrix clauses that have undergone the *kakarimusubi* conversion. In contrast, the object NP of conclusive verbs appears without the particle. Beginning in the early post-OJ period, verb inflection began to change, a change that, by the fifteenth century, had transformed the language into one similar to modern Japanese. The major force behind this change was the assimilation of the conclusive form by the attributive form. When the change was completed, only the original attributive form remained in the language, having taken over those positions originally occupied by the conclusive form. This change affected all verbs except the two irregular verbs *sinu* 'die' and *inu* 'leave'. Before the change, attributive and conclusive forms were clearly distinguished; even for those types of verbs that had the same shape for the two forms (quadrigrade, upper monograde, and lower monograde; cf. note 9), the two forms apparently differed in accentuation (Leon Serafim, personal communication). After the change, with the exception of the two verbs noted, all verbs took on the original attributive form of the verb for both conclusive and attributive inflections. The diagram in (46), based on a similar diagram in Matsunaga 1983, shows the inflected portions before and after the change.

(46)

	Inflection type				
	I	II	III	IV	V
Before the change					
Conclusive	-u	-i	-iru	-eru	-u
Attributive	-u	-u	-iru	-eru	-uru
After the change					
Conclusive	-u	-u	-iru	-eru	-uru
Attributive	-u	-u	-iru	-eru	-uru

The traditional Japanese labels for these inflection types are as follows: I is *yodan;* II is *ra-gyoo henkaku,* which, after the change, was assimilated into the *yodan* category; III is *kami-ichidan;* IV is *shimo-ichidan;* and V includes the four classes *kami-nidan, shimo-nidan, ka-gyoo henkaku,* and *sa-gyoo henkaku.*

The cause of this change is generally attributed to the *kakarimusubi* construction. As discussed earlier, the *kakarimusubi* rule, which is triggered by a *kakari* particle, converts the matrix conclusive form into the attributive form. The *kakarimusubi* construction is common in literary texts of both the OJ and post-OJ periods. This construction effected the change in the verbal system illustrated in (46) in the following way. In OJ, the *kakarimusubi* rule is always triggered by a *kakari* particle, but in post-OJ, *kakarimusubi* constructions without any *kakari* particle *(rentai-dome)* began to appear. In other words, the occurrence of the matrix attributive form became independent of the *kakari* particle, which led to the attributive form taking over the position of the conclusive form until the latter ultimately disappeared from the language.

From our point of view, what matters is that this change in the verbal system naturally led to the spread of the accusative particle *-o* throughout the language. In OJ, whenever a transitive attributive form occurs with its object NP, the NP is accompanied by the particle *-o.* Because the attributive form occurs in subordinate clauses and in *kakarimusubi* constructions, the occurrence of *-o* is in effect limited to these types of clauses as far as the attributive verb is concerned. But once the attributive form is established as the matrix-clause verb independently of the *kakari* particle, the particle *-o* becomes obligatory in matrix as well as subordinate clauses, thereby naturally increasing the occurrence of *-o* (Matsunaga 1983; Miyagawa and Matsunaga 1986). This hypothesis straightforwardly accounts for the increased frequency of the accusative marker *-o* in post-OJ. The hypothesis receives support from the fact that the gradual increase in the frequency of *-o* corresponds in time to the gradual transition of the verbal system from its OJ form, which clearly distinguishes conclusive and attributive verbs, to the later system in which the original attributive shape is used for both forms. In the next section, I present comparative data from two different texts of the *Tale of the Heike* to further demonstrate the change toward an increased use of *-o*. Unlike what we have seen so far, the data give us a view of the ongoing change from the fourteenth to the sixteenth centuries.

Before proceeding to the next section, a few brief remarks are in order about the time period during which the verbal system incurred the change. Most traditional studies assume that the change took place over a period of some three hundred years, from the thirteenth to the fifteenth centuries. But the increased frequency of *-o* began as early as the tenth century, as documented by Matsuo (1938). Part of this increase surely reflects the influence from *kanbun*. But it is also a fact that *kakarimusubi* constructions without any *kakari* particle are attested in the texts of the late Heian period, that is, the eleventh and twelfth centuries (Sato 1977). The verbal system thus began to change much earlier than the thirteenth century, contrary to what is generally assumed in traditional studies. Overall, the combination of *kanbun* influence and the beginnings of the transition of the verbal system can account for the increased frequency of *-o* in the early post-OJ period. These two forces triggered a change in Japanese, from a language that utilized abstract case for some instances of the accusative case to a language in which all instances of the accusative case are realized by an overt case marker.

8 FURTHER EVIDENCE: THE *TALE OF THE HEIKE*

The textual data to be presented here from the *Tale of the Heike* represent a time period that spans more than two hundred years, from the latter part of the fourteenth century to the end of the sixteenth century. This time span in fact covers the part of the language's history when major linguistic changes in the verbal system took a firm hold, transforming the language into one that closely resembles modern Japanese. The *Tale of the Heike* is a war epic set in the declining years of the Heian period. The Heian period (A.D. 794–1185) was, until near the end, a time of peace, when the arts flourished, all owing primarily to the extraordinary power wielded by the Fujiwara family, who, by means of strategic marriages, ruled through puppet emperors. In time, their power waned, giving way to chaos and, ultimately, the usurpation of rule by the most powerful military clan, the Heike (whose Japanese name was *Taira*). The *Tale of the Heike* covers the years 1131–1221, but it focuses on the short span of history from the time Kiyomori, the leader of the Heike, ascended to power in 1167 to the defeat of the Heike at the hands of the Genji clan in 1185 at Dan-no-ura.[17]

The stories in the *Tale of the Heike* are oral literature in that they were disseminated orally by blind monks who accompanied their storytelling with the *biwa* lute. It is believed that the *Tale of the Heike* was written by Yukinaga, a courtier who lived in the thirteenth century. The original text no longer exists, and scholars utilize the text produced in 1371 by Kakuichi, a blind monk who recited the *Tale of the Heike* for many years and who, months before his death, is said to have dictated his *Heike* for use by his disciple. Today, this version is the most authoritative text of the *Heike*; thus, the language found in this text possibly reflects the era in which Kakuichi lived as much as it reflects the original, thirteenth-century era of Yukinaga.

The second text of the *Tale of the Heike* used here is commonly referred to as the *Amakusa Heike*, and was published in 1592 in the town of Amakusa. This text, which contains many but not all of the stories of the *Heike*, was intended as a textbook for teaching Japanese to foreign missionaries, most of them from Portugal. In accordance with its purpose, the text is written in Portuguese-style romanization, and the language is believed to reflect the spoken Japanese of the late sixteenth century. The original *Amakusa Heike* text is thought to have been written by Fabian Fukan, a native Japanese-language instructor at a mission school in Amakusa where the text was published.[18] By comparing the older *Heike* text with the *Amakusa Heike*, it is possible to witness the change from the latter part of the fourteenth century, when Kakuichi dictated his *Heike* stories, to the end of the sixteenth century, when Fukan transformed them into the spoken style of his time. As we shall see, the data reveal a clear trend toward an increased use of *-o*. In this chapter, I use the shorthand forms *Heike* and *H* to refer to the older text based on Kakuichi's dictation and *Amakusa Heike* and *AH* to refer to the sixteenth-century text.

8.1 Comparison of the use of *-o* in the *Heike* and *Amakusa Heike*

I begin the discussion of the data with a pair of examples that illustrate the dramatic increase in the use of *-o* over the two hundred years between the *Heike* and *Amakusa Heike*. Unless otherwise noted, the *Heike* examples are from Ichiko 1973–1975 and the *Amakusa Heike* examples are from Kamei and Sakata 1966; the English translations are from Kitagawa and Tsuchida 1975.[19]

(47) *H:* Sono yo ha yomosugara, Yasuyori nyuudoo to futari,
AH: Sono yo wa yomosugara, Yasuyori nyuudoo to futari
that night all night Yasuyori both

H: haka-no mawari-o gyoodoosi-te nenbutu __ moosi,
AH: haka-no mawari-o gyoodoosi-te nenbutu-**o** moosi,
grave perimeter walked around prayers-ACC chanting

H: akenureba, atarasyuu dan __ tuki, kuginuki __ sasete,
AH: akureba atarasyuu dan-**o** tuite, kuginuki nado-**o** mo sesase,
day new tomb-ACC made fence of stakes-ACC made

H: mae ni kariya __ tukuri, sitiniti sitiya nenbutu __
AH: mae ni kariya-**o** tukuri, sitiniti sitiya nenbutu-**o**
front in hut-ACC made seven days seven nights prayers-ACC

moosi
moosi,
chant

H: kyoo __ kaite. (Book 3, *Shooshoo miyakogaeri*; vol. 1, 222)
AH: kyoo-**o** kaite. (67)
sutras-ACC transcribe

'All that night Naritsune and Yasuyori walked round and round the grave, continually chanting Buddhist prayers. When day came, they made a tomb and enclosed it with a fence of stakes. In front of the tomb they built a temporary hut, where they continued to chant prayers and to transcribe sutras for seven days and nights.'

In just this fragment, we find six direct objects that are without *-o* in the *Heike* but are accompanied by the case marker in the *Amakusa Heike*. Note that every one of the six bare NPs is adjacent to the verb in the *Heike* version, which confirms again that the object NP in older Japanese is commonly licensed by abstract case assignment under adjacency. It is also important to point out that every one of the six verbs is in the conjunctive form. As we saw earlier (Section 5.2), the conjunctive form *optionally* assigns abstract case, and it is common in OJ examples to find an object NP with *-o* with a conjunctive verb as well as without *-o*. Recall, too, that in relation to the optionality of abstract case assignment, we observed a "parallelism" requirement in which the direct objects of conjunctive forms in a sentence either all have the case particle or all lack the particle. We can see this parallelism in the *Heike* example above: the object NPs all lack the case marker.

But before we conclude that this text sample indeed exemplifies the parallelism requirement, it is important to consider the occurrence of *-o* in the segment *haka-no mawari-o gyoodoosi* 'walked around (the perimeter of) the grave'. Observe that the NP *haka-no mawari* has *-o* and thus constitutes an apparent counterexample to the parallelism requirement. One possible account of this offending *-o* is that, unlike the other NPs which are true object NPs of transitive verbs, the NP in question is adverbial in function, since the verb, *gyoodoosuru,* is a motion verb, and the NP with *-o* designates the location of action. By this account, this *-o* is different in nature from the pure accusative case marker, hence it would not behave the same in the parallelism situations. I have been unable to locate relevant additional data to confirm this hypothesis, so the adverbial characterization is at present merely speculative.

8.2 Suzuki's study

To compare the two texts, *Heike* and *Amakusa Heike,* it is of course necessary to study the two texts line by line the way we did with one fragment in the previous section. Fortunately, Suzuki (1973) has already pursued such a study and provides results that we can use directly. I first report on her findings and then present data of my own from the two texts in order to expand on the points that come out of Suzuki's work.

Through close scrutiny of the *Heike* and *Amakusa Heike* texts, Suzuki identifies 1,850 pairs of examples involving the accusative marker *-o,* with each pair consisting of a sentence from *Heike* and its corresponding sentence from *Amakusa Heike*. She categorizes these pairs into three groups, as shown in (48). (For presentation here, Suzuki's "B" and "C" groups are reversed and the percentage of each group is provided, rounded off to the nearest percentage point.) The plus sign indicates use of *-o* and the minus sign absence of *-o*.

(48)

	Text		Pairs	
Group	*H*	*AH*	N	%
A	+	+	1,430	77
B	–	+	400	22
C	+	–	20	1
			1,850	100

As shown, 1,430 pairs, or 77 percent of the total, have *-o* in both of the corresponding sentences (group A). These paired examples reflect the part of the grammar that did not undergo the change from abstract to overt case, but rather the part in which the verb is incapable of assigning abstract case to begin with, because, for example, it is in the attributive form. If we assume that the language of the *Heike* reflects that of Kakuichi, the fourteenth-century blind monk who dictated the most authoritative extant text, we can suppose that by Kakuichi's time, the language had already begun to shift toward consistently marking the accusative case with the overt case marker. From this view, some of the *Heike* examples in group A already reflect the language change from abstract to overt case marking, though we have no way of knowing which ones.

In contrast, the 400 pairs of examples in group B reflect a shift from abstract to overt case during the more than two hundred years that separate the two texts. These instances represent direct evidence for the main thesis of this chapter, that Japanese shifted from being a language (OJ) that used predominantly abstract case assignment for the accusative case to one in which all instances of the accusative case are realized overtly. On the other hand, the small number of pairs in group C appear to represent a reverse shift, from overt to abstract case assignment. As I show later, however, Suzuki demonstrates that for virtually all of these pairs there is an independent reason why *-o* occurs in the *Heike* example but not in the *Amakusa Heike* counterpart. I want to first discuss group B using examples that Suzuki provides. Then, in Section 8.6, I discuss the apparent counterexamples represented by group C.

8.3 Group B: Suzuki's representative examples

Despite the fact that the shift from abstract to overt case had started by the time Kakuichi dictated the *Heike* text in 1371, it is easy to see that this shift did not finish with the *Heike,* but continued without interruption for the next two hundred years, to the time when the *Amakusa Heike* was produced in 1592. This is evidenced by the examples in group B, which are sentences whose accusative case assignment shifts from an abstract mode of assignment to an overt mode. This group represents 22 percent, over one-fifth, of the examples examined. Suzuki provides ten representative pairs from group B. All ten are given here in (49)–(58). Since there are some discrepancies in the actual choice of words between the two texts, I provide a word-for-word English gloss only for the *Heike* example. I have also changed the order of the examples from that in which they are presented in Suzuki 1973, 106–107.

(49) *H:* "Sigemori koso tenka-no daizi-o bessite kikiidasitare.
Shigemori under heaven crisis-ACC special heard
'Ware-o ware to omowan mono domo wa, mina
me-ACC I think retainers all
mononogusite hasemaire' to, hiroose yo" to notamaeba,
arm come quickly inform order
kono yosi __ **hiroosu.** (Book 2, *Hooka no sata*; vol. 1, 152)
this inform$_{\text{CONCL}}$

AH: "Sigemori koso tenka no daizi-o kikiidaitare, 'ware-o ware to omoo mono domo wa mina mononogusite hasemaire' to hiroose yo" to geziserarureba kono yosi-o hiroosita. (43)

'"[Shigemori] ordered: 'I have learned that the country is now in a state of crisis. Let all my retainers hear these words: "You who consider yourselves truly loyal to Shigemori—arm and gather here!"' [So Morikuni informed the retainers of this.]'

(50) *H:* Sono toki ni uta __ **yomu**-byoo wa nakarisika domo,
that moment poem compose$_{\text{CONCL}}$ not
wakoo yori anagati ni suitaru miti nareba, saigo no
youth from wholeheartedly be found road was last
toki mo wasuretamawazu. (Book 4, *Miya no gosaigo*; vol. 1, 331–332)
moment could not forget

AH: Sono toki uta-**o** yomareuzuru koto dewa nakere domo,
wakai toki kara, anagati ni tasinami sukareta miti zya ni yotte,
saigo made mo wasurerarenanda to kikoete gozaru. (112)

'No ordinary man could compose a poem at such a moment. For Yorimasa, however, the writing of poems had been a constant pleasure since his youth. And so, even at the moment of his death, he did not forget.'

(51) *H:* Heike ima wa miyako-o sadame, Dairi __ **tukuru** beki yosi sata
Heike now capital decided palace build$_{\text{CONCL}}$
arisini, Koreyosi-ga muhon to kikoesikaba,
Koreyoshi-NOM revolt heard
ikani to sawagare keri. (Book 8, *Dazaifuochi*; vol. 2, 135)
what to do upset

AH: Heike wa ima kuni o sadamete Saigoku ni mata Dairi-**o** tukuroo
to sataseraretare domo, Ogata-ga muhon to kikoetareba, nani to
syoozo to yuute, sawagiawareta tokoro de. (169)

'No sooner had the Heike decided on the site of a new capital at Dazaifu than they heard that Koreyoshi had turned against them.'

(52) *H:* Yooyoo ni itawari, yudono situraina(n)do site,
various kindness bath make
oyu __ **hikasetatematuru.** (Book 10, *Senju no mae*; vol. 2, 304)
bath take$_{\text{CONCL}}$

AH: Munesige wa nasake no aru mono de, samazama ni itawari
nagusame tatematuri, yudono-o kamae, oyu-**o** hikasetatematuri
nado sita. (253)

'. . . was a compassionate man. . . . He first offered Shigehira a hot bath.'

(53) *H:* Isogi izu beki yosi, sikiri ni notamoo aida, hakinogoi
quickly go repeated command clean
tiri __ **hirowase,** migurusiki mono domo torisitatamete,
trash pick up$_{\text{CONJ}}$ unsightly things put away
izubeki ni koso **sadamari kere.** (Book 1, *Gioo*; vol. 1, 54)
go *KIKARI* decided$_{\text{PERF}}$

AH: Isoide ideyo to sikiri ni ooseraruru ni yotte,
haki no goi tiri-**o** hirowase, migurusii mono domo
torisitatamete zyoozuru ni sadamatta. (83)

'Thus receiving Kiyomori's brutal and repeated commands to go, she made up her mind to obey only after having first put her room in order so that she would leave nothing unsightly or unbecoming behind her.'

(54) *H:* Saikoo Hoosi kono koto __ **kii-te,** waga mi no ue to ya
Saikoo this matter heard$_{\text{CONJ}}$ my fate
omoikemu, muti-o age, in no gosyo Hoozyuuzidono e
thought whip strike Cloistered Place
hasemairu. (Book 2, *Saikoo ga kirare*; vol. 1, 125)
galloped$_{\text{CONCL}}$

AH: Saikoo wa kono koto-**o** kii-te, sate wa waga mi no ue zya to
omoote, muti-o utte in no gosyo ni hasemairu tokoro ni. (23)

'Priest Saikoo, hearing of their arrest, may have thought that his fate would be the same. He galloped off toward the Cloistered Palace at Hoojuu-ji.'

(55) *H:* Miyako nite ooku-no kotugainin __ **misika domo,**
capital many beggars saw$_{\text{CONJ}}$
kakaru mono o ba imada mizu. (Book 3, *Arioo*; vol. 1, 229)
this kind people before not seen$_{\text{CONCL}}$

AH: Miyako de amata-no kotugainin-**o** mitaredomo kono yoo na
mono o ba mada mita koto ga nai. (73)

'Then he saw that what had been rumored about the island by the people of the capital could not compare with actuality—Kikai-ga-shima was horrible beyond description.'

(56) *H:* Akureba 16 niti, Takakura-no miya-no gomuhon __
next day revolt
okosase tamai-te, usesasetamainu to moosu hodo koso arikere.
raise$_{\text{CONJ}}$ disappear$_{\text{CONCL}}$ said
Miyako zyuu-no soodoo nanomenarazu. (Book 4, *Kioo*;
capital all commotion not normal vol. 1, 299)

AH: Akureba 16 niti Takakura-no miya wa gomuhon-**o** okosaserarete
usesaserareta to yuu hodo koso are, miyako no uti ga soodoo
suru koto wa obitadasikatta. (97)

'By sunrise of the next day, the sixteenth, the rumor had already spread that Prince Mochihito had attempted to raise a revolt, had been discovered, and had gone into hiding. The news caused great commotion among the people of the capital.'

(57) *H:* Genzi wa asoko ni zin to(t)te uma __ **yasume,** kokoni
Genji over there horse rest$_{\text{CONJ}}$ here
zin to(t)te uma __ **kai** nado sikeru hodo ni isogazu.
horse fed$_{\text{CONJ}}$ not hurry$_{\text{CONCL}}$
(Book 9, *Rooba*; vol. 2, 218)

AH: Genzi wa nanoka no u no koku yaawase to sadamattareba, kasiko ni zin tori, uma-**o** yasume, koko ni zin tori, uma-**o** kai nando site isoganu ni. (217)

'As the Genji calmly rested and fed their horses, they seemed to have courage in reserve.'

(58) *H:* Kumagai wa uma-no futohara __ **isase-te,** hanureba asi o
Kumagai horse's stomach shot$_{\text{CONJ}}$ reared legs
koete oritattari. (Book 9, *Ichi-ni no kake*; vol. 2, 226)
leaped stood$_{\text{CONCL}}$

AH: Kumagai wa uma-no hara-**o** isase-te sikiri ni hanetareba, kyuuzyoo tuite oritatta. (222)

'When [Kumagai's] horse was shot in the belly and reared in pain, he leaped to the ground and fought on foot.'

8.4 Conclusive form and abstract case assignment

We can divide these ten pairs into two groups. The first group consists of the first four pairs, (49)–(52), and the second group consists of (54)–(58). Example (53) does not fall into either of the two groups; as we shall see, it is an exception to the generalization that I wish to propose. In the *Heike* examples in the first group, the bare NP occurs as the object of a transitive verb in the conclusive form. These are, in other words, the stereotypical examples of abstract case assignment. The following review gives just the object–verb portions of these examples:

(49′) kono yosi __ **hiroosu**
this inform$_{\text{CONCL}}$

(50′) uta __ **yomu**-byoo wa
poem compose$_{\text{CONCL}}$

(51′) Dairi __ **tukuru** beki
palace build$_{\text{CONCL}}$

(52′) oyu __ **hikasetatematuru**
bath take$_{\text{CONCL}}$

These four examples are evidence that the OJ property of abstract case assignment is observable in the *Heike* text, and, as expected, the object NP licensed by abstract case appears adjacent to the verb. Certainly, it is not at all surprising to find this property, since the Kakuichi text of 1371, from which the above examples are taken, clearly distinguishes between the conclusive form, which assigns abstract case, and the attributive form, which lacks this capability. In fact, it is not difficult to find instances of the latter, in which the overt case marker *-o* appears with an attributive form, as in the following three examples:

(59) Fumi-o **toriiruru** koto mo naku. (Book 1, *Gioo*; vol. 1, 55)
letter-ACC accept$_{\text{ATTRIB}}$ no need
'There was no need to accept the letter.'

(60) kassen-no sidai-o **sirusimoosareru** ni (Book 9, *Kawara kassen*; vol. 2, 187)
fight's result-ACC report$_{\text{ATTRIB}}$
'reported the result of the fight'

(61) onnamida-o **nagasasetamoo** ni (Book 11, *Kagami*; vol. 2, 417)
tears-ACC cried out$_{\text{ATTRIB}}$
'cried out in tears'

8.5 Conjunctive form and overt case marking

Turning to the second set of representative group B examples from Suzuki's study, in (54)–(58) the bare object NPs occur not with a conclusive form but with a conjunctive form. Let us extract just the object NP–conjunctive verb segments in the *Heike* versions of these examples.

(54′) kono koto __ **kii-te**
this matter heard$_{\text{CONJ}}$

(55′) ooku-no kotugainin __ **misika domo**
many beggars saw$_{\text{CONJ}}$

(56′) gomuhon __ **okosase tamai-te**
revolt raise$_{\text{CONJ}}$

(57′) uma __ yasume . . . uma __ **kai**
horse rest$_{\text{CONJ}}$ horse fed$_{\text{CONJ}}$

(58′) uma-no futohara __ **isase-te**
horse's stomach shot$_{\text{CONJ}}$

As we have already seen (Section 5.2), the conjunctive forms appear to *optionally* assign abstract case, since we commonly find both overtly cased and abstractly cased object NPs with this form. The text segments in (54)–(58) exemplify conjunctive forms that assign abstract case. The conjunctive forms in these examples either take the "bare verb stem" form, as in (55) and (57), or the bare verb stem plus *-te,* as in (54), (56), and (58). The conjunctive suffix *-te* clearly does not affect the case-assigning property of the conjunctive form, since abstract case assignment is implemented regardless of whether the suffix is present.[20]

The question here is whether there is a pattern to those instances in which the conjunctive form assigns abstract case or whether the distribution of abstract case is purely random. I wish to propose that there is in fact a generalization to be captured here. Consider what a conjunctive form is. In its simplest form without the suffix *-te,* it is a bare verb stem (Sansom 1928, 137); in essence, that is the form of the verb before suffixation occurs. This verb form therefore lacks any of the meaning represented by verbal suffixation, such as tense, and even with *-te,* the conjunctive form cannot by itself express tense. Despite the conjunctive verb's "incomplete" nature, it is nevertheless able to participate in linguistic expressions because the finite verb in the sentence provides the necessary information. If the finite verb is interpreted as past, then the conjunctive verb, too, is interpreted as referring to an action or event in the past. In short, the conjunctive form depends on the information borne by the suffix of the finite verb in the sentence. This can be diagrammed as follows, using tense as an example.

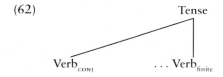

(62)

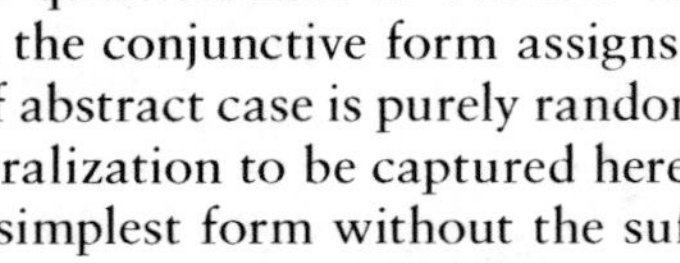

What (62) indicates is that the tense suffix on the finite verb has scope over not only the finite verb but also the conjunctive verb, a reasonable assumption given that the tense of the conjunctive form is strictly dependent on the tense inflection of the finite verb.

If the tense element on the finite verb has scope over the conjunctive verb, it is fairly predictable that other suffixal elements on the finite verb also have scope over the conjunctive verb. A natural candidate along with tense is the "conjugation" inflection, that is, the inflection that distinguishes among the different verbal forms such as the conclusive and the attributive. Under this hypothesis, if the finite verb is conclusive, the conjunctive verb will share properties of a conclusive verb. And an attributive inflection on the finite verb will likewise characterize the conjunctive verb as attributive in relevant properties. What are these properties? An obvious candidate is abstract case assignment. If conclusive, the verb has the ability to assign abstract case. In contrast, we have seen ample evidence that a verb in either the attributive or the perfect form does not have this capability, resulting in the appearance of the overt case marker *-o* on the object NP. If the hypothesis regarding the scope of the finite-verb suffix is correct, we can predict that when the finite verb is conclusive in form, the conjunctive form will, like the conclusive form, be able to assign abstract case; the object NP of the conjunctive form will therefore be able to appear without the overt case marker *-o*. Accordingly, we can also predict that when either an attributive suffix or the perfect suffix is on the finite verb, the conjunctive is deprived of the ability to assign abstract case; the object NP of the conjunctive verb therefore will need the overt case marker *-o*.

On the whole, the data uphold these predictions. In (54)–(58), which are examples of abstract case assignment implemented by a conjunctive form, the relevant finite verb is conclusive in form. I have extracted the relevant portions of these examples in the following review:

(54″) kono koto __ kii-te . . . hasemairu
this matter heard$_{\text{CONJ}}$ galloped$_{\text{CONCL}}$

(55″) ooku no kotugainin __ misika domo . . . mizu
many beggars saw$_{\text{CONJ}}$ not seen$_{\text{CONCL}}$

(56″) gomuhon __ okosase tamai-te, usesasetamainu
revolt raise$_{\text{CONJ}}$ disappear$_{\text{CONCL}}$

(57″) uma __ yasume . . . uma __ kai . . . isogazu
horse rest$_{\text{CONJ}}$ horse fed$_{\text{CONJ}}$ not hurry$_{\text{CONCL}}$

(58″) uma-no futohara __ isase-te . . . oritattari
horse's stomach shot$_{\text{CONJ}}$ stood$_{\text{CONCL}}$

As an example, segment (57″), which has two transitive conjunctive forms, can be diagrammed as follows:

(63)

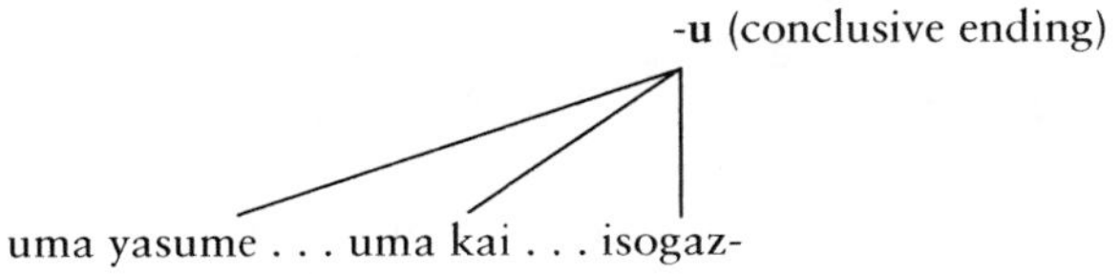

As shown, the conclusive ending *-u* has scope over not only the finite verb *isogaz-* 'not hurry' to which it attaches but also the conjunctive forms *yasume* 'rest' and *kai* 'feed', giving the latter two forms a "conclusive" status as far as abstract case assignment is concerned. Consequently, the object NPs of these conjunctive forms are licensed by abstract case assignment, so they appear without overt case marking.

The examples in (64)–(68) contrast with those that we have just seen. Each example contains a conjunctive form accompanied by an overtly cased object NP. As indicated, the finite verb in each example is either in the attributive or the perfect form, neither of which allows abstract case assignment. (Examples (64)–(66) are from Book 1, *Tenjoo-no yamiuchi*, and found in Ichiko 1973–1975, vol. 1, 39–40.)

(64) . . . sore mo hyoosi-**o** kaete, "ana kuroguro, kuroki too
rhythm-ACC change$_{CONJ}$ ah dark dark head
ka na, ikanaru hito-no urusi nurikemu" to zo **hayasare keru.**
how what person lacquer paint *KAKARI* tease$_{ATTRIB}$
'. . . [the spectators] improvised verses, teasing him with the following words: "Ah, how darkly the black man's head is blackened. What kind of man could have lacquered him so dark?"'

(65) "Soreyuukemu-**o** taisite kuen ni ressi, hyoozyoo-**o**
ceremonial sword-ACC wear$_{CONJ}$ banquet attend$_{CONJ}$ weapon-ACC
tamawatte miyazyuu-o **syutunyuu suru** wa . . ."
equip palace go in and out$_{ATTRIB}$
'[A man who is allowed to] attend formal banquets, one who is allowed to wear a ceremonial sword and go in and out of the palace . . .'

(66) Hayaku mifuda-**o** kezutte, kekkan tyoonin seraru **beki yosi**.
quickly name card-ACC exclude$_{CONJ}$ service dismissed must$_{ATTRIB}$
'His name must be stricken immediately from the court rolls, and he must without fail be rusticated or dismissed permanently from service.'

(67) Namida-**o** nagasi sode-**o** **siboranu** wa nakari keri.
tears-ACC flow$_{CONJ}$ sleeve-ACC not wring$_{ATTRIB}$ no one
'There was no one who did not cry.'
(Book 3, *Shooshoo miyako gaeri*; vol. 1, 222)

(68) Yaya atte okiagari, namida-**o** osaete **moosi** **keru** wa . . .
little later set up tear-ACC hold back$_{CONJ}$ said
'Then he rose and, controlling himself, said, . . .'
(Book 3, *Sooji shikyo*; vol. 1, 232)

In these examples, the final verb lacks the lexical property to assign abstract case; hence the conjunctive form also lacks this property. I should add that the analysis just presented accounts for the parallelism noted by Zenno (1987), who demonstrates that the object NP of a conjunctive form has the case particle *-o* if the object NP of the final verb also has the particle. If the object NP in the final clause does not have the particle, the object NP of the conjunctive form likewise is devoid of the particle. Zenno also notes that the presence/absence of the particle correlates with the kind of verbal form found in the second clause: if it is conclusive, the case particle *-o* does not appear, whereas the particle does appear if the verbal form is attributive or perfect.

Of course, when one is dealing with a language that is as much in transition as is the one in the *Heike,* no generalization can escape counterexamples. There are in fact two kinds of counterexamples within the group B data. The first kind, exemplified in (69), consists of only *possible* counterexamples:

(69) Sikaru o Tadamori Bizen-no kami tarisi toki,
but Tadamori Bizen governor COP-PAST when

Toba-in no gogan, Tokuzyoozyu-in-**o** zoosin site,
Toba Tokujooju-in-ACC build$_{\text{CONJ}}$

sanzyuu-san-gen-no midoo-**o** tate, sen-it-tai-no mihotoke-**o**
thirty-three-ken hall-ACC dedicate$_{\text{CONJ}}$ 1,001 Buddhas
sue tatematuru. (Book 1, *Tenjoo-no yamiuchi*; vol. 1, 36)
installed

'Now when Tadamori was governor of Bizen Province, he ingratiated himself with the abdicated emperor Toba by building the Tokujooju-in temple. Here he dedicated a hall 33 ken long, in which he installed 1,001 statues of Buddhas.'

The text segment in (69) is a possible counterexample because *-o* appears with the object NP of the conjunctive forms, yet the finite verb appears to be in the conclusive form. I say that this is only a *possible* counterexample because the finite verb, *sue tatematuru,* is quadrigrade, hence it is actually ambiguous between conclusive and attributive; if the former, it is a true counterexample, but if the latter, it naturally follows our hypothesis. There are many examples of this sort. Without some definitive method to determine the actual inflection, conclusive or attributive, these examples cannot be said to negate our hypothesis.

The second group consists of clear-cut counterexamples. One member of this group is example (53) above. Of Suzuki's ten representative pairs of text segments from group B, listed in (49)–(58), all follow the generalization proposed here except (53). In (53), the final verb form, *kere,* is in the perfect *(izen),* because of the presence of the *kakari* particle *koso.* As I noted earlier in the chapter, the perfect form apparently does not assign abstract case, hence (53) must be seen as an exception.

Note also the following example:

(70) Hitobito kore-**o** kiite, mina namida-**o** **nagasare keri.**
people this-ACC hear$_{\text{CONJ}}$ all tear-ACC flow$_{\text{CONCL}}$
'All of those with him wept.'
(Book 8, *Natora*; vol. 2, 124)

The verb with the ending *keri,* a perfect tense marker, is without doubt in the conclusive form; the attributive form of this ending is *keru.* Nevertheless, the object NP of the conjunctive form, *kore* 'this', is marked with *-o,* a clear counterexample to our hypothesis that a conjunctive verb in a sentence with a finite conclusive form should assign abstract case. Interestingly, the object NP of the conclusive form itself, *namida* 'tears', is overtly cased with *-o* as well, which is also a counterexample, this time to the hypothesis that the conclusive form assigns abstract case.

8.6 Group C: Apparent counterexamples

I now proceed to the final point regarding the *Tale of the Heike.* As Suzuki (1973) found, there are twenty *Heike–Amakusa Heike* pairs in which the *Heike* example has the overt case marker *-o* but the corresponding *Amakusa Heike* example does not, with the object phrase occurring as a "bare" phrase instead. These examples, called group C in (48), are apparent counterexamples to the hypothesis that the direction of change proceeds from abstract case assignment to overt case marking. As noted there, these paired examples represent only 1 percent of the entire data set of 1,850 pairs. Because the number is so small, these examples do not seriously jeopardize our hypothesis. The problem posed by these examples is even further minimized when we take into consideration the points noted by Suzuki that independently account for at least some of the data.

As Suzuki observes, some of the examples that manifest a "reversed" trend can be accounted for by the difference in style between the *Heike* and *Amakusa Heike;* the former employs a literary language whereas the latter employs something closer to the spoken language of the sixteenth century. As a result, some *Heike* phrases that are formal and literary by virtue of having *-o* are changed to a less literary, more idiomatic style without *-o* in the *Amakusa Heike.* An example of this is the phrase *inoti(-o) ikiru* 'to live a life'. This phrase, which is found as early as the *Man'yōshū,* occurs most commonly in the *Heike* without *-o.* According to Suzuki, there are sixteen occurrences of this phrase without *-o* and only three occurrences with *-o* among the 1,850 *Heike* examples that she looked at. The following text segment is one of the three that contain the *-o*:

(71) *H:* Dainagon-ga kirare soorawan ni oite ha, Naritune totemo
Dainagon-NOM execute
kainaki **inoti-o ikite** nani ni kawasi sooroo beki?
worthless life live what for
(Book 2, *Shooshoo koiuke*; vol. 1, 142)

AH: Naritika ga kiraryoozuru ni oite wa, Syoosyoo totemo,
kainai **inoti** __ **ikite** nani ni tukamaturoo zo? (36)

'But since he is to be executed this evening, what am I to live for?'

Suzuki reasons that the phrase without *-o* is more idiomatic, thus is more compatible with the spoken style of the *Amakusa Heike*. Of the three occurrences of this phrase with *-o*, the example above is the only one that loses the *-o* in the *Amakusa Heike*. It should also be emphasized that the absence of *-o* here is an option that exists even in the *Heike*; it is therefore possible to view the pair in (71) as a case in which the option to have *-o* is exercised in the *Heike*, and the option to exclude the case marker is exercised in the *Amakusa Heike*, the latter for a stylistic reason. In this way, we need not view the example as a counterexample to the hypothesis that the nature of accusative case changed from a mixture of abstract case and overt case marking in OJ to strictly overt case marking in post-OJ.[21]

Another type of sentence in group C that is similar to (71) involves an NP that is optionally marked with *-o* and followed by the pro-verb *su* 'do'.[22] When the *-o* fails to occur, the NP and *su* together form a verbal compound; with *-o*, the construction is a straightforward object NP–verb construction with essentially the same meaning. In the *Heike*, there are 148 occurrences of this construction without *-o*, and 9 occurrences with *-o* (Suzuki 1973). Of the nine instances, three "lose" the case marker in the corresponding *Amakusa Heike* example. An example of this is *asizuri(-o) suru* 'stamping (the floor)', which appears with *-o* in the *Heike* (Book 3, *Ashizuri*; vol. 1, 206) but is absent in the *Amakusa Heike* (65). The apparent "reversed" direction here is nothing more than a difference in choice: in the *Heike*, the less common NP-*o su* version is chosen in nine instances, whereas in the the *Amakusa Heike*, three of these are changed to the more common verb–compound construction with essentially the same meaning.[23] This type of example and the first type discussed in relation to (71) account for eight of the twenty pairs in group C.

The third type of sentence contains a numeral quantifier. If a numeral quantifier occurs alone, without an antecedent, it can be either with or without case marking. There are three instances in the *Heike* where a numeral quantifier has *-o* and the corresponding segments in the *Amakusa Heike* lack the case marker, for example, *zyuugo-ki(-o) idaite* 'sent fifteen mounted soldiers'.[24] The presence of the particle on the numeral quantifier has the effect of emphasizing the quantity; without the particle, the sentence is a neutral statement without such emphasis. If we follow Suzuki's explanation, the absence of *-o* in the *Amakusa Heike* example simply reflects the decision of the writer of this text to deemphasize the numeral. Here again, in the original *Heike*, one has the choice to use or not use the particle; in the *Heike*, three numeral quantifiers happen to have the particle, whereas the corresponding segments in the *Amakusa Heike* do not.

In all three types of examples just discussed, what we see is a *Heike* phrase that has two manifestations, one with *-o*, the other without. In all three, it is possible to regard the *Heike* examples in group C as containing the phrase with *-o* and the *Amakusa Heike* counterparts as containing the same phrase without *-o*. By this account, these examples do not pose a problem for the hypothesis that historical change occurred unidirectionally from abstract case assignment to overt case marking.

These three sentence types cover eleven of the twenty paired examples in group C, leaving nine pairs unaccounted for. Suzuki argues that seven of these pairs need not count as counterexamples, thereby leaving only two without any explanation.

According to Suzuki's argument, five of the pairs occur in battle scenes where the absence of *-o* can be considered a rhetorical device. In particular, she suggests that the absence of *-o* gives the expression a sense of instability and excitement, as befitting a battle cry. One example is as follows:

(72) *H:* Yosi, oto na se so. Kataki ni uma-no asi-**o** tukarakasase yo.
hey sound quiet enemy horse-GEN legs become tired
(Book 9, *Ichi-ni no kake*; vol. 2, 224)

AH: Yosi, oto na si so. Tada kataki ga uma-no asi __ tukarakasasei. (220)

'Keep silent! Let their horses be worn out!'

Presumably, the absence of *-o* in *Amakusa Heike* also gives the utterance more of a spoken flavor, an effect that is made possible because the language has, by this time, transitioned to uniformly overt marking of the accusative case; the absence of the case marker therefore serves in this instance as a rhetorical device to enhance the excitement of the battle.[25]

The final group of sentences that Suzuki attempts to account for consists of two pairs of sentences that contain the word *kore* 'this'. This word is marked with *-o* in the *Heike* examples. Suzuki argues that the word *kore* in the *Amakusa Heike* is used commonly as a vocative, that is, in calling out, hence the word is best analyzed as an independently occurring expression and not as a direct object. The following example constitutes one of the two pairs;[26] note that even the translation by Kitagawa and Tsuchida (1975) of the *Heike* example reflects the vocative nature of *kore*.

(73) *H:* Kore-**o** mitamae, toogoku-no tonobara, Nippon iti-no
this look east warriors Japan number one
goo no mono no zigaisuru tehon. (Book 9, *Kiso no saigo*;
mighty one end to self way vol. 2, 199)

AH: Kore __ miyo goo no mono no zigaisuru sama, tehon ni sei,
toogoku no mono bara. (208)

'You, warriors of the east, see how the mightiest warrior in Japan puts an end to himself!'

Out of the original twenty pairs of sentences in group C, this leaves just two pairs without an explanation. They are as follows:

(74) *H:* Tada ware ni omoiyurusite, naisidokoro-o miyako e
quickly I permit Three Sacred Treasures capital to
kaesiiretatemature. (Book 10, *Ukebumi*; vol. 2, 289)
send back

AH: Haya naisidokoro __ kaesiiretatematutte . . . (245)

'I pray you to send back the Three Sacred Treasures to the capital!'

(75) *H:* Hiziri wakagimi-o uketoritatematurite, yo-o hi ni tuide
take day night into
hasenoboru hodo ni. (Book 12, *Hase rokudai*; vol. 2, 485)
hurry up

AH: Hiziri wa wakagimi __ uketori, yo o hi ni site noboru hodo ni. (328)

'Mongaku hurried with the young lord and retainers up to the capital, traveling both day and night.'

An interesting point to note in passing is that, in (74), the direct object marked with *-o* in the *Heike* occurs away from the verb, but the corresponding direct object in the *Amakusa Heike,* which lacks the particle, occurs adjacent to the transitive verb, suggesting an "abstract case" effect in sixteenth-century Japanese. Whether abstract case is in fact the culprit here—and, indeed, whether abstract case is still operative in sixteenth-century Japanese—is, at this point, an open question. The data that we have looked at are overwhelmingly in the direction of overt case, though the data do not explicitly rule out residual effects of the OJ abstract case.

As we have seen here, virtually all of the twenty paired sentences in Suzuki's group C that ostensibly represent counterexamples to the unidirectional shift from abstract case to overt case can be accounted for. Although some explanations are more compelling than others, Suzuki's account only leaves two pairs, (74) and (75), without an explanation. Therefore, the hypothesis defended throughout this chapter—that the abstract case assignment of accusative case in OJ is supplanted uniformly by overt case marking in post-OJ—can be safely assumed.

9 MODERN JAPANESE -*O*

Before closing this chapter, I want to briefly discuss the case marker *-o* in modern Japanese in the light of its historical development. There are two issues to deal with. The first is the question of precisely where in the grammar *-o* arises. The second is the condition under which *-o* can occur.

9.1 *-o* as a D-structure case marker

The first question, that of the "location" of *-o* in the grammar, arises because of the modular nature of the theory that I am assuming. In particular, the theory postulates a multilevel representation of syntax: D-structure, S-structure, phonological form (PF), and logical form (LF), as shown in (76) (cf. Chomsky 1981, 1982; Chomsky and Lasnik 1977).

(76)

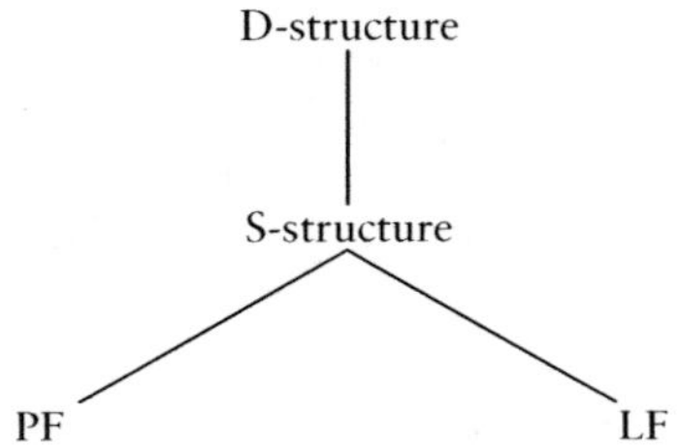

Chomsky (1986a), for example, proposes that case is realized at S-structure in most instances.[27] A clear example in Japanese of S-structure case is the nominative *-ga*. This case marker appears on the subject NP of a direct passive, which originates in the object position at D-structure and is moved to the subject position at S-structure.

(77) Kuruma-ga$_i$ [$_{VP}$ doroboo-ni t_i nusum-are-ta]
car-NOM thief-by steal-PASS-PAST
'A car was stolen by a thief.'

The fact that *-ga* appears on this moved NP is evidence that the case particle arises at S-structure, after movement has applied.

What about the case particle *-o*? On first blush, nothing comes to mind that would compel us to deal with it any differently than with *-ga*. Therefore, it appears to be a case marker that arises at S-structure. But now, let us reflect on its historical development. As stated at the beginning of this chapter, the historical source of this particle is found in the emphatic/exclamatory particle *-o*. The latter particle surely presented itself at D-structure simply because there is no systematic way in which it can be inserted later, not to mention the problem in semantic interpretation that such an insertion would cause. If, indeed, the case particle *-o* developed out of this emphatic/exclamatory marking, one might suspect that the case marker *-o*, even in modern Japanese, appears at D-structure instead of S-structure (though, of course, historical change is not constrained from shuffling items from one component to another).

In fact, there is one piece of evidence to support this notion. An "adverbial" particle such as *-mo* 'too' can attach to NPs with "semantic" postpositions, as in (78). it can never appear with the nominative case marker *-ga*, as shown in (79).

(78) Gakusei-ga Tookyoo-kara-**mo** kita.
students-NOM Tokyo-from-too came
'Students came from Tokyo, too.'

(79) a. Gakusei-**mo** kita.
students-too came
'Students came, too.'

b. *Gakusei-ga-**mo** kita.

We can make the reasonable assumption that *-mo* 'too' can only appear with particles present at D-structure. *-mo* itself is assumed to arise at D-structure, and no other particle can occur between it and the NP unless it is there to begin with at D-structure.

Remarkably, the nominative and accusative do not pattern alike with respect to *-mo*. The following example, taken from a linguistics book (Inoue 1983, vii), shows that *-o*, unlike *-ga*, can co-occur with *-mo*.

(80) Honsyo-no naiyoo-wa, sippitu sinakatta kenkyuu buntansya,
this book-GEN content-TOP writing not researchers
kyooryokusya-no kenkyuu seika ya tiken-**o-mo** hanei sita mono ni
assistants-GEN researcher result knowledge reflect work
natte iru.
is

'The content of this book reflects not only the work of the authors, but also the information and research results provided by other researchers and assistants.'

It is not at all uncommon to find *-o* occurring with *-mo* in modern Japanese, which strongly suggests that *-o* is present in D-structure.

9.2 When does *-o* occur?

In past analyses of the particle, *-o* is seen as transformationally inserted onto the "second" or the "rightmost" NP (Kuroda 1965; Kuno 1973). More recently, Saito (1983, 1985) has argued that *-o* is a phonetic realization of abstract case assigned by a transitive verb under government. He notes, for example, that *-o* can optionally drop under adjacency.[28]

(81) Taroo-wa nani-o/__ katta no?
Taro-TOP what-ACC bought Q
'What did Taro buy?'

(82) Nani-o/?*__ Taroo-wa katta no?
what-ACC Taro-TOP bought Q
'What did Taro buy?'

Saito argues that *-o* in (81) can drop because the NP is adjacent to the verb, hence abstract case assignment licenses the NP. On the other hand, in (82), the object NP has been scrambled away from the verb, which necessitates the appearance of the overt particle *-o* on the NP. Because abstract case assignment occurs, Saito argues that *-o* is simply a phonetic realization of this case assignment.

There is a problem with Saito's analysis. A number of linguists have noted that it is not only *-o* that can drop; under appropriate conditions, the nominative *-ga* can drop as well (Masunaga 1987; Takezawa 1987; Tsutsui 1984). To illustrate, in the following example, the nominative marker that marks the "object" of the stative predicate is dropped.

(83) Kimi-wa nani __ iru no?
you-TOP what need Q
'What do you need?'

Whatever the correct analysis may be, clearly the case-drop phenomenon fails to attest the existence of abstract accusative case in modern Japanese.

Looking at the historical development of *-o* provides a radically different view than that of either Saito or the early transformational treatments of Kuroda and Kuno. Recall that in OJ, the case marker *-o* and abstract case are in complementary distribution. The case marker occurs with attributive and perfect forms, whereas the conclusive form assigns abstract case. Both overt and abstract case require a case-assigning feature on the verb; it just so happens that this feature manifests itself differently, either as an overt case marker or as abstract case. According to my analysis, what survives in modern Japanese is the overt manifestation of the accusative-case-assigning feature. The option to assign abstract case disappeared when the conclusive form died out in post-OJ. As we have also seen, *-o* appears to be inserted at D-structure, contrary to Kuroda (1965) and Kuno (1973).

What, then, is the condition under which *-o* occurs? Based on the prior discussion, I conclude that this condition is the same as the condition that dictates the occurrence of *-o* in OJ: *-o* occurs if the accusative-case-assigning feature is contained in the verb. In OJ, the option to overtly manifest this case is exercised by the attributive and perfect forms, but, in modern Japanese, this option is now an obligatory feature of the morphosyntactic system of case. This analysis of the modern accusative *-o* has historical validity. Moreover, it explains why one does not find "accusative" abstract case in modern Japanese.

10 SUMMARY

In this chapter, I argued that the infrequency of the overt case particle *-o* on direct objects in OJ stems from the availability of abstract case assignment by the verb. As long as the direct object is adjacent to the verb, the verb can license the direct object by abstract case assignment, which allows the direct object to appear as a bare NP without a case particle. Although the infrequency of OJ *-o* has often been commented on by traditional grammarians, an important insight of this chapter is that the occurrence of *-o* is not random, as has been suggested by a number of grammarians. The distribution of the particle depends on the type of inflection found on the transitive verb, as summarized in (84).

(84) Distribution of the particle *-o* according to verb inflection
- (i) *-o* need not occur if the verb is in the conclusive form.
- (ii) *-o* occurs if the verb is in the attributive or perfect form.
- (iii) With the conjunctive form, the occurrence of *-o* depends on the form taken by the tensed verb in the subsequent clause—the particle need not occur if the tensed verb is in the conclusive form, but it occurs if the verb is in the attributive or perfect form.

The conclusive form assigns abstract case to its direct object, in turn making it possible for the noun phrase to occur without the particle *-o*. On the other hand, with the attributive and perfect forms of the verb, the case must be manifested overtly, since *-o* is nominal-like in its distribution, though it is not a purely nominal case. Finally, as stated in (iii), the behavior of the conjunctive form with regard to case depends on the tensed verb: if the verb is in the conclusive form, it is likely that the conjunctive form can also assign abstract case; in contrast, the occurrence of an attributive or perfect verb entails that the conjunctive form does not assign abstract case, hence the object noun phrase must be accompanied by *-o*. Although counterexamples are inevitable, what is given in

(84) is the general pattern observed in the poetry and prose of the OJ texts that are investigated here.

The hypothesis put forth that only the conclusive form (and the conjunctive form occurring with the conclusive form) assigns abstract case does more than account for the distribution of the particle *-o* in OJ. It also provides a compelling reason for the linguistic change that transformed OJ, which frequently had bare direct-object NPs licensed by abstract case, into the Japanese of today, in which the direct object is virtually always overtly case-marked. Traditional grammarians have argued that the increased frequency of *-o* is due to the influence of *kanbun*. Although we cannot exclude the possibility that *kanbun*, with its ever-present *-o* on the direct object, contributed to the frequency of *-o*, this literary tradition alone cannot account for such a dramatic change. Based on the analysis of OJ *-o*, I argued that there is a purely linguistic factor involved. The bare object NPs in OJ are licensed by abstract case assignment. If this ability to assign abstract case is lost, we naturally predict that all object NPs must have the overt accusative case marker *-o*, and this is precisely what happened in post-OJ. As early as the Heian period, the verbal system began to undergo a fundamental change. The particular change relevant to our discussion is the loss of the conclusive form, which was an abstract case assigner, and its replacement with a verbal form that corresponds to the attributive form. The attributive form in OJ did not assign abstract case; by virtue of its taking over the conclusive form, the Japanese language in effect lost the ability to assign abstract case to the direct-object NP, thereby necessitating the increased appearance of the particle *-o*. This change, which took several hundred years, transformed the OJ of the eighth and ninth centuries into the uniform overtly case-marked Japanese of the late sixteenth century and beyond.

In the last section of this chapter, I documented this change by presenting data from two texts of the *Tale of the Heike*, the fourteenth-century *Heike* text and the late-sixteenth-century *Amakusa Heike* text. What we found was that in the earlier text, abstract case as well as the overt particle *-o* mark the accusative case. Their distribution was seen to be highly predictable from the form of the verb. The conclusive form, or the conjunctive form occurring with a tensed conclusive form, assigns abstract case, whereas the attributive and perfect forms, or the conjunctive form occurring with one of these forms, require the overt case marker *-o* on the object NP. The shift to a more uniform, overtly cased language is seen in the *Amakusa Heike* text; there, the frequency of occurrence of the particle is more than 20 percent greater than in the *Heike* text. The *Amakusa Heike* is believed to reflect the language of its era (Suzuki 1973). Clearly, then, the accusative-case-marking system of the late sixteenth century had lost the OJ property of abstract case assignment, giving way to the modern Japanese system of uniformly marking the object with the overt particle *-o*.

I also showed that the historical treatment of *-o* pursued in this chapter provides a fresh perspective on the modern particle *-o*, one that is radically different from the early transformational analysis (Kuroda 1965; Kuno 1973) and the more recent proposal in the Government and Binding theory (Saito 1983, 1985).

The study of the historical development of the accusative case in Japanese demonstrates a fundamental point about diachronic change. Diachronic change—at least in part—is guided by the principles of universal grammar. The particular change observed in this study has to do with a shift in the way in which the requirement of case theory is implemented: the language shifted from assigning case by abstract means (for many sentences) in OJ to uniformly assigning case by an overt case marker (*-o*) in post-OJ. This shift was motivated by an independent change in the verbal system that deprived the language of the verbal form (the conclusive) capable of assigning abstract case. Without such a verbal form, there was no option but to always overtly mark the accusative case with the case particle *-o*. In other words, the frequency of the particle *-o* increased dramatically in post-OJ to keep meeting the universal requirement imposed by case theory that every overt NP be case-marked, a requirement that in OJ was met just as often by abstract case assignment as by overt case marking, if not more often.

The principles of universal grammar are formulated to accommodate the synchronic variations among modern languages. What I have shown is that these principles are pertinent—indeed, crucial—to characterizing historical change. This is not at all surprising, since a language at any given point in time instantiates universal grammar, and any historical change must conform to the requirements imposed by the principles of universal grammar. Therefore, diachronic variation (at least the kind examined here) and synchronic variation are, in principle, one and the same. Both demonstrate various ways in which a particular universal principle is instantiated. The particular historical phenomenon of interest in this chapter is a perfect example of the nondistinctness of diachronic and synchronic variation. The difference between abstract case assignment in OJ and overt case marking in modern Japanese is precisely the same difference that one finds between modern Japanese and modern English. Whereas overt case is utilized in modern Japanese, abstract case assignment licenses the direct-object NP in modern English, very much like the direct-object NP in OJ. With regard to historical change, it is interesting to note that Japanese and English changed precisely in the opposite direction: Japanese shifted from abstract case assignment to overt case marking, and English shifted from the rich overt-case system of its ancient Germanic ancestor to the abstract-case system of today. As shown in (85), with regard to accusative case marking, OJ "is" modern English, and modern Japanese "is" Old English, a graphic example of the nondistinctness of diachronic and synchronic variation.

(85) Accusative case in Japanese and English

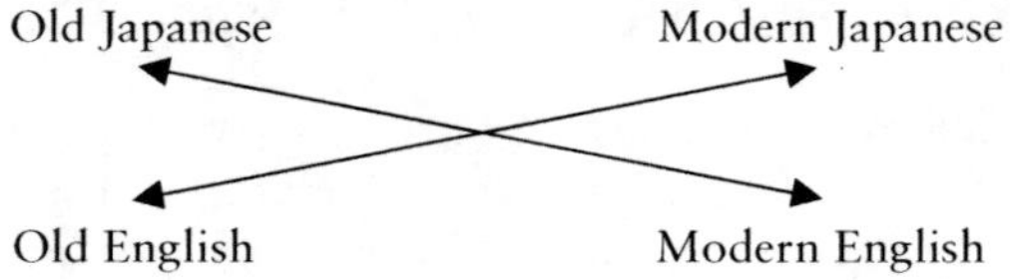

The diagram in (85) represents the fact that OJ and modern English depend on abstract case for marking the direct object (at least some of the time), whereas Old English and modern Japanese count on overt case marking. In this way, the two languages developed precisely in the opposite direction with regard to accusative case.

10 The Old Japanese accusative revisited
Realizing all the universal options

1 INTRODUCTION

One thing that is certain about human language is that it continuously changes. A point that is almost too obvious even to mention is that however a language changes through time, it must remain a human language. In other words, the changes cannot be random in nature. An important idea put forth by some linguists is that the changes are predetermined in the sense that diachronic variation within a particular language directly reflects variations found across contemporary languages; diachrony is synchrony when it comes to variations that can occur. In a clear expression of this idea, Lightfoot (1979, viii) observes that the formulation of "a possible grammar will provide the upper limits to the way in which a given grammar may change historically, insofar as it cannot change into something which is not a possible grammar." In a similar vein, Joseph (1980, 346), in addressing the loss of the infinitive form in Greek, notes that "[u]niversal constraints which hold in synchronic grammars are used to explain the direction taken by certain changes in syntax."

In Chapter 9, I tested this hypothesis about language change by looking at how the accusative case marking of objects in eighth-century Old Japanese (OJ) changed into the familiar system we find today. A noun phrase must, as a universal requirement, have case (Chomsky 1981). Across languages, we typically find two different ways of case-marking the object: morphological case marking, as in German, modern Japanese, and Latin, and what is sometimes referred to as abstract case, or the absence of any overt case form, which characterizes English, Romance languages, and a host of others. What I argued is that in OJ, we find both morphological and abstract case, but language change transformed the language into a strictly morphological-case-marking language, which is what we find today. The choice between morphological case and abstract case in OJ is not random, as sometimes assumed, but is predicted by the inflection found on the verb, a point first noted by Matsunaga (1983). Specifically, the conclusive form of the verb, which is found typically in the main clause, but also in certain subordinate clauses, allows abstract case, so that its object occurs bare without any case marking. In contrast, morphological case marking must appear if the verb has attributive inflection, which occurs commonly in subordinate clauses but can also occur in the main clause in what is called the *kakarimusubi* construction, as we will see later.

(1) Distribution of abstract and morphological case (Chapter 9, Section 3.3)
The conclusive form assigns abstract case, while the case-assigning feature of the attributive form must be manifested overtly as *-wo*.[1]

This is exemplified below from the *Man'yōshū*, a collection of poems compiled in the eighth century.

(2) Ware-ha imo __ omohu.
I-TOP wife think$_{\text{CONCL}}$
'I think of my wife.'

(3) [sima-**wo** miru] toki
island-ACC look$_{\text{ATTRIB}}$ time
'when I look upon the island'

In (2), the verb 'think' is in the conclusive form, and the object 'wife' has no overt case marking, which arguably indicates that it is licensed abstractly. In (3), the verb 'look' is in the attributive, and the object 'island' is accompanied by the OJ accusative case marker *-wo*. We can see from Matsuo's (1938) work that both abstract case and morphological case were common in the *Man'yōshū*.

(4) Frequency of the case marker *-wo* in the *Man'yōshū*

	Object NP with *-wo*	Without *-wo*
Man'yōshū (Book 17)	51	96

The fact that *-wo* does not always appear has led some to suggest that the OJ *-wo* was unstable as a case marker (Kobayashi 1970, 226), or that it was simply optional (Wrona and Frellesvig 2009). However, close examination shows that the distribution of OJ *-wo* is highly predictable and it clearly functions as a case marker.

It is important to point out that the difference between abstract and morphological case is not a difference between main and subordinate clauses, as might be suggested from looking at (2) and (3). Although the conclusive form, which assigns abstract case, occurs largely in the main clause, it also occurs in subordinate clauses with the complementizer *to*. The following example is from the *Tosa diary*, written in the Early Middle Japanese of the tenth century.[2]

(5) Kono hito [uta __ **yoman** to] omofu kokoro
this person poem compose-intend$_{\text{CONCL}}$ COMP think mind
arite narikeri.
exist COP
'This person had the intention to compose poems.'

As shown, the object *uta* 'poem' is bare, indicating that the verb has assigned abstract case.

Similarly, while the attributive form occurs typically in subordinate clauses, it can also occur in the main clause in a construction called *kakarimusubi*. This is the construction in which a *kakari* focus particle occurs sentence-medially, and the verb must be in the attributive form (or, with one type of *kakari* particle, namely *koso*, in the perfect form). The example below, taken from Sansom 1928, illustrates this rule for the *kakari* particles *zo* and *ya* (*zo* is used for emphasis, something akin to 'indeed', while *ya* is commonly used for rhetorical questions).

(6) a. Isi-wa kawa-ni otu. Conclusive
rock-TOP river-in fall
'Rocks fall into the river.'

b. Isi **zo** kawa-ni **oturu.** Attributive

c. Isi **ya** kawa-ni **oturu.** Attributive

Among 208 examples in a sample of the *Man'yōshū* (Takagi et al. 1962, 55–109), 34 are *kakarimusubi* constructions with a transitive verb and an object NP. All 34 are main clauses, and, the particle *-wo* marks the object NP without exception (Matsunaga 1983). The following is one such example.

(7) Kimi-ga mi-fune-**wo** itu to ka matamu?
you-NOM fine-boat-ACC when *KAKARI* wait$_{\text{ATTRIB}}$
'When may we await your fine boat back?'

Another feature of the analysis presented in Chapter 9, following Matsunaga (1983) and Miyagawa and Matsunaga (1986), is that the change from the mixed case system of OJ to one that uses morphological case across the board is predictable from the way the verbal inflection changed from around the tenth century to the fifteenth century. During this period, the language lost the conclusive form, and the attributive form moved into its place. This is shown below, based on a table in Matsunaga 1983.

(8) Changes in the verbal inflection

Before the change					
Inflection type	I	II	III	IV	V
Conclusive	-u	-i	-iru	-eru	-u
Attributive	-u	-u	-iru	-eru	-uru
After the change	-u	-u	-iru	-eru	-uru

Before the change, conclusive and attributive inflections had different forms in Types II and V, and, more importantly, this difference identified the two inflections as distinct across the language. But after the change, the distinction was lost, and where there were differences earlier, the new form took on the shape of the old attributive form, indicating that it is the attributive inflection that won out. This naturally led to the spread of morphological case because the attributive form requires morphological case, and its distribution expanded due to language change, from a more restricted distribution in OJ, mostly in subordinate clauses, to a much broader distribution, including the main clause, in modern Japanese.

In this chapter, I will take up criticisms by Kinsui (1993) of Chapter 9's analysis of the distribution of OJ abstract and morphological case. I will answer them drawing on the work of Miyagawa and Ekida (2003; M&E) and also Yanagida (2007) and Yanagida and Whitman (2009). As we will see particularly from Yanagida 2007 (see also Yanagida and Whitman 2009), OJ had a third way to license case on the object along with abstract and morphological case.

Kinsui (1993, 202) accepts the distinction I drew between abstract case and morphological case marking for OJ. He concludes by saying that he "believe[s] that we can accept, as a tendency, the absence of *wo* on the main clause object and its presence in the subordinate clause object, as Miyagawa asserts" (209). He is, however, reluctant to accept it at face value because there are "numerous counterexamples" (208). He criticizes the theory in Chapter 9 as "too rigid and unable to account for the counterexamples," raising three main issues.

(9) Kinsui's criticisms

(i) Versification
Ninety percent of the poems in the *Man'yōshū* consist of the *tanka*, a verse form that has five lines of five or seven moras, 5–7–5–7–7 (Nippon Gakujutsu Shinkokai 1965). In poetry it is possible that the occurrence of the case marker *-wo* is governed in part by the rigid versification.

(ii) There are examples in which the object has the morphological *-wo* despite the fact that the verb is in the conclusive form.

(iii) There are examples in which the object does not have morphological *-wo* despite the fact that the verb is in the attributive form.

I will take up each of these; I will combine (i) and (ii) in the next section, and in Section 3, I will take up (iii) by drawing on recent work by Yanagida (2007) and Yanagida and Whitman (2009).

2 THE CONCLUSIVE FORM IN OJ PROSE: MIYAGAWA AND EKIDA 2003

Kinsui's point that versification may sometimes dictate whether *-wo* appears or not seems to find confirmation in the following *waka*-poetry example taken from the *Izumi Shikibu diary*, a literary work of the tenth century (see M&E). The *waka* versification is the 5–7–5–7–7 *tanka* pattern commonly found in the *Man'yōshū*. The translation is from Cranston 1969.

(10)	Ookata ni	Nothing remarkable—
	Samidaruru to ya	The same old rain that pelts us
	Omouran	Every year, you think?
	Kimi __ koiwataru	These are my tears of love
	Kyoo no nagame o	Falling in a deluge all day long!

In the fourth line, morphological *-wo* fails to occur on the object *kimi* 'you' although its verb, *koiwataru* 'longing for', is in the attributive form. The absence of *-wo* makes it possible to maintain the versification of five or seven moras—in this case seven. I will return to this example later.

To see whether poetic versification somehow skewed the distribution of *-wo* in the *Man'yōshū*, M&E looked at several major works of literature from the Heian period (A.D. 794–1185), all written in prose with some poetry sprinkled through the text; they excluded the poetry. The two primary texts taken up are the *Izumi Shikibu diary* and the *Murasaki Shikibu diary*, both written by Heian court ladies in the tenth century. M&E also drew from the *Tale of Genji* by Murasaki Shikibu, the most important literary work of the Heian period, as well as the *Sarashina diary* (tenth century) to further confirm certain points observed in the other two texts. In this chapter, I will focus on the *Murasaki Shikibu diary* (*MSD*) to demonstrate M&E's point that we find the same distribution of abstract and morphological case in prose as in poetry.

The *MSD* occupies eighty-three pages in the Iwanami Bunko series (Ikeda and Akiyama 1984), and was written by Murasaki Shikibu, the celebrated Heian writer and court lady who also authored the *Tale of Genji*. This diary, which does not contain very many *waka* poems (which were, in any case, excluded for consistency), "has to do chiefly with the birth of two sons to the empress, events of political importance, since she was the daughter of Michinaga and through his royal grandchildren Michinaga got an unshakable grip on the imperial house" (Seidensticker 1981, viii).

2.1 The text of the *Murasaki Shikibu diary*

M&E found 382 pertinent sentences with a direct object in the *MSD*. I first give the raw data below according to verbal inflection. M&E deal with four inflections, the conclusive, attributive, perfect, and conjunctive. I will skip the perfect inflection but will include the conjunctive, which is found in a number of environments, including as the verbal form for conjuncts. I include it because M&E use it to make an argument regarding the conclusive form.

(11) *Murasaki Shikibu diary*: Preliminary

Inflection	Object NP with -*wo*	Object NP without -*wo*
Conclusive	30	56
Attributive	53	46
Conjunctive	90	92

These raw data from *MSD* offer many apparent counterexamples to the distribution statement in (1). There are thirty object NPs with -*wo* occurring with the conclusive form. Also, there are forty-six instances of an object NP without -*wo* occurring with the attributive form. What we see with the conjunctive form is that this form freely selects between the morphological case marker and abstract case, so the two possibilities are virtually even, a point that becomes important for dealing with some of the apparent counterexamples.[3]

As noted by M&E, once the raw data above are analyzed and certain special cases are eliminated, the results are much more in tune with what Chapter 9 argued based on the *Man'yōshū* (see also Matsunaga 1983; Miyagawa and Matsunaga 1986). It is possible to eliminate twenty-five of the conclusive examples that are deviant and thirty-seven of the attributive examples that are deviant.

(12) *Murasaki Shikibu diary*: Final

Inflection	Object NP with -*wo*	Object NP without -*wo*
Conclusive	5 (9%)	56 (91%)
Attributive	53 (85%)	9 (15%)
Conjunctive	90 (49%)	92 (51%)

The conclusive form overwhelmingly selects abstract case, while there is a strong tendency for the attributive form to select the morphological case marker -*wo*. The conjunctive form remains split virtually evenly between the morphological case marker and abstract case, showing that it optionally assigns abstract case.[4] The final data show that the observation originally made in Chapter 9 (and Matsunaga 1983) based on the poetry of the *Man'yōshū* is upheld even for prose. This responds to Kinsui's criticism that poetic versification may have skewed the distribution of abstract and morphological case independent of verbal inflection. As we will see later in the chapter, one interesting possibility does arise where the occurrence of *-wo* may be conditioned by versification without violating any grammatical principles.

Below, I will summarize some of M&E's discussion of how they dealt with the apparent counterexamples involving the occurrence of *-wo* with the conclusive form, keeping the attributive form in abeyance until Section 3. First, as M&E note, there are a number of lexical idiosyncrasies that force the occurrence of *-wo* regardless of verbal inflection. There are, for example, a number of idioms that are frozen in form with the *-wo* particle, and these account for some of the thirty deviant conclusive examples. I will not deal with these lexical idiosyncrasies in this chapter. What I will deal with are three types of apparent counterexamples that have a common character, namely, examples in which the conclusive form is prevented from assigning abstract case, so *-wo* is inserted to meet the requirement of case for the object NP.

To set the stage, I will briefly review the difference between conclusive and attributive forms that gives rise to the different case-marking possibilities. The conclusive form is a "true verb form" used to predicate an action, property, or state (Sansom 1928, 130). As a pure verb, we can surmise that it has all of the properties of a verb, including the capability to assign abstract case.[5] In contrast, the attributive inflection has "substantive" properties, which makes it similar to a nominal. Konoshima (1962), for example, notes that the attributive inflection has a nominalizing function. The following example from Sansom 1928, 136, demonstrates three substantive qualities of the attributive form.[6]

(13) hito-no **mitogamuru**-wo sirazu
people-GEN blaming$_{\text{ATTRIB}}$-ACC not know
'not knowing that others blamed them'

First, the attributive form *mitogamuru* 'blaming' has a substantive interpretation similar to that of the English gerund. Second, the particle *-wo* attaches to it to make the phrase an argument of the verb *sirazu* 'not know'. Third, the subject of *mitogamuru* has the genitive case marker, which is a hallmark of NP arguments in nominal clauses. These three properties make the attributive form appear nominal in nature. It would be incorrect, however, to identify it as a pure nominal, because it has verbal and adjectival properties as well. For example, it is able to modify a noun without the prenominal genitive particle *-no*. In (3) above, for example, if the attributive form *miru* 'look' were a pure nominal, we would expect the prenominal modification particle *-no* between it and the relative head.

In Chapter 9, a parallel is drawn between the substantive nature of the attributive form and the gerund in English. The latter requires insertion of *of* for case.

(14) the teaching *of* calculus

The idea is that, due to its substantive nature, the attributive form is also unable to assign abstract case, and *-wo* is inserted to meet the case requirement, just as *of* is inserted in (14). In modern theory, this nominalizing behavior of the attributive inflection would naturally be viewed as nominalizing the "small *v*" (Yanagida and Whitman 2009), in turn depriving the predicate of the ability to assign abstract case. However, to be consistent with Chapter 9, I will continue to speak of the attributive form itself as lacking this ability.

Below, we will see that some of the apparent counterexamples to the idea that the conclusive form assigns abstract case are examples in which the conclusive form is somehow prevented from exercising its normal abstract-case-assigning function, forcing *-wo* to be inserted.

2.2 When *-wo* occurs with the conclusive form

As shown in (11), there are thirty examples of this type that seem to contradict the prediction that objects of the conclusive form should not have *-wo* because the verb is able to assign abstract case. M&E account for all but five of these. I will summarize three of M&E's accounts, which have the common property of demonstrating a way in which the conclusive form is prevented from assigning abstract case.

2.2.1 Exceptional Case Marking (ECM)

A defining property of abstract case is that it must be assigned under adjacency with the verb (Stowell 1981). Thus, in English, normally nothing can intervene between the verb and its object, unless the object is made "heavy" and is able to undergo heavy-NP shift.

(15) a. *John read yesterday a book.
b. John read yesterday a book with 23 chapters. Heavy-NP shift

One of the *MSD* examples in which the object has *-wo* despite the verb being in the conclusive form is the following.

(16) Sakizaki-no miyuki-**wo** nadote meiboku-arite-to
past-GEN visits-ACC why honor-COP-COMP
omohi-tamahi-kemu. (36.11)
think-honor-PAST$_{\text{CONCL.SPECULATIVE}}$
'Why did I feel my previous visits as such an honor?'

We can see that this is an ECM construction because it is the subordinate subject 'previous visits' that is marked with *-wo*, and the matrix verb 'think' is a typical ECM verb. Similar examples occur in modern Japanese (Kuno 1976).

(17) a. Taroo-ga Hanako-ga tensai-da-to omotteiru.
Taro-NOM Hanako-NOM genius-COP-COMP think
'Taro thinks Hanako is a genius.'

b. Taroo-ga Hanako-o tensai-da-to omotteiru. ECM
Taro-NOM Hanako-ACC genius-COP-COMP think

The accusative subject is licensed by the matrix verb 'think' in both the OJ example (16) and in the modern-Japanese example (17b). The accusative NP in (16), by virtue of being embedded in an ECM clause, does not occur adjacent to the matrix verb, which therefore cannot assign abstract case to it. For this reason, morphological case is inserted on the subordinate subject.

This eliminates one of the potential counterexamples from the *MSD*. One of Kinsui's (1993) putative counterexamples from the *Man'yōshū* is also an ECM construction, as he himself notes.

(18) Yononaka-**wo** usi-to yasasi-to omohe domo
world-ACC unpleasant-COMP shame-COMP think although
tobitachi kane tsu tori ni shi ara ne ba.
fly away cannot bird be NEG
'Although I feel the world as being unpleasant and unbearable, I cannot fly away as I am not a bird.'

2.2.2 Emphasis

A number of the apparent counterexamples involve an object that is marked by *-wo* because the object is emphasized; *-wo* is known to have this emphatic function.

(19) sore-**wo** ware masarite iha-mu-to (78.6)
it-ACC I more than speak-intend-COMP
'that I speak about it more than (others do)'

This happens to be an example in which the conclusive form occurs in a subordinate clause, something made possible by the complementizer form *-to*. Is it the case that *-wo* is freely inserted on accusative objects whenever emphasis is desired? Note that the object in (19) occurs at a distance from the verb 'speak'. This suggests that emphasis may have the effect of moving the object away from its original position and hence away from the verb; this makes assignment of abstract case impossible, so *-wo* is inserted, just like in the ECM construction. In the following example, the object is, on the surface, adjacent to the verb, but we can surmise that it has moved away from its original complement position.

(20) . . . mi-tyau-no uti-**wo** tohora-se-tamahu. (43.11)
screen-GEN inside-ACC pass-CAUS-honor
'Let . . . pass inside the screen.'

See Yanagida 2006 for an argument that in OJ, all *-wo*-marked phrases move to a position outside the verbal projection; this may be related to a role for *-wo* in marking definiteness (Motohashi 1989) or specificity (Yanagida and Whitman 2009).

2.2.3 Compounding

Five of the apparent counterexamples involve compound verbs. Compounding apparently deprives the verb of its ability to assign abstract case, forcing *-wo* to be inserted. Following is one such example.

(21) Sirokane-no su-**wo** hitobito **tuki-sirohu.** (25.1)
silver-GEN cover-ACC people poke-each other
'People laugh amongst themselves at the silver cover.'

The verb *tuki-sirohu* is made up of 'poke' and 'each other'. M&E note that compound verbs almost always require *-wo* on the object regardless of the verbal inflection, suggesting that compounding somehow deprives the verb of assigning abstract case. In this example, the object with *-wo* has moved above the subject, which also makes it impossible to assign abstract case. There are examples where the object stays adjacent to the verb; nevertheless, *-wo* is required even if the verb is in the conclusive form. This is true for the *MSD*, and it is also true for the other major work that M&E analyzed, the *Izumi Shikibu diary*. The evidence M&E give has to do with the conjunctive inflection. Recall that the conjunctive form optionally assigns abstract case, and in the literary works analyzed, objects with and without *-wo* are evenly split; we can see this even split in (12) (ninety to ninety-two). M&E report a similar even distribution in the *Izumi Shikibu diary*. However, when we look at compounds in the conjunctive inflection, there is a clear pattern of obligatory *-wo*. The following is data from the *Izumi Shikibu diary* taken from M&E.

(22) Conjunctive compounds in the *Izumi Shikibu diary*

Object NP with *-wo*	Object NP without *-wo*
10 (91%)	1 (9%)

Just as with ECM and emphasis, the verb's apparent inability to assign abstract case when it is a compound, even when it has conclusive inflection, leads to *-wo* being inserted. Although M&E do not give an explanation, the phenomenon may be similar to what we see with gerunds in English, in that adding certain morphological structure to a verb (*-ing* in English, compounding or attributive inflection in Japanese) eliminates the possibility of assigning abstract case. That is not an explanation, of course, and I will leave the issue open.

2.3 Interim conclusion

See M&E for accounts of other apparent counterexamples to the idea that conclusive form assigns abstract case. All told, M&E account for all but five of the thirty apparent counterexamples in the *MSD*.

Finally, let us return to the question of versification and the poem from the *Izumi Shikibu diary* given in (10) above, which is repeated below.

(23)	Ookata ni	Nothing remarkable—
	Samidaruru to ya	The same old rain that pelts us
	Omouran	Every year, you think?
	Kimi __ koiwataru	These are my tears of love
	Kyoo no nagame o	Falling in a deluge all day long!

The fourth line contains the object *kimi* 'you' in its bare form without *-wo* despite the fact that the verb *koiwataru* 'longing for' is in the attributive. The absence of *-wo* makes it possible to fit the line into a seven-mora metrical pattern, as required by the *tanka* verse form. As an alternative to the idea that *-wo* is omitted here for the sake of the meter—or as an explanation of what permits the omission of *-wo* for the sake of the meter—M&E note that the use of the verb *koiwataru* is largely limited to poetry, and it typically occurs with *kimi* 'you' or *imo* 'wife', so that the combination *kimi koiwataru* formed a "poetic expression" independent of the verbal inflection. This is one possible explanation. Below, we turn to the work of Yanagida (2007; see also Yanagida and Whitman 2009), which provides a very different analysis, in line with the idea that *-wo* can be excluded here to respect versification because the case requirement is met by a means other than abstract or morphological case.

3 INCORPORATION AND THE ATTRIBUTIVE: YANAGIDA 2007 AND YANAGIDA AND WHITMAN 2009

In this section, I turn to the attributive form, specifically addressing apparent counterexamples to the hypothesis that the attributive form, being nominal in nature, cannot assign abstract case and therefore requires the morphological case marker *-wo* to accompany the object. As we saw in (11), the *MSD* contains a number of superficially deviant cases where the object occurs bare despite the verb being in the attributive inflection. While there are fifty-three instances of the attributive *-wo*, which is what we expect, there are forty-six examples where the object of the attributive is bare. Kinsui (1993) notes similar potential counterexamples from the *Man'yōshū*. M&E provide various explanations for all but five of the forty-six *MSD* putative counterexamples. For example, three of them contain an object NP with the adverbial particle *-nado* 'such as' and one contains an object NP with *-bakari* 'only'; these adverbial particles make it unnecessary for morphological case marking to appear even in modern Japanese.

3.1 Yanagida's discovery

Yanagida (2007) proposes a unified explanation for most of the OJ examples of bare objects with the attributive, one that cuts across the case-by-case accounts in M&E, based on her study of the *Man'yōshū* (see also Yanagida and Whitman 2009). Yanagida found that, in the *Man'yōshū*, there are ninety examples of transitive clauses that contain a bare object, and of these, fifty-five have the attributive form. The following is an example of the latter from her article (quoted in Yanagida and Whitman 2009; I retain their orthographic system, while adjusting the glosses in minor ways).

(24) Saywopimye-no kwo-ga pire puri-si yama. (5.868)
Sayohime-GEN child-NOM scarf wave$_{\text{ATTRIB}}$ hill
'the hill where Sayohime waved her scarf'

Here the verb *puri-si* 'wave' is in the attributive form and yet its object, *pire* 'scarf', occurs without *-wo*. Here is Yanagida's discovery.

(25) Yanagida's (2007) discovery

Of the fifty-five examples from the *Man'yōshū* where bare objects occur with the attributive form, in fifty-four (all but one) the objects are nonbranching nouns—single words, in other words.

We see an example in (24) above, in which the object *pire* is a single word. Why should this be the case? Yanagida (2007) argues that this overwhelming tendency for bare objects of attributive forms to be nonbranching indicates a third way in which objects can be licensed to meet the case requirement.

Baker (1988) shows that in a number of languages, the case requirement on the object is met not by abstract or morphological case, but by the object *incorporating* into the verb. This is shown in the Chukchee example below, taken from Spencer 1999 and cited in Yanagida and Whitman 2009 (I have simplified the glosses).

(26) a. Muri myt-ineretyrkyn kimitʔ-e.
we we-are carrying load-INSTR
'We are carrying the load.'

b. Ytlygyn qaa-tym-gʔe.
father deer-killed-3SG
'The father killed a deer.'

In (26a) the object occurs with an overt case marker (instrumental), but in (26b), the single-word object *qaa* 'deer' (a nonbranching N) has incorporated into the verbal structure in order to meet the case requirement. It is an important fact that incorporation occurs only with a head, because it is a kind of morphological process occurring in syntax. If Yanagida is correct in attributing some OJ bare objects to head incorporation, it means that in OJ we find three ways to license case on the object.

(27) Licensing case on the OJ object
(i) Abstract case
(ii) Morphological case
(iii) Head incorporation

While the first two ways were noted in Chapter 9, the third is a new insight that cuts across most of the example-by-example explanations offered by M&E and provides a unified and dramatic account of much of the problem data related to the attributive form.

In the remainder of the chapter, I will attempt to replicate Yanagida's discovery made on the basis of poetry in the *Man'yōshū* by looking again at the Heian prose studied in M&E.

3.2 Replicating Yanagida's discovery in Heian literature

M&E list in appendices all of the potential counterexamples from the *MSD* and also the *Izumi Shikibu diary*. I examined these examples to see if it is possible to replicate in tenth-century Heian prose the generalization stated in (25) that Yanagida made on the basis of poetry in the eighth-century collection the *Man'yōshū*. Setting aside the examples mentioned earlier of objects with an adverbial particle such as *-nado* 'such' and *-bakari* 'only', which do not require case marking, the following are the numbers of bare objects with an attributive verb divided into nonbranching (single word) and branching (phrasal) types.

(28) Nonbranching and branching bare objects with the attributive

	Nonbranching	Branching
Murasaki Shikibu diary	44	7
Izumi Shikibu diary	13	6

The *MSD* clearly evidences the pattern of Yanagida's discovery: of the fifty-one bare objects with the attributive form, only seven are branching. An equally striking pattern worth mentioning is that, among the examples that M&E were unable to account for with their case-by-case explanations, of which there are nine, only one is branching. Unlike the *MSD*, the *Izumi Shikibu diary* does not show a clear pattern of incorporation: of the nineteen relevant examples, almost a third are branching. However, there is something noteworthy about all six of the branching examples. All involve the formal nominalizer *koto*. An example is given below.

(29) mutukasiki **koto** __ ifu-o kikosimesi te (444.9)
disturbing things say-ACC hear-honor
'hear that (someone) says disturbing things'

M&E note this fact as well, and simply stipulate that a phrase with the formal nominalizer *koto* does not require case. If we exclude these examples, the *Izumi Shikibu diary* replicates Yanagida's discovery without exception. I also note that in the *MSD*, of the seven branching bare objects, two are of this type in which the object is headed by *koto*. Of the remaining five, two involve the light verb *su* or its related causative form, and M&E note that these verbs tend to allow the object to occur without -*wo* in any inflection.[7]

Why should the occurrence of *koto* (or its voiced alternate form *goto*) allow an object that branches to occur without -*wo* even when the verb is in the attributive form? One possibility is that the clause headed by *koto* is not an NP, but a CP, and CPs do not require case. This is simply a speculation, but the idea that *koto* may function as either C or N has been proposed for modern Japanese by Whitman (1992).

Finally, let us return one more time to the poem from the *Izumi Shikibu diary* (23) in which the object, *kimi* 'you', occurs without -*wo* despite the fact that the verb *koiwataru* 'longing for' is in the attributive, allowing the line to adhere to the seven-mora requirement.

(30) Kimi __ koiwataru

The object is a single word, which means that its case requirement can be met by incorporation. In a case like this, with an attributive verb and a nonbranching object, there is an option of incorporation or assigning -*wo* to the object, and this option gives the poet the license to choose between them in order to respect the versification.

4 CONCLUSION

I demonstrated that the systematic distribution of abstract and morphological case argued for in Chapter 9 finds further support from the work of M&E and of Yanagida (2007) and Yanagida and Whitman (2009). Most of the putative counterexamples to the proposed distribution, including those pointed out by Kinsui (1993), find explanation in independently motivated notions such as adjacency for abstract case assignment and head incorporation to fulfill the case requirement. One interesting result that came out of applying Yanagida's head-incorporation analysis was an account of the limited optionality of *-wo*: so long as the verb is attributive and the object is nonbranching, the poet in the OJ era could select either of the applicable licensing options in order to respect the versification of poetry of the time while being fully compliant with the grammar of OJ.

Notes

NOTES TO THE INTRODUCTION

1. The UNESCO report mentioned above is about the rapid loss of languages that is endangering this diversity.
2. The ability of a dative marker to function as either a case marker or a P is found in other languages. For example, Cuervo (2003a) shows that the dative marker in Spanish may function as a case marker or a preposition depending on whether the dative phrase is doubled by a clitic.
3. My work on *-kata* nominalization owes a great deal to Kishimoto's (2006) earlier work on this construction, although he gives a different judgment based on other examples similar to (11b).
4. Hiraiwa (2005) suggests that when the genitive case marker occurs, the clause that contains it is nominalized.

NOTES TO CHAPTER 1

1. A number of people contributed directly to the ideas in and the writing of the book from which this chapter is drawn (Miyagawa 1989). They include Noam Chomsky, Peter Culicover, Ken Hale, Nobuko Hasegawa, Robbie Ishihara, Brian Joseph, and Hiroaki Tada. I wish to thank my students who commented on earlier ideas, including some that were hatched the night before, and also patiently evaluated grammaticality of sentences. These include Naoya Fujita, Setsuko Matsunaga, Mari Nakamura, Naoko Nemoto, Hideo Tomita, and Tomo Yoshida.
2. Some NQs are idiosyncratic. For example, as shown in (1), the regular classifier for people is *-nin*; however, for counting one or two people, the "native Japanese numbers" *hito* 'one' and *futa* 'two' are used in combination with the classifier *-ri (hito-ri* 'one$_{\text{PEOPLE}}$', *futa-ri* 'two$_{\text{PEOPLE}}$'). Beginning with the number three, the numeral system borrowed from Chinese is used in combination with the regular classifier *-nin*. This classifier is also borrowed from Chinese.

   Some numeral–classifier combinations undergo phonological change. For example, the initial *h* of the classifier *-hon*, which is used to count long, slender objects as shown in (4), changes to *b* when attached to the numeral *san* 'three' *(san-bon)*. This change, which is obligatory, is conditioned by the final nasal element in *san*. For reasons unknown, when the same classifier attaches to the numeral *yon* 'four', which also has a final nasal element, the *h* → *b* change does not occur: *yon-hon/*yon-bon*.
3. *Postscript.* In principle, the syntactic independence of NP and NQ may be derived or base-generated, and both analyses have been pursued. In this chapter, I develop a base-generation approach. In Chapter 2, I present an analysis in which the NP and NQ start out as a single phrase. Neither analysis assumes the rule of quantifier float mentioned below.

4. Unlike *raw* and *nude* in (10) and (11), which do not receive a thematic role from the verb, some "predicates" in English do function as arguments of the verb. For example, the lower clause in (i), *to go*, is considered to have the thematic role *goal* (cf. Culicover and Wilkins 1986).

   (i) John tried **to go.**

   See the above reference and also Gruber 1965, 1976 and Jackendoff 1972 for an extensive discussion of different thematic roles assigned by particular verbs.

   One controversy pertaining to examples such as (i) is whether the lower clause is a full S or simply a VP. The former view assumes that the clause contains PRO in the subject position. We will not enter into this controversy since NQs do not occur as the main predicate of a clause, hence there is no justification for positing a PRO. For the analysis of the infinitival clause as a full S, see Williams 1980; Chomsky 1981; Koster and May 1982; Manzini 1983; among others. For the "VP analysis" of infinitival clauses, see Brame 1975; Hasegawa 1981; Bresnan 1982a; Culicover and Wilkins 1986; among others.

   There is one case in which a NQ can occur in an argument position.

   (ii) Ano **san-nin**-ga mata kita.
   those three-CL-NOM again came
   'Those three (people) came again.'

   (iii) Kono **ni-mai**-o Tanaka-san-ni ageru.
   these two-CL-ACC Tanaka-to give
   'I'll give these two (sheets) to Tanaka.'

   These are only apparent counterexamples to the generalization that, as a predicate, a NQ must occur in combination with a name (antecedent). Note that the demonstratives *ano* 'those' in (ii) and *kono* ' these' in (iii) indicate that the antecedent is clearly understood in context. These are, in other words, elliptical expressions in which the clearly understood antecedent of the NQ is left unsaid. Without any indication that the antecedent is recoverable from context, these expressions would be infelicitous, as shown in (iv) and (v).

   (iv) ***San-nin**-ga kita.
   three-CL-NOM came
   'Three came.'

   (v) ***Ni-mai**-o Tanaka-san-ni ageru.
   two-CL-ACC Tanaka-to give
   'I'll give two to Tanaka.'

5. I first proposed the predication-theory analysis in Miyagawa 1986, 1988. Ueda (1986) independently has made the same proposal.
6. *Postscript*. In the original publication of this chapter (Miyagawa 1989, chap. 2), I used the term *ergative*, following Burzio (1986). However, the standard name for this type of verb has come to be *unaccusative*, so I have changed the term throughout to reflect the present practice.
7. *Postscript*. I have left out two additional sections from the original for reasons of space. Section 5 gave evidence that the semantic notion of affectedness plays an important role in the construal of the NQ. Section 6 looked at the consequences of the present analysis of the NQ for long-distance movement and for the topic/contrastive *-wa* construction.
8. The judgment "?" is mine. The judgment of sentences in which a NQ modifies the indirect object of *ageru* 'give' varies from speaker to speaker. For example, Haig (1980) reports that his informants accept this sentence while Tomoda (1982) marks it as ungrammatical. The three native speakers that I consulted varied in their judgments as well: one completely rejects it, another accepts it, and the third detects a slight awkwardness.

9. The relationship between grammatical relations and quantifier float is investigated in detail in the literature on relational grammar (e.g., Postal 1976).
10. Kuroda (1965) first proposed that the antecedent of the reflexive *zibun* must be the subject. See Inoue 1976b and Kitagawa 1980 for counterexamples. Harada (1976b) proposes that the honorification morpheme *o-* . . . *-ni-nar* is triggered by the subject NP. See Kitagawa 1980 for some counterexamples.
11. One problem with Shibatani's analysis concerns sentences such as (17) and (19), which are cited by Harada in support of the grammatical-relations hypothesis. In these grammatical examples, the antecedent of the NQ is a subject marked by the dative *-ni* in violation of Shibatani's "surface nominative/accusative" generalization. Curiously, Shibatani (1977, n. 14) accounts for their grammaticality by stating that these NPs with the dative case "function as embedded NOM subjects before they are made into datives in the main clauses following Predicate Raising." Such an analysis goes against his assertion that what counts is the *surface* case marking.
12. The following example, pointed out to me by Peter Culicover (personal communication), is a problem for the mutual-c-command requirement for predication:

    (i) John swims nude, and Mary does too.

    In the original analysis by Williams (1980), the predicate *nude* is analyzed as being directly dominated by S, hence it and the subject NP *John* c-command each other. However, as Culicover notes, such an analysis is dubious in light of (i). In (i), presumably VP deletion has deleted the VP of the second conjunct. As we can see, the predicate *nude* is a part of the deleted VP. If, contrary to this, we adopt Williams's analysis, *nude* should not be deletable under VP deletion. I leave this as a problem for future analysis.
13. Haig (1980) and Kuroda (1980) independently note examples such as (44). Saito (1983) suggests the " trace" analysis to account for the grammaticality, though he does not explicitly propose an analysis of the NQ.
14. To complete the picture, it is necessary to note that a postposition provides case as well as a thematic role to its object NP, an assumption commonly made in the Government and Binding framework. In GB, it is stipulated that lexical items with the feature [–N] are case assigners (Chomsky 1981; Kayne 1981). The following is the lexical-feature specification for the four major categories verb, noun, adjective, and preposition/postposition (Chomsky 1970):

Verb	[+V, –N]
Noun	[–V, +N]
Adjective	[+V, +N]
Preposition	[–V, –N]

    As shown, verbs and prepositions (or postpositions) share the [–N] feature that designates case assigners.
15. *Postscript.* Some speakers pointed out to me that (57a) and (58a) are not so bad for them.
16. *Postscript.* As I mentioned earlier (note 6), in the original 1989 publication of this chapter I used *ergative* instead of *unaccusative*, but the field since then has adopted the latter term.
17. *Postscript.* See next chapter for discussion of how examples such as (86a) and the others given below can be improved if interpreted in a certain aspect.

NOTES TO CHAPTER 2

1. NQs occur in a number of constructions (see Kamio 1977 and Watanabe 2006, among others). In this chapter, I focus on the NP(-case)–NQ sequence as well as cases of NQ stranding.

2. See discussion in the next section that opens up the possibility that examples like (5b) may actually be grammatical under one interpretation.
3. See Levin and Rappaport Hovav 2005 for discussion of three types of telicity. In this chapter, I will not subdivide telicity into different types.
4. There are examples superficially very similar to the ungrammatical (9a) that for some people are not so bad, with a special interpretation.

   (i) (*)Tomodati-ga itizikan futa-ri odotta.
   friend-NOM one hour two-CL danced
   ('Two friends danced per hour.')

   For those who accept this sentence, the special interpretation is that every hour, two friends danced. This is a telic interpretation, and the grammatical nature of it is predicted. To get this interpretation, 'one hour' and the NQ must be pronounced as a prosodic unit. The following pseudocleft example shows that the two comprise a phrase (thanks to Hiroki Maezawa for pointing this out).

   (ii) Tomodati-ga odotta-no-wa itizikan futa-ri da.
   friend-NOM danced-NL-TOP one hour two-CL COP
   'It's two each hour that friends danced.'

   This example only has the interpretation that friends danced two at a time each hour. In the ungrammatical (9a), combining 'ten minutes' with the NQ is more difficult for reasons that I don't understand.
5. After the completion of this chapter, Tanaka's (2006) paper was brought to my attention, which makes similar observations about NQ stranding and telicity (Tanaka calls it "boundedness"). I thank Željko Bošković for pointing me to the paper.
6. It is possible that TEA could follow from independent considerations, if we consider the possibility that in the ungrammatical atelic examples, what intervenes between the subject NP and the subject NQ is an element that structurally belongs below Spec,*v*P, and thus the stranded subject NQ is not supported by the copy of the subject in *v*P. This would allow us to account for the ungrammatical (and grammatical) cases without stipulating something like TEA. One point in favor of this is that the following atelic example is fine.

   (i) Gakusei-ga kinoo san-nin sake-o nonda.
   student-NOM yesterday three-CL sake-ACC drank
   'Three students drank sake yesterday.'

   This is an atelic example, yet stranding is possible. The reason may be that the temporal adverb 'yesterday' is above Spec,*v*P, and the NQ *san-nin* is in Spec,*v*P along with the copy of the subject 'students'. However, there are a number of examples, such as the pairs due to Tsujimura given in (6)–(7) and the activity–accomplishment minimal pair in (9), that are not readily amenable to this kind of structural analysis. I will therefore assume TEA, but with the idea that it may be possible to derive it from basic structural considerations.
7. If we follow Borer (2005), the phrase 'in ten minutes' begins below Asp_QP and moves to Spec,Asp_QP, leaving behind a variable that it binds to give the required quantificational structure for telic aspect.
8. Nobuaki Nishioka has pointed out to me that the ungrammatical (16a) can be improved by adding a locative PP.

   (i) ?Tomodati-ga **butai-de** zyup-pun futa-ri odotta.
   friend-NOM stage-on ten minutes two-CL danced
   'Two friends danced for ten minutes on the stage.'

I agree that this sentence is much better than (16a). It appears very much like the example in (8a), where the addition of a bounded event location with *-de* adds telicity and allows stranding.

9. Occurrence of two stranded NQs, as in this and the following example, is, for some speakers, mildly awkward, although acceptable. Also, this example shows that in Japanese, it is possible to strand a NQ in a θ-position, contrary to the analysis in Bošković 2004.
10. Nakanashi pairs (32) with the following example:

    (i) Gakusei-ga kinoo san-nin Peter-o tatai-ta.
    student-NOM yesterday three-CL Peter-ACC hit-PAST
    'Three students hit Peter yesterday.'

    Unlike with 'kill' in (32), the act of hitting Peter can take place multiple times, hence the sentence is felicitous.
11. Most speakers I consulted about these examples were able to get the inverse scope. A few speakers note that as soon as they hear *dareka* 'someone' in the subject position, they immediately imagine a specific person; for these speakers, inverse scope is not available.

NOTES TO CHAPTER 3

1. This chapter was originally published as an article in the *Journal of East Asian Linguistics*. We are grateful to a large number of people for providing valuable comments at various points in its writing. They include Elena Anagnostopoulou, Rajesh Bhatt, Joan Bresnan, Noam Chomsky, Sandy Chung, Cristina Cuervo, Heidi Harley, Nobuko Hasegawa, Hisa Kitagawa, Jim Huang, Sabine Iatridou, Eloise Jelinek, Simin Karimi, Jaklin Kornfilt, Alec Marantz, Jim McCloskey, Martha McGinnis, David Pesetsky, Liina Pylkkänen, Norvin Richards, Mamoru Saito, Koichi Takezawa, and Kazuko Yatsushiro. Versions were presented at MIT's Argument Structure and Syntax class and at linguistics colloquiums at Kanda University of International Studies, Syracuse University, Tsukuba University, University of Arizona, University of Calgary, and UC Santa Cruz. We thank the participants for giving us suggestions and raising a variety of issues. Finally, we thank the two anonymous *JEAL* reviewers for their valuable comments.
2. In the above example, the existential quantifier occurs in the lower position and the universal quantifier in the higher position. The ambiguity obtains even if the higher quantifier (the "scrambled" quantifier) is existential and the lower one is universal.

    (i) Taroo-ga nanika-o dono-tomodati-ni-mo okutta.
    Taro-NOM something-ACC every friend sent
    'Taro sent something to every friend.'
    'some' > 'every', 'every' > 'some'

3. Hoji's (1985) observation is based on Kuroda's (1970) observation that one only gets scope ambiguity between subject and object with movement of the object across the subject. There are a number of technical implementations of how the existence of the trace leads to inverse scope (e.g., Aoun and Li 1989; Hoji 1985; Hornstein 1995; Johnson and Tomioka 1997). We will not attempt to argue for one particular approach.
4. We gloss the *-ni* here as 'to' to reflect the notion, to be defended, that when inanimate, the goal is a PP.
5. Marantz's (1993) QR-based analysis runs into a problem when we introduce the small *v*. We would predict wrongly that a transitive sentence with subject

and object quantifiers would not be scopally ambiguous. Bruening (2001) addresses this issue directly by suggesting that we can uphold many parts of Marantz's analysis if we assume that QR is subject to superiority, like any other movement. See his paper for details. We will assume this QR-with-superiority analysis for the different quantifier-scope facts in the Japanese DOC and the *to*-dative construction.

6. *Postscript.* As noted in Chapter 1, speakers vary as to whether they accept a numeral quantifier associated with a dative phrase. Both authors of this chapter accept it, and we will go with that judgment.
7. An anonymous reviewer indicates that in (17), *kokkyoo* 'borders' and the classifier *-tu* are "not quite compatible." However, both authors feel that this combination is fine, although possibly not optimal, and, in fact, there really is no other choice of classifier. We also checked with others, and they do not object to this combination.
8. The *-ni* particle also occurs on the source phrase, as in the following.

   (i) Taroo-ga Hanako-ni tegami-o moratta.
   Taro-NOM Hanako-*NI* letter-ACC received
   'Taro received a letter from Hanako.'

   This "source" *-ni* can be replaced with the full postposition *-kara*.

   (ii) Taroo-ga Hanako-kara tegami-o moratta.
   Taro-NOM Hanako-from letter-ACC received
   'Taro received a letter from Hanako.'

   We speculate that the *-ni/-kara* alteration is similar to the goal alternation, except that with the goal both alternants can be *-ni*. See Section 4.2, in which we discuss the goal postposition *-e* 'to'. Finally, speakers vary on the judgment of (16), the example in which a numeral quantifier floats off an animate goal phrase. Both authors feel that it is grammatical, as do many others we have consulted. However, there are those who do not accept this example with the verb *okuru* 'send'. Kishimoto (2001b) develops an analysis in which the goal phrase with this verb is strictly a PP. Our analysis is based on the judgment of speakers who accept this quantifier float.
9. We are grateful to Masaki Sano for suggesting the possibility of the two-goal construction in Japanese, although he himself finds it somewhat awkward (see discussion in note 11).
10. Many ditransitive verbs do not allow the two-goal construction, e.g., *ageru* 'give', *syookaisuru* 'introduce'. To allow the two-goal construction, a verb apparently must be associated with some sort of a "path," such as *okuru* 'send'.

    Toshinobu Mogi (personal communication) pointed out to us that the verb *todokeru* 'deliver' is, for him, much better with two goals than the verb we have used, *okuru* 'send'. As far as we can see, *todokeru* behaves in every way the same as *okuru*, so for speakers who find the two-goal example with *okuru* awkward, we suggest that they replace it with *todokeru*. See Cuervo 2003b for discussion of similar examples in Spanish.
11. We have been told by a few speakers that they reject two occurrences of *-ni* altogether (hence, they reject the two-goal construction). We do not know if this is a dialectal or idiolectal variation. The two authors of this article do not have this restriction.

    Some English speakers find two-goal sentences mildly awkward while others reject them.

    (i) ?/*John sent Mary a package to her office.

    We don't know why.

Postscript. Richard Larson (personal communication) informed us that the sentence improves (somewhat) if the locative phrase has a pronoun that is coreferential with the goal.

(ii) John sent Mary a package to her office.

A similar improvement is found in Japanese for at least some who find the two-goal sentence unacceptable.

(iii) Taroo-ga Hanako-ni kinoo kanozyo-no ofisu-ni
Taro-NOM Hanako-DAT yesterday she-GEN office-to

nimotu-o okutta.
package-ACC sent

'Taro sent Hanako a package to her office yesterday.'

12. Takezawa (2000) makes some extremely interesting observations about the possessive construction that are directly pertinent to our discussion. He observes that the possessor in the possessive construction with *aru* is marked by the dative *-ni*.

(i) Taroo-ni bessoo-ga aru.
Taro-DAT country house-NOM have
'Taro has a country house.'

If it is correct to assume that the goal of the DOC is a possessor, the fact that it has dative case marking falls out naturally from the fact that the possessor in Japanese is marked by the dative. As Takezawa notes, this, in turn, would be a natural consequence of adopting Harley's (1995b) approach to the DOC, in which HAVE is assumed to be present in the structure. Although Takezawa himself does not point out the possibility of a two-goal construction, he notes that it is possible to have a location along with the possessor in the possessive construction.

(ii) Taroo-ni(-wa) Karuizawa-ni bessoo-ga aru.
Taro-DAT(-TOP) Karuizawa-in country house-NOM have
'Taro has a country house in Karuizawa.'

13. Most speakers we have consulted judge this sentence to be ill formed. However, there are a few who accept it with only a slight hesitation. As we argue in Section 6.1, for those who allow this movement, it may be, like in Greek, a VP-internal A′-movement. The availability of this movement for some speakers is not inconsistent with our analysis, as we will show. It is not clear to us why there is an apparent idiolectal variation in how readily a speaker accepts this A′-movement (in Japanese and also in Greek—see Section 6.1).
14. Takano argues that the movement must be overt because covert short scrambling is disallowed.
15. In a recent presentation, Bresnan and Nikitina (2003) provide data that could shed light on this preference. Using the parsed SWITCHBOARD corpus, they looked at occurrences of the DOC and the *to* dative. For the verb *give*, they found that out of its 261 occurrences, 226, or 87%, were the DOC while only 35 were the *to* dative. The DOC is clearly the "preferred syntactic expression" for *give*, possibly because, with an animate goal, it is preferable to construe the goal as the possessor.
16. There are variations on Marantz's proposal. There is a version of the DOC proposal by Pylkkänen (2002) that more directly captures the possessive relationship by postulating an applicative head that takes the possessor (*Mary*) as its specifier and the possessee (*a package*) as its complement

(Pylkkänen uses Kratzer's [1996] "Voice" instead of little *v*; this difference does not concern us).

(i)

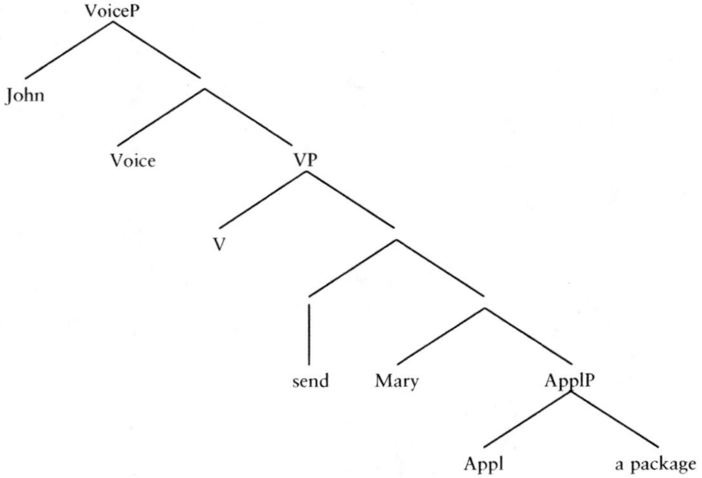

The applicative head has the meaning of "possession," and it relates the possessor, Mary, to the possessee, a package. In this way, this alternative proposal is more attractive in capturing the possessive nature of the high goal. It also captures the fact that this kind of "low" applicative head only occurs with transitive verbs because it occurs with an object (cf. Pylkkänen 2002). Nevertheless, in this article, we will use the earlier version by Marantz because it readily accommodates a two-goal construction.

Also, Bruening (2001) proposes a different structure for the *to* dative.

(ii)

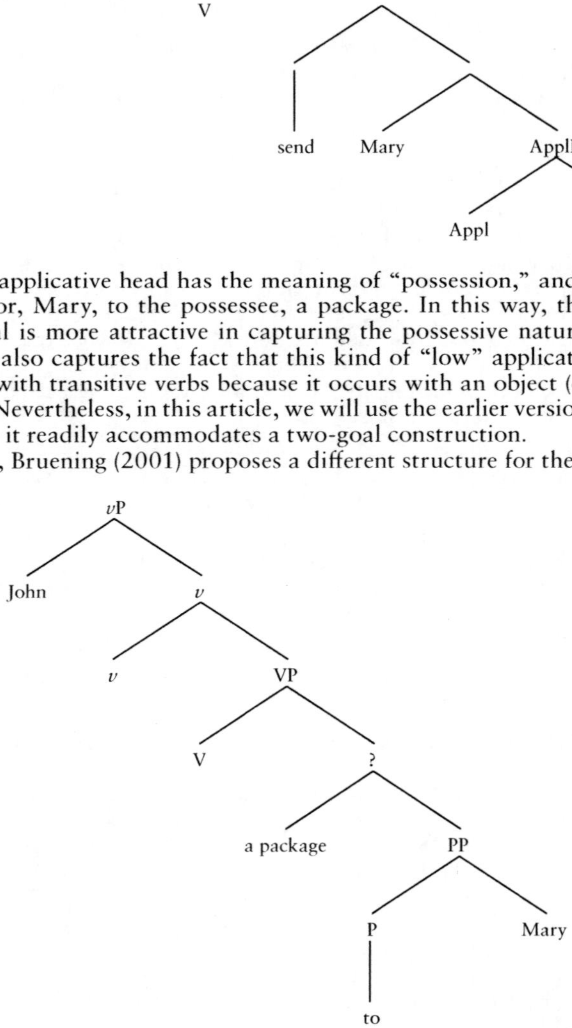

In this structure for the *to* dative, the theme and the PP goal are symmetrical; they are directly dominated by the node that Bruening marks with ?. This node is some sort of a small clause, we presume. An advantage to this structure over Marantz's is that it makes structurally transparent the word-order permutation we find in Japanese between the theme and the low goal (the PP goal). We will argue that this permutation is base-generated. While Bruening's structure may ultimately turn out to be correct, we will continue to use Marantz's structure for the sake of consistency.

17. The applicative head imposes the possessor-animacy requirement, thereby capturing the observation that the goal must be animate in the DOC but not in the *to* dative. What about the other argument-structure difference we noted? As pointed out at the beginning of the article, the DOC in English may have a causative meaning but not the *to* dative (Oehrle 1976).

    (i) a. The article gave me a headache.
    b. *The article gave a headache to me.

    In Japanese, there are several verbs for 'give', and in no case do we get the kind of distinction we find in English. For example, the verb *ataeru* 'give' may have the ostensible causative interpretation in either order.

    (ii) a. Ano-kozin-koogeki-no-ronbun-ga boku-ni zutuu-o
    that-personal-attack-GEN-article-NOM me-*NI* headache-ACC
    ataeta.
    gave
    'That personal-attack article gave me a headache.'

    b. (?)Ano-kozin-koogeki-no-ronbun-ga zutuu-o boku-ni
    that-personal-attack-GEN-article-NOM headache-ACC me-*NI*
    ataeta.
    gave

    Both authors feel that (iib) is not as good, but it is still grammatical. If in fact we replace *zutuu* 'headache' with *zutuu-no-tane* 'a seed for a headache', the sentence is perfect even in the theme–goal order.

    In fact, even in English, the *to*-dative version improves if the goal phrase is made "heavier" (Alec Marantz, personal communication).

    (iii) That article gave a headache to every person who had the misfortune of reading it.

    The issues appear quite complex, and we will not pursue this "causative" argument structure further in our article.

18. One of the anonymous reviewers notes that with the verb 'give', there seems only to be the meaning of possession regardless of the word order. The example the reviewer gave is the following.

    (i) kodomo-ni kyouhusin-o ataeru.
    child-DAT scared feeling-ACC give
    'make a child scared'

    As the reviewer correctly notes, in either order the interpretation must be possession. This seems on the surface to be a counterexample to the idea that in the theme–goal order, the construction must be the *to* dative, hence it only implies location, not possession. However, it is well known that even in English, the verb *give* implies possession even in the *to* dative. This may be due to a special meaning of *give*, say, that it is associated with the causative meaning of 'cause to have' (cf. Harley 1995b; Richards 2001).

19. As one of the anonymous reviewers notes, this analysis faces a problem with the subject–object quantifier ambiguity. Marantz proposed his theory before the small *v* was well established as a head for the external argument. If we assume *v*P for a transitive construction, then Marantz's theory would incorrectly predict lack of ambiguity for subject–object. See

Bruening 2001 for an interesting alternative to the DOC scope freezing that does overcome the subject–object problem. Our analysis is completely compatible with Bruening's proposal.

20. There is a question as to whether the theme generated below the locative goal first moves to the position of the "higher" locative goal before externalizing to Spec,TP. We will not argue for or against this possibility. See Takano 1998 for relevant discussion.
21. For an unusual and surprising piece of evidence for the base-generation analysis, see Aldridge 2001. Aldridge makes use of *hentai kanbun*, a particular written form of Classical Japanese.
22. The idioms presented are those of the "rigid" type, in which no chunk of the idiom can be moved. This is similar to *kick the bucket* in English. In contrast, Miyagawa (1995, 1997) used idioms that allow a chunk to be moved by A-scrambling, such as *X-ni te-o nobasu* lit. 'extend one's hand to X; expand one's reach to X'. This type of idiom is like *take advantage*, which allows *take* to be moved, for example, by passivization. Thanks to an anonymous reviewer for noting the distinction between the idioms in this article and those in Miyagawa 1997.
23. It is worth noting that Rizzi (1986) gives the reciprocal as being subject to the Chain Condition.
24. See Reinhart 1983 among others for the distinction between coreference and binding. See Hoji 1995 for an example of work on Japanese that essentially assumes Reinhart's approach.
25. An anonymous reviewer wonders if the facts in Yatsushiro 1998, 2003 cannot be dealt with by some other means, such as reconstruction or, if one is not fond of A-chain reconstruction, by a derivational application of Condition C. Such approaches face serious challenges from examples such as the following.

    (i) Hanako-ga [Taroo-no$_i$ syasin]-o kare-ni$_i$ okuri-kaesita.
    Hanako-NOM Taro-GEN photograph-ACC him-to sent-back
    'Hanako returned Taro's photograph to him.'

    This is in the theme–goal order, which, in the standard analysis, involves movement. The fact that the intended construal is fine, as opposed to, say, the following, is indication that there is no reconstruction/Condition C effect.

    (ii) *Hanako-ga kare-ni$_i$ [Taroo-no$_i$ syasin]-o okuri-kaesita.
    Hanako-NOM him-to Taro-GEN photograph-ACC sent-back

26. One possible avenue to explore is the interaction of *kare-zisin* with Condition B. It is well known that Condition B violation with overt pronouns in Japanese is weak, or for some speakers, even essentially nonexistent (cf. Hoji 1995).

    (i) ?Taroo-ga$_i$ kare-o$_i$ hihan-sita.
    Taro-NOM him-ACC criticized
    'Taro criticized him.'

    In the ditransitive construction, there appears to be a difference depending on word order. For the following examples, we don't indicate the grammatical judgment.

    (ii) a. Hanako-ga (kagami-o tukatte) Taroo-ni$_i$ kare-o$_i$
    Hanako-NOM (mirror-ACC using) Taro-DAT him-ACC
    miseta.
    showed
    'Hanako showed Taro him (using a mirror).'

b. Hanako-ga (kagami-o tukatte) Taroo-o$_i$ kare-ni$_i$
Hanako-NOM (mirror-ACC using) Taro-ACC him-DAT
miseta.
showed
'Hanako showed Taro to him (using a mirror).'

We are not certain how good—or bad—(iia) is. To the extent that it is interpretable, we feel that the theme–goal order in (iib) is worse, although it is a delicate judgment. If something like this turns out to be the case, we need to look at all of Yatsushiro's data with Condition B–type violation in mind. We will not pursue this issue further in this chapter, particularly given the delicate nature of the judgment.

27. To be more precise, McGinnis (2002) argues that in a language with what Pylkkänen (2002) calls a low applicative, the applicative phrase is not a phase, while the applicative phrase of a high applicative is a phase.
28. Fukui's proposal also faces the well-known counterexample of Slavic, which is a head-initial language, yet scrambling is allowed to the left, against the grain of head projection.
29. There are Greek speakers who find this scrambled version much worse than "?" (Sabine Iatridou, personal communication), reflecting the "*" judgment that the two coauthors of this chapter attribute to the two-goal constructions in Japanese in which the theme has moved to the left of the high goal.
30. This A′ analysis of the VP-internal scrambling may also shed light on a possible counterexample to our analysis. Takano (1998) points out that it is possible for the theme in the theme–goal order to strand a numeral quantifier; he gives Koizumi (1995) credit for first noting this.

(i) Taroo-ga nimotu-o Hanako-ni futa-tu okutta.
Taro-NOM package-ACC Hanako-*NI* two-CL sent
'Taro sent two packages to Hanako.'

Our analysis would predict that this structure should be impossible. However, if this is A′-movement, we have already seen that such movement is not subject to the routine locality found with A-scrambling. On this account this would be something like a focus movement as suggested in Miyagawa 1997.

NOTES TO CHAPTER 4

1. For earlier versions of the dual-base analysis, see Kitagawa 1994 and Miyagawa 1995.
2. Koizumi and Tamaoka (2010), supporting this analysis, give experimental evidence that when the object precedes the subject, the subject may stay in Spec,*v*P.
3. See Chapter 3, Section 4.2 (example (45)) on the possibility of ambiguity in the goal–theme order even when the goal is animate.
4. Harley (1995b), for example, argues that the double-object verb contains an abstract *have*. On this assumption, the double-goal construction in (19) is, in a way, predicted from Takezawa's (2001) study of the possessive construction with *-aru* 'have'. As he notes, this possessive verb may allow both a possessor and a location.

(i) Taroo-ni Hakone-ni bessoo-ga aru.
Taro-DAT Hakone-in villa-NOM have
'Taro has a villa in Hakone.'

5. According to Ito (2007), only certain types of ditransitives allow both of the goals to surface in the same sentence; these are what Matsuoka (2003) calls 'pass'-type ditransitive verbs. See Ito's work for elaboration. Ito notes that for him, an example such as (21), in which the accusative theme occurs before the high goal, is fine. This judgment may be a case of a special A′-movement discussed in Chapter 3, Section 6, based on Anagnostopoulou's (1999, 2003) analysis of Greek ditransitive constructions.
6. This has an important consequence for quantifier scope in ditransitive constructions. As noted earlier, the theme–goal order leads to quantifier-scope ambiguity, which Hoji (1985) attributes to movement of the theme across the goal. However, what we just observed is that the goal in the theme–goal order must be the low goal, which would make this order comparable to the English dative construction. As noted earlier, the English dative construction has scopal ambiguity, although English does not have scrambling. A view that English in fact does have some such movement is given by Takano (1998). In any case, it is clear that we do not have the final word on the source of the scopal ambiguity.
7. See Ito 2007 for a different judgment on (23b). If the movement of the accusative theme phrase can be A′-movement (see Chapter 3, Section 6), it is possible to have a reasonably grammatical structure even for (23b), although such an A′-movement requires a special stress pattern.
8. The particle *-ni*, which has many existences, including the dative case, the postposition 'to'/'from'/'at', temporal marking 'at', and so forth, never occurs in nominals with the genitive, a point that, as far as I know, was first observed by Harada (1976b).
9. Kitagawa (1994) was the first to propose a type of decomposition for the double-object construction in Japanese; he suggested that a double-object ditransitive verb decomposes into CAUSE and HAVE. See also Harley 1995b.
10. Miyamoto and Takahashi (2002) were the first to suggest that such an object–verb adjacency condition may hold in processing, something they proposed on the basis of work on the adjacency condition found in languages such as English (Stowell 1981).
11. The examples in (9)–(10) are presented with Kishimoto's judgments. See Tsujioka 2011 for more discussion, including some differences in judgment.
12. Kishimoto characterizes them as the Type III and IV tough clauses discussed in Inoue 1978a. However, see Tsujioka 2011.

NOTES TO CHAPTER 5

1. This chapter is from a 2011 special issue of *Lingua* on nominalization. I am grateful to the two editors of the special issue, Jaklin Kornfilt and John Whitman, and an anonymous reviewer for extensive comments that helped to shape the final version. Jaklin also helped with the Turkish data and discussed this project with me from its inception. I also benefited from discussions with Jun Abe, Yasuaki Abe, Masatake Arimoto, Noam Chomsky, Yoshio Endo, Nobuko Hasegawa, Jim Huang, Sabine Iatridou, Kazuko Inoue, Eunju Kim, Hiroki Maezawa, Hideki Maki, Roger Martin, Takashi Masuoka, Keiko Murasugi, Heizo Nakajima, Masao Ochi, Mamoru Saito, Hiromu Sakai, Peter Sells, Yasutada Sudo, Hiroaki Tada, Asako Uchibori, Azusa Yokogoshi, and Tomo Yoshida. Earlier versions were presented at the Workshop on Altaic Formal Linguistics 4 at Harvard University and at Hiroshima University, Kanda University of International Studies, MIT, Nagoya University, and Yokohama National University.

2. I am using *Altaic* more as a typological label than to presume an actual genetic relation among the languages named.
3. Another example of the diversity of licensing of genitive subjects is found in the so-called genitive of negation, in which negation apparently licenses the genitive on the subject of certain verbs in languages such as Russian (see Pesetsky 1982 and Chapter 6 of this volume).
4. See Kornfilt 2008 for other languages that fall into the category of what I call D-licensing.
5. Hale (2002, 112) also mentions in passing that there apparently is case alternation in the Dagur RC between the genitive and accusative case markers when the subject is pronominal. He does not pursue this issue.
6. The term *subjunctive* is probably not the appropriate one to use here since languages that have a distinct subjunctive form typically do not freely allow the subjunctive in constructions such as the RC. In this respect, Hiraiwa's own term *C-T amalgam* would more appropriately express the intent of the analysis.
7. Another example of a difference between *-ga* and *-no* is found in a recent study by Maki, Tsubouchi, and Hamasaki (2007). They surveyed 464 undergraduate students, who were asked to rate *-ga/-no* sentences from 5 to 1, with 5 being fully grammatical. Statistically significant differences arose between *-ga* and *-no*. Following is one such difference.

   (i)

Structure	Average rating
[(AdvP) NP-NOM (AdvP) V] N	4.23
[(AdvP) NP-GEN (AdvP) V] N	2.51

   When an adverb (AdvP) is placed in front of a nominative subject or after it, the sentence was judged as essentially acceptable (4.23), but if the subject is genitive, there was a clear perception of grammatical degradation, again showing that there is a fundamental difference between the nominative and genitive case markings on the subject. Crucially, these researchers chose "active" verbs—transitives and unergatives—for their study (there are a couple that are questionable as "active," such as a verb of motion). We return to this issue of verbal type below.
8. See Lees 1965 for an analysis of Turkish similar to Maki and Uchibori's, positing a null nominal head; see Kornfilt 1984, 2003 for counterarguments to Lees's analysis of Turkish, and an alternative that I assume for Turkish in this paper.
9. As *Lingua*'s editors noted, we might be able to explain example (13) under D-licensing without adopting the Maki and Uchibori analysis. While Maki and Uchibori postulate a silent nominal head, what D-licensing minimally requires is the D head. If D can directly select clauses, such as the comparative *-yori* clause in (13), in addition to selecting NPs, we would have a solution to (13). One such example of a D directly selecting a clause without an NP is found in the RC analysis of Vergnaud and Kayne (see Bianchi 1999).
10. *Postscript.* A number of native speakers have informed me that they do not share the judgment in (16), with either both examples being equally awkward or both being fine. However, with the following, most of these speakers get the distinction.

    (i) a. Mary-no$_i$ [kinoo kanozyo-**ga**$_i$ yatotta] gakusei
    Mary-GEN yesterday her-NOM hired student
    'Mary's student that she hired yesterday'

    b. ??Mary-no$_i$ [kinoo kanozyo-**no**$_i$ yatotta] gakusei
    Mary-GEN yesterday her-GEN hired student

In this example, the verb has been changed to the active 'hire' from the experiencer verb 'hear' in the original. As we will see in the next chapter, certain nonagentive verbs allow an entirely different genitive that can occur in a CP instead of a bare TP; this other genitive would allow the construal intended in (16b). For reasons that I do not understand, the distinction in judgment also becomes clearer if 'Mary' and 'she' are separated, in this case, by 'yesterday'.

11. See Lasnik and Saito 1991 for arguments that the ECM subject may optionally stay in situ in Spec,TP (cf. the argument in Section 3.1 for the in situ status of the genitive subject in Japanese). What we see in (19) is that even if the ECM subject stays inside the TP, Condition B is still violated (there is no grammatical reading of (19) with coreference), which indicates that the defective TP does not function as a binding domain. This is somewhat different from Lasnik and Saito's prediction based on anaphor binding.
12. While I use D′ for the node that immediately dominates the RC, this is strictly for convenience, and I stay neutral as to the precise nature of the projection. Murasugi (1991) argues that the Japanese RC is a TP in all cases, but what we are advocating is that this is true only when the subject is genitive; if the subject is nominative the RC is a full CP.
13. The universal quantifier in (23) is contained in *v*P, and we must assume that it is able to escape this *v*P by first adjoining to it. See Johnson 2000, for example, for some relevant discussion.
14. The lack of ambiguity in (24a) indicates that there is no operator movement in this noun-complement construction, unlike the counterpart in English (Miyagawa 1993). A possible alternative to the QR analysis of (24b) is that for the wide-scope reading, the genitive subject is in Spec,DP to begin with, as the possessor of 'reason', and from this position it takes scope over the head noun. Evidence in favor of this "possessor" analysis is that for many speakers, placing an adverb such as 'tomorrow' to the left of the genitive subject deprives the genitive subject of its wide-scope reading (Ochi 2001).

    (i) [Asita [Taroo-ka Hanako]-no kuru] riyuu-o osiete.
    tomorrow Taro-or Hanako-GEN come reason-ACC tell me
    'Tell me the reason why Taro or Hanako will come tomorrow.'
    (*)'Taro or Hanako' > 'reason'

    The adverb belongs to the TP, so that it rules out the genitive subject occurring in Spec,DP, in turn preventing the subject from taking scope over the head noun.

    Another way to view (i) is that an adverb at the left edge encourages a one-event reading—an event that will happen tomorrow—whereas the wide-scope reading requires a two-event reading. Evidence in favor of the QR analysis is the following.

    (ii) [Syatyoo-no [[Taroo-ka Hanako]-no syusse-suru] riyuu]-o
    president-GEN Taro-or Hanako-GEN be promoted reason-ACC
    osiete.
    tell me
    'Tell me the president's reason for why Taro or Hanako will be promoted.'
    'Taro or Hanako' > 'reason'

    In this example the possessor position is filled by 'president', so that the genitive subject has to be within TP. Nevertheless, the wide-scope reading of this subject is still allowed, suggesting that the genitive subject undergoes QR to take the wide scope. (As expected, the wide-scope reading is difficult, if not impossible, for the nominative version of (ii).) It is important to note that a double-possessor reading is not possible: **syatyoo-no Taroo-no riyuu* (intended: 'the president's Taro's reason'). This excludes the genitive subject from being in the lower Spec,DP position in a double-possessor construction.

15. Since Watanabe (1996) and Hiraiwa (2001) identify "subjunctive" as the form that licenses genitive subjects, it is worth noting that the subjunctive in English does not lead to scope ambiguity.

    (i) Someone asked that every car be washed.

16. The example with 'fortunately' and genitive subject improves markedly if the predicate is unaccusative or passive (see next chapter).

17. *Postscript.* There is a potential problem with example (28b). The analysis I present predicts that if the intervening elements occur to the left of the genitive subject, leaving the genitive subject adjacent to the verb, the sentence should be fine. However, one of the intervening elements, 'vigorously', is not natural even if placed before the genitive subject.

    (i) ??ikioi-yoku kodomotati-no kake-nobotta kaidan
    vigorously children-GEN run-climb up stairway
    'the stairway that those children ran up vigorously'

    As was pointed out to me at my talk at Nagoya University in June 2011, another adverb, 'foolishly', works better for our purpose.

    (ii) a. *kodomotati-no orokanimo kake-nobotta kaidan
    children-GEN foolishly run-climb up stairway

    b. orokanimo kodomotati-no kake-nobotta kaidan
    foolishly children-GEN run-climb up stairway
    'the stairway that those children ran up foolishly'

    As shown, if 'foolishly' intervenes between the genitive subject and the verb (iia), the relative clause is degraded, but if the adverb occurs before the genitive subject (iib), the relative clause is fine.

18. One might wonder why some formal feature from D isn't inherited by T here. The technical specification of C and T is that they are merged together into the structure as if they are a single lexical item (Chomsky 2007, 2008), and it is only when this happens that a probe can appear on C and be inherited by T. T and D, on the other hand, are never merged together.

19. In Miyagawa 2008, I claimed that the transitivity restriction does not apply in noun-complement clauses, suggesting that the complement clause is a CP even when it contains a genitive subject.

    (i) Gapless construction

    (?)[Taroo-**no** Hanako-o susumeta] riyuu-o osiete.
    Taro-GEN Hanako-ACC recommend reason-ACC tell me
    'Tell me the reasons why Taro recommended Hanako.'

    However, it appears that this claim was incorrect. When we place an adverb in front of the genitive subject, the effects of the transitivity restriction clearly emerge (thanks to Hiroki Maezawa for pointing this out to me).

    (ii) *[Kinoo Taroo-**no** Hanako-o susumeta] riyuu-o
    [yesterday Taro-GEN Hanako-ACC recommend reason-ACC
    osiete.
    tell me
    (Intended: 'Tell me the reasons why Taro recommended Hanako yesterday.')

    Apparently, in (i) the genitive subject is located in Spec,DP, in the possessor position.

20. To account for the transitivity restriction, Hiraiwa (2001, 115) proposes that assignment of the accusative in one phase requires the assignment of the nominative in the next phase. Although there is some empirical data that might be taken to support this, in the end, it is a stipulation that awaits a more principled explanation.
21. *Postscript*. Another way to view (40) is that it is similar to the French example in (37a), in which the object has been extracted from *v*P by *wh*/operator movement. Thanks to David Hill for pointing this out.
22. Our proposal that the genitive-subject construction has some type of stative interpretation contrasts with the claim in Horie and Kang 2000 that the genitive-subject construction is nonstative in nature. See Nambu 2007 for evidence against Horie and Kang's claim.
23. The novels are *Byakuya Soshi* (1976) by Itsuki Hiroyuki, *Hoshibosi no Kanashimi* (1984) by Miyamoto Teru, *Koibumi* (1987) by Renjo Mikihiko, and *Fukai Kawa* (1996) by Endo Shusaku.
24. Nambu (2007) presents another extensive corpus study of *ga–no* conversion based on the minutes of the national Diet (parliament). While the overall percentage of genitive subjects is smaller than in Kim's study (a fact that may reflect the formal style of the Diet minutes), Nambu's results echo Kim's in showing that the genitive subject occurs far more frequently with adjectives (27.8%) than with verbs (10.6%).
25. For adjectives, I am assuming the CP–TP/nominative–genitive distinction as argued earlier. However, it is possible—even likely—that the adjective also has a simple Adjective Phrase projection (see, e.g., Yamakido 2000). It is possible that a purely stative unaccusative verb may also have something similar, such as a Modifier Phrase, as proposed by Ogihara (2004). I will simply note this possibility but will not incorporate it into the analysis in this paper.
26. Example (46) may also be purely stative if the "present tense" *-ru* has this property in RCs, a possibility that has been noted (thanks to Yasu Sudo for this point).
27. The paucity of genitive subjects with transitives and unergatives recalls Terada's (1987) contention that the genitive subject only occurs with unaccusatives (she did not consider adjectives). Although her generalization is not quite true, it does capture a clear tendency towards favoring unaccusatives (and, even more, adjectives) over transitives and unergatives as Kim (2009) shows. Unfortunately, the actual example that Terada (1987, 636) gives is an instance of the transitivity restriction, so the empirical evidence she provides is not appropriate. The example is the following.

    (i) *?Perry-no Tokyo-o kengakusiteita toki-wa orisimo
    Perry-GEN Tokyo-ACC sightsee time-TOP seasonably
    yuki-ga hutteita.
    snow-NOM falling
    'At the time when Perry did sightseeing of Tokyo, it was seasonably snowing.'

NOTES TO CHAPTER 6

1. In Miyagawa 2010, I give arguments that the effect of EPP only shows up when there are relevant formal features on the head (e.g., T).
2. Some speakers do not find (12a) so bad with the genitive subject. It is possible that these speakers are topicalizing the 'when' phrase, keeping the topic marker *-wa* silent, which is an option (see Kuno 1973). The topic marker

functions like a case marker in turning *toki* into an N. These speakers are thus parsing (12a) in a way that allows D-licensing of the genitive. One such speaker I checked with does not allow 'fortunately', a sure sign that the genitive is being D-licensed.

(i) [Saiwai-ni minna-ga/?*-no odotta toki](-wa) nigiyaka-ni
fortunately all-NOM/-GEN danced when(-TOP) lively
natta.
became
'When everyone fortunately danced, it became lively.'

The sentence with the genitive is fine without 'fortunately' if *-wa* occurs overtly or, as it appears, covertly. Another possibility besides *-wa* is that these speakers are silently assuming *-ni*; *-ni* can occur optionally on temporal clauses and it has the same effect of turning *toki* into a nominal.

3. These examples were organized by Jason Merchant in a handout.
4. Other unaccusatives in his examples include *kureru* 'goes down' and *tatsu* 'passes'. There are also examples that involve transitive/unergative verbs such as *yomu* 'read' and *omou* 'think', but in other constructions, such as the comparative. I will comment on those examples later.
5. This raises a question about QR in English, in particular, how can the object quantifier take scope over the subject quantifier in examples such as *Someone loves everyone*, if the object is inside *v*P, presumably a phase? Johnson and Tomioka (1997) and Johnson (2000) give arguments that the object takes scope over the copy of the subject in Spec,*v*P, rather than the pronounced copy in Spec,TP as in previous accounts. If so, the object quantifier need not raise out of *v*P to take inverse scope.
6. There are dialects on the southern island of Kyushu that allow the genitive case in nominative positions even in the matrix clause. See Kato 2007 and Yoshimura 1994.
7. See note 9 for a suggestion that only a subset of dependent tense licenses the GDT.
8. In Slavic, the genitive of negation may occur on the object of transitive verbs; I assume that when this happens, the small *v* is somehow partially defective in that it fails to assign accusative case. See Section 5 for more on this.
9. There is a complication here in that there is another conditional, *-tara*, which contains the "past" morpheme *-ta* and shows dependent-tense interpretation, yet a genitive subject is still not allowed.

(i) Hanako-ga/*-no ki-tara, osiete kudasai.
Hanako-NOM/-GEN come-if tell me please
'Please let me know if Hanako comes.'

Similarly, the conditional *-to* requires the nonpast inflection on the preceding predicate, which is dependent-tense marking, but blocks genitive case.

(ii) Hanako-ga/*-no kuru-to, paatii-ga motto tanosiku naru.
Hanako-NOM/-GEN come-if party-NOM more fun become
'If Hanako comes, the party will become more fun.'

Chiharu Kikuta pointed out to me that *nara* 'if' and *node* 'because' can occur with dependent tense, yet they never allow the GDT. All this points to the possibility that what licenses GDT is a subset of dependent tense that goes with such temporal notions as 'when' and 'until'. I leave this issue open.

10. In an earlier version of Chapter 5, I mistakenly said that some of the examples in (48) are not very good, but it has become clear that they are basically fine after checking with a large number of native speakers.

NOTES TO CHAPTER 7

1. This paper appeared in *Lingua* in 1984. I am grateful to Adrian Akmajian, Ken Hale, Morris Halle, Richard Oehrle, Mamoru Saito, Susan Steele, and Yasushi Zenno for discussing the subject matter contained in this paper at various points in its development. The research for this paper was partially funded by NIMH lF32NH08 24–01.

   This paper was partially based on my 1980 University of Arizona doctoral dissertation. The dissertation was supervised by the late Adrian Akmajian, who died of illness in the summer of 1983. The paper is dedicated to him.
2. Historically, the *-sas* form "gave rise to the *sase* form around the 12–15th centuries" (Shibatani 1973; see also Miyaji 1969).
3. Shibatani states that the distinction in the meaning of V-*sas* he points out is applicable only to speakers from the Kanto (Tokyo) region. Those from Kansai (Osaka) do not make the distinction. The analysis of V-*sas* in this chapter will likewise reflect the use of V-*sas* in the Kanto region.
4. There are some problems with Aronoff's data. For example, *furiosity* is listed as a bona fide word in *Walker's rhyming dictionary* (I am grateful to Morris Halle for this information).
5. Bruce Miller (personal communication) provided the Mitla Zapotec examples. His phonological transcription is used for the examples. I have also taken two examples from Briggs 1961.
6. See Farmer 1980, Miyagawa 1980, and Ostler 1980 for extensive discussions of the lexical approach to the Japanese causative construction.
7. I am grateful to Mamoru Saito (personal communication) for pointing out the advantages of a parallel-structure approach to the V-*sase*. A similar proposal has been made for the French causative by Zubizarreta (1982).

NOTES TO CHAPTER 8

1. In Marantz's (1997) system, what is found at the position of V in (25) is instead a root that, once raised to *v*, takes on the category of a verb. I will comment more on this later.
2. This subsection is new; it does not appear in Miyagawa, in press, the previous version of this chapter.
3. There is a third approach based on the notion of paradigms (Miyagawa 1980, 1984a [= Chapter 7], 1989; Stump 2001). I believe that the two approaches I take up can subsume most, or all, of the advantages of the approach based on paradigms.

NOTES TO CHAPTER 9

1. Like Chapter 1, the present chapter is taken from Miyagawa 1989. In addition to the help with that book that I gratefully acknowledged in Chapter 1, note 1, Takashi Ogawa and Yasushi Zenno assisted generously with the Old Japanese data in this chapter.
2. There are four situations in which the direct object appears without the accusative particle *-o*. The first is when the direct object has a particle such as the topic marker *-wa* or *-mo* 'also'.

   (i) Kabu-**wa** katta.
   stocks-TOP bought
   'As for stocks, (I) bought (them).'

The second involves sentences that have an empty category in the object position (cf. Kuroda 1965; Huang 1984), which makes it impossible for the particle *-o* to appear because no particle in Japanese can appear with an empty element.

(ii) Boku-ga ***e*** katta.
me-NOM bought
'I bought (it).'

Third, the direct object can be marked by the nominative *-ga* if the predicate is stative (cf. Kuno 1973).

(iii) Boku-ga BMW-**ga** kai-tai.
me-NOM BMW-NOM buy-want
'I want to buy a BMW.'

Fourth, the accusative *-o* can be optionally dropped in colloquial speech if the direct object is adjacent to the transitive verb (Saito 1983; Masunaga 1987).

(iv) Kimi-wa nani katta no?
you-TOP what bought Q
'What did you buy?'

See Section 6 for more on the first and fourth possibilities.

3. The *Man'yōshū* data in this chapter are, for the most part, based on Miyagawa and Matsunaga 1986, which is indebted for its data to Matsunaga's (1983) Ohio State University master's thesis. However, this chapter includes significantly more new data.
4. See Travis 1984 and Lumsden 1987 for a similar view of historical change within the Government and Binding theory.
5. Two common case assigners are verbs and prepositions, which share the lexical feature [–N] (cf. Chomsky 1970, 1981). The "adjacency condition" on abstract case assignment, which I assume here, is adopted from Stowell 1981. See Kayne 1984 for an alternative formulation.
6. There is apparently a parametric variation on how strictly a language follows the adjacency condition. English is quite strict, but see Stowell 1981 for a discussion of languages with a comparatively loose requirement for adjacency.
7. I represent the particle as *-o* instead of *-wo* throughout this chapter, though the actual pronunciation of the particle in OJ is most likely the latter. This phonological distinction between *wo* and *o* began to erode in the early eleventh century (Mabuchi 1971).
8. The first two of the four exceptions are as follows:

(i) Katusika-no Mama-no irie-ni utinabiku
Katsushika-in Mama bay-in bending and yielding
[tamamo __ karikemu] Tekona si omooyu. (*KT* 433)
fine seaweed will have cut Tekona recollect
'Recollect Tekona, who will have cut and reaped the fine seaweed bending and yielding (with the waves) in the bay of Mama in Katsushika.'

(ii) Arae-no Fuzie-no ura-ni [suzuki __ turu] ama to ka
(epithet) Fujie bay-in [perch fish fisherman
miramu tabiyuku ware o. (*KT* 252)
consider traveling I
'Would they consider me as a fisherman angling perch in the bay of Fujie minding of course hempen cloth, I who am traveling?'

In (i), *tamamo karikemu Tekona* 'Tekona, who will have cut and reaped the fine seaweed' is a relative-clause construction, thus the object NP *tamamo* should have *-o* by our analysis. Its absence is possibly explained by the fact that *tamamo karu* is an idiomatic expression (Matsunaga 1983). In (ii), *suzuki turu ama* 'fisherman angling perch' is also a relative-clause construction. One possible way out of this exception is to view *suzuki turu* as a quasi noun–verb compound, along the lines of modern-Japanese compounds such as *sakana-turi* 'fish angling' (fishing). The remaining two exceptions given in (iii) and (iv) might also be accounted for as compounds, though further study is needed to establish this.

(iii) Omiya-no uti-made kikoyu abikisu to
Imperial Palace inside-to hear draw net
[ago __ totonouru] ama-no yobigoe. (*KT* 238)
fisherboys arrange fishermen's cry
'Oh! The fishermen's cries calling together and arranging in order the fisherboys and -girls saying: "We are going out to draw the nets!" They resound onto the inner part of the Imperial Palace.'

(iv) Ana miniku sakasira o su to [sake __ nomanu] hito-o
ugly try to be smart sake not drink person
yoku mireba saru ni kamo niru. (*KT* 344)
carefully see if monkey resemble
'If one observes carefully such people who do not drink sake thinking "I will play the sage!" how ugly it is; surely they will resemble monkeys.'

9. There are four major types of verbs in OJ, categorized on the basis of their inflection. The following examples are taken from Sansom 1928, 91.

	Quadrigrade	Lower bigrade	Middle bigrade	Unigrade
Conclusive	yuku 'go'	tabu 'eat'	otu 'fall'	miru 'see'
Attributive	yuku	taburu	oturu	miru

Note that the conclusive and attributive forms clearly differ in shape for lower bigrade and middle bigrade but not for quadrigrade and unigrade. For the latter two categories, the two forms are distinguished by accentuation (Leon Serafim, personal communication).

10. This example, quoted in Sansom 1928, xi, is from the *Shoku Nihongi*, which contains "certain Imperial edicts in pure Japanese" and was completed A.D. 797.

11. There is one situation in which the overt case marker *must* appear although the verb is conclusive. The -*o* becomes obligatory on the object of the conclusive verb if the object is an attributive verb clause (Sansom 1928, 321), like in (20). In the following example from the same Sansom source, although the verb *matu* is in the conclusive form, the particle -*o* is nevertheless used:

(i) yo-no fukuru-**o** matu
night fall wait
'to wait until the night falls'

How can we deal with this? If the argument is a noun phrase instead, the case marker need not occur. One solution is to use the crucial distinction between NPs and clauses, stipulating that abstract case can only be assigned to an NP, never to a clause.

(ii) Stipulation on abstract case assignment
Abstract case can only be assigned to a nominal.

This is intuitively plausible because abstract case is always assigned to an argument of the case assigner, and an argument is nearly always a nominal.

12. There is one particle, the emphatic *koso*, that turns the conclusive into not the attributive but the perfect form. I deal with this *koso* form in Section 5.1.
13. Kuno (1973) originally studied the phenomenon of case drop in relation to the topic marker *-wa*, as in the following example:

    (i) Taroo __/-wa itta?
    'Did Taro go?'

    How can we be certain that the "dropped" particle in (43) is the accusative *-o* and not the topic marker *-wa?* If it is the latter, the particleless sentence has no bearing on the claim that abstract case assignment appears to happen in modern Japanese as well. Actually, the "dropped" particle in (43) cannot be *-wa* because the object NP is a *wh*-word, and it is well known that the topic marker does not occur with *wh*-words (Kuno 1973; but see Miyagawa 1987b). If a particle were to occur in (43), it could only be the accusative case, so the sentence does indeed suggest abstract case assignment (cf. Saito 1983, 1985).
14. Another question about Matsuo's data is that he counted object NPs that occur with particles such as *-mo* 'also' in the same category as NPs without *-o*. Even in modern Japanese, a particle such as *-mo* 'also' does not allow *-o* to occur with it.

    (i) Hanako-wa hon-mo katta.
    Hanako-TOP book-also bought
    'Hanako also bought a book.'

    An NP marked by *-mo* is free to move within the sentence, unlike a true "bare" NP, which must occur adjacent to the verb. Consequently, from the perspective of case marking, *-mo* appears to provide case to its NP without the kind of dependence seen in abstract case assignment. In considering the phenomenon of case, then, these object NPs with particles but without *-o* should be excluded from those licensed by abstract case assignment. The figures in (44) in the "without *-o*" column are therefore larger than they should be. In the absence of the actual examples, it is not clear what the actual figures should be. For our purposes, the figures given by Matsuo nevertheless provide evidence for the trend of increasing use of *-o* from the eighth century to the tenth century. There is nothing about the *Man'yōshū* that would cause it to have more, or fewer, NPs with *-mo* (and other particles like *-mo*) than do the *Tales of Ise* and the *Tosa diary*.
15. See Miller 1967, 117–120, for other aspects of *kanbun*, including the various subtraditions that arose through the ages.
16. Because all officials were male, in effect only males were required to use Chinese in writing, not females. As a result, virtually all Japanese literary masterpieces from the ninth to the twelfth centuries were authored by women because they were free to use their native tongue in writing while the men were forced to use a foreign language that was rarely completely mastered (Morris 1969).
17. This information on the *Tale of the Heike,* including the historical description of the time period, is gleaned from the translators' preface to Kitagawa and Tsuchida 1975.
18. This information on the *Amakusa Heike* is from Kiyose 1986 and Suzuki 1973.
19. For the *Heike* extracts, I give the book number and its Japanese title, followed by the volume number (either 1 or 2) and page number in Ichiko

1973–1975. For the *Amakusa Heike,* I simply give the page number in Kamei and Sakata 1966.

20. *-te* is the conjunctive form of the suffix *-tsu,* which appears to signify "that the action or state described by the verb is definite and complete" (Sansom 1928, 174). One difference between having the conjunctive suffix *-te* and not having it is that its presence implies a stronger "bond" between the conjoined clauses than that which exists without it (Kuno 1973).

21. Suzuki claims that the following four pairs fall into the same category as (71) in that the *-o* in the *Heike* does not occur in the *Amakusa Heike* because of the latter's spoken style. Unfortunately, she fails to show that the absence of *-o* in the phrase in these four pairs is an option in the *Heike*. Her argument to exclude these as counterexamples is therefore considerably weaker than for (71).

(i) *H:* Yumiya-**o** toru narai, kataki-no te ni kakatte inoti-o
bow and arrow have enemy hand fall into life
usinau koto, mattaku hazi nite hazi narazu.
loose quite disgraceful disgraceful not
(Book 10, *Senju no mae*; vol. 2, 303–304)

AH: Yumiya __ toru mi no te ni torawarete horobosaruru koto, mukasi kara mina aru koto de. (252)

'It is not a disgrace at all for a man of bow and sword to fall into the hands of his enemy and be put to death.'

(ii) *H:* Kooya nite ongusiorosi, soreyori Kumano e mairaseowasimasi,
take tonsure then Kumano to go
gose-no koto-**o** yokuyoku moosasetamai, Nati-no oki nite
afterlife prayed Nachi off the shore
onmi-o nagesasetamaite sooroo. (Book 10, *Mikka heiji*;
himself drowned vol. 2, 338)

AH: Kooya de gosyukke ari, sono noti Kumano e mairaserare, koosei-no koto __ yokuyoku inoraserarete noti, tui ni onmi-o nagesaserareta. (271)

'There he took the tonsure and then made a pilgrimage to the Kumano Shrine. After he had prayed for his afterlife, he drowned himself off the shore of Nachi.'

(iii) *H:* Ooitono, wakagimi-no ongusi-**o** kakinade, namida-o
Munemori hair caress tears
harahara to nagaite, syugo-no busi domo ni notamaikeru wa . . .
rapidly wept warriors to said
(Book 11, *Fukushoo kirare*; vol. 2, 421)

AH: Yagate osoba ni yoraseraruru o hiza ni kakinose kami __ kakinade, syugo no busi domo ni ooseraruru wa . . . (298)

'Caressing him, Munenori wept and said: . . .'

(iv) *H:* Owasikeru (tokoro), niwa-**o** hitotu hedatete mukae naru oku ni
yard one separated the other side
suetatematuri . . . (Book 11, *Ooito no kirare*; vol. 2, 401)
entered

AH: Ooitono no fusi oba Yoritomo no gozatta tokoro kara niwa __ hitotu hedatete, tai no ya ni okitatematuri: . . . (302)

'He was given a seat in a room separated by a courtyard from the room in which Yoritomo was seated.'

22. See Kageyama 1977, 1982 and Miyagawa 1987a for discussions of this construction in modern Japanese.
23. One of these three *Heike* examples has already been cited earlier in the paragraph. The other two, according to Suzuki (1973), are as follows.

(i) *H:* Hyooenosuke, uma yori ori, kabuto-o nugi,
Yoritomo horse from get off helmet take off
tyoozu ugai-**o** site, oozyoo-no hoo-o fusiogami . . .
mouth wash do capital bowed
(Book 5, *Gosetsu no sata*; vol. 1, 406)

AH: Yoritomo uma kara tonde orite kabuto-o nugi, tyoozu ugai __ site, miyako-no hoo-o fusiogoode . . . (128)

'Yoritomo alighted from his horse, took off his helmet, washed his hands, and rinsed his mouth. Kneeling and facing the capital, he bowed his head down to the ground . . .'

(ii) *H:* Tada kore yori yamazutai ni miyako e nobotte, koisiki
only now from mountains to capital to cross loving
mono domo o ima itido mi mo si, miete no noti, zigai-**o** sen
wife and children once more see seeing after suicide do
ni wa sikazi. (Book 10, *Kubiwatasi*; vol. 2, 278)
all I can do

AH: Saraba korekara miyako e nobotte saisi o mite noti, moonen o hanarete zigai __ siyoo ni wa sikumazii. (244)

'. . . All I can do is dare to cross over the mountains to the capital and see my wife and children but once more. Then let me put an end to my life.'

24. The following example in Suzuki 1973 is the source of all three instances of *-o* appearing on a numeral quantifier in the *Heike* but not in the *Amakusa Heike* counterparts, including the one just cited.

(i) *H:* Heike mata hakari koto tomo sirazu,
Heike again ruse matter not knowing
zyuugo-ki-**o** idaite, zyuugo-no kabura-o ikaesu. Genzi
fifteen horsemen send fifteen arrows shoot Genji
sanzyun-ki-**o** idaite isasureba, Heike 30-ki-o idaite
thirty horsemen send and shoot arrows Heike 30 horsemen send
30-no kabura-o ikaesu. Gozyun-ki-**o** idaseba gozyuu-ki-o
30 arrows shoo fifty horsemen send fifty horsemen
idasiawase . . . (Book 7, *Kurikaraotoshi*; vol. 2, 56)
sent in return

AH: Heike mo 15-ki __ idaite 15-no kabura-o imaziwaseba,
Genzi mata 30-ki __ daite 30-no kabura-o isasetareba,
30-no kabura-o ikaeyasu. 50-ki daseba 50-ki a dasiawase . . .
(139)

'In reply, the Heike, not knowing the real intentions of the Genji, sent fifteen of their strongest bowmen to shoot arrows at the Genji. When the Genji sent thirty horsemen, the Heike sent the same number. When fifty rode from the Genji, fifty of the Heike appeared to meet them . . .'

25. The other four examples Suzuki gives are as follows:

(i) *H:* Kaziwara sa mo aruran to ya omoiken, sou-no abumi-**o** (fumi)
Kagesue heed the warning both stirrups kicked
sukasi, tazuna-o uma-no yugami ni sute, harubi-o
reins horse mane throw girth
toite zo simetari keru. (Book 9, *Ujigawa no senjin*; vol. 2, 184)
loosen tighten

AH: Kaziwara makoto to omootaka, . . . soo no abumi __ fumisukaite, tazuna-o uma-no koogami ni sutete, harubi-o toite simuru aida ni. (197)

'Heeding his warning, Kagesue dropped his reins, kicked his feet from the stirrups, leaned forward in the saddle, loosened the girth and tightened it afresh.'

(ii) *H:* Hatakeyama uma-no hitai-o nobukani isasete, yowareba,
horse face deeply hit weakened
kawanaka-yori yunzue-**o** tuite oritattari.
river-from pole vault dismounted

(Book 9, *Ujigawa no senjin*; vol. 2, 185)

AH: Hatakeyama uma-no hitai-o nobukani isasete, uma oba kawa no naka-yori nagaite yunzue __ tuite oritatu ni. (198)

'His horse, however, was hit in the forehead (by an arrow that had been loosened by Yamada no Jiroo from the far bank). The horse weakened, and so Shigetada dismounted, using his bow as a pole to vault from the saddle.'

(iii) *H:* Kuraoki uma-o oiotosu. Aruiwa asi-**o** utiotte,
saddled horses chase down some leg break
koronde otu. Aruiwa sooinaku otite yuku mo ari.
fall down some safely climb down

(Book 9, *Sakaotosi*; vol. 2, 235)

AH: Yositune kuraoki uma-o ni-hiki oiotosaretareba, ip-piki wa asi __ utiotte korobioti, ip-piki wa sooinoo Heike no siro no usiro ni otituki. (227)

'He then drove some of his saddle horses down the cliff. Some lost their foothold halfway, breaking their legs; but others reached the bottom, scrambling down safely.'

(iv) *H:* Yoiti kabura-**o** totte tugai, yoppiite hyoodo hanatu.
arrow take place on bow drew with all his might fly

(Book 11, *Nasu no yoichi*; vol. 2, 372)

AH: Kohyoo nare domo, zyuusan zoku no kabura __ totte tugai, sibasitamotte hanasuni. (282)

'Taking the turnip-headed arrow, he drew his bow with all his might and let fly.'

26. The other example given by Suzuki is the following:

(i) *H:* Kore-**o** kiki tamae tonobara, kimi ni onkokorozasi
this hear everyone lord to loyalty
omoimairasetamawan hitobito wa, kore yori izuti e mo otii.
show people now from wherever go

(Book 9, *Higuti no kirare*; vol. 2, 200)

AH: Kore __ okiki are onoono, yo wa sude ni koozya, inoti no osikaroo hitobito wa izukata e mo otisaserarei. (209)

'Hear this, everybody! Any among you who wishes to show his loyalty to our lord, Yoshinaka, may leave here and go wherever he pleases.'

27. Chomsky distinguishes between "structural" case and "inherent" case, the former being realized at S-structure and the latter at D-structure.
28. See Tsutsui 1984 and Masunaga 1987 for a detailed treatment of case drop in Japanese.

NOTES TO CHAPTER 10

1. In Chapter 9, I used *-o* as the form of the accusative case marker, for uniformity with the modern language, but in this chapter I will use *-wo*, which reflects the original labial glide present in OJ and earlier forms of Japanese.
2. The text for the *Tosa diary* is Ikeda 1930. This particular example is noted in Zenno 1987.
3. For more on the conjunctive form, see the previous chapter. There I argue (Section 8.5) that the type of case licensing for objects of the conjunctive is actually determined by the matrix verb.
4. On this optionality with the conjunctive, see note 3.
5. In recent theory, accusative case assignment is done not directly by the V, but by what is called a "small *v*" that selects VP (e.g., Chomsky 1995). I will assume this, but will continue to describe case assignment in terms of verbs to be consistent with Chapter 9.
6. This example is from *Shoku Nihongi*, a work that contains "certain Imperial edicts in pure Japanese" and was completed in 797.
7. The three remaining exceptions from the *MSD* are the following.

(i) mono-no kazukazu __ kaki-taru fumi (27.3)
thing-GEN many write-PERF document
'document in which (one) wrote many things'

(ii) hito-no hazi __ mi-haberi-si yo (29.1)
person-GEN disgrace see-humble-PAST night
'the night that (someone) saw a person's disgrace'

(iii) sodeguti-no ahahi __ warou kasane-taru hito (88.1)
sleeve-GEN coloration bad lay-PERF person
'a person who layered (her) sleeves in an unpleasant manner'

References

Abe, Y. 1993. Dethematized subjects and property ascription in Japanese. In *Language, information, and computation: Proceedings of the Asian Conference, Seoul, 1992*, ed. C. Lee, B. Kang: 132–144. Seoul: Thaehaksa.

Aikawa, T. 1995. Remarks and replies: "Reflexivity" by Reinhart and Reuland (1993). Ms., MIT, Cambridge, Mass.

Aldridge, E. 2001. *Hentai kanbun* perspective on short scrambling. *Journal of East Asian Linguistics* 10: 169–200.

Alexiadou, A., Anagnostopoulou, E. 1998. Parametrizing AGR: Word order, V-movement, and EPP-checking. *Natural Language and Linguistic Theory* 16: 491–539.

Alexiadou, A., Anagnostopoulou, E. 2001. The subject-in-situ generalization and the role of Case in driving computations. *Linguistic Inquiry* 32: 193–231.

Alexiadou, A., Anagnostopoulou, E. 2007. The subject-in-situ generalization revisited. In *Interfaces + recursion = language? Chomsky's minimalism and the view from syntax-semantics*, ed. H.-M. Gärtner, U. Sauerland: 31–60. Berlin: Mouton de Gruyter.

Anagnostopoulou, E. 1999. On clitics, feature movement, and double object alternations. In *NELS 29: Proceedings of the twenty-ninth annual meeting of the North East Linguistic Society,* vol. 2, *Papers from the poster session*, ed. P. N. Tamanji, M. Hirotani, N. Hall: 40–55. Amherst, Mass.: GLSA Publications.

Anagnostopoulou, E. 2003. *The syntax of ditransitives.* Berlin: Mouton de Gruyter.

Aoun, J., Li, Y.-H. A. 1989. Constituency and scope. *Linguistic Inquiry* 20: 141–172.

Aronoff, M. 1976. *Word formation in generative grammar.* Cambridge, Mass.: MIT Press.

Asarina, A., Hartman, J. 2011. Genitive subject licensing in Uyghur subordinate clauses. In *Proceedings of the seventh Workshop on Altaic Formal Linguistics (WAFL 7)*, ed. A. Simpson: 17–31. Cambridge, Mass.: MITWPL. (MIT Working Papers in Linguistics 62.)

Babby, L. H. 1980. *Existential sentences and negation in Russian.* Ann Arbor, Mich.: Karoma.

Babyonyshev, M. A. 1996. Structural connections in syntax and processing: Studies in Russian and Japanese. Doctoral thesis, MIT, Cambridge, Mass.

Bach, E. 1989. *Informal lectures on formal semantics.* Albany, N.Y.: SUNY Press.

Bailyn, J. F. 1997. Genitive of negation is obligatory. In *Annual workshop on formal approaches to Slavic linguistics: The Cornell meeting, 1995*, ed. W. Browne, E. Dornsich, N. Kondrashova, D. Zec: 84–114. Ann Arbor, Mich.: Michigan Slavic Publications.

Baker, M. 1988. *Incorporation: A theory of grammatical function changing.* Chicago: University of Chicago Press.

Baker, M. 1996. *The polysynthesis parameter.* Oxford: Oxford University Press.

Barss, A., Lasnik, H. 1986. A note on anaphora and double objects. *Linguistic Inquiry* 17: 347–354.

Bedell, G. 1972. On *no*. In *Studies in East Asian syntax*, ed. G. Bedell, K. Hirakouji, R. Rodman, S. A. Thompson, K. Watanabe: 1–20. Los Angeles: University of California. (UCLA Papers in Syntax 3.)

Belletti, A., Rizzi, L. 1981. The syntax of *ne*: Some theoretical implications. *The Linguistic Review* 1: 117–154.

Bianchi, V. 1999. *Consequences of antisymmetry: Headed relative clauses.* Berlin: Mouton de Gruyter.

Bjeljac-Babic, R. 2000. Six thousand languages: An embattled heritage. *UNESCO Courier*, April: 18–19.

Bobaljik, J. 2003. Floating quantifiers: Handle with care. In *The second Glot International State-of-the-Article book*, ed. L. Cheng, R. Sybesma: 107–148. Berlin: Mouton de Gruyter.

Boeckx, C. 2003. *Islands and chains: Resumption as stranding.* Amsterdam: John Benjamins.

Borer, H. 2005. *The normal course of events.* Oxford, New York: Oxford University Press.

Borsley, R., Kornfilt, J. 2000. Mixed extended projection. In *The nature and function of syntactic categories*, ed. R. Borsley: 101–131. San Diego: Academic. (Syntax and Semantics 32.)

Bošković, Ž. 2004. Be careful where you float your quantifiers. *Natural Language and Linguistic Theory* 22: 681–742.

Brame, M. 1975. On the abstractness of syntactic structures: The VP controversy. *Linguistic Analysis* 1: 191–203.

Bresnan, J. 1973. The syntax of the comparative clause construction in English. *Linguistic Inquiry* 4: 275–343.

Bresnan, J. 1978. Class notes, October 12, MIT, Cambridge, Mass.

Bresnan, J. 1982a. Control and complementation. *Linguistic Inquiry* 13: 343–434.

Bresnan, J. 1982b. *The mental representation of grammatical relations.* Cambridge, Mass.: MIT Press.

Bresnan, J., Nikitina, T. 2003. Categoricity and gradience in the dative alternation. Ms., Stanford University, Stanford, Calif. Presented at MIT on May 4, 2003.

Briggs, E. 1961. *Mitla Zapotec grammar.* Mexico City: Instituto Lingüístico de Verano and Centro de Investigaciones Antropológicas de México.

Bruening, B. 2001. QR obeys Superiority: Frozen scope and ACD. *Linguistic Inquiry* 4: 275–343.

Burzio, L. 1981. Intransitive verbs and Italian auxiliaries. Doctoral thesis, MIT, Cambridge, Mass.

Burzio, L. 1986. *Italian syntax: A government-binding approach.* Dordrecht, the Netherlands: Reidel.

Carstens, V. 2003. Rethinking complementizer agreement: Agree with a case-checked goal. *Linguistic Inquiry* 34: 393–412.

Chomsky, N. 1965. *Aspects of the theory of syntax.* Cambridge, Mass.: MIT Press.

Chomsky, N. 1970. Remarks on nominalization. In *Readings in English transformational grammar*, ed. R. A. Jacobs, P. S. Rosenbaum: 184–221. Waltham, Mass.: Ginn.

Chomsky, N. 1975. *The logical structure of linguistic theory.* New York: Plenum.

Chomsky, N. 1977. On WH-movement. In *Formal syntax*, ed. P. Culicover, T. Wasow, A. Akmajian: 71–132. New York: Academic.

Chomsky, N. 1981. *Lectures on government and binding: The Pisa lectures*. Dordrecht, the Netherlands: Foris.
Chomsky, N. 1982. *Some concepts and consequences of the theory of government and binding*. Cambridge, Mass.: MIT Press.
Chomsky, N. 1986a. *Knowledge of language: Its nature, origin, and use*. Praeger: New York.
Chomsky, N. 1986b. *Barriers*. Cambridge, Mass.: MIT Press.
Chomsky, N. 1993. A minimalist program for linguistic theory. In *The view from Building 20*, ed. K. Hale, S. J. Keyser: 1–52. Cambridge, Mass.: MIT Press.
Chomsky, N. 1995. *The Minimalist Program*. Cambridge, Mass.: MIT Press.
Chomsky, N. 2000. Minimalist inquiries. In *Step by step: Essays on minimalism in honor of Howard Lasnik*, ed. R. Martin, D. Michaels, J. Uriagereka: 89–155. Cambridge, Mass.: MIT Press.
Chomsky, N. 2001. Derivation by phase. In *Ken Hale: A Life in language*, ed. M. Kenstowicz: 1–52. Cambridge, Mass.: MIT Press.
Chomsky, N. 2005. Three factors in language design. *Linguistic Inquiry* 36: 1–23.
Chomsky, N. 2007. Approaching UG from below. In *Interfaces + recursion = language? Chomsky's minimalism and the view from syntax-semantics*, ed. H.-M. Gärtner, U. Sauerland: 1–29. Berlin: Mouton de Gruyter.
Chomsky, N. 2008. On phases. In *Foundational issues in linguistic theory*, ed. R. Freidin, C. Otero, M.-L. Zubizarreta: 133–166. Cambridge, Mass.: MIT Press.
Chomsky, N., Lasnik, H. 1977. Filters and control. *Linguistic Inquiry* 8: 425–504.
Chujo, K. 1983. Nihongo tanbun-no rikai katei—Bunrikai sutoratejii no sougo kankei [The interrelationships among strategies for sentence comprehension]. *Japanese Journal of Psychology* 54: 250–256.
Cinque, G. 1999. *Adverbs and functional heads*. Oxford: Oxford University Press.
Cirillo, R. 2009. *The syntax of floating quantifiers: Stranding revisited*. Utrecht, the Netherlands: LOT.
Clark, E. V., Clark, H. H. 1979. When nouns surface as verbs. *Language* 55: 767–811.
Collins, C. 2003. The internal structure of vP in Ju|'hoansi and ǂHoan. *Studia Linguistica* 57: 1–25.
Collins, C., Branigan, P. 1997. Quotative inversion. *Natural Language and Linguistic Theory* 15: 1–41.
Cranston, E., trans. 1969. *Izumi Shikibu diary*. Cambridge, Mass.: Harvard University Press.
Cuervo, M. C. 2003a. Datives at large. Doctoral thesis, MIT, Cambridge, Mass.
Cuervo, M. C. 2003b. Structural asymmetries but same word order: The dative alternation in Spanish. In *Symmetry in grammar*, vol. 1, *Syntax and semantics*, ed. A. M. Di Sciullo: 117–144. Amsterdam: John Benjamins. (Linguistik Aktuell/Linguistics Today 57.)
Culicover, P., Wilkins, W. 1984. *Locality in linguistic theory*. New York: Academic.
Culicover, P., Wilkins, W. 1986. Control, PRO, and the Projection Principle. *Language* 62: 120–153.
Déprez, V. 1990. Two ways of moving the verb in French. In *Papers on Wh-movement*, ed. L. Cheng, H. Demirdache: 47–85. Cambridge, Mass.: MITWPL. (MIT Working Papers in Linguistics 13.)
Diesing, M. 1992. *Indefinites*. Cambridge, Mass.: MIT Press. (Linguistic Inquiry Monograph 20.)
Doetjes, J. 1997. *Quantifiers and selection*. The Hague: Holland Academic Graphics.

Downing, P. 1984. Japanese numeral classifiers: A syntactic, semantic, and functional profile. Doctoral thesis, University of California, Berkeley.
Dowty, D. 1989. On the semantic content of the notion "thematic role." In *Properties, types, and meaning*, vol. 2, *Semantic issues*, ed. G. Chierchia, B. Partee, R. Turner: 69–129. Dordrecht, the Netherlands: Kluwer.
Dowty, D. 1991. Thematic proto-roles and argument selection. *Language* 67: 547–619.
Embick, D. 2007. Blocking effects and analytic/synthetic alternations. *Natural Language and Linguistic Theory* 25: 1–37.
Embick, D., Marantz, A. 2008. Architecture and blocking. *Linguistic Inquiry* 39: 1–53.
Embick, D., Noyer, R. 2001. Movement operations after syntax. *Linguistic Inquiry* 32: 555–595.
Farmer, A. K. 1980. On the interaction of morphology and syntax. Doctoral thesis, MIT, Cambridge, Mass.
Fitzpatrick, J. 2006. Two types of floating quantifiers and their A/A-bar properties. In *NELS 36: Proceedings of the thirty-sixth annual meeting of the North East Linguistic Society*, ed. C. Davis, A. R. Deal, Y. Zabbal: 253–266. Amherst, Mass.: GLSA Publications.
Folli, R., Harley, H. 2005. Flavors of *v*: Consuming results in Italian and English. In *Aspectual inquiries*, ed. P. Kempchinsky, R. Slabakova: 95–120. Dordrecht, the Netherlands: Springer.
Fujita, N. 1988. Genitive subject in Japanese and Universal Grammar. Master's thesis, Ohio State University, Columbus.
Fujita, N. 1994. On the nature of modification: A study of floating quantifiers and related constructions. Doctoral thesis, University of Rochester, Rochester, N.Y.
Fukui, N. 1993. Parameters and optionality. *Linguistic Inquiry* 24: 399–420.
Fukushima, K. 1991. Generalized floating quantifiers. Doctoral thesis, University of Arizona, Tucson.
Greenberg, J. 1972. Numeral classifiers and substantival number: Problems in the genesis of a linguistic type. *Working Papers on Language Universals* 9: 1–39.
Grimshaw, J. 1990. *Argument structure*. Cambridge, Mass.: MIT Press.
Grimshaw, J. 1991. Extended projection. Ms., Brandeis University, Waltham, Mass.
Grimshaw, J. 2000. Locality and extended projection. In *Lexical specification and insertion*, ed. P. Coopmans, M. Everaert, J. Grimshaw: 115–133. Amsterdam, Philadelphia: John Benjamins.
Gropen, J., Pinker, S., Hollander, M., Goldberg, R., Wilson, R. 1989. The learnability and acquisition of the dative alternation in English. *Language* 65: 203–257.
Gruber, J. 1965. Studies in lexical relations. Doctoral thesis, MIT, Cambridge, Mass.
Gruber, J. 1976. *Lexical structures in syntax and semantics*. New York: North-Holland.
Gunji, T., Hasida, K. 1998. Measurement and quantification. In *Topics in constraint-based grammar of Japanese*, ed. T. Gunji, K. Hasida: 39–79. Dordrecht, the Netherlands: Kluwer.
Hagiwara, H., Caplan, D. 1990. Syntactic comprehension in Japanese aphasics: Effects of category and thematic role order. *Brain and Language* 38: 159–170.
Haig, J. H. 1980. Some observations on quantifier floating in Japanese. *Linguistics* 18: 1065–1083.
Hale, K. 2002. On the Dagur object relative: Some comparative notes. *Journal of East Asian Linguistics* 11: 109–122.
Hale, K., Keyser, S. J. 1993. On argument structure and the lexical expression of syntactic relations. In *The view from Building 20: Essays in honor of Sylvain Bromberger*, ed. K. Hale, S. J. Keyser: 53–108. Cambridge, Mass.: MIT Press.

Halle, M., Marantz, A. 1993. Distributed morphology and the pieces of inflection. In *The view from Building 20: Essays in honor of Sylvain Bromberger*, ed. K. Hale, S. J. Keyser: 111–176. Cambridge, Mass.: MIT Press.
Harada, S.-I. 1971. *Ga–no* conversion and idiolectal variations in Japanese. *Gengo Kenkyu* 60: 25–38.
Harada, S.-I. 1973. Counter Equi-NP Deletion. *Annual Bulletin* (Research Institute of Logopedics and Phoniatrics, University of Tokyo) 7: 113–147.
Harada, S.-I. 1976a. *Ga–no* conversion revisited: A reply to Shibatani. *Gengo Kenkyu* 70: 23–38.
Harada, S.-I. 1976b. Honorifics. In *Japanese generative grammar*, ed. M. Shibatani: 499–562. New York: Academic. (Syntax and Semantics 5.)
Harada, S.-I. 1976c. Quantifier float as a relational rule. *Metropolitan Linguistics* (Linguistic Circle, Tokyo Metropolitan University) 1: 44–49.
Harada, S.-I. 1977. Nihongo-ni henkei-wa hituyō da [Transformations are needed in Japanese]. *Gengo* 6: 11–12.
Harley, H. 1995a. *Sase* bizarre: The structure of Japanese causatives. In *Proceedings of the 1995 annual conference of the Canadian Linguistic Association*, ed. P. Koskinen: 225–235. Toronto: Linguistics Graduate Course Union, University of Toronto.
Harley, H. 1995b. Subjects, events, and licensing. Doctoral thesis, MIT, Cambridge, Mass.
Harley, H. 2008. On the causative construction. In *The Oxford handbook of Japanese linguistics*, ed. S. Miyagawa, M. Saito: 20–53. New York: Oxford University Press.
Hasegawa, N. 1981. A lexical interpretive theory with emphasis on the role of subject. Doctoral thesis, University of Washington, Seattle.
Hashimoto, S. 1969. *Joshi jodōshi-no kenkyū* [Particles and auxiliary verbs]. Tokyo: Iwanami Shoten.
Higginbotham, J. 1983. Logical form, binding, and nominals. *Linguistic Inquiry* 16: 547–593.
Hiraiwa, K. 2001. On nominative–genitive conversion. In *A few from Building E39: Papers in syntax, semantics, and their interface*, ed. E. Guerzoni, O. Matushansky: 66–125. Cambridge, Mass.: MITWPL. (MIT Working Papers in Linguistics 39.)
Hiraiwa, K. 2002. Nominative–genitive conversion revisited. In *Japanese/Korean linguistics*, vol. 10, ed. N. M. Akatsuka, S. Strauss: 546–559. Stanford, Calif.: CSLI Publications.
Hiraiwa, K. 2005. Dimensions of symmetry in syntax: Agreement and clausal architecture. Doctoral thesis, MIT, Cambridge, Mass.
Hirohama, F. 1966. On *o*. *Kokugogaku-to Kokubungaku*.
Hoji, H. 1985. Logical form constraints and configurational structures in Japanese. Doctoral thesis, University of Washington, Seattle.
Hoji, H. 1995. Demonstrative binding and Principle B. In *NELS 25: Proceedings of the twenty-fifth annual meeting of the North East Linguistic Society*, ed. J. N. Beekman: 255–271. Amherst, Mass.: GLSA Publications.
Horie, K., Kang, B. 2000. Action/state continuum and nominative–genitive conversion in Japanese and Korean. In *Modern approaches to transitivity*, ed. R. Kikusawa, K. Sasaki: 93–114. Tokyo: Kuroshio.
Hornstein, N. 1995. *Logical form: From GB to minimalism*. Oxford: Blackwell.
Hoshi, H. 2006. Functional categories and configurationality. *Memoirs of the Faculty of Education and Human Studies* (Natural Science, Akita University) 61: 1–38.
Huang, C.-T. J. 1982. Logical relations in Chinese and the theory of grammar. Doctoral thesis, MIT, Cambridge, Mass.
Huang, C.-T. J. 1984. On the distribution and reference of empty pronouns. *Linguistic Inquiry* 15: 531–574.

Iatridou, S., Anagnostopoulou, E., Izvorski, R. 2001. Observations about the form and meaning of the perfect. In *Ken Hale: A life in language*, ed. M. Kenstowicz: 189–238. Cambridge, Mass.: MIT Press.

Ichiko, T., ed. 1973–1975. *Heike monogatari* [The tale of the Heike]. 2 vols. Tokyo: Shōgakukan. (Nihon Koten Bungaku Zenshu 29–30.)

Ikeda, K., ed. 1930. *Tosa nikki* [The Tosa diary]. Tokyo: Iwanami Shoten.

Ikeda, K., Akiyama, K., eds. 1984. *Murasaki Shikibu nikki* [The Murasaki Shikibu diary]. Tokyo: Iwanami Shoten. (Iwanami Bunko.)

Inoue, K. 1976a. *Henkei-bunpō-to nihongo* [Transformational grammar and Japanese]. Tokyo: Taishūkan Shoten.

Inoue, K. 1976b. Reflexivization: An interpretive approach. In *Japanese generative grammar*, ed. M. Shibatani: 117–200. New York: Academic. (Syntax and Semantics 5.)

Inoue, K. 1978a. *Nihongo-no bunpō kisoku* [Grammar rules in Japanese]. Tokyo: Taishūkan Shoten.

Inoue, K. 1978b. "Tough sentences" in Japanese. In *Problems in Japanese syntax and semantics*, ed. J. Hinds, I. Howard: 122–154. Tokyo: Kaitakusha.

Inoue, K., ed. 1983. *Nihongo-no kihon kōzō* [The structure of Japanese]. Tokyo: Sanseidō.

Ishii, Y. 1998. Floating quantifiers in Japanese: NP quantifiers vs. VP quantifiers, or both? In *Researching and verifying an advanced theory of human language: Grant-in-aid for COE research report 2*, ed. K. Inoue: 149–171. Kanda, Japan: Kanda University of International Studies.

Ito, A. 2007. Argument structure of Japanese ditransitives. *Nanzan Linguistics* (Nanzan University, Nagoya, Japan) 3: 127–150.

Ito, K. 1990. *Kodomo-no kotoba: Shūtoku-to sōzō* [Children's language: Acquisition and creation]. Tokyo: Keisō Shobō.

Ito, T., Sugioka, Y. 2002. *Go-no shikumi-to gokeisei* [The structure of words and word formation]. Tokyo: Kenkyūsha.

Jackendoff, R. S. 1972. *Semantics in generative grammar*. Cambridge, Mass.: MIT Press.

Jacobsen, W. 1992. *The transitive structure of events in Japanese*. Tokyo: Kuroshio.

Jaeggli, O. 1986. Passive. *Linguistic Inquiry* 17: 587–622.

Johnson, K. 2000. How far will quantifiers go? In *Step by step: Essays on minimalism in honor of Howard Lasnik*, ed. R. Martin, D. Michaels, J. Uriagereka: 187–210. Cambridge, Mass.: MIT Press.

Johnson, K., Tomioka, S. 1997. Lowering and mid-size clauses. In *Reconstruction: Proceedings of the 1997 Tübingen workshop*, ed. G. Katz, S.-S. Kim, H. Winhart: 185–205. Tübingen, Germany: Universität Tübingen. (Arbeitspapiere des Sonderforschungsbereichs 340, Bericht Nr. 127.)

Joseph, B. 1980. Linguistic universals and syntactic change. *Language* 56: 345–370.

Kageyama, T. 1977. Lexical structure: A comparative study of Japanese and English. Doctoral thesis, University of Southern California, Los Angeles.

Kageyama, T. 1982. Word formation in Japanese. *Lingua* 57: 215–258.

Kageyama, T. 1993. *Bunpō-to gokeisei* [Grammar and word formation]. Tokyo: Hitsuji Shobō.

Kamei, T., Sakata, Y., eds. 1966. *Heike monogatari: Habiyan-shō, Kirishitan-ban* [The tale of the Heike]. Tokyo: Yoshikawa Kōbunkan.

Kamide, Y., Altmann, G., Haywood, S. 2003. The time-course of prediction in incremental processing: Evidence from anticipatory eye movements. *Journal of Memory and Language* 49: 133–156.

Kamio, A. 1977. Sūryōshi-no syntakkusu [The syntax of numeral quantifiers]. *Gengo* 8: 83–91.
Kato, S. 2007. Scrambling and the EPP in Japanese: From the viewpoint of the Kumamoto dialect of Japanese. In *FAJL 4: Proceedings of the fourth conference on formal approaches to Japanese linguistics*, ed. Y. Miyamoto, M. Ochi: 113–124. Cambridge, Mass.: MITWPL. (MIT Working Papers in Linguistics 55.)
Kayne, R. S. 1976. French relative *que*. In *Current studies in Romance linguistics*, ed. M. Luján, F. Hensey: 255–299. Washington, D.C.: Georgetown University Press.
Kayne, R. S. 1981. On certain differences between French and English. *Linguistic Inquiry* 12: 349–372.
Kayne, R. S. 1984. *Connectedness and binary branching*. Dordrecht, the Netherlands: Foris.
Kayne, R. S., Pollock, J.-Y. 1978. Stylistic inversion, successive cyclicity, and Move NP in French. *Linguistic Inquiry* 9: 595–621.
Kayne, R. S., Pollock, J.-Y. 2001. New thoughts on stylistic inversion. In *Subject inversion and the theory of universal grammar*, ed. A. Hulk, J.-Y. Pollock: 107–162. New York: Oxford University Press.
Kim, E. 2009. Gendaigo-no rentai-shushokusetsu-ni okeru joshi 'no' [The particle *-no* in the modificational construction in modern Japanese]. *Nihongo Kagaku* (National Institute for Japanese Language and Linguistics, Tokyo) 25: 23–42.
Kinsui, S. 1993. Kotengo-no 'wo' ni tuite [On Classical Japanese *-wo*]. In *Nihongo-no kaku-o megutte* [Case in Japanese], ed. Y. Nitta: 191–224. Tokyo: Kuroshio.
Kinsui, S. 1994. Rentai shushoku-no 'ta' ni tuite [On *-ta* in nominal modification]. In *Nihongo-no meishi shūshoku hyōgen* [Nominal modification in Japanese], ed. Y. Takubo: 29–65. Tokyo: Kuroshio.
Kiparsky, P. 1973. "Elsewhere" in phonology. In *A festschrift for Morris Halle*, ed. P. Kiparsky, S. Anderson: 93–106. New York: Holt, Rinehart and Winston.
Kiparsky, P. 1982. Lexical morphology and phonology. In *Linguistics in the morning calm: Selected papers from SICOL-1981*, ed. Linguistic Society of Korea: 3–91. Seoul: Hanshin.
Kiparsky, P. 2005. Blocking and periphrasis in inflectional paradigms. In *Yearbook of morphology 2004*, ed. G. Booij, J. van Marle: 113–135. Dordrecht, the Netherlands: Springer.
Kishimoto, H. 2001a. Binding of indeterminate pronouns and clause structure in Japanese. *Linguistic Inquiry* 32: 597–633.
Kishimoto, H. 2001b. The role of lexical meanings in argument encoding: Double object verbs in Japanese. *Gengo Kenkyu* 120: 35–65.
Kishimoto, H. 2006. Japanese syntactic nominalization and VP-internal syntax. *Lingua* 116: 771–810.
Kishimoto, H. 2008. Ditransitive idioms and argument structure. *Journal of East Asian Linguistics* 17: 141–179.
Kitagawa, C. 1980. Review of *Problems in Japanese syntax and semantics* (ed. J. Hinds and I. Howard). *Language* 56: 435–440.
Kitagawa, H., Tsuchida, B. T., trans. 1975. *The tale of the Heike*. Tokyo: University of Tokyo Press.
Kitagawa, Y. 1986. Subjects in Japanese and English. Doctoral thesis, University of Massachusetts, Amherst.
Kitagawa, Y. 1994. Shells, yolks, and scrambled e.g.s. In *NELS 24: Proceedings of the twenty-fourth annual meeting of the North East Linguistic Society*, ed. M. Gonzàlez: 221–239. Amherst, Mass.: GLSA Publications.
Kitagawa, Y., Kuroda, S.-Y. 1992. Passive in Japanese. Ms., University of Rochester, Rochester, Md., and University of California, San Diego.

Kitahara, H. 2002. Scrambling, case, and interpretability. In *Derivation and explanation in the Minimalist Program*, ed. S. D. Epstein, T. D. Seely: 167–183. Oxford: Blackwell.

Kitazume, S. 1996. Middles in English. *Word* 47: 161–183.

Kiyose, R. 1986. Amakusa-bon [The Amakusa text]. *Kokubungaku* 31: 112–113.

Kobayashi, Y. 1970. *Nihon bunpō-shi* [History of Japanese grammar]. Tokyo: Tōkō Shoin.

Koizumi, M. 1994. Nominative objects: The role of TP in Japanese. In *FAJL 1: Proceedings of the first conference on formal approaches to Japanese linguistics*, ed. M. Koizumi, H. Ura: 211–230. Cambridge, Mass.: MITWPL. (MIT Working Papers in Linguistics 24.)

Koizumi, M. 1995. Phrase structure in minimalist syntax. Doctoral thesis, MIT, Cambridge, Mass.

Koizumi, M. 2005. Syntactic structure of ditransitive constructions in Japanese: Behavioral and imaging studies. *The proceedings of the sixth Tokyo Conference on Psycholinguistics*, ed. Y. Otsu: 1–25. Tokyo: Hitsuji Shobō.

Koizumi, M. 2008. Nominative object. In *The Oxford handbook of Japanese linguistics*, ed. S. Miyagawa, M. Saito: 141–164. Oxford: Oxford University Press.

Koizumi, M., Tamaoka, K. 2004. Cognitive processing of Japanese sentences with ditransitive verbs. *Gengo Kenkyu* 125: 173–190.

Koizumi, M., Tamaoka, K. 2010. Psycholinguistic evidence for the VP-internal subject position in Japanese. *Linguistic Inquiry* 41: 663–680.

Konoshima, T. 1962. Chūkogo-ni okeru yōgen rentaikei-no yōhō [The use of the participial adjective in medieval Japanese]. *Kokugogaku* 48: 102–107.

Koreshima, M. 1966. *Kokugo joshi-no kenkyū* [A study of particles in Japanese]. Tokyo: Ōfūsha.

Kornfilt, J. 1984. Case marking, agreement, and empty categories in Turkish. Doctoral thesis, Harvard University, Cambridge, Mass.

Kornfilt, J. 2003. Subject case in Turkish nominalized clauses. *In Syntactic structures and morphological information*, ed. U. Junghanns, L. Szucsich: 129–215. Berlin, New York: Mouton de Gruyter.

Kornfilt, J. 2008. Subject case and *Agr* in two types of Turkic RCs. In *Proceedings of the fourth Workshop on Altaic Formal Linguistics (WAFL 4)*, ed. S. Ulutas, C. Boeckx: 145–168. Cambridge, Mass.: MITWPL. (MIT Working Papers in Linguistics 56.)

Koster, J., May, R. 1982. On the constituency of infinitives. *Language* 58: 116–143.

Kratzer, A. 1994. The event argument and the semantics of voice. Ms., University of Massachusetts, Amherst.

Kratzer, A. 1996. Severing the external argument from its verb. In *Phrase structure and the lexicon*, ed. J. Rooryck, L. Zaring: 109–137. Dordrecht, the Netherlands: Kluwer.

Krause, C. 2001. On reduced relatives with genitive subjects. Doctoral thesis, MIT, Cambridge, Mass.

Krifka, M. 1989. Nominal reference, temporal constitution, and quantification in event semantics. In *Semantics and contextual expressions*, ed. R. Bartsch, J. van Benthem, P. van Emde Boas: 75–115. Dordrecht, the Netherlands: Foris.

Krifka, M. 1992. Thematic relations as links between nominal reference and temporal constitution. In *Lexical matters*, ed. I. A. Sag, A. Szabolcsi: 29–53. Stanford, Calif.: Center for the Study of Language and Information.

Kubo, M. 1992. Japanese syntactic structures and their constructional meanings. Doctoral thesis, MIT, Cambridge, Mass.

Kuno, S. 1973. *The structure of the Japanese language*. Cambridge, Mass.: MIT Press.

Kuno, S. 1976. Subject raising. In *Japanese generative grammar*, ed. M. Shibatani: 17–49. New York: Academic. (Syntax and Semantics 5.)

Kuno, S. 1978. Theoretical perspectives on Japanese linguistics. In *Problems in Japanese syntax and semantics*, ed. J. Hinds, I. Howard: 213–285. Tokyo: Kaitakusha.

Kuno, S., Takami, K.-I. 2003. Remarks on unaccusativity and unergativity in Japanese and Korean. In *Japanese/Korean linguistics*, vol. 12, ed. W. McClure: 280–294. Stanford, Calif.: CSLI Publications.

Kuroda, S.-Y. 1965. Generative grammatical studies in the Japanese language. Doctoral thesis, MIT, Cambridge, Mass.

Kuroda, S.-Y. 1970. Remarks on the notion of subject with reference to words like *also*, *even*, or *only*, illustrating certain manners in which formal systems are employed as auxiliary devices in linguistic descriptions. Part 2. *Annual Bulletin* (Logopedics and Phoniatrics Research Institute, University of Tokyo) 4: 127–152.

Kuroda, S.-Y. 1971. Two remarks on pronominalization. *Foundations of Language* 7: 183–198.

Kuroda, S.-Y. 1980. Bun kōzō-no hikaku [The comparison of sentence structures]. In *Nichi-eigo hikaku kōza 2: Bunpō* [Lectures on Japanese–English comparative studies 2: Grammar], ed. T. Kunihiro: 23–61. Tokyo: Taishūkan Shoten.

Kuroda, S.-Y. 1981. Some recent trends in syntactic theory and the Japanese language. In *Proceedings of the Arizona conference on Japanese linguistics: The formal grammar sessions*, ed. A. K. Farmer, C. Kitagawa: 103–122. Tucson, Ariz.: University of Arizona Linguistics Circle. (Coyote Papers 2.)

Kuroda, S.-Y. 1988. Whether we agree or not: A comparative syntax of English and Japanese. *Lingvisticae Investigationes* 12: 1–47.

Kuroda, S.-Y. 1993a. Lexical and productive causatives in Japanese: An examination of the theory of paradigmatic structure. *Journal of Japanese Linguistics* 15: 1–82.

Kuroda, S.-Y. 1993b. On the scope principle and scope ambiguities in Japanese. Ms., University of California, San Diego, and Kanda University of International Studies, Makuhari, Japan.

Larson, R. 1988. On the double object construction. *Linguistic Inquiry* 19: 335–391.

Lasnik, H., Saito, M. 1991. On the subject of infinitives. In *Papers from the twenty-seventh regional meeting of the Chicago Linguistic Society*, vol. 1, *The general session*, ed. L. M. Dobrin, L. Nichols, R. M. Rodriguez: 324–343. Chicago: Chicago Linguistic Society.

Lees, R. B. 1965. Turkish nominalizations and a problem of ellipsis. *Foundations of Language* 1: 112–121.

Levin, B., Rappaport, M. 1989. An approach to unaccusative mismatches. In *Proceedings of the nineteenth annual meeting of the North Eastern Linguistics Society*, ed. J. Carter, R. M. Déchaine: 314–328. Amherst, Mass.: GLSA Publications.

Levin, B., Rappaport Hovav, M. 1995. *Unaccusativity: At the syntax-lexical semantics interface*. Cambridge, Mass.: MIT Press.

Levin, B., Rappaport Hovav, M. 2005. *Argument realization*. Cambridge: Cambridge University Press. (Research Surveys in Linguistics.)

Lieber, R. 1980. On the organization of the lexicon. Doctoral thesis, MIT, Cambridge, Mass.

Lightfoot, D. 1979. *Principles of diachronic syntax*. Cambridge: Cambridge University Press.

Link, G. 1983. The logical analysis of plurals and mass terms: A lattice-theoretical approach. In *Meaning, use, and interpretation of language*, ed. R. Bäuerle, C. Schwarze, A. von Stechow: 302–323. Berlin: de Gruyter.

Link, G. 1987. Algebraic semantics for event structures. In *Proceedings of the sixth Amsterdam colloquium*, ed. J. Groenendijk, M. Stokhof, F. Veltman: 243–262.

Amsterdam: Institute for Language, Logic, and Information, University of Amsterdam.
Lumsden, J. 1987. Syntactic features: Parametric variation in the history of English. Doctoral thesis, MIT, Cambridge, Mass.
Mabuchi, K. 1971. *Kokugo oninron* [Japanese phonology]. Tokyo: Kasama Shoten.
Mahajan, A. 1990. The A/A-bar distinction and movement theory. Doctoral thesis, MIT, Cambridge, Mass.
Maki, H., Tsubouchi, K., Hamasaki, M. 2007. Gendai nihongo-no shukaku/zokkaku kōtai-no ANOVA bunseki: Kaizai kōka-to sono gani [An ANOVA analysis of the nominative–genitive alternation in modern Japanese: An intervention effect and its implications]. In *Proceedings of the 135th meeting of the Linguistic Society of Japan*: 160–165. Kyoto: Linguistic Society of Japan.
Maki, H., Uchibori, A. 2008. *Ga/no* conversion. In *The Oxford handbook of Japanese linguistics*, ed. S. Miyagawa, M. Saito: 192–216. Oxford: Oxford University Press.
Manning, C., Sag, I., Iida, M. 1999. The lexical integrity of Japanese causatives. In *Studies in contemporary phrase structure grammar*, ed. R. D. Levine, G. M. Green: 39–79. Cambridge: Cambridge University Press.
Manzini, M. R. 1983. On control and control theory. *Linguistic Inquiry* 14: 421–446.
Marantz, A. 1984. *On the nature of grammatical relations*. Cambridge, Mass.: MIT Press.
Marantz, A. 1993. Implications of asymmetries in double object constructions. In *Theoretical aspects of Bantu grammar*, ed. S. Mchombo: 113–150. Stanford, Calif.: CSLI Publications.
Marantz, A. 1997. No escape from syntax: Don't try morphological analysis in the privacy of your own lexicon. In Proceedings of the twenty-first annual Penn Linguistics Colloquium, ed. A. Dimitriadis, L. Siegel, C. Surek-Clark, A. Williams: 201–225. Philadelphia: Penn Linguistics Club. (University of Pennsylvania Working Papers in Linguistics 4.2.)
Martin, S. 1961. *Dagur Mongolian grammar, texts, and lexicon*. Bloomington: Indiana University Press. (Uralic and Altaic Series 4.)
Martin, S. 1975. *A reference grammar of Japanese*. New Haven, Conn., London: Yale University Press.
Masunaga, K. 1987. Non-thematic positions and discourse anaphora. Doctoral thesis, Harvard University, Cambridge, Mass.
Matsumoto, Y. 2000. On the crosslinguistic parameterization of causative predicates: Implications from Japanese and other languages. In *Argument realization*, ed. M. Butt, T. Holloway King: 135–169. Stanford, Calif.: CSLI Publications.
Matsunaga, S. 1983. Historical development of case marking in Japanese. Master's thesis, Ohio State University, Columbus.
Matsuo, O. 1938. Heian shoki-ni okeru kakujoshi o [The case marker *-wo* in early Heian]. *Kokugo-to Kokubungaku* 15: 1389–1412.
Matsuo, O. 1969. O-kakujoshi (kotengo, gendaigo) [The case marker *-o* in Classical Japanese and modern Japanese]. In *Joshi jodōshi yōsetsu* [Theory of case marking and auxiliary verbs], ed. A. Matsumura. Tokyo: Gakutōsha.
Matsuoka, M. 2003. Two types of ditransitive constructions in Japanese. *Journal of East Asian Linguistics* 12: 171–203.
May, R. 1977. The grammar of quantification. Doctoral thesis, MIT, Cambridge, Mass.
Mazuka, R., Itoh, K., Kondo, T. 2002. Cost of scrambling in Japanese sentence processing. In *Sentence processing in East Asian languages*, ed. M. Nakayama: 131–166. Stanford, Calif.: CSLI Publications.
Mazurkewich, I., White, L. 1984. The acquisition of the dative alternation: Unlearning overgeneralizations. *Cognition* 16: 261–283.

McCawley, J. 1978. Conversational implicature and the lexicon. In *Pragmatics*, ed. P. Cole: 245–260. New York: Academic. (Syntax and Semantics 9.)
McCloskey, J., Hale, K. 1983. On the syntax of person–number inflection in modern Irish. *Natural Language and Linguistic Theory* 1: 487–533.
McGinnis, M. 1998. Locality in A-movement. Doctoral thesis, MIT, Cambridge, Mass.
McGinnis, M. 2002. Object asymmetries in a phase theory of syntax. In *Proceedings of the 2001 annual conference of the Canadian Linguistic Association*, ed. J. T. Jensen, G. van Herk: 133–144. Ottawa: Department of Linguistics, University of Ottawa.
Mihara, K.-I. 1998. Sūryōsi renketu kōbun-to 'kekka'-no gan'i [Quantifier linking construction and the implication of "resultative"]. Parts 1–3. *Gengo* 27, no. 6: 86–95; no. 7: 94–102; no. 8: 104–113.
Miller, R. A. 1967. *The Japanese language*. Chicago: University of Chicago Press.
Miyagawa, S. 1980. Complex verbs and the lexicon. Doctoral thesis, University of Arizona, Tucson.
Miyagawa, S. 1984a. Blocking and Japanese causatives. *Lingua* 64: 177–207.
Miyagawa, S. 1984b. Restructuring and the purpose expression in Japanese. Ms., Ohio State University, Columbus.
Miyagawa, S. 1986. Syntactic movement, semantic roles, and predication. Ms., Ohio State University, Columbus. Paper presented at the Japanese Syntax Workshop, Center for the Study of Language and Information, Stanford University.
Miyagawa, S. 1987a. Lexical categories in Japanese. *Lingua* 73: 29–51.
Miyagawa. S. 1987b. *Wa* and the WH phrase. In *Perspectives on topicalization: The case of Japanese* wa, ed. J. Hinds, S. K. Maynard, S. Iwasaki: 185–217. Amsterdam: John Benjamins.
Miyagawa, S. 1988. Predication and numeral quantifier. In *Papers from the second International Workshop on Japanese Syntax*, ed. W. Poser: 157–192. Stanford, Calif.: Center for the Study of Language and Information.
Miyagawa, S. 1989. *Structure and case marking in Japanese*. New York: Academic. (Syntax and Semantics 22.)
Miyagawa, S. 1993. Case-checking and Minimal Link Condition. In *Papers on case and agreement 2*, ed. C. Phillips: 213–254. Cambridge, Mass.: MITWPL. (MIT Working Papers in Linguistics 19.)
Miyagawa, S. 1994. *(S)ase* as an elsewhere causative. In *Program of the Conference on Theoretical Linguistics and Japanese Language Teaching: Seventh symposium on Japanese language*: 61–76. Tokyo: Tsuda University.
Miyagawa, S. 1995. Scrambling as an obligatory movement. In *Proceedings of the Nanzan University International Symposium on Japanese Language Education and Japanese Language Studies*: 81–92. Nagoya, Japan: Nanzan University.
Miyagawa, S. 1996. Word order restrictions and nonconfigurationality. In *FAJL 2: Proceedings of the second conference on formal approaches to Japanese linguistics*, ed. M. Koizumi, M. Oishi, U. Sauerland: 117–141. Cambridge, Mass.: MITWPL. (MIT Working Papers in Linguistics 29.)
Miyagawa, S. 1997. Against optional scrambling. *Linguistic Inquiry* 28: 1–26.
Miyagawa, S. 1998. *(S)ase* as an elsewhere causative and the syntactic nature of words. *Journal of Japanese Linguistics* 16: 67–110.
Miyagawa, S. 2001. The EPP, scrambling, and *wh*-in-situ. In *Ken Hale: A life in language*, ed. M. Kenstowicz: 293–338. Cambridge, Mass.: MIT Press.
Miyagawa, S. 2003a. A-movement scrambling and options without optionality. In *Word order and scrambling*, ed. K. Simin: 177–200. Malden, Mass.: Blackwell.
Miyagawa, S. 2003b. QR/scrambling correlations and the notion of phase. Ms., MIT, Cambridge, Mass.

Miyagawa, S. 2005. On the EPP. In *Perspectives on phases*, ed. M. McGinnis, N. Richards: 201–236. Cambridge, Mass.: MITWPL. (MIT Working Papers in Linguistics 49.)
Miyagawa, S. 2006. Genitive subject in Japanese and Turkish. Paper presented at the Nominalization Workshop, Syracuse University, Syracuse, N.Y., March.
Miyagawa, S. 2008. Genitive subjects in Altaic. In *Proceedings of the fourth Workshop on Altaic Formal Linguistics (WAFL 4)*, ed. C. Boeckx, S. Ululas: 181–198. Cambridge, Mass.: MITWPL. (MIT Working Papers in Linguistics 56.)
Miyagawa, S. 2009. Meishika-to kō-kōzō [Nominalization and argument structure]. In *Goi-no imi-to bunpō* [Meaning of words and grammar], ed. Y. Yumoto, H. Kishimoto: 473–494. Tokyo: Kuroshio.
Miyagawa, S. 2010. *Why agree? Why move? Unifying agreement-based and discourse-configurational languages.* Cambridge, Mass.: MIT Press. (Linguistic Inquiry Monograph 54.)
Miyagawa, S. 2011a. Genitive subjects in Altaic and specification of phase. *Lingua* 121: 1265–1282. (Special issue, "Nominalizations in linguistic theory," ed. J. Kornfilt, J. Whitman.)
Miyagawa, S. 2011b. Optionality. In *The Oxford handbook of linguistic minimalism*, ed. C. Boeckx: 354–376. Oxford, New York: Oxford University Press.
Miyagawa, S. In press. Blocking and causatives. In *FAJL 5: Proceedings of the fifth conference on formal approaches to Japanese linguistics.* Cambridge, Mass.: MITWPL. (MIT Working Papers in Linguistics.)
Miyagawa, S., Arikawa, K. 2007. Locality in syntax and floating numeral quantifiers. *Linguistic Inquiry* 38: 645–670.
Miyagawa, S., Ekida, F. 2003. Historical development of the accusative case marking in Japanese as seen in classical literary texts. *Journal of Japanese Linguistics* 19: 1–105.
Miyagawa, S., Matsunaga, S. 1986. Historical development of the accusative case in Japanese. *Journal of Asian Culture* 9: 87–101.
Miyagawa, S., Tsujioka, T. 2004. Argument structure and ditransitive verbs in Japanese. *Journal of East Asian Linguistics* 13: 1–38.
Miyaji, H. 1969. *Seru, saseru*—shieki. In *Kotengo, gendaigo joshi, jodōshi shōsetsu* [A detailed explanation of historic and modern particles and auxiliary verbs], ed. A. Matsumura. Tokyo: Gakutōsha.
Miyamoto, E. T., Nakamura, M. 2005. Unscrambling some misconceptions: A comment on Koizumi and Tamaoka 2004. *Gengo Kenkyu* 128: 113–129.
Miyamoto, E. T., Takahashi, S. 2002. Sources of difficulty in processing scrambling in Japanese. In *Sentence processing in East Asian languages*, ed. M. Nakayama: 167–188. Stanford, Calif.: CSLI Publications.
Miyata, S. 1998. Question acquisition in a Japanese child: The analysis of KII (1;4–3;0) data using CHILDES. *Bulletin of Aichi Shukutoku Junior College* 37: 209–218.
Morris, I. 1969. *The world of the shining prince: Court life in ancient Japan.* Baltimore: Penguin.
Motohashi, T. 1989. Case Theory and the history of the Japanese language. Doctoral thesis, University of Arizona, Tucson.
Muraoka, S. 2006. Nihongo-no bunrikaikatei-ni okeru mokutekigomeishiku-no kakujoshi-no eikyō [The effects of case-marking information on processing object NPs in Japanese]. *Cognitive Studies* 13: 404–416.
Murasugi, K. 1991. Noun phrases in Japanese and English: A study in syntax, learnability, and acquisition. Doctoral thesis, University of Connecticut, Storrs.
Murasugi, K., Fuji, C., Hashimoto, T. 2008. A VP-shell analysis for the undergeneration and the overgeneration in the acquisition of Japanese causatives and potentials. *Nanzan Linguistics* 4: 21–41.

Myers, S. 1984. Zero-derivation and inflection. In *Papers from the January 1984 MIT workshop in morphology*, ed. M. Speas, R. Sproat: 53–69. Cambridge, Mass.: Department of Linguistics and Philosophy, MIT. (MIT Working Papers in Linguistics 7.)

Nakai, S. 1980. A reconsideration of *ga–no* conversion in Japanese. *Papers in linguistics* 13: 279–320.

Nakanishi, K. 2004. Domains of measurement: Formal properties of non-split/split quantifier constructions. Doctoral thesis, University of Pennsylvania, Philadelphia.

Nakanishi, K. 2007a. *Formal properties of measurement constructions*. Berlin: Mouton de Gruyter.

Nakanishi, K. 2007b. Measurement in the nominal and verbal domains. *Linguistics and Philosophy* 30: 235–276.

Nakanishi, K. 2008. Syntax and semantics of floating numeral quantifiers. In *The Oxford handbook of Japanese linguistics*, ed. S. Miyagawa, M. Saito: 287–319. Oxford, New York: Oxford University Press.

Nakayama, S. 1982. On English and Japanese pronouns. Master's thesis, University of Tokyo.

Nambu, S. 2007. Teiryōteki-bunseki-ni motozuku 'ga/no' kōtai saikō [Another look at *ga–no* conversion based on statistical analysis]. *Gengo Kenkyu* 131: 115–149.

Nambu, S. 2010. Nominative/genitive alternation in Japanese: A quantitative study and its theoretical implications. Ms., University of Pennsylvania, Philadelphia.

Nippon Gakujutsu Shinkōkai. 1965. *The Man'yōshū*. New York: Columbia University Press.

Nishigauchi, T., Uchibori, A. 1991. Japanese bare NPs and syntax–semantics correspondences in quantification. Ms., Osaka University and University of Connecticut, Storrs.

Ochi, M. 2001. Move F and *ga/no* conversion in Japanese. *Journal of East Asian Linguistics* 10: 247–286.

Oehrle, R. 1976. The grammatical status of the English dative alternation. Doctoral thesis, MIT, Cambridge, Mass.

Oehrle, R., Nishio, H. 1981. Adversity. In *Proceedings of the Arizona conference on Japanese linguistics: The formal grammar sessions*, ed. A. K. Farmer, C. Kitagawa: 163–186. Tucson, Ariz.: University of Arizona Linguistics Circle. (Coyote Papers 2.)

Ogihara, T. 1994. Adverbs of quantification and sequence-of-tense phenomena. In *Proceedings from Semantics and Linguistic Theory* 4, ed. M. Harvey, L. Santelmann: 251–267. Ithaca, N.Y.: Department of Modern Languages and Linguistics, Cornell University.

Ogihara, T. 2004. Adjectival relatives. *Linguistics and Philosophy* 27: 557–608.

Ohki, M. 1987. Nihongo-no yūru sūryōsi-no danwa kinō-ni tuite [On discourse functions of floating quantifiers in Japanese]. *Shichōkaku Gaikokugokyōiku Kenkyū* 10: 37–68.

Okutsu, K. 1969. Sūryōteki hyōgen-no bunpō [The grammar of quantified expressions]. *Nihongo Kyōiku* 14: 42–60.

Okutsu, K. 1974. *Seisei nihon bunpōron* [Generative grammatical studies in Japanese]. Tokyo: Taishūkan Shoten.

Oshima, S. 1979. Conditions on rules: Anaphora in Japanese. In *Explorations in linguistics: Papers in honor of Kazuko Inoue*, ed. G. Bedell, E. Kobayashi, M. Muraki: 432–448. Tokyo: Kenkyusha.

Ostler, N. D. M. 1980. A non-transformational analysis of Japanese case-marking and inflexion. In *Theoretical issues in Japanese linguistics*, ed. Y. Otsu, A. K. Farmer: 63–91. Cambridge, Mass.: Department of Linguistics and Philosophy, MIT. (MIT Working Papers in Linguistics 2.)

Perlmutter, D. 1978. Impersonal passives and the unaccusative hypothesis. In *Proceedings of the fourth annual meeting of the Berkeley Linguistics Society*, ed. J. Jaeger, A. Woodbury, F. Ackerman, C. Chiarello, O. Gensler, J. Kingston, E. Sweetser, H. Thompson, K. Whistler: 157–189. Berkeley, Calif.: University of California, Berkeley.

Pesetsky, D. 1982. Paths and categories. Doctoral thesis, MIT, Cambridge, Mass.

Pesetsky, D. 1995. *Zero syntax: Experiencers and cascades*. Cambridge, Mass.: MIT Press.

Pierson, J. L. 1931. *The Manyôśû*, vol. 2. Leiden, the Netherlands: E. J. Brill.

Pinker, S. 1989. *Learnability and cognition: The acquisition of argument structure*. Cambridge, Mass.: MIT Press.

Poser, W. 1992. Blocking of phrasal constructions by lexical items. In *Lexical matters*, ed. I. Sag, A. Szabocsi: 111–130. Stanford, Calif.: CSLI Publications.

Postal, P. 1976. Avoiding reference to subject. *Linguistic Inquiry* 7: 151–191.

Pylkkänen, L. 2002. Introducing arguments. Doctoral thesis, MIT, Cambridge, Mass.

Rappaport Hovav, M. 2008. Lexicalized meaning and the internal temporal structure of events. In *Crosslinguistic and theoretical approaches to the semantics of aspect*, ed. S. Rothstein: 13–42. Amsterdam: John Benjamins.

Rappaport Hovav, M., Levin, B. 2005. Change of state verbs: Implications for theories of argument projection. In *The syntax of aspect*, ed. N. Erteschik-Shir, T. Rapoport: 274–286. Oxford: Oxford University Press.

Reinhart, T. 1979. Syntactic domains for semantic rules. In *Formal semantics and pragmatics for natural language*, ed. F. Guenthner, S. J. Schmidt: 107–130. Dordrecht, the Netherlands: Reidel.

Reinhart, T. 1983. *Anaphora and semantic interpretation*. London: Croom Helm.

Richards, N. 1997. Competition and disjoint reference. *Linguistic Inquiry* 28: 178–186.

Richards, N. 2001. An idiomatic argument for lexical decomposition. *Linguistic Inquiry* 32: 183–192.

Rizzi, L. 1986. On chain formation. In *The syntax of pronominal clitics*, ed H. Borer: 65–95. New York: Academic. (Syntax and Semantics 19.)

Rizzi, L. 1990. *Relativized minimality*. Cambridge, Mass.: MIT Press.

Rothstein, S. 1983. The syntactic form of predication. Doctoral thesis, MIT, Cambridge, Mass.

Ruwet, N. 1991. On the use and abuse of idioms in syntactic argumentation. In *Syntax and human experience*, N. Ruwet, ed. and trans. John Goldsmith: 171–251. Chicago: University of Chicago Press.

Sadakane, K., Koizumi, M. 1995. On the nature of the "dative" particle *ni* in Japanese. *Linguistics* 33: 5–33.

Sag, I. 1978. Floating quantifiers, adverbs, and extraction sites. *Linguistic Inquiry* 9: 146–150.

Saito, M. 1982. Case marking in Japanese: A preliminary study. Ms., MIT, Cambridge, Mass.

Saito, M. 1983. Case and government in Japanese. In *Proceedings of the second West Coast Conference on Formal Linguistics*, ed. M. Barlow: 247–259. Stanford, Calif.: Department of Linguistics, Stanford University.

Saito, M. 1985. Some asymmetries in Japanese and their theoretical implications. Doctoral thesis, MIT, Cambridge, Mass.

Saito, M. 1992. Long distance scrambling in Japanese. *Journal of East Asian Linguistics* 1: 69–118.

Saito, M., Fukui, N. 1998. Order in phrase structure and movement. *Linguistic Inquiry* 29: 439–474.

Saito, M., Hoji, H. 1983. Weak crossover and Move α in Japanese. *Natural Language and Linguistic Theory* 1: 245–259.

Sakai, H. 1994. Complex NP constraint and case-conversions in Japanese. In *Current topics in English and Japanese*, ed. M. Nakamura: 179–200. Tokyo: Hitsuji Shobō.

Sanches, M., Slobin, L. 1973. Numeral classifiers and plural marking: An implicational universal. *Working Papers on Language Universals* 11: 1–22.

Sano, M. 1985. LF movement in Japanese. *Descriptive and Applied Linguistics* 18: 245–259.

Sansom, G. B. 1928. *A historical grammar of Japanese*. Oxford: Clarendon.

Sato, A., Kahraman, B., Ono, H., Sakai, H. 2009. Expectation driven by case-markers: Its effect on Japanese relative clause processing. In *The proceedings of the tenth Tokyo Conference on Psycholinguistics*, ed. Y. Otsu: 215–237. Tokyo: Hitsuji Shobō.

Sato, K. 1977. *Kokugogaku kenkyu jiten* [Dictionary of Japanese grammar]. Tokyo: Meiji Shoin.

Seidensticker, E. 1981. Introduction to *The tale of Genji*, trans. E. Seidensticker. New York: Alfred A. Knopf.

Shibatani, M. 1973. Semantics of Japanese causativization. *Foundations of Language* 9: 327–373.

Shibatani, M. 1977. Grammatical relations and surface cases. *Language* 53: 789–809.

Shibatani, M. 1978. Mikami Akira and the notion of "subject" in Japanese grammar. In *Problems in Japanese syntax and semantics*, ed. J. Hinds, I. Howard: 52–67. Tokyo: Kaitakusha.

Shirai, Y., Miyata, S., Naka, N., Sakazaki, Y. 2001. The acquisition of causative morphology in Japanese: A prototype account. In *Issues in East Asian language acquisition*, ed. M. Nakayama: 182–203. Tokyo: Kuroshio.

Shlonsky, U. 1991. Quantifiers as functional heads: A study of quantifier float in Hebrew. *Lingua* 84: 159–180.

Simpson, J. 1983. Resultatives. In *Papers in lexical-functional grammar*, ed. L. Levin, M. Rappaport, A. Zaenen: 143–157. Bloomington: Indiana University Linguistic Club.

Snyder, W. 1992. Chain-formation and crossover. Ms., MIT, Cambridge, Mass.

Spencer, A. 1999. Chukchee homepage. Online course notes, University of Essex, Colchester, England. http://privatewww.essex.ac.uk/~spena/Chukchee/CHUKCHEE_HOMEPAGE.html.

Sportiche, D. 1988. A theory of floating quantifiers and its corollaries for constituent structure. *Linguistic Inquiry* 19:425–449.

Stowell, T. 1981. Origins of phrase structure. Doctoral thesis, MIT, Cambridge, Mass.

Stowell, T. 1982. The tense of infinitives. *Linguistic Inquiry* 13: 561–570.

Stump, G. 2001. *Inflectional morphology: A paradigm structure approach*. Cambridge: Cambridge University Press.

Sudo, Y. 2009. Invisible degree nominals in Japanese clausal comparatives. In *Proceedings of the fifth Workshop on Altaic Formal Linguistics (WAFL 5)*, ed. R. Shibagaki, R. Vermeulen: 285–295. Cambridge, Mass: MITWPL. (MIT Working Papers in Linguistics 58.)

Sugioka, Y. 1984. Interaction of derivational morphology and syntax in English and Japanese. Doctoral thesis, University of Chicago.

Sugioka, Y. 1992. On the role of argument structure in nominalization. *Language, Culture, and Communication* (Keio University) 10: 53–80.

Suzuki, T. 1973. *Heike monogatari, Amakusa-bon Heike monogatari* taihi-ni yoru kaku hyōgen kattatsu katei-no ichi danmen [Comparison for case marking of the

Tale of the Heike and the *Amakusa Tale of the Heike*]. *Kokugogaku Ronsetsu Shiryō* 10.
Svenonius, P. 2004. On the edge. In *Syntactic edges and their effects*, ed. D. Adger, C. de Cat, G. Tsoulas: 261–287. Dordrecht, the Netherlands: Kluwer.
Tada, H. 1992. Nominative objects in Japanese. *Journal of Japanese Linguistics* 14: 91–108.
Tada, H. 1993. A/A-bar partition in derivation. Doctoral thesis, MIT, Cambridge, Mass.
Tada, H. 1999. Attracting categorial features. *Fukuoka University Review of Literature and Humanities* 31: 97–110.
Takagi, I., et al., trans. and eds. 1957. *Man'yōshū*, vol. 1. Tokyo: Iwanami Shoten. (Nihon Koten Bungaku Taikei 4.)
Takagi, I., et al., trans. and eds. 1962. *Man'yōshū*, vol. 4. Tokyo: Iwanami Shoten. (Nihon Koten Bungaku Taikei 8.)
Takahashi, H. 2010. Adverbial clauses and nominative/genitive conversion in Japanese. In *Proceedings of the sixth Workshop on Altaic Formal Linguistics (WAFL 6)*, ed. H. Maezawa, A. Yokogoshi. Cambridge, Mass.: MITWPL. (MIT Working Papers in Linguistics 61.)
Takami, K.-I. 1998. Nihongo-no sūryōsi yūri-ni tuite [On quantifier float in Japanese]. Parts 1–3. *Gengo* 27, no. 1: 86–95; no. 2: 86–95; no. 3: 98–107.
Takano, Y. 1998. Object shift and scrambling. *Natural Language and Linguistic Theory* 16: 817–889.
Takano, Y. 2008. Ditransitive constructions. In *The Oxford handbook of Japanese linguistics*, ed. S. Miyagawa, M. Saito: 423–455. London, New York: Oxford University Press.
Takezawa, K. 1987. A configurational approach to case-marking in Japanese. Doctoral thesis, University of Washington, Seattle.
Takezawa, K. 2000. Kūkan-hyōgen-no tougoron: Kou-to jutsubu-no tairitsu-ni motozuku apurōchi [The syntax of location expressions: An approach based on the tension between the predicate and the clause]. In *Kūkann hyōgenn-to bunpō* [Location expressions and grammar], ed. S. Aoki, K. Takezawa. Tokyo: Kuroshio.
Takezawa, K. 2001. Aru-no tōgoteki nimen-sei [On the syntax of the verb of existence *aru*]. In *Higashi-azia-gengo-bunka-no Sōgōkenkyū*: 75–100. Tsukuba, Japan: University of Tsukuba.
Tanaka, T. 2006. Boundedness condition and Japanese floating numeral quantifiers. Ms., University of Connecticut, Storrs.
Tenny, C. 1987. Grammaticalizing aspect and affectedness. Doctoral thesis, MIT, Cambridge, Mass.
Tenny, C. 1994. *Aspectual roles and the syntax–semantics interface.* Dordrecht, the Netherlands: Kluwer.
Terada, M. 1987. Unaccusativity in Japanese. *Proceedings of NELS 17*, ed. J. McDonough, B. Plunkett: 619–640. Amherst, Mass.: GLSA, University of Massachusetts, Amherst.
Teramura, H. 1982. *Nihongo-no shintakkusu-to imi 2* [Japanese syntax and meaning 2]. Tokyo: Kuroshio.
Tomoda, S. 1982. Analysis of quantifiers in Japanese. In *Studies on Arabic, Basque, English, Japanese, Navajo, and Papago*, ed. T. Larson. Tucson, Ariz.: University of Arizona Linguistic Circle. (Coyote Papers 3.)
Travis, L. 1984. Parameters and effects of word order variation. Doctoral thesis, MIT, Cambridge, Mass.
T'sou, B. 1976. The structure of nominal classifier systems. In *Austroasiatic studies*, part 2, ed. P. N. Jenner, L. C. Thompson, S. Starosta: 1215–1247.

Honolulu, Hawaii: University of Hawaii Press. (Oceanic Linguistics Special Publication 13.)

Tsujimura, N. 1990a. Ergativity of nouns and case assignment. *Linguistic Inquiry* 21: 277–287.

Tsujimura, N. 1990b. Unaccusative mismatches in Japanese. In *ESCOL '89: Proceedings of the sixth annual meeting of the Eastern States Conference on Linguistics*, ed. K. DeJong, Y. No: 264–276. Columbus: Ohio State University.

Tsujioka, T. 2001. The syntax of possession in Japanese. Doctoral thesis, Georgetown University, Washington, D.C.

Tsujioka, T. 2011. Idioms, mixed marking in nominalization, and the base-generation hypothesis for ditransitives in Japanese. *Journal of East Asian Linguistics* 20: 117–143.

Tsutsui, M. 1984. Particle ellipses in Japanese. Doctoral thesis, University of Illinois, Urbana–Champaign.

Ueda, M. 1986. On quantifier float in Japanese. In *Oriental linguistics*, ed. N. Hasegawa, Y. Kitagawa: 263–309. Amherst, Mass.: GLSA, University of Massachusetts, Amherst. (University of Massachusetts Occasional Papers in Linguistics 11.)

Ura, H. 1999. Checking theory and dative subject constructions in Japanese and Korean. *Journal of East Asian Linguistics* 8: 223–254.

Vendler, Z. 1967. *Linguistics and philosophy*. Ithaca, N.Y.: Cornell University Press.

Visser, F. T. 1963. *An historical syntax of the English language*, part 1, *Syntactical units with one verb*. Leiden, the Netherlands: Brill.

Voalis, D., Dupuis, F. 1992. On the status of verbal traces in French: The case of stylistic inversion. In *Romance languages and modern linguistic theory*, ed. P. Hirschbühler, P. Koerner: 325–338. Amsterdam: John Benjamins.

Walker's rhyming dictionary. 1936. New York: Dutton.

Watanabe, A. 1993. AGR-based case theory and its interaction with the A-bar system. Doctoral thesis, MIT, Cambridge, Mass.

Watanabe, A. 1996. Nominative–genitive conversion and agreement in Japanese: A cross-linguistic perspective. *Journal of East Asian Linguistics* 5: 373–410.

Watanabe, A. 2006. Functional projections of nominals in Japanese: Syntax of classifiers. *Natural Language and Linguistic Theory* 24: 241–306.

Whitman, J. 1992. String vacuous V to Comp. Ms., Cornell University, Ithaca, N.Y. Paper presented at the 1991 GLOW.

Williams, E. 1980. Predication. *Linguistic Inquiry* 11: 203–238.

Williams, E. 1981a. Argument structure and morphology. *The Linguistic Review* 1: 81–114.

Williams, E. 1981b. On the notions "lexically related" and "head of a word." *Linguistic Inquiry* 12: 245–274.

Wrona, J., Frellesvig, B. 2009. The Old Japanese case system: The function of *wo*. In *Japanese/Korean linguistics*, vol. 17, ed. S. Iwasaki, H. Hoji, P. M. Clancy, S.-O. Sohn: 565–579. Stanford, Calif.: CSLI Publications.

Yamakido, H. 2000. Japanese attributive adjectives are not (all) relative clauses. In *WCCFL 19: Proceedings of the nineteenth West Coast Conference on Formal Linguistics*, ed. R. Billerey, B. D. Lillehaugen: 588–602. Somerville, Mass.: Cascadilla Press.

Yanagida, Y. 2006. Word order and clause structure in Early Old Japanese. *Journal of East Asian linguistics* 15: 37–68.

Yanagida, Y. 2007. Miyagawa's (1989) exceptions: An ergative analysis. In *FAJL 4: Proceedings of the fourth conference on formal approaches to Japanese linguistics*, ed. Y. Miyamoto, M. Ochi: 265–276. Cambridge: MITWPL. (MIT Working Papers in Linguistics 55.)

Yanagida, Y., Whitman, J. 2009. Alignment and word order in Old Japanese. *Journal of East Asian Linguistics* 18: 101–144.

Yatsushiro, K. 1998. Structure within VP in Japanese. In *Japanese/Korean linguistics*, vol. 8, ed. D. Silva: 501–514. Stanford, Calif.: CSLI Publications.

Yatsushiro, K. 2003. VP internal scrambling. *Journal of East Asian Linguistics* 12: 141–170.

Yokoyama, M. 1991. Yōzi-wa naze mokutekigo-o kakuzyosi ga de hyōzi suru ka [Why children mark object with the case marker *-ga*]. In *Syakai-ni okeru gengo kinō-no syosō*, ed. F. C. Peng et al.: 144–163. Tokyo: Bunka Hyoron.

Yoshimura, N. 1994. 'Ga' no mondai [Issues of *-ga*]. *Henyō-suru Gengo Bunka Kenkyū* (University of Shizuoka): 13–28.

Zenno, Y. 1983. Verb phrase idioms and paradigmatic structures. Ms., Ohio State University, Columbus.

Zenno, Y. 1985. The paradigmatic structure and Japanese idioms. Master's thesis, Ohio State University, Columbus.

Zenno, Y. 1987. Object case marking in Old Japanese. Ms., University of California, Los Angeles.

Zubizarreta, M. L. 1982. On the relationship of the lexicon to syntax. Doctoral thesis, MIT, Cambridge, Mass.

Index

A

Abe, Y., 141, 142
accomplishments, 48–49, 61
accusative case: in modern Japanese, 252–255; in Old Japanese, 12–15, 217, 219, 221, 222–251
acquisition, 206–208
activities, 48–49, 61
adjacency, 14, 19, 26, 220–221, 231, 237, 254. *See also* locality
adjuncts, 25, 32, 34, 35, 151–152
adverbs: floating quantifiers as, 57; as test for size of clause, 133–134, 147, 153, 159, 163–164, 167
affectedness, 276n7
agents, 38, 40, 43
Agree, 126, 127, 137
agreement: in ϕ-features, 8, 123–124, 134; Spec–head, 124; *wh*-agreement, 127
Aikawa, T., 87
Akiyama, K., 263
Aktionsart, 140–141, 144, 149
Aldridge, E., 284n21
Alexiadou, A., 95, 137–138
Altaic languages, genitive subjects in, 122
Altmann, G., 114
A-movement, 3, 21, 36–38, 41, 45
A'-movement, 90, 281n13, 286n5, 286n7
Anagnostopoulou, E., 88, 89–90, 95, 137–138, 144, 149, 286n5
anaphors, 65, 84–87
animacy: in causative constructions, 10, 171–172, 173; in ditransitive constructions, 4, 65, 66–67, 69, 70, 72, 74, 96–97, 139, 283n17
antecedents of numeral quantifiers, 22–25, 29–32
Aoun, J., 69, 73, 98, 279n3
applicatives, 66–67, 75, 77, 88, 99, 105
arguments, 32; and adjuncts, 25, 32, 35, 151–152; clausal, 276n4, 294n11; elements that are not, 20; external, 44, 47, 49–50, 58; internal, 88–89, 154; quasi-objects as, 34
Arikawa, K., 3, 45, 47, 48, 55
Aronoff, M., 11, 169, 170, 173–174, 197, 213, 292n4
Asarina, A., 6
aspect: stative, 140–144, 149; telic, 44, 47–54, 59, 60–61
AspP, 8, 51–52, 57, 122, 124, 130
attributive verb form in Old Japanese, 13, 224–227, 233–235, 259–262, 264, 265–266, 269–273

B

Babby, L. H., 154
Babyonyshev, M. A., 154
Bach, E., 51
Bailyn, J. F., 154
Baker, M., 14, 104, 139, 270–271
Bantu: agreement, 1; applicatives, 66, 99
Barss, A., 65–66, 73
base generation: of syntactically independent numeral quantifiers, 21, 25, 275n3; of word-order permutation in ditransitives, 73, 74, 81–88, 91, 92–93, 95–101, 102
Bedell, G., 122, 123, 126, 127, 146
Belletti, A., 40
Bianchi, V., 287n9
binding: of anaphors, 65; and coreference, 87; of variables, 73, 87. *See also* Condition B; Condition C
Bjeljac-Babic, R., 1

blocking: accounts compared, 212–215; and causatives, 11, 170, 172–176, 197–202, 213; in English, 173–174, 194, 213–215; and the lexicon, 169–170, 177, 193–194, 195, 202; nominalization as test for, 179; vs. nonoccurrence, 174, 177; paradigms and, 172–176
Bobaljik, J., 57
Boeckx, C., 123
Borer, H., 44, 51–52, 53–54, 278n7
Borsley, R., 130
Bošković, Ž., 3, 50, 278n5, 279n9
Brame, M., 276n4
Branigan, P., 137, 138
Bresnan, J., 4, 65, 69, 96, 214, 276n4, 281n15
Briggs, E., 292n5
Bruening, B., 66, 69, 77, 98, 280n5, 282–283n16, 284n19
Burzio, L., 21, 40–41, 43, 276n6
Burzio's Generalization, 43
'by' phrases, 38–39

C

Caplan, D., 112
Carstens, V., 123
case drop in colloquial Japanese, 231, 254, 293n2
case filter, 33, 220
case licensing: and phasehood, 123, 132, 134; with defective T, 131; at D-structure or S-structure, 252–253; by *v*, 299n5; variation and change, 12–15, 217, 220–221, 257–258
case marking: of antecedent of numeral quantifier, 22–25, 30, 34, 35, 70, 97–98; lack of syntactic projection, 30–31, 33; movement and, 73–74; thematic role not assigned by, 31–32, 33
case theory, 33, 220–221
categorial status: case markers vs. postpositions and, 30–32; of goals in ditransitives, 69–70, 72–73, 78–80, 96–98, 101, 139, 279n4; numeral quantifiers as test for, 5, 30–32, 69–70, 74–75, 78–79, 81, 97, 139; passivization as test for, 78–79
causatives: acquisition of, 206–208; adversity, 180–181; analytical vs. lexical, 10–11, 171–172, 173, 176, 177, 195–197, 202–206, 208–211, 215; and blocking, 170, 172–176, 177, 179, 193–194, 195, 197–202, 213; of ditransitives, 106; double, 198–200; English, 110, 203, 208–212, 213, 215; in idioms, 11, 179–180, 182, 184–185, 196, 200–202, 206, 209–211; Mitla Zapotec, 174–177; nominalization of, 110–111, 177–179, 182–183, 196, 203; structural analysis, 11–12, 106, 110–111, 185–193, 197, 202–206; synthetic (*see* analytical vs. lexical); unaccusatives alternating with, 10–11, 196, 201, 203, 209–210, 215
c-command, 27; in double-object construction, 65–67; mutual, of NPs and numeral quantifiers, 27–40, 41; quantifier scope and, 45
Chain Condition, 83–87
change. *See* language change
Chinese influence on Japanese, 232–233
Chomsky, N., 1, 21, 25, 32, 33, 36, 38, 86, 87, 88, 89, 95, 110, 123, 124, 126, 131, 134, 137, 155, 169, 188, 189, 202–203, 217, 219, 220, 252, 259, 276n4, 277n14, 289n18, 293n5, 299n27, 299n5 (Chap. 10)
Chujo, K., 112
Chukchee incorporation, 271
Cinque, G., 133, 147
Cirillo, R., 57
Clark, E. V., 169
Clark, H. H., 169
classifiers, 17–18, 51, 57, 280n7
C-licensing of genitive case: in Japanese, 7, 123, 126, 127–130, 138, 146, 149–150; in Turkish, 123, 124–125, 139–140
clitics and cliticization, 40–41
Collins, C., 137, 138
compounding, Old Japanese accusative and, 223, 228–229, 268–269
conclusive verb form in Old Japanese: abstract case with, 13, 224, 225, 242–243, 259–261; loss of, 233–234, 261–262, 264;

morphological case with, 264, 266–269; purely verbal nature of, 224, 265
Condition B, 130–131, 148–149, 189–190, 191, 284n26
Condition C, 284n25
conjunctive verb form in Old Japanese, 229, 237, 243–248, 264, 268
cooperative principle, 202, 215
copies (traces): of external arguments, 3, 47, 50, 53, 58–59, 61–62; identified by numeral quantifiers, 21, 28, 29, 37–38, 41, 44, 45, 46; of internal arguments, 58–59; in scope relations, 61–62, 68, 291n5
copy theory of movement, 87
coreference, 87
corpus studies: English and Old English, 211–212; Japanese, 140–144, 148; Old Japanese, 232, 235–251, 260, 263–273, 281n15
Cranston, E., 263
Cuervo, M. C., 287n2 (Intro.), 280n10
Culicover, P., 20, 22, 276n4, 277n12

D

Dagur genitive subjects, 6, 7, 122–123, 124, 130, 134
dative construction: c-command relations in, 73; English, 64–67, 96, 103–104, 286n6; Greek, 89–90; in idioms, 117; passivization of theme, 80; scrambling in, 73; semantics, 64, 65, 67; scope relations in, 69, 73, 77
datives: as antecedents of numeral quantifiers, 22–25, 34, 35, 69–70, 280n6; DP or PP, 5; Spanish, 275n2 (Intro.)
defective T, 131–132, 140–144, 149, 153
delimitedness. *See* telicity
dependent tense, 9, 149, 151, 158–159, 160
Déprez, V., 137
derivation, morphological, 105–106, 110, 204–205, 213
Diesing, M., 49
direct objects, 22, 33–34, 161–166
Distributed Morphology, 12, 204–205, 212
ditransitives: animacy in, 65, 66–67, 69, 70, 72, 74, 96–97, 139, 283n17; causativization of, 106; dual argument structures, 4–6, 64–88, 92–93, 95–101, 112–121; English, 64–67, 71, 73, 77, 80, 96, 286n6; Greek, 89–90; in idioms, 82–83, 116–121; Japanese, 3–4, 67–70; nominalization of, 5–6, 101–106; processing, 112–116; scope relations in, 68–69, 73, 75, 77, 90–91, 98–99, 286n6; semantics, 64–67, 69, 283nn17–18; word order in, 3–4, 67–68, 70–72, 73, 81–88, 99–100, 101, 116
D-licensing of genitive case: in Dagur, 8, 123, 124; in Japanese, 7–8, 126–127, 129, 130–140, 146, 149–151, 163, 167–168
Doetjes, J., 57
Double-*o* Constraint, 197
double-object construction: animacy restriction, 4, 65, 66–67, 96, 283n17; causative semantics, 64, 66, 69, 283n17; c-command relations in, 65–67; English, 4, 64–67, 96, 103–104; Greek, 89–90; in idioms, 117; scope relations in, 69, 75
Downing, P., 17
Dowty, D., 47, 48, 108
D-structure, 41
dual-base analysis of ditransitives, 4–6, 64–88, 92–93, 95–101, 112–121
Dupuis, F., 138

E

-e 'to', 79–80, 100, 280n8
ECM construction, 7, 131, 135, 149, 266–267
economy, 135, 148
Ekida, F., 14, 262, 263–265, 266–269, 271–272
elsewhere morphemes, 205–214
Embick, D., 195, 212, 214–215
emphatic *-(w)o* in Old Japanese, 221–222, 252, 267–268
endpoints. *See* telicity
English: case marking, 220–221, 257–258; causatives, 110, 203, 208–215; ditransitive constructions, 4, 64–67, 96, 103–104, 286n6; ECM construction, 7, 131, 135, 149; external arguments, 50;

floating quantifiers, 3, 45, 50–51; nominalization, 103–104, 106; quantifier scope in, 60, 61–62, 69, 156, 291n5; small clauses, 20, 104; *win*, 35
EPP movement, 56, 88, 95, 135, 290n1
ergatives. *See* unaccusatives
exclamatory *-(w)o* in Old Japanese, 221–222, 252, 267–268
experiencers, 36, 39
extended grammatical-relations hypothesis on quantifier float, 21–22, 24–25, 34
external arguments, 44, 47, 49–50, 58, 206

F

Farmer, A. K., 202, 292n6
features: EPP, 88–89, 95, 135, 290n1; lexical, 277n14; *ϕ*-features, 8, 123–124, 134
filters: blocking and, 170, 176–177, 202, 212, 214–215; case filter, 33, 220
Fitzpatrick, J., 57
floating quantifiers, 3, 44, 45, 50, 57. *See also* numeral quantifiers, stranded or floating
focus, 90
Folli, R., 50
Frellesvig, B., 13, 260
French: quantifier float, 3, 45, 50–51; *que–qui* complementizer alternation, 125; stylistic inversion, 137–138
Fuji, C., 203, 206–208
Fujita, N., 9, 51, 56, 57, 151, 152, 155
Fukui, N., 68, 89, 91, 285n28
Fukushima, K., 49, 57

G

G (abstract preposition), 104–105
ga–no conversion, 6–9, 125–149
genitive case licensing, 6–9, 122–168; in Dagur, 6, 8, 122–123, 124, 130, 134; in nominalizations, 93; on objects, 161–166; phases and, 7–8, 123–124, 134, 137, 157; scope relations and, 132–133, 156–158, 164–166; and syntactic position of subjects, 126–127, 134–136, 147–148; in Turkish, 122, 123, 124–125, 134, 139–140, 287n8
genitive of dependent tense, 8–9, 152–168
genitive of negation in Slavic, 9, 149, 151, 154–155, 159, 161, 287n3
goals: animacy, 4, 65, 69, 70, 72, 74, 96–97, 139, 283n17; clausal, 276n4; in ditransitives, 65, 67, 69–91, 96, 99, 101, 139; DP or PP, 4–5, 69–70, 72–73, 96–98, 101, 279n4; locative/low and possessive/high, 4–5, 65, 67, 69, 70–73, 96, 99; passivization of, 39, 78–79; and telicity, 48, 49, 59
Government and Binding, 44, 45, 51, 197, 219, 277n14
grammatical relations, 21–23, 24, 30, 32, 33
Greek: ditransitives, 89–90; scrambling, 90, 281n13
Greenberg, J., 18
Grimshaw, J., 108, 130
Gropen, J., 64
Gruber, J., 276n4
Gunji, T., 55

H

Hagiwara, H., 112
Haig, J. H., 2, 19, 45–46, 47, 72, 276n8, 277n13
Hale, K., 6, 7, 8, 122, 123, 124, 130, 146, 202, 203, 204, 211, 213, 216, 287n5
Halle, M., 12, 204, 212, 292n4
Hamasaki, M., 287n7
Harada, S.-I., 6, 22, 23, 49, 108, 122, 123, 125, 126, 128, 129, 134–135, 136, 137, 138, 139, 145, 146, 148, 190–191, 197, 231, 277nn10–11, 286n8
Harley, H., 4, 12, 50, 64, 65, 66, 70, 73, 96, 202, 203, 205, 281n12, 283n18, 285n4, 286n9
Hartman, J., 6
Hasegawa, N., 35, 276n4, 279n1
Hashimoto, S., 221, 222
Hashimoto, T., 203, 206–208
Hasida, K., 55
Haywood, S., 114
Higginbotham, J., 108
Hill, D., 290n21
Hiraiwa, K., 7, 8–9, 122, 123, 124, 127–129, 134, 139, 140, 145, 146, 149–151, 155, 164, 167, 275n4, 287n6, 289n15, 290n20

Hirohama, F., 221, 233
historical development. *See* language change
Hoji, H., 4, 60, 68, 87, 91, 92–93, 96, 98, 99, 116, 279n3, 284n24, 284n26, 286n6
Horie, K., 290n22
Hornstein, N., 279n3
Hoshi, H., 93
Huang, C.-T. J., 25, 293n2

I

Iatridou, S., 144, 149, 285n29
Icelandic transitive expletive construction, 1
Ichiko, T., 236, 246, 295–296n19
idioms: causatives in, 11, 179–180, 182, 184–185, 196, 200–202, 206, 209–211; ditransitives in, 82–83, 116–121; and locality, 82, 116; nominalization of, 107, 118–121; Old Japanese accusative and, 223
Iida, M., 202
Ikeda, K., 263, 299n2
Inada, T., 61
incorporation, 14, 104, 107, 269–272
indirect objects, 22, 25. *See also* datives
indirect passive, 35–36, 39–40
individual-level predicates, 49
inherent case, 299n27
inheritance, 123, 131, 135, 148
Inoue, K., 22, 24–25, 34, 120, 189, 253, 277n10, 286n12
Ishii, Y., 57
Italian: external arguments, 50; unaccusatives and *ne* cliticization, 40–41
Ito, A., 286n5, 286n7
Ito, K., 206
Ito, T., 93, 102
Itoh, K., 112
Izvorski, R., 144, 149

J

Jackendoff, R. S., 276n4
Jacobsen, W., 195, 205
Jaeggli, O., 38–39
Johnson, K., 61, 62, 132, 156, 279n3, 288n13, 291n5
Joseph, B., 219, 259

K

Kageyama, T., 93–94, 102, 106, 110, 297n22
kakarimusubi, 225–227, 261
Kakuichi, 236, 238, 239, 243
Kamei, T., 236, 296n19
Kamide, Y., 114
Kamio, A., 26, 277n1
kanbun kundoku, 232–233
Kang, B., 290n22
Kansai and Kanto dialects of Japanese, 292n3 (Chap. 7)
-*kara* 'from', 30, 31, 32–33, 280n8
-*kata* 'way', 6, 93–94
Kato, S., 291n6
Kayne, R. S., 5, 103–104, 110, 137, 138, 277n14, 287n9, 293n5
Keyser, S. J., 202, 203, 204, 211, 216
Kikuta, C., 291n9
Kim, E., 140–141, 143, 290n24, 290n27
Kinsui, S., 13–14, 142, 262, 263, 264–265, 267, 270, 273
Kiparsky, P., 174, 195, 202, 205, 212, 213, 214–215
Kishimoto, H., 70, 73, 93, 94–95, 101–103, 105–106, 107, 108, 109, 111, 112, 117–120, 135, 164, 275n3 (Intro.), 280n8, 286nn11–12
Kitagawa, C., 277n10
Kitagawa, H., 236, 250, 295n17
Kitagawa, Y., 57, 70, 73, 74, 202, 285n1, 286n9
Kitahara, H., 95, 135
Kitazume, S., 212
Kiyose, R., 295n18
Kobayashi, Y., 13, 221–222, 260
Koizumi, M., 5, 84, 98, 112–113, 116, 138, 164, 285n30, 285n2 (Chap. 4)
Kondo, T., 112
Konoshima, T., 265
Koreshima, M., 232
Kornfilt, J., 6, 122, 123, 124–125, 130, 140, 287n4, 287n8
Koster, J., 276n4
Kratzer, A., 142, 149, 206, 282n16
Krause, C., 122, 124
Krifka, M., 51
Kubo, M., 78
Kuno, S., 10, 22, 23, 35, 36, 48, 163, 186, 253, 254, 257, 267, 290n2, 293n2, 295n13, 296n20
Kuroda, S.-Y., 2, 3, 10, 11–12, 19, 44, 45, 46, 47, 50, 57, 60, 62, 74, 95, 185, 186–187, 188, 194,

197, 198, 202, 253, 254, 257, 277n10, 277n13, 279n3, 293n2

L

language acquisition, 206–208
language change, 218–220, 259; English, 211–212; Japanese, 12–15, 232–251, 256–258, 259
language variation, 1, 68, 92, 218
Larson, R., 64, 66, 82, 99, 100, 116, 117, 281n11
Lasnik, H., 65–66, 73, 252, 288n11
Lees, R. B., 287n8
Levin, B., 47, 48, 50, 210, 211, 278n3
Lexicalist Hypothesis, 169
lexicon, 169–170, 176–177, 187–188
Li, Y.-H. A., 69, 73, 98, 279n3
Lieber, R., 169
Lightfoot, D., 219, 259
Link, G., 51
literature, Japanese, 218: and Chinese influence, 232–233; Heian period, 263; *Man'yōshū*, 218; *Tale of the Heike*, 235–236
little *v*. *See v*
locality: in chains, 84, 85; idioms and, 82, 116; movement and, 54, 80, 89, 136; numeral quantifiers and, 2–3, 19, 26, 44–45, 46, 53; passivization and, 80
long-distance movement, 276n7
Lumsden, J., 293n4

M

Mabuchi, K., 293n7
Mahajan, A., 90
Maki, H., 129, 150, 151, 158, 167, 168, 287nn7–9
Manning, C., 202
Manzini, M. R., 276n4
Marantz, A., 12, 32, 65, 66–67, 69, 71, 75–77, 98, 99, 105, 195, 203, 204, 206, 210, 212, 279–280n5, 281–283n16, 283n17, 283n19, 292n1 (Chap. 8)
Martin, S., 122, 198
Masunaga, K., 254, 293n2, 299n28
Matsumoto, Y., 205
Matsunaga, S., 13, 223, 226, 233–235, 259, 261, 264, 293n3, 294n8
Matsuo, O., 221, 232, 233, 235, 260, 295n14
Matsuoka, M., 112, 286n5
May, R., 61, 132, 156, 276n4
Mazuka, R., 112
Mazurkewich, I., 4, 65, 96
McCawley, J., 195, 198, 202, 208–209, 215
McCloskey, J., 213
McGinnis, M., 87, 88, 285n27
Merchant, J., 291n3
metalinguistic comparison, 214–215
Mihara, K.-I., 48, 49
Miller, B., 292n5
Miller, R. A., 295n15
Minimalist Program, 44, 45, 51, 197
Mitla Zapotec causatives, 174–177
mixed projections, 130
Miyagawa, S., 3, 7, 9, 12, 14, 37, 40, 45, 47, 48, 50, 55, 56, 59, 62, 70, 72, 73, 74, 78, 79, 81, 82, 83, 85, 88, 89, 90, 92–93, 95, 96, 101, 112, 123, 126, 130, 131, 132, 135, 138–139, 146, 151, 152, 156, 157, 163, 165, 189, 198, 199, 200, 201, 202, 205, 214, 217, 235, 261, 262, 263–265, 266–269, 271–272, 276nn5–6, 284n22, 285n30, 285n1 (Chap. 4), 288n14, 289n19, 290n1, 292n6, 292nn2–3 (Chap. 8), 293n3, 295n13, 297n22
Miyaji, H., 292n2 (Chap. 7)
Miyamoto, E. T., 112, 113, 114, 286n10
Miyata, S., 207
Mogi, T., 280n10
morphology, 105–106, 110, 169, 204–205
Morris, I., 295n16
Motohashi, T., 268
Move α, 41, 231
movement: A-movement, 3, 21, 36–38, 41, 45; A′-movement, 90, 281n13, 286n5, 286n7; and case, 54; copy theory, 87; covert, 126; EPP movement, 56, 88, 95, 135, 290n1; long-distance, 276n7; in passives, 21, 36–38, 46, 58; and telicity, 52–53; and type mismatch, 61; in unaccusatives, 41, 46–47, 58. *See also* scrambling
Muraoka, S., 114
Murasugi, K., 139, 203, 206–208, 288n12
mutual-c-command requirement, 27–40, 41
Myers, S., 93, 105–107, 109–111

Myers's Generalization, 93, 105–111

N
Nakai, S., 126–127
Nakajima, H., 133, 147
Nakamura, M., 113, 114
Nakanishi, K., 49, 51, 56–57
Nakayama, S., 87
Nambu, S., 148, 290n22, 290n24
negative polarity items, 66
-ni (particle), 5, 98, 118–119, 138–139, 286n8
Nikitina, T., 281n15
Nippon Gakujutsu Shinkōkai, 218, 262
Nishigauchi, T., 49
Nishio, H., 180–181
Nishioka, N., 278n8
nominalizations, 93; of causatives, 110–111, 177–179, 182–183, 196, 203; of ditransitives, 5–6, 101–106; of idioms, 107, 118–121; lack of scrambling in, 95, 101; syntactic analysis, 93–95, 106–109, 130
nominative–genitive conversion, 6–9, 125–149
Noyer, R., 195, 214
numeral quantifiers, 2, 17–19, 277n1; as adverbs, 57; antecedent of, 22; classifiers used, 17–18, 280n7; construal with NP, 18–19, 20; with dative antecedents, 22–25, 34, 35, 69–70, 276n8, 280n6; identifying NPs/DPs vs. PPs, 5, 30–32, 69–70, 74–75, 78–79, 81, 97, 139; lack of thematic role, 20; and locality, 2–3, 19, 26, 44–45, 46, 53; in NP-modifier position (nonfloating), 19–20, 70, 97; in Old Japanese, 249; and plural marking, 18; and predication, 20, 27–28; and rule of quantifier float, 20, 21–22; and small clauses, 20; stranded or floating, 44, 45–51, 54–57, 69–70, 78–79; syntactic independence from NP, 19–20, 21, 25

O
objects: direct, 22, 33–34, 161–166; indirect, 22, 25 (*see also* datives); quasi-, 24–25, 34
Ochi, M., 123, 126, 132, 146, 156, 288n14
Oehrle, R., 64, 180–181, 283n17
Ogihara, T., 142, 158–159, 164, 290n25
Ohki, M., 49
Okutsu, K., 20, 22
Old English causativization, 211
Old Japanese: accusative case, 12–15, 217, 219, 221, 222–251; exclamatory *-o*, 221–222; verbal inflections, 13, 223–251, 255–256
One-Component Hypothesis, 202
Optimality Theory, 212
Oshima, S., 189
Ostler, N. D. M., 292n6

P
Pāṇini, 205, 212
Paradigmatic Structure, 169–170, 172–185, 292n3 (Chap. 8)
parameters, 219–220
particles: case vs. postpositional, 30–32; *kakari*, 225–226
partitives, 40–41
passives: 'by' phrase in, 38–39; with genitive subjects, 153–154; Japanese direct, 23, 35–39, 46; Japanese indirect, 23, 35–36, 39–40; lexical analysis, 37; movement analysis, 21, 36–38, 46, 58
'pass'-type verbs, 112–113, 116, 286n5
perfect verb form in Old Japanese, 228–229
Perlmutter, D., 21, 40, 41, 42
Pesetsky, D., 6, 64, 65, 73, 93, 98, 99, 103, 104–106, 110, 111, 154, 203, 287n3
phases: and applicatives, 88; and genitive licensing, 7–8, 123–124, 134, 137, 157
ϕ-feature agreement, 8, 123–124, 134
Pierson, J. L., 218
Pinker, S., 4, 64, 65, 96
plural marking, 18
poetry, 218, 262–263, 264–265, 269
Pollock, J.-Y., 137, 138
Poser, W., 214
possessive construction, 281n12, 285n4
Postal, P., 277n9
postpositions: case assigned by, 277n14; syntactic projection of, 30–31; thematic roles assigned by, 32–33
Predicate Raising, 186, 189

predicate-internal subject position, 3, 44, 45, 47, 50–51, 58. *See also* external arguments
predication, theory of, 20, 28
probes, 124, 131, 134
processing, 112–116
Projection Principle, 188
pseudoclefts, 278n4
Pylkkänen, L., 64, 65, 66, 67, 99, 202, 281–282n16, 285n17

Q

quantifier float, 3, 44, 45, 50, 57; rule of, 20, 21–22. *See also* numeral quantifiers, stranded or floating
Quantifier Raising, 69, 77, 132–133, 156–157
quantifier scope: in ditransitives, 68–69, 74, 77–78, 90–91, 98–99, 286n6; and genitive licensing, 132–133, 156–158, 164–166; (non)rigidity in Japanese, 44, 45, 60, 68; and telicity, 45, 60, 61–62
quasi-objects, 24–25, 34

R

Rappaport Hovav, M., 47, 48, 50, 278n3
reciprocals, 84–85
reconstruction, 284n25
reduced structures, 8, 122, 124, 129–134, 146–147
reflexives, 23, 85–87, 186
Reinhart, T., 27, 284n24
relational grammar, 277n9
restructuring, 189–190, 191
resultative phrases, 59
Richards, N., 64, 87, 117, 283n18
Rizzi, L., 40, 83–87, 125, 284n23
roots, category-neutral, 206, 292n1 (Chap. 8)
Rothstein, S., 20
Russian. *See* Slavic
Ruwet, N., 210

S

Sadakane, K., 5, 98, 138
Sag, I., 57, 202
Saito, M., 35, 68, 87, 89, 123, 146, 231, 254, 257, 277n13, 288n11, 292n7, 293n2, 295n13
Sakai, H., 130–131, 132, 148–149
Sakata, Y., 236, 296n19
Sakha genitive subjects, 6
Sanches, M., 18
Sano, M., 164, 280n9
Sansom, G. B., 224, 225–226, 228, 230, 244, 261, 265, 294nn9–10
-sas (causative suffix), 9, 170–171, 172–174, 181–185, 191–193
-sase (causative suffix), 9–11, 106, 110–111, 170–171, 177–191, 196–197, 204–208
Sato, A., 112, 113–116
Sato, K., 235
scope. *See* quantifier scope
scrambling: absent in *-kata* nominalization, 95; characteristic of Japanese, 3–4, 62, 68, 92; covert, 61; double, 56; in English *to*-dative construction, 73, 286n6; feature-driven, 89, 91, 95; in Greek, 90; in Japanese ditransitives, 3–4, 68, 73, 92, 96, 100, 286n6; in Slavic, 285n28
Seidensticker, E., 263
semantic drift. *See* idioms
Serafim, L., 234, 294n9
Shibatani, M., 10–11, 20, 22, 23–24, 35, 69, 97, 171–172, 197, 277n11, 292nn2–3
Shirai, Y., 206, 207
Shlonsky, U., 57
'show'-type verbs, 112–113, 116
Simpson, J., 59
Slavic: genitive of negation, 9, 149, 151, 154–155, 159, 161, 287n3; scrambling, 285n28
Slobin, L., 18
small clauses, 20, 104, 282–283n16
small *v*. *See* *v*
Snyder, W., 84
source (thematic role), 280n8
Spanish datives, 275n2 (Intro.)
Spec–head agreement, 124
Spell-Out, 137
Spencer, A., 271
Sportiche, D., 3, 45, 50, 57
S-structure, 41
stage-level predicates, 49
Standard Theory, 197, 219
stative predicates, 140–144, 149, 161–162
Stowell, T., 14, 33, 140, 188, 217, 220, 266, 286n10, 293nn5–6
stranding of numeral quantifiers, 3, 44, 45–51, 54–57
structural case, 299n27

Stump, G., 195, 292n3 (Chap. 8)
stylistic inversion in French, 137–138
subcategorization, 24–25, 38–39, 188
subject honorification, 23, 108–109, 190–191
subject-in-situ generalization, 137–140
subjects, 32, 33–34; as antecedent of numeral quantifiers, 22; dative, 24, 35; genitive, 6–9, 122–154; predicate-internal, 3, 44, 45, 47, 50–51, 58
"subjunctive" C, 127–128, 146, 289n15
Sudo, Y., 129, 167, 290n26
Sugioka, Y., 93, 102, 107, 111, 120
surface-case hypothesis on quantifier float, 21–22, 23–24, 25, 30, 35
Suzuki, T., 238–243, 247, 248–251, 256, 295n18, 296n21, 297–298nn23–26
Svenonius, P., 124

T

T: defective, 8, 131–132, 140, 149, 161–162; EPP feature on, 95, 135, 290n1; role in case licensing, 6, 123, 127, 131–132, 134, 137, 146, 161. *See also* tense
T'sou, B., 18
Tada, H., 50, 61, 68, 90, 164, 165
Takagi, I., 218, 223, 226, 261
Takahashi, H., 8–9, 150–151, 155–158, 166, 167
Takahashi, S., 112, 286n10
Takami, K.-I., 48, 56
Takano, Y., 68, 73–74, 281n14, 284n20, 285n30, 286n6
Takezawa, K., 146, 164, 254, 281n12, 285n4
Tamaoka, K., 112–113, 116, 285n2
Tanaka, T., 278n5
telicity, 3, 44, 47–54, 59, 60–61
Tenny, C., 51, 54
tense: dependent, 9, 149, 151, 158–159, 160; independent, 160; interpretation of defective T, 140–144; as test for size of clause, 95, 109, 124, 130, 132–133. *See also* T
Terada, M., 151, 290n27
Teramura, H., 142
textual data. *See* corpus studies
thematic roles: ablative, 32–33; agent, 38, 40, 43; assigned by postposition, 32–33; of clauses, 276n4; elements that do not receive, 20; experiencer, 36, 39; external, 38–39, 43; goal, 39, 276n4; internal, 43; not assigned by case markers, 31–32; numeral quantifiers' lack of, 20; in passives, 38–39; source, 280n8; theme, 40, 42
Tomioka, S., 61, 279n3, 291n5
Tomoda, S., 276n8
traces. *See* copies
transitivity restriction on *ga–no* conversion, 125–126, 136–140
traversal objects, 24, 34
Travis, L., 293n4
Tsubouchi, K., 287n7
Tsuchida, B. T., 236, 250, 295n17
Tsujimura, N., 47–48, 49, 59, 278n6
Tsujioka, T., 4, 5, 95, 96–97, 112, 119–121, 139, 286nn11–12
Tsutsui, M., 254, 299n28
Turkish genitive subjects, 122–123, 124–125, 134, 139–140, 287n8
two-goal construction, 71–72, 76–78, 100, 285n29
type mismatch, 61

U

Uchibori, A., 49, 129, 150, 151, 158, 167–168, 287nn8–9
Ueda, M., 37, 44, 46, 276n5
Uighur genitive subjects, 6
unaccusatives: causatives and, 10–11, 196, 201, 203, 209–210, 215; with genitive arguments, 9, 150–151, 152–155; in Italian, 40–41; movement analysis, 21, 40–41, 46–47, 58
unergatives, 42–43, 46–47, 48, 59, 152
universal grammar, 21; and language change and variation, 1, 15, 92, 218–220, 257–258, 259
Ura, H., 164

V

v: case licensing by, 299n5; causativization and, 203–206; genitive arguments with, 149, 151, 155, 159, 162; in nominalizations, 94–95, 106–109; and Quantifier Raising, 279n5, 283n19
variation. *See* language variation
Vendler, Z., 48
verbal inflection in Old Japanese, 223–251, 255–256

Vergnaud, J.-R., 287n9
verse, 218, 262–263, 264–265, 269
visibility, 50, 53, 58–59, 62
Visser, F. T., 211
Voalis, D., 138
VP-internal subject position. *See* predicate-internal subject position
VP shells, 66

W

Wakayama, M., 143
Walker's rhyming dictionary, 292n4
Watanabe, A., 7, 8, 70, 72, 73, 123, 125, 127–128, 129, 130, 136–137, 138, 145, 146, 147, 149–150, 151, 166–167, 277n1, 289n15
wh-agreement, 127
White, L., 4, 65, 96
Whitman, J., 14, 151–152, 262, 263, 266, 268, 269–273
Wilkins, W., 20, 22, 276n4
Williams, E., 20, 28, 37, 169, 276n4, 277n12
word formation. *See* morphology; causatives; nominalizations
word order: in Japanese ditransitives, 3–4, 67–68, 70–72, 73, 81–88, 99–100, 101, 116; in Old Japanese, 229–231
Wrona, J., 13, 260

X

X-bar theory, 188

Y

Yamakido, H., 290n25
Yanagida, Y., 14, 262, 263, 266, 268, 269–273
Yatsushiro, K., 68, 74, 82, 83, 85–86, 88, 91, 284n25, 285n26
Yokoyama, M., 207
Yoshimura, N., 291n6

Z

Zenno, Y., 11, 179, 182, 201, 222, 225, 226, 227, 228, 229, 246–247, 299n2
Zubizarreta, M. L., 292n7